New Directions in Criminological Theory

This edited collection brings together established global scholars and new thinkers to outline fresh concepts and theoretical perspectives for criminological research and analysis in the twenty-first century. Criminologists from the UK, USA, Canada and Australia evaluate the current condition of criminological theory and present students and researchers with new and revised ideas from the realms of politics, culture and subjectivity to unpack crime and violence in the precarious age of global neoliberalism.

These ideas range from the micro-realm of the 'personality disorder' to the macro-realm of global 'power-crime'. Rejecting or modifying the orthodox notion that crime and harm are largely the products of criminalisation and control systems, these scholars bring causes and conditions back into play in an eclectic yet thematic way that should inspire students and researchers to once again investigate the reasons why some individuals and groups elect to harm others rather than seek sociability. This collection will inspire new criminologists to both look outside their discipline for new ideas to import, and to create new ideas within their discipline to reinvigorate it and further strengthen its ability to explain the crimes and harms that we see around us today.

This book will be of particular interest to academics and both undergraduate and postgraduate students in the field of criminology, especially to those looking for theoretical concepts and frameworks for dissertations, theses and research reports.

Steve Hall is Professor of Criminology at the Social Futures Institute, Teesside University.

Simon Winlow is Senior Lecturer in Sociology at the University of York.

New Directions in Criminological Theory

Edited by Steve Hall and Simon Winlow

Routledge
Taylor & Francis Group

LONDON AND NEW YORK

First published 2012
by Routledge
2 Park Square, Milton Park, Abingdon, Oxon, OX14 4RN

Simultaneously published in the USA and Canada
by Routledge
711 Third Avenue, New York, NY 10017

*Routledge is an imprint of the Taylor & Francis Group, an informa
business*

British Library Cataloguing in Publication Data
A catalogue record for this book is available from the British Library

Library of Congress Cataloging in Publication Data
New directions in criminological theory/edited by Steve Hall and Simon
   Winlow.—1st ed.
     p. cm.
   Includes bibliographical references and index.
   1. Criminology.   I. Hall, Steve, 1995-   II. Winlow, Simon.
   HV6025.N4933 2012
   364.01—dc23
                                                           2011047915

ISBN: 978–1–84392–914–7 (hbk)
ISBN: 978–1–84392–913–0 (pbk)
ISBN: 978–0–203–11786–6 (ebk)

Typeset in Times by
RefineCatch Limited, Bungay, Suffolk

MIX
Paper from
responsible sources
FSC
www.fsc.org   FSC® C004839

Printed and bound in Great Britain by
TJ International Ltd, Padstow, Cornwall

Step forward: we hear that you are a good man.
You cannot be bought, but the lightning
Which strikes the house, also
Cannot be bought.
You hold to what you said.
But what did you say?
You are honest, you say your opinion.
Which opinion?
You do not consider your personal advantages.
Whose advantages do you consider then?
You are a good friend.
But are you a good friend of the good people?
Hear us then: we know
You are our enemy. This is why we shall
Now put you in front of a wall. But in consideration
of your merits and good qualities
We shall put you in front of a good wall and shoot you
With a good bullet from a good gun and bury you
With a good shovel in the good earth.

Bertolt Brecht

Contents

Contributors

Kate Burdis is a final year criminology Ph.D. student at the University of York. Her research interests include theoretical criminology, social theory, consumer culture and crime, political economy and crime, and crimes of the powerful. Her current research, *Illicit Investment Schemes: Criminal Motivations and Cultural Contexts*, explores the subjectivity of those involved in illegitimate high-yield investment schemes. The project is ultimately a theoretical piece but is empirically grounded in interviews with offenders and is funded by the ESRC. Kate has taught theoretical criminology courses at York, Glasgow and Northumbria universities.

Pat Carlen is Visiting Professor at Kent University, Editor-in-Chief of the *British Journal of Criminology*, co-founder of the UK campaigning group Women in Prison, and has published nineteen books and many articles on criminal and social justice. Selected works have been translated into Dutch, Japanese, Norwegian, Portuguese and Spanish. In 1997 she was awarded the American Society of Criminology's Sellin-Glueck Prize for Outstanding International Contributions to Criminology, in 2010 the British Society of Criminology's Award for Outstanding Achievement, and in 2011 an Honorary Doctorate in Law from Lincoln University.

Walter S. DeKeseredy is Professor of Criminology at the University of Ontario Institute of Technology (UOIT). He has published sixteen books and over 100 scientific journal articles and book chapters on violence against women and other social problems. In 2008, the Institute on Violence, Abuse and Trauma gave him the Linda Saltzman Memorial Intimate Partner Violence Researcher Award. He also jointly received the 2004 Distinguished Scholar Award from the American Society of Criminology's (ASC) Division on Women and Crime and the 2007 inaugural UOIT Research Excellence Award. In 1995, he received the Critical Criminologist of the Year Award from the ASC's Division on Critical Criminology (DCC) and in 2008 the DCC gave him the Lifetime Achievement Award.

Jeff Ferrell is currently Professor of Sociology at Texas Christian University, USA, and Visiting Professor of Criminology at the University of Kent, UK.

He is the author of the books *Crimes of Style*, *Tearing Down the Streets*, *Empire of Scrounge*, and, with Keith Hayward and Jock Young, *Cultural Criminology: An Invitation* (winner of the 2009 Distinguished Book Award from the American Society of Criminology's Division of International Criminology), and co-editor of the books *Cultural Criminology*, *Ethnography at the Edge*, *Making Trouble*, *Cultural Criminology Unleashed*, and *Cultural Criminology: Theories of Crime*. He is also the founding and current editor of the New York University Press book series *Alternative Criminology*, and one of the founding editors of the journal *Crime, Media, Culture: An International Journal*, winner of the Association of Learned and Professional Society Publishers' 2006 Charlesworth Award for Best New Journal. In 1998 he received the Critical Criminologist of the Year Award from the Division of Critical Criminology of the American Society of Criminology.

Steve Hall is Professor of Criminology at the Social Futures Institute, Teesside University. After dropping out of university in 1974 he became a nomadic musician, general labourer and avid reader of anything political or philosophical. In the 1980s he worked with young offenders in the de-industrialising northeast of England, and he was active politically during the steelworks and mine closures in County Durham. In 1988 he returned to university, and, after graduating in 1991 began teaching, researching and publishing. Essentially a sociologist, he has also published in the fields of history and radical philosophy. He is the co-author of *Violent Night* (Berg, 2006), his recent co-authored book *Criminal Identities and Consumer Culture* (Willan/Routledge, 2008) has been described as 'an important landmark in criminology', and he is also the author of *Theorizing Crime and Deviance: A New Perspective* (Sage, 2012).

Keith J. Hayward is Professor of Criminology and Sociology at the University of Kent, UK. He has published widely in the areas of cultural criminology, criminological theory (in particular the relationship between consumer culture and crime), popular culture, social theory, and terrorism. He is the author of *City Limits: Crime, Consumer Culture and the Urban Experience* (RoutledgeCavendish, 2004), the co-author of *Cultural Criminology: An Invitation* (Sage, 2008), and the co-editor of *Cultural Criminology Unleashed* (RoutledgeCavendish, 2004), *Criminology* (Oxford University Press, 2nd Edition 2009), *Framing Crime: Cultural Criminology and the Image* (Routledge, 2009), and *Fifty Key Thinkers in Criminology* (Routledge, 2010).

Dick Hobbs is Professor of Sociology at the University of Essex. He is the author of *Doing the Business: Entrepreneurship, The Working Class and Detectives in the East End of London* (Oxford University Press, 1988), *Bad Business: Professional Crime in Modern Britain* (Oxford University Press) and co-author of *Bouncers: Violence and Governance in the Night-time Economy* (Oxford University Press). His recent publications include: *The Eternal Recurrence of Crime and Control* (co-edited with Tim Newburn and David

Downes) (Oxford, 2010), *Securing the Olympic Site* (co-authored with Jon Coaffee, Gary Armstrong and Pete Fussey) (Ashgate, 2011), *Ethnography in Context* (Sage, 2011), and *Lush Life: Constructing Organised Crime in the UK* (Oxford University Press, 2012).

David W. Jones is Principal Lecturer in Psychosocial Studies at the University of East London. He is author of *Understanding Criminal Behaviour: Psychosocial Approaches to Criminality* (Willan, 2008); *Myths, Madness and the Family* (Palgrave, 2002) and co-editor of *Emotion: New Psychosocial Perspectives* (Palgrave, 2009).

Gabe Mythen is Senior Lecturer in Criminology at the University of Liverpool. His work on risk and regulation is located at the intersection between criminology and sociology. His current research is focussed around the construction, mediation and regulation of the terrorist threat and the effects of UK counter-terrorism legislation on Muslim minority groups.

Tim Owen currently lectures in Criminology and Criminal Justice at the University of Central Lancashire. He previously lectured in Sociology at the University of Liverpool, and the Open University in the North West, UK. He recently co-edited *Reconstructing Postmodernism: Critical Debates* with Jason L. Powell (Nova Science Publishers), and wrote *Social Theory and Human Biotechnology* (Nova Science Publishers). His main research interest lies in building bridges between the social and biological sciences, and he has published many articles and book chapters in the areas of criminology, sociology and social policy. Tim is currently engaged in writing his third book, *Criminological Theory: Beyond Postmodernism* for Palgrave Macmillan.

Robert Reiner is Professor of Criminology in the Law Department, London School of Economics. He is author of *The Blue-Coated Worker* (Cambridge University Press, 1978), *The Politics of the Police* (Wheatsheaf, 1985; 2nd Edition 1992; 3rd Edition Oxford University Press, 2000; 4th Edition 2010), *Chief Constables* (Oxford University Press, 1991), *Law and Order: An Honest Citizen's Guide to Crime and Control* (Polity Press, 2007); *Policing, Popular Culture and Political Economy: Towards a Social Democratic Criminology* (Ashgate, 2011). He has co-edited: *Beyond Law and Order* (Macmillan, 1991), *Accountable Policing* (Institute for Public Policy Research, 1993), *Policing* (Dartmouth, 1996), and *The Oxford Handbook of Criminology* (Oxford University Press, 1994; 2nd Edition 1997; 3rd Edition 2002; 4th Edition 2007). He was President of the British Society of Criminology from 1993 to 1996, received the British Society of Criminology Outstanding Achievement Award in 2011. He has been Director of the LSE Mannheim Centre for Criminology, 1995–98, and since 2009. He is an Academician of the Academy of Social Sciences.

Colin Sumner is the Editor of *CrimeTalk*, an e-zine on crime and justice that can be found at www.crimetalk.org.uk. A former lecturer at the University of Cambridge and professor of sociology, criminology and law at the University of East London, he has authored several books, including *Reading Ideologies*; *The Sociology of Deviance: An Obituary*; *Crime, Justice and Underdevelopment*; *Censure, Violence and Culture*; and the *Blackwell Companion to Criminology*. He co-founded the international journal *Theoretical Criminology*.

Steve Tombs is Professor of Sociology at Liverpool John Moores University. He has a long-standing interest in the incidence, nature and regulation of corporate crime, and in particular the regulation and management of health and safety at work. Recent publications include *Regulatory Surrender: Death, Injury and the Non-Enforcement of Law* (Institute of Employment Rights, 2010), *A Crisis of Enforcement: The Decriminalisation of Death and Injury at Work* (Centre for Crime and Justice Studies, 2008) and *Safety Crimes* (Willan, 2007), all co-authored with Dave Whyte. He co-edited: *State, Power, Crime* (Sage, 2009); *Beyond Criminology? Taking Harm Seriously* (Pluto Press, 2004), *Criminal Obsessions* (Crime and Society Foundation, 2005, 2008); *Unmasking the Crimes of the Powerful: Scrutinising States and Corporations* (Peter Lang, 2003); and *Risk, Management and Society* (Kluwer-Nijhoff, 2000). He is also the co-author of *Corporate Crime* (Longman, 1999), *Toxic Capitalism* (Ashgate, 1998, Canadian Scholars' Press, 1999), and *People in Organisations* (Blackwell, 1996). He was Chair of the Centre for Corporate Accountability, 1999–2009.

Sandra Walklate is currently Eleanor Rathbone Chair of Sociology at the University of Liverpool, where she has been since January 2006, having held previous posts at Manchester Metropolitan University, Keele, Salford and Liverpool John Moores. She has written extensively on criminal victimisation, latterly in the particular context of terrorism.

Colin Webster is Professor of Criminology at Leeds Metropolitan University and Visiting Research Fellow at Teesside University. His publications include *Poor Transitions: Social Exclusion and Young Adults* (Policy Press, 2004) and *Understanding Race and Crime* (Open University Press, 2007). He is co-authoring *Youth on Religion: The Development, Negotiation and Impact of Faith and Non-Faith Identity* (Routledge, 2012), *Low-pay, No-pay: Work and Poverty at the Bottom of the UK Labour Market* (Policy Press, 2012), and is co-editing *New Directions, New Generations: Ethnicity, Crime and Justice* (Routledge, 2013).

Michel Wieviorka is currently Administrateur (President) of the Fondation Maison des Sciences de l'Homme (Paris), and Professor at the Ecole des Hautes Etudes en Sciences Sociales (Paris), where he served as director of CADIS (Centre d'Analyse et d'Intervention Sociologiques) from 1993 to 2009. He was President of the International Sociological Association (2006–10). His main research deals with social movements, racism, terrorism, violence, democracy, cultural identities and multiculturalism. Among some forty books in French, several have been translated into various languages, including English: *The Working Class Movement* (with Alain Touraine, Cambridge University Press), *The Arena of Racism* (Sage), *The Making of Terrorism* (University of Chicago Press), *The Lure of Antisemitism* (Brill), *Violence: A New Approach* (Sage), and *Evil: A Sociological Perspective* (Polity Press, forthcoming).

David Wilson is Professor of Criminology at Birmingham City University, and Director of the university's Centre for Applied Criminology. He is the Editor of the *Howard Journal of Criminal Justice*, Vice Chair of the Howard League for Penal Reform and Vice President of New Bridge. A former prison governor, he has written extensively on serial murder and has championed a structural – as opposed to a medical-psychological – approach to understanding this phenomenon. He appears regularly in the print and broadcast media. His most recent book is *Looking For Laura: Public Criminology and Hot News* (Waterside Press).

Eric Wilson is senior lecturer of public law at Monash University, Melbourne, Australia. He received a Doctorate in History from Cambridge University in 1991 and a Doctorate of Juridical Science from the University of Melbourne in 2005. He is the author of *The Savage Republic* (Martinus Nijhoff, 2008). He is currently editing a series of volumes on critical criminology devoted to the relationships between covert government agency, organized crime, and extra-judicial forms of governance. The first volume in the series, *Government of the Shadows: Parapolitics and Criminal Sovereignty*, was published by Pluto Press in 2009. Eric's research interests are critical criminology, the history and philosophy of international law, the comparative law of Southeast Asia, cultural studies, and critical jurisprudence. His next book, *The Dual State: Parapolitics, Carl Schmitt, and the National Security Complex*, will be released by Ashgate Publishing in 2012.

Simon Winlow is Senior Lecturer in Sociology at the University of York. He is the author of *Badfellas: Crime, Tradition and New Masculinities* (Berg, 2001), and co-author of *Bouncers: Violence and Governance in the Night-time Economy* (Oxford University Press, 2003), *Violent Night: Urban Leisure and Contemporary Culture* (Berg, 2006), *Criminal Identities and Consumer Culture: Crime, Exclusion and the New Culture of Narcissism* (Willan/ Routledge, 2008) and the forthcoming *Rethinking Social Exclusion* (Sage, 2012).

Majid Yar is Professor of Sociology at the University of Hull. His research interests include crime and deviance, media/new media, social theory and sexual culture. His publications include *Cybercrime and Society* (2006), *Key Concepts in Criminology* (2008), *The Handbook on Internet Crime* (2009), *Community and Recognition* (2009), and *The Politics of Misrecognition* (2011).

Acknowledgements

The editors would like to thank all those who found the time and exerted considerable effort to contribute to this volume. In these dark days of relentless governmental agendas and institutional audits, many social scientists are box-pressed into a situation that forces them to think twice about contributing to collections such as this one. A powerful behaviourist system of penalties and incentives bears down on individual academics, ushering them politely yet firmly onto the factory floor to produce work that is – to use the latest ugly neologism to make its way into the lexicon of the marketised British university – 'REFable': that is, likely to be considered valuable by those drawn from our peer group to populate disciplinary assessment panels, whose subjective opinion of our work is somehow transposed into the objective distribution of institutional research funding. For so many academics working in today's high-pressure research environment, contributing to an edited collection represents wasted time that could have been spent drafting another article for a 'high-impact' journal. Many of these journals marginalise searching and innovative theoretical work in favour of a constant stream of situational evidence-based policy research. This is of course valuable work in its own right, but affording it such privilege has the effect of prolonging orthodox philosophical and theoretical frameworks rather than encouraging new and revised positions that can furnish us with the explanatory power and research agendas we need to face the rapidly changing times in which we live. We are heartened that so many world-leading and up-and-coming criminologists agreed to put these matters to one side for the time that it took to write the thoughtful essays that comprise this collection. We are convinced that, in the longer term and at a deeper level, it will be writings such as these that have the higher 'impact'. We also extend our heartfelt thanks to all of the M.A. and Ph.D. students we have taught and supervised over the years; perhaps more than anything, the enthusiasm they have shown when exposed to powerful ideas has sustained our conviction that reflexive theory still resides at the heart of social science.

As we write these words our thoughts turn to Bob Lilly, who had agreed to contribute to this volume but was prevented from doing so by illness. Our very best wishes go to Bob and his family.

Introduction

The need for new directions in criminological theory

Steve Hall and Simon Winlow

Whatever happened to new ideas?

Criminology is an unusual academic discipline. Ethics, justice, self-governance, external control and the nature of social order have been subject to serious intellectual consideration in the West since Hesiod, but this vast historical continuum of thought failed to coalesce into a distinct academic discipline until midway through the twentieth century. We have seen self-styled 'criminologists' appearing on the scene since the early nineteenth century, but they had always learnt their trade in other disciplines – statistics, psychiatry, medicine, law, philosophy and so on – and studied crime as something of a sideline. Thus the exact 'origin' of criminology as an academic discipline is difficult to pin down, and this is partly a reflection of the contested nature of its history in the West. Here in Britain, early criminological thought tended to be state-centred, positivistic and interested in the actual causes of crime only insofar as they fitted neatly into existing or developing governmental projects. Classical liberal legalists insisted on crime as an act of free will and choice, medics insisted on delving into the individual's genetic and neurological systems, and social-liberal welfarists focused on economic disruption, poverty and faulty forms of moral and social reproduction. All shared a common concern with internal and external forms of governance, and thus during this period it would have perhaps been more fitting to call the discipline 'contrology' rather than 'criminology' (Ditton, 1979). In this mode of thinking aetiology is a mere convenience, something to be explained away in a manner that affirms the political and governmental projects of the day or their approved sub-dominant opposition. This tradition still dominates criminology today, where the classical-liberal mainstream maintains its dominant discourse of free will and faulty socialisation in long-running tension with social liberalism's discourse of poverty and social inequality. Any alternative explanation must fight hard for survival in the interstices of this rather unspectacular and tedious clash of the weary Titans, with, it must be said, little support from a predominantly left-liberal criminological discipline that shuns aetiology and applies most of its effort to the analysis of the control system and the protection of the individual's rights within it. Indeed, such was the dominance of 'controlology' that some influential theories – such as symbolic interactionism, labelling theory and Foucauldian theory – were imported whole to posit criminality and deviance as the products of social reaction and the constitutive and reproductive power of the control system. Look no further; everything criminological springs from the process of control itself. Without diminishing the importance of a thorough and ongoing critique of the control system and its human rights issues, we must address the problem that this intellectual neglect not only diminishes criminology's political and cultural importance but also leaves the aetiological field wide open to crude, populist forms of biological determinism and classical-liberal individualism. Since the Second World War, the criminological aircraft has tried to fly on one wing, and therefore it simply cannot get off the runway.

In the light of this aetiological entropy and dismissal of intellectual curiosity, perhaps we might begin to question left-liberal criminology's self-constructed heroic mythology. In the late 1960s, so the story goes, intrepid sociologists with an interest in deviance began to challenge the dominant conservative and administrative narratives. In keeping with the times, many of these new academic criminologists were left-liberals keen to criticise the intrusiveness of the modernist state and the oppressively restrictive nature of the social structure, whilst simultaneously identifying the grotesque injustices of an increasingly global capitalist economy. Their critique of mainstream criminological positivism was of course aimed at a hard-to-miss target, and conservative and liberal factions continue to duke it out for the hearts and minds of aspiring academic criminologists to this day. Much of this work has been quite productive, and we do not want to begin this book with an indiscriminate swipe at all that has gone before. Indeed, in the race between administrative and left-liberal criminologists to produce intellectually nourishing work the latter win hands down; it could be said that they were the only ones really trying. However, the ongoing battle between the dourness and sluggishness of positivistic 'evidence-based policy research' and the boundless romanticism of left-liberal criminology has clearly created something of a disciplinary impasse, which, together with a broad range of historical contingencies that emanate from outside the academy, has ground the project to a virtual halt. Criminology these days has lost much of the intellectual vitality that is commonly associated with the discipline up to the 1970s, and even where that vitality remains it must be said that it experiences difficulty in leaving these decades behind and producing analyses that explain the shape and motivational background of criminality in the current crisis-ridden epoch of advanced global capitalism. Despite high student interest in undergraduate criminology courses, there is little sense of any real forward momentum in the aetiological-theoretical sphere. In the rest of this short introduction we want to outline why this sense of disciplinary inertia has arisen, how it is reflected in contemporary academic practice, and what we might begin to do about it.

Textbookification

The intellectual history of academic criminology is now clear for all to see. All one has to do is to pick up one of the dazzling array of criminology textbooks and a surprisingly clear and rather linear history of the discipline is laid out for academics to reproduce *ad infinitum* in lecture theatres and seminar rooms across the West. The story starts with Bentham's utilitarianism and Beccaria's model for an enlightened criminal justice system, before moving on through Lombrosan 'scientific' criminology towards the early sociology of the Chicago School, glossing over or missing out entirely interesting thinkers such as Simmel and Veblen, the early European socialist thought of Engels, Bonger, and the early Freudians such as Adler, Aichhorn, Fromm and Lacan. At this point, so the story goes, we started to think seriously about crime, its social roots and its connections to the immediate environment, yet the foundation of criminological theory was – once the break with Durkheim had been made by the Chicago School of sociology – limited to early American liberal-progressivism, with its symbolic interactionist core. This is then followed by a quick look at Sutherland's theory of differential association before moving swiftly on to the American sub-cultural theory of Cloward and Ohlin, Miller and Cohen. A disinterested glance is cast at conservative control theory before we move on swiftly to arrive in the 1960s, that celebrated decade when people apparently threw off the shackles of modernist ideology, fought against the authoritarian state and constructed the dazzling new ideas that would transform both the academy and the world beyond. Here the story slows down to a crawl as we investigate labelling theory, Matza's theories of drift and neutralisation and Becker's classic text of that era, *Outsiders*. From this point the story cuts its ties to the United States and ventures across the Atlantic to investigate the radical liberalism of Britain in the swinging sixties, the deviancy conferences and the establishment of critical criminology, feminist criminology and the roots of what is now cultural criminology as permanent and tenaciously oppositional sub-disciplines. After that not much of note happens: a few famous studies here and there, the development of yet more disciplinary sub-categories, but nothing really seismic. Left realism, postmodernism and risk theory entered the stage, but – with some notable exceptions (see Young, 1999; Lea, 2002; Currie, 2007; 2010) – were rapidly absorbed into the 'contratology' tradition.

What we have presented here is of course a quick caricature, but our point is to draw the reader's attention to the fundamental artificiality and selectivity of the standard textbook narrative. Criminology has created its history not as a developing, incremental, cohesive project, but in retrospect, looking backwards to pick out the key ideas and intellectual themes that form the basis of a narrative that allows the discipline to establish a clear identity and history, a story of who we are and how we got here. The most challenging aspect of this combined creation and evolutionary myth is that it necessarily involves numerous acts of exclusion (see Hall, 2012). It is often textbook writers who play a key role in determining what counts in the history of the discipline. As they leaf through articles, monographs, policy documents and, of course, older textbooks in their search for material, they also, by a process of elimination, play an active role in deciding not simply what will be preserved for posterity, but also what will be lost in the mists of time. This process becomes more problematic when we enter the contemporary world of mass higher education and burgeoning undergraduate populations who must be provided with accessible introductory texts that are not too intellectually taxing and contain, in one volume, everything they need to know about criminology. One gets a sense that contemporary textbook writers primarily consult other textbooks in order to tell the story of twentieth-century criminology, and a gradual, lazy consensus builds in relation to the roots and boundaries of our discipline. These textbooks then become the primary source of information for harried lecturers who must, at the same time as facing rising teaching and administration loads, construct visually entrancing PowerPoint presentations for demanding students who, now, in their new role of empowered consumers reversing the traditional structure of relations in the university, sit in judgment of the disciplinary experts who are employed to teach and generally satisfy the newly forged desire of students for a 'positive university experience'.

The next stage of this mutating educational simulacrum arises with the production of the subsequent generation of academic criminologists who, in some cases at least, have failed to read classic texts in the original. Grade inflation, the rise of new electronic teaching media and a general decline in the level of traditional academic skills that students bring with them upon entry all mean that it is now possible to pass criminology degrees – although perhaps not with flying colours – without ever entering a library and without reading the canon, never mind what the canon's guardians systematically excluded. Institutional pressures make it very difficult to fail students, lest their departure from the university contributes to a decline in league table positions. We can add to this the very real occupational problems faced by younger criminologists as they set out to build their all-important intellectual profiles. Teaching and administration loads have risen considerably since the golden age of the 1960s academy, and a subtle but insistent magnetic force tends to draw talented younger academics towards the higher-profile established research universities that still cling on to research assessment as an 'income stream'. Many of those who remain too long in Britain's post-1992 New University sector are likely to be too weighed down by admin-istration and high teaching loads to be able to build a publishing career with anything like the ease and the rapidity of those in the research sector. Thus it is no surprise that lecturers are forced to deliver lectures on topics that do not lie within their particular academic specialism, and neither is it unreasonable to claim that lecturers turn to textbooks when faced with the prospect of delivering yet another lecture in a full-to-bursting teaching schedule.

Textbook writers usually adopt the position of the objective and politically neutral presenter of basic facts or 'contested' ideas. Very rarely do they display any overt ideological or political affiliation, and of course 'contested' means an interminable simulated war of mutual deconstruction, in which there can never be either a winner or a consensual platform on which we can move forward. Thus we no longer construct theories – what's the point? – but proliferating 'theoretical frameworks' to sell to students, who can then begrudgingly shoehorn their hurriedly informed choices into their dissertations, no matter how awkward the fit, so the appropriate box can be ticked on the mark sheet. New criminologists adopt this bearing in relation to the grand intellectual ideas of our discipline. The worst examples of this sort of thing can be seen in those textbooks that offer a basic description of a theory, then follow it up with bullet-point criticisms. In this way, the reader is encouraged to acknowledge that Marx made a few good points, but communism ultimately failed and his analysis did not leave enough space for individual agency. Adorno's analysis of the culture industry is useful in understanding the development of post-war popular culture, but ultimately his model is too deterministic and restrictive. Merton's strain theory is good in some ways, bad in others. Taylor was right about this, wrong about that. On and on we go until it becomes obvious that the core message, deeply indicative of our times, is that students are increasingly being instructed that there is *nothing* – even in a complex synthetic form – to which one can fully commit. This should be quite acceptable; indeed the constant reflexive critique of older ideas is an essential aspect of scientific and philosophical development, but this is a useful exercise *only* when the scientific-philosophical community is committed to the principle that we can actually develop better ideas that explain the social world in genuinely insightful ways. However, the current dominance of liberal-pluralist, postmodernist, Weberian constitutionalist and pragmatic risk 'theories' has eroded this basic goal. Today the proper comportment of the intellectual is to be fully without belief, to be sceptical and cynical about *everything* that has existed, exists now and will exist in the future; except scepticism itself and its complex ideological roots: being sceptical about that would just be going too far.

All truth claims come with the overarching textbook master-caveat that no idea is perfect, and every intellectual position attracts criticism with no end in sight. Instead, readers are encouraged to treat criminological knowledge as a veritable smorgasbord of phenomenological forms and theoretical 'frameworks', none of which are really much good when it comes down to explaining the 'complex' empirical world. We should take from Merton what is useful, put it together with what is useful in Park, weave in a little bit of Young, and doff one's cap to Becker, but the end result is usually not a positive synthesis of ideas but gloomy resignation to the notion that if all these ideas are largely wrong there is little point in having ideas in the first place. As for reviving ideas already rejected by the discipline's elite group of established anti-establishmentarians for reasons that no-one can quite remember . . . well, forget it. Students are encouraged to occupy the rather depressing, apathetic and far from intellectually taxing realm of the 'middle ground', creating 'balanced' arguments without ever knowing that this amounts to compulsory liberalism, the ideology whose cleverness lies in its ability to deny that it is an ideology. They should risk nothing and ensure that they don't alienate the marker of assignments with actual intellectual commitment. Essays should be pitched as a review of the literature, and, like the textbooks that are used as a guide, every position should be criticised. All essay conclusions must avoid 'determinism', 'reductionism', 'essentialism' and so on, acknowledge alternative positions, and balance themselves securely with elegant poise on the fence. And, of course, lest we forget, today's students are tomorrow's academics, to whom all ideas are, it seems, reduced to the sad status of mere opinions. The wellspring of theoretical criminology – curiosity and the drive to understand – has not naturally run dry; it has been quite deliberately filled up and blocked off in a huge postmodernist earth-moving operation, leaving us with the interminable simulated contestation of what we already have. Thus we can 'do criminology' by placing arbitrarily chosen theoretical frameworks around our hallowed empirical data like the wrapping paper on birthday presents. The more the merrier, lest some of us begin to settle on a set of ideas that seem to make sense of what's going on around us. This is the way we wash our hands, on a cold and frosty morning.

At this stage we are willing to risk a tentative conclusion that this trend – to say nothing important lest it devalues one's intellectual credentials – is creeping into the mainstream of academic publishing. Crime, and its causes and control, is an intellectually demanding area of study that should draw from the deepest wells of philosophy, social theory, psychology, history and rapidly evolving empirical reality. Yet, in the hands of some academic criminologists the field becomes an almost tortuous collection of meaningless micro-analyses, irritating social research jargon and statistical obscurantism followed by banal conclusions that continue to hold out the hope of tentative truth claims, further down the road, perhaps after another round of grant applications and field research.

This is not a problem that afflicts only criminology's positivists and criminal justice specialists. Even those who position themselves as critical, cultural or radical criminologists can find themselves trapped on a carousel where the conclusions of the past come round and round again to demand their validation. Rather than looking at an external world of perpetual crisis and mutating forms, a world of quite incredible injustices and harms, we continue our perpetual fetishistic rediscovery of moral panics, sub-cultural resistance and the aggressive labelling and demonisation of the powerless. Is this all we have now, the constant reiteration of what already exists? Is this the limit of our creativity? Shouldn't we be encouraging our colleagues and students to *rethink the entire problem* of crime, deviance and social order in ways that relate to today's changing world? And – dare we say it – could some of the ideas arbitrarily rejected in the past by the dominant post-war liberal–conservative alliance be reworked to create more illuminating theories of crime and harm?

This act of rethinking has also been made difficult in the practical sense. Not only are academic criminologists compelled to engage in a ceaseless cycle of grant applications, administration, teaching, research and publication – occupational control measures that act as a counterforce to the possibility that someone somewhere might, even accidentally, have an original thought – but we also face the task of swimming against a powerful current that pushes us towards reasserting key disciplinary tropes, concepts and 'theories'. It's not that the Anglo-American research elite don't like theories – although some have been heard to say precisely that, quite unequivocally, at conferences and seminars – but that they are quite happy working with the official theoretical frameworks that have been handed down to them; it's just that they don't like to call their theories theories, and even when they do it's difficult to know whether they really want to take the theories they are allowed to call theories seriously. In this act of denial the established philosophical principles and socio-psychological theories that really do inform research agendas and data analysis melt into the background to become *doxa*, ideological forms that resemble traditional creation myths, the invisible common sense that nobody bothers to question. In this climate, actually risking a genuinely new idea can be quite disconcerting. One immediately has to face up to being caught up in the Schopenhauerian shuffle; each new idea will be first laughed out of court, then met with symbolic violence should even a few start taking it too seriously; then it will become the received wisdom that everyone knew about anyway. Finally, the idea can fulfil its true destiny by joining the *doxa* and gradually disappearing into the ether; in the liberal *doxa*, everything is swept up in a Derridean vortex of endless scepticism and deconstruction, where everything is born to be finished when it's unfinished and to have a brief and fleeting meaning only in the process of rendering it meaningless. To the liberal mind, settling on a meaning can be politically dangerous, not to mention personally painful and scary because it might demand some truly *political* action in the real world. What the theorist is left with is the prospect that the new idea, no matter how good or bad it is, will be derided either mockingly or quite viciously by a colleague – often an expert in a specialist field and with a vested interest in censoring alternative viewpoints – during the anonymous peer review process; published reviews are usually far less harsh, because of course our brave defenders of the framework have to put their real names on them. It is far easier to publish an article that offers support for the dominant mode of explanation, or criticises some aspect of the dominant mode of thinking without ever daring to suggest a complete replacement, than to publish an article that directly challenges that orthodoxy at its deepest intellectual and political roots. Criminology's preferred image of reflexivity, we must suspect, is largely cosmetic.

To *rethink* the problem of crime, deviance and social order means to withdraw from the immediacy of the debate. Rather than rushing to judgement, one should redouble one's efforts to discover the truth of the event. This act of rethinking means that one should countenance the possibility that orthodox positions are not just wrong, but may be actual impediments to understanding, or ideological constructions produced to 'cover up' reality. It means a refusal to engage with the expectation that one must endorse one or another of the existing ideas, and instead holds out the possibility of constructing an entirely new or at least thoroughly revised mode of explanation. It means diligently excavating the political and ideological background of truth claims. It means that, rather than rushing to answer social and governmental anxieties about crime and justice, one should actively attempt to discover new problems for society to be concerned about or encourage society to understand existing problems in new ways. This willingness to take on the difficult intellectual task of extracting oneself from the prevailing disciplinary logics of contemporary criminology is essential if we are to rejuvenate and reengage the disciplinary dialectic that we need to drive criminological theory forward. If Hegel and Adorno were right that the dialectic's antitheses do not come from elsewhere but lie immanent in the contradictions of the thesis itself, we must suspect that for some political-ideological reason or other they are being held in protective custody. To be sure, this might demand a few sacrifices: a few senior administrators might become a little disgruntled, a few promotions might be missed, senior figures in the discipline might get a bit upset, and friendships and networks might be tested. But the potential outcome is that we once again become capable of actually taking an academic lead on the key issues of our time. Taking on this task can create a new period of intense intellectual curiosity, and make criminology once again vital and vigorous, capable of shaping critical social analysis well into the twenty-first century.

The first step is to abandon criminology's weirdly postmodern, self-referential gaze. In the last decade or so, and for the first time in its history, criminology has sought to establish firm parameters on what is and what is not classed as 'criminology'. It does this by creating a myth about its own history and then enshrining it as 'fact'. For years criminology was happy to acknowledge that it was essentially an importer of ideas and theories from cognate fields and more firmly established academic disciplines across the social sciences and humanities. It also acted as a meeting place of sorts, an intellectual space into which academics from different disciplinary backgrounds could come to debate the causes and control of crime and social harm. In recent years there seems to have been a gradual erosion of this very positive intellectual firmament. This seems to be partly a reflection of the huge growth of university teaching and research programmes in criminology and criminal justice across the West, a process that demands a clear curriculum in order to assess student achievement in any given field. There are also a broad range of factors at work here that emanate from outside the academy and are beyond the remit of this brief introduction; suffice it to say that criminologists encounter their main obstacle each time they try to obtain funding from an external body for a *really* interesting research question. But our claim is that criminologists – especially those criminologists with an interest in reforming the theoretical frameworks in whose construction we were not involved but in whose maintenance we are actively involved whether we like it (or indeed know it) or not – must once again envision our discipline as both an importer and a generator of cutting-edge ideas relevant to the world today, as well as a meeting place that welcomes lively, cross-disciplinary discussion.

For instance, in the last few years radical philosophy and theoretical psychoanalysis have produced important new ideas that can help us to understand postmodern subjectivity, historical continuity and stasis, the nature of postmodern capitalism and the transformation of politics. These are ideas that should, indeed must, be fully integrated into theoretical criminology if we are to progress from this point. There are also important new ideas coming on stream in political theory, psychology, cultural studies and the humanities, and the same is true of any number of associated disciplines, including new analyses from the natural sciences on what is material or immaterial in the human world. Instead of embracing these ideas and drawing them into the field of criminological analysis we have tended to dismiss them as overly abstract, and 'detached from reality' (see for instance Young, 2011). It is quite a salutary thought that Young, one of the most influential figures in post-war criminology, indulges in the sort of lampooning of theory that conceals a deep fear of it and an inability to work with it in a constructive way, and demands that we continue on without ever constructing new ideas. It is far easier to dismiss everything that occurs as yet another moral panic, or identify in the bland homogeneity of consumer culture new forms of political resistance in the semiology of the latest corporate youth fashion, or partake in the tedious and interminable mud-slinging skirmish between the left- and right-wing liberals who make up the criminological mainstream. Young would have critical criminologists think a little harder than the 'datasaurs' of abstract empiricism, but not quite as hard as the 'theorodactyls' who 'soar above reality in an endless quest for a fashionable perch' (ibid.: 218). Young's cautionary tale is a stern warning for us to fall into line and dutifully apply ourselves to the endless regurgitation of the once-radical liberal-left theories of the 1960s and 1970s, as if those ideas are incapable of improvement or replacement and there is no point in trying. Young does not really dislike the 'theorodactyls'; in fact he is beholden to them and more worried about new creatures coming along to blow his own exalted and venerable flying dinosaurs out of the sky.

On the contrary, we feel the time is now ripe for new ideas. The perpetual crises of the early twenty-first century, which occur against the background of the absolute triumph of liberal-capitalism, demand to be taken seriously. We cannot put this contemporary period and its criminological forms into theoretical relief with the old ideas of the 1960s and 1970s, and certainly not with the defeatist pragmatism of the 1980s and 1990s. These crises fully deserve deep theoretical interventions, and we cannot continue to theorise crime and harm conveniently *as if* the end of history has really arrived and no alternative is possible; nothing is more intellectually restrictive than the assumption of the eternal recurrence of *what is* and the adoption of all thought to its pragmatic management. We have seen this assumption reduce politics to post-political homogeneity; to allow this to happen to intellectual life in general would be grossly negligent, the realisation of the totalitarian dream in the most improbable of forms. We no longer live in the 1960s, and whilst we should respect some of the major theoretical accomplishments of the past, we should not slavishly regard this particular period as the pinnacle of human thought and attempt to make its theories fit into a very different political, economic, cultural and ideological climate. Instead, we should, in an exercise shorn of sentimental attachment and vested interests, take from those theories what remains vital and pertinent before redoubling our efforts to make sense of the world both as it is and as it could be. It is only in the gap between what is and what is not that true thought can actually take place (Badiou, 2001).

All that might seem like a tall order. This is only one edited collection, and its aim is not to lay down a blueprint or manifesto for a universal criminological theory of the future. Books that attempt to perform that task tend to be premature and rather one-dimensional, and even those that offer more modest and feasible manifestos for specific positions (see for instance Ferrell *et al.*, 2008; O'Malley, 2010) lack the inter-disciplinary breadth and the philosophical and empirical depth to put forward a convincing case. What the authors of this collection have done is put into question the way criminological knowledge is produced, evaluate the current condition of theory, and suggest possible ways forward towards new theories that will be relevant to the current shape and trajectory of crime and harm in today's globalising neoliberal world, and, perhaps, in some ways commensurable in the sense that their main concepts can somehow 'speak' to each other through their walls. Without theory, data is simply a disconnected jumble of dubious and fleeting factoids. The construction of theory is a collective organic process; it is the responsibility of researchers to once again become theorists, and theorists to become researchers, and construct new and more relevant analyses as they go along. One thing is certain, though: past explanations no longer hold much water, and paramount amongst these failures is the postmodernist–deconstructionist paradigm that claims that no theories can hold any water at all except for a brief moment in time at the local micro-level. Many of the essays in this collection attempt to move away from that paradigm.

Structure of the book

It must be emphasised that this small collection can only scratch the surface of the huge task before us and provide a few pointers to possible *directions* that our thought can take, hence the title. If others decline to take up the baton and expand the discussion, the project is dead. Our collection starts at the foundations, with an attempt to dig down and investigate some of criminology's underlying disciplinary practices and philosophical and political contexts. In the first section four essays are loosely drawn together under the title 'Epistemological and Political Reflections'. In Chapter 1 Pat Carlen examines the epistemological context for the collection in an essay that addresses the tricky yet profoundly important foundational issues of the production of knowledge and political activism within academic criminology. Chapter 2 is offered by Robert Reiner, an important and – given the turmoil caused by the current global crisis in the capitalist economy – very timely call to criminologists to return to political economy in analyses of crime, policing and punishment. In Chapter 3, Majid Yar begins with the observation that post-'68 critical criminology failed to incorporate the towering achievements of European critical theory into its corpus. Yar focuses on the developing field of zemiology, or the social harm perspective, and suggests persuasively that aspects of contemporary critical theory, especially in the area of social recognition, can provide a richer theoretical basis for analyses of social harm. In Chapter 4, Walter DeKeseredy offers an expert and highly illuminating dissection of the current state of criminological theory in North America. DeKeseredy notes the onward march of what Elliot Currie (2007) has called 'So what? Criminology' and the consequent marginalisation of theoretical criminology in the major academic institutions in the United States, but also identifies some signs of life in both Canada and the US, one of which is the relatively recent development of cultural criminology.

The second section addresses 'Criminological Theory, Culture and the Subject' and draws together six very different papers. The first, Chapter 5, is written by Tim Owen, whose 'post-postmodern' analysis attempts to bridge the gap between criminological theory, evolutionary psychology and behavioural genetics with a preliminary analysis that presents an enlightened view of their interaction and suggests ways forward for their eventual incorporation into criminological theory. Chapter 6 is the work of Michel Wieviorka, notable French social theorist and former president of the International Sociological Association. Here he offers a short and accessible introduction to his account of the decline of the social and the rise of personal subjectivity as the basis of his theoretical intervention into our understanding of violence. In Chapter 7, Colin Webster addresses the place of 'race' in criminological theory. Webster is particularly concerned with the relationship between 'race' and class in Britain and sees these forms of discrimination as 'mutually compounding'. Here he attempts to create an innovative theoretical framework that might allow us to generate some momentum and move beyond the largely empiricist nature of much criminological thinking on 'race' and crime in the UK. In Chapter 8, Keith Hayward assesses new ideas in cultural geography and how they might encourage criminologists to think in a more informed manner about the relationship between space and crime. For Hayward, the influence of the Chicago School continues to shape criminological accounts of space, but here he claims that a new theoretical approach that foregrounds a cultural analysis of the internal dynamics of space might be a more productive means of developing this area of criminological analysis. Steve Hall is the author of Chapter 9, a topical assessment of the recent riots that swept across England during the summer of 2011. He uses the riots' political failure and rapid slide into 'aggravated shopping' and haphazard skirmishes to enjoin criminologists to move beyond the standard intellectual battlements of the 'left' and 'right' as they now appear on a truncated post-political spectrum. To this end criminology must reject many of its underlying philosophical foundations, draw upon Continental philosophy and construct new theories that link today's nihilistic consumer-centred forms of criminality with the new forms of ideology and subjectivity that dominate the neoliberal world. In Chapter 10, Colin Sumner, originator of the concept of *social censure*, a useful home-grown idea unwisely neglected by criminology's narrowband mainstream, replies to his neo-conservative US critics who want to resurrect the defunct idea of deviant behaviour from a moral absolutist position. Also commenting on the recent UK riots, he argues that little about what was censured as rioting can be called deviance; much of this form of capital destruction was minor compared to that which followed recent investment banking failures. The censure of the riots reflects the absence of moral authority in government rather than political or economic deviance amongst the 'rioters'.

Our third section addresses the theme of 'Criminological Theory and Violence'. In the first essay in this section, Chapter 11, David Jones argues perceptively for the reintroduction of psychological theory into twenty-first century criminological thought to create links with more socially orientated theories. With this in mind, Jones offers an exposition of 'personality disorders' and suggests ways in which a new interdisciplinary framework might help us to better understand the dynamics of inclusion and exclusion, humiliation and violence. Simon Winlow follows up with Chapter 12, a critique of the production of contemporary criminological knowledge that moves on to present an advanced psychosocial theory of subjective violence. David Wilson writes the final chapter in this section, Chapter 13. Wilson, Britain's foremost commentator on serial killing, furnishes us with broader view that looks down below the visceral subjective foreground of violent predatory crime to offer a reflective account of the social, economic and cultural contexts in which such crime takes place.

The final section is entitled 'Crime and Criminological Theory in the Global Age' and contains six chapters from another group of notable criminologists who provide us with examples of the ways in which theories can be applied to crimes and harms in the age of global neoliberal capitalism. First, in Chapter 14 cultural criminology's leading North American exponent, Jeff Ferrell, unveils a new theoretical means of grasping the profound sense of rootlessness and flux that seems endemic in our economy, culture and society as we encounter the disruptive forces of global capitalism. Ferrell is of course a noted ethnographer as well as a theorist, and this paper is of particular note as it furnishes us with a clear indication of Ferrell's willingness to integrate political economy into the project of cultural criminology. Next, in Chapter 15 Dick Hobbs, another notable ethnographer and Britain's most astute commentator on organised and professional crime in its cultural and economic contexts, offers a multi-dimensional analysis of contemporary organised crime and governmental attempts to control it. In Chapter 16 Kate Burdis, a doctoral researcher and Steve Tombs, a leading international commentator on social harm and the 'crisis of enforcement' that hampers the regulation of powerful corporate and state organisations, investigate the social harms occurring in the wake of the current global financial crisis. They call for a concerted attempt to understand criminal subjectivities, constructed in the shadow of global neoliberalism, that energise and reproduce this plutocratic system. In Chapter 17, Eric Wilson, from Monash University in Australia, investigates the world of parapolitics, the 'in-determinate space(s) of convergence among the state, national security agencies, and criminal cartels'. Borrowing heavily from Paul Virilio's theory of *dromology*, based on the concept of 'speed as power', and using the example of the recent financial crisis, Wilson argues that twenty-first century critical criminology must extend its remit and begin to analyse these crucial spaces, where covert state–criminal associations operate with ruthless and potentially harmful dromological efficiency. The final chapter in our collection is written by Gabe Mythen and Sandra Walklate. In 'Global Terrorism, Risk and the State', the authors firmly connect criminology to global politics as they investigate the rise of securitisation and the discourse of 'the new terrorism'. They argue that the failed, disproportionate and socially harmful 'war on terror' has been driven not by real extant threats but by imagined future attacks, and conclude by suggesting that critical criminology turn its theoretical gaze onto the 'uses and abuses of political violence'.

References

Badiou, A. (2001) *Ethics: An essay on the understanding of evil*. London: Verso.

Currie, E. (2007) 'Against Marginality: Arguments for a public criminology', *Theoretical Criminology*, 11, 175–90.

——(2010) 'Plain Left Realism: An appreciation and some thoughts for the future', *Crime, Law and Social Change*, 54, 111–24.

Ditton, J. (1979) *Controlology: Beyond the new criminology*. London: Macmillan.

Ferrell, J., Hayward, K. and Young, K. (2008) *Cultural Criminology: An invitation*. London: Sage.

Hall, S. (2012) *Theorizing Crime and Deviance: A new perspective*. London: Sage.

Lea, J. (2002) *Crime and Modernity: Continuities in left realist criminology*. London: Sage.

O'Malley, P. (2010) *Crime and Risk*. London: Sage.

Young, J. (1999) *The Exclusive Society*. London: Sage.

——(2011) *The Criminological Imagination*. Cambridge: Polity.

Part I

Epistemological and political reflections

1 Criminological knowledge

Doing critique; doing politics[1]

Pat Carlen

The role of academics in society has been of perennial interest to philosophers, scientists and social scientists. In 2005, however, the debate in social science was given fresh impetus by the publication of Michael Burawoy's 2004 presidential address to the American Sociological Association, entitled 'For Public Sociology' (Clawson *et al.* 2007). Since then, debate about the desirability of a 'public criminology' has become one of the staples of criminological polemic (e.g. Uggen and Inderbitzen 2006; Loader and Sparks 2010). However, the term 'public' has proved to be something of a dead weight as far as this particular debate is concerned, since it could reasonably be claimed that with the majority of criminologists engaged in publication, teaching, campaigning or government consultancy, criminology has always been primarily 'public' (see Ericson 2005 for a similar view). None the less, much of the debate has got bogged down with discussion about how to define 'public', rather than with addressing the main issue as to the desirable and possible roles for academic criminologists in penal politics. That is why the term 'public criminology' is used sparingly in this chapter. Instead, the phrase 'doing politics' is routinely employed. It refers, specifically, to debates and oppositional struggles between players involved in the development of criminal justice and penal policies, including: local and national politicians, civil servants, campaigners on crime and penal justice issues, crime victims, religious groups, media, and academic criminologists – each arguing from a different mix of political, ideological, epistemological and ethical standpoints, and, from each of these standpoints, often developing internally logical crimin-ologies. Academic criminology, in the political context, is but one criminology among many (see Carlen 2010).

The arguments which follow stem from an assumption that although critique is inevitably political, critique and politics are separately embedded in the opposi-tional discourses of altruism and vested interest. Two questions then arise. First: is it either desirable and/or possible for academic criminologists to engage in critique *and* penal politics? Second: how can criminologists possibly work with the contradictions between altruistic critique and a penal politics democratically embedded in the different and legitimate interests of all parties involved?

The rest of the chapter will be divided into four parts. First, 'Criminological Critique and Penal Politics: Are They Compatible?' puts forward the argument that, although doing academic criminology and doing politics are logically incompatible activities, because of the existential force of those same fundamental contradictions, academic criminologists have no choice: if they do critique, they also do politics. Second, 'Doing Critique, Doing Politics: Hard Choices' discusses, with examples, some of the strategic difficulties and dilemmas inherent in the inevitable clash of professional ethics and political interests which confront criminologists engaged in both deconstructive critique and reconstructive criminal justice politicking. Third, 'Beware the Search for Truth' identifies and warns against some contemporary threats to criminological critique and a democratic penal politics. Finally, 'New Directions for Criminological Knowledge' concludes the chapter by arguing that although criminology as a profession should see itself as a service industry producing academic criminological expertise, its appropriate sphere of political activity, *as a profession*, is within universities rather than within the political arena. Criminologists enter the political arena with values and agendas other than those developed under the auspices of science.

Criminological critique and penal politics: are they compatible?

Academic criminology is different from other perspectives on lawbreaking and criminal justice because, like other scientific disciplines, it is professionally bound to engage in analytic critique according to the scientific and legitimated methodological protocols of its discipline; and independently of political pressures and self-interest. Accordingly, it attempts to forge analyses which provide accounts for the ever-changing faces of crime and the social, cultural, economic and political conditions in which lawbreaking is seen, or not seen, to be a social issue. This is a complex task, the product of which (like much scientific work) does not easily lend itself to sound-bite description and political rhetoric. To add to the complexity of critique, academic criminologists do not speak with one voice. Insofar as its practitioners (variously) consider the causes of crime to be embedded in an individual's psychological or psycho-social make-up and/or a jurisdiction's local and global politics, economy or culture, academic criminology broadens out to become an interdisciplinary and cross-disciplinary social science, albeit one with no definitive epicentre. The contested meanings of the concepts of crime and justice result in the theoretical and investigative terrains of criminology being constituted and continuously transformed by a range of academic disciplines: sociology, law, economics, psychology, geography, philosophy, statistics and history. All have their experts specialising in crime, and within these groupings a miscellany of investigative methodologies and modes of analysis are deployed.

Cutting across the traditional disciplines, and mushrooming as the preconditions for crime continuously change and regroup, are a bewildering number of specialist academic criminologies: comparative, critical, cultural, environmental, feminist, global, Marxist, psycho-social, crime science, harm reduction, and many more, each fashioned and continuously refashioning, to meet the new demands of changing times (see Carlen 1998, 2010). Yet, however inclusive or exclusive the disciplinary umbrella under which an academic criminologist works, the critical aim is always to interrogate the changing preconditions of specified aspects of crime and criminal justice so that, via discovery and critique, new knowledge might be produced. Criminology's parameters thus expand or shrink according to the conceptual framework within which any individual research project is pursued. This seeming individuality and difference in pursuit of knowledge, however, emanates, contradictorily, from the altruism of the collective ethic of independence and lack of compromise in critique. Given, therefore, that critique necessarily calls into question the status quo, and altruism declines to pursue personal interest, is it desirable for a professional, academic criminologist to engage in both critique and penal politics? Is it possible? And if, as I shall argue, it is both desirable and possible, what are the implications for doing critique and doing politics? For while all criminology is public, doing critique and doing politics is engaged in by individuals who, though they work under a collective professional ethic, hold a variety of religious, cultural and political beliefs about the nature of crime and punishment and a variety of epistemologies (or anti-epistemologies) about the nature of research, knowledge and ideology. Thus, although it might be common sense to assume that the main reason for doing criminology is to create new, more effective and more just ways of doing penal justice, the desirability and/or possibility of criminologists simultaneously doing critique and doing politics (in the sense of making effective interventions into criminal justice issues) has been hotly contested by both criminologists and government administrators. Criminologists have worried about the corruption and distortion of academic theory by policymakers paying lip service to new criminological knowledge, arguments and findings while at the same time, incorporating them into justifications for retrogressive policies (Smart 1989; Carlen 2002: 155–72; Walters 2003). A further concern, moreover, has been provoked by the recurring summary dismissal by governments of theories and research findings which have not meshed with political desire (Hope 2008).

Policymakers, for their part, have been equally frustrated: either by a criminological pursuit of research not seen as being obviously relevant to immediate and pressing crime and justice issues; or by analyses seen as most probably entailing penal policies involving political suicide for any political party willing to endorse them, and professional suicide for any individual officials rash enough to persevere in proposing them in face of media and popular opposition. There is also a more generally held suspicion that academic criminologists are insufficiently concerned about taking seriously non-academic views on crime and punishment.

The main stumbling block to greater collaboration between academics and policy makers inheres in an historical and fundamental difference in their missions. Under the auspices of science the professional mission of academic criminologists is to engage in constant critique of the taken-for-granted meanings of crime and punishment within which the policy issues are framed. Civil servants, conversely, are employed to advise on, and implement, the policies of their governments. Not all academics and not all civil servants, of course, see their missions in such stark or oppositional terms, and criminological perspectives have, over the years, helped shape many penal policies. Even so, within criminology, there is such a strong feeling that policy formation and critique are incompatible that one of the strongest groupings, or strands of thought, within academic criminology has been loosely termed 'critical criminology' – to distinguish it from criminological work more committed to policy formation than to critique.

The concept of critique being inherent in science, at first sight it might be seen as being nothing more than a spurious claim to political probity for any academics to claim that they engage in critical analysis. None the less, many contemporary criminologists do feel obliged to make that claim. And the main reason for such academic self-branding is because, insofar as the criminology of official agencies is oriented towards problem solving, it cannot usually call into question the official definitions or priorities embedded in the construction of policy issues in the first place. Even when civil servants and agency administrators are very much committed to deriving deconstructive practical lessons from the arguments or findings of academic criminology, recent experience, in the UK, at any rate, suggests that the final arbiter of criminological research relevance will be party political expediency rather than, say, 'the public good', 'the cause of justice' or 'ethical considerations' (see, for recent UK examples, Lewis 1997; Ramsbotham 2003). So much is obvious, and it is not a dilemma peculiar to criminology, or even to social science research in particular. All academic research has political, cultural and economic conditions of existence which are beyond the control and often even the knowledge of the players (see Lyman and Scott 1970: 58–66 on information games).

The determination of critical criminologists in universities to resist erosion of their professional obligation to do independent research has, moreover, been strengthened during the last couple of decades by the acceleration and intensification of government demands that universities make the direction, quality and quantity of their research explicitly relevant and accountable to the priorities of government funding councils, with the concepts of quality and quantity always being contentiously defined and, too often, conflated. In the jurisdictions where these demands have been made, the amount of government funding of specific academic institutions has been made conditional upon the extent to which the researches of academic personnel have been seen to meet governmental 'relevance' and 'quality' criteria. Consequently, the political demands for, and definitions of, 'relevance' and 'quality' have been buttressed by an institutional acquiescence and collusion inimical to the independent critique previously valued as a defining characteristic of academic research. Criminological research environments have thus become much more overtly politicised at the local, national and trans-national levels.

Overall, the responses of criminologists to this state of affairs have been pragmatic. Most academics have had little choice but to acquiesce in their employing university's injunctions to chase grants. But while some policy-oriented criminologists have seen the demand for 'relevance' as being sufficient justification for doing as much grant-funded agency research as possible, some critical criminologists have also viewed policy-related research as endowing them with both greater authority and opportunities for making effective interventions into the related policy debates. Either way, universities have encouraged policy-related research because government and local authority invitations to tender often result in the large (and often repeat) contracts which swell university coffers. At the same time, a steep increase in the number of university students has, in the UK, resulted in academics having more teaching and administrative duties and less time to do the types of research that are intensely time-consuming. Smaller-scale, solely theoretical and/or ethnographic studies have, as a consequence, been seen by criminologists as being less productive of career rewards (Wacquant 2002).

Yet, although policy research (such as evaluation studies) is usually not seen as contributing much in the way of new knowledge of crime and criminal justice, criminologists who promote and encourage it may well justify problem-solving research on the following grounds: that the extra funding it attracts has a significant spill-over effect for individual criminology departments by subsidising research of a more theoretical kind; that academics, especially critical criminologists, have a public duty to develop policies directed at the reduction of certain crimes (feminists, for example, may be eager to do agency research which they hope will lead to a reduction in crimes against women). On the other hand, and in direct opposition to the agency-funded pragmatists, theoretical altruists, primarily concerned that their research should be independent and fundamentally critical of prevailing concepts of criminal justice, may well insist that the only justification for criminologists working in a university (as opposed to a government agency research institute) is that they should engage in constant criminological critique independently of populist, political or institutional considerations.

Meantime, the terms 'critical', 'pragmatist', 'policy-oriented' and 'altruistic' criminologists are, of course, ideal-typical constructions and few criminologists can be characterised as being deserving of only one categorisation. (See Loader and Sparks 2010: 134–44 for a more detailed and nuanced typology which ingeniously demonstrates the complexity of the discursive moves that professionals can make in interpreting their professional mission.) Pragmatic and altruistic strategies for the development of research projects and programmes are often practised alternately or even at the same time by individual criminologists compelled to do criminology in conditions not of their own making. Moreover, and as I have argued elsewhere, a policy-oriented criminologist 'working on a small canvas according to conventional technical protocols (e.g. statistical analysis) may well contribute as much (or more) to new knowledge about the working of contemporary criminal justice as the self-consciously critical theorist' (Carlen 2010). However, if criminologists attempt academic critique at the same time as doing penal politics, their dilemmas are likely to be both multiple and kaleidoscopic – as we shall see below. But why should academic criminologists do both critique and politics?

The loftiest and most logical answer is that as 'altruism' is historically seen to be a professional value, professional criminologists have an inalienable obligation to contribute to the construction of penal justice. Indeed, invoking such altruistic professionalism, some criminologists have put the blame for contemporary punitive excess on the aloofness of too many academic criminologists from policy issues. A more down to earth answer might be that as universities in many countries are publicly funded institutions, academics have a duty to produce knowledge that is seen to be useful. My own view is that today, when the academy is under threat and attack from all sides, academic criminologists should be very robust in defence of critique and knowledge production which may or may not be seen to have policy applications, and that they should not feel obliged to justify theoretical work on the grounds of its relevance to immediate crime issues – which, as has already been pointed out, are characterised by the very definitions of crime (and relevance) that critical criminologists aim to call into question. However, though we might not feel professionally *obliged* to justify our work by its policy relevance, many of us will still wish to intervene in policy issues – either as campaigners or as trans-national, national or local policy consultants. And then the much more vexed question arises: even if it is desirable to combine criminological critique and penal politics, is it possible?

In one sense criminologists have no choice but to engage in crime and justice politics. Crime is a political construct and any criminologist publishing a critical or novel analysis of any aspect of crime or punishment can expect it to be assessed and critiqued by people whose interests in crime are entirely different to those of the author. Critical writings on crime and justice will necessarily be opposed to other critical or non-critical viewpoints. But, as the history of criminology indicates, criminologists have always gone way beyond their academic mission to produce new knowledge of crime and criminal justice, and have constantly attempted to intervene in penal politics. Some have called this activity 'educating the public', others have called it 'government consultancy'; and even more have called it 'campaigning'. All of which diverse interventionist criminology, together with the stance taken by the very few non-interventionist 'theoretical altruists', has given birth to the ideological declension which is sometimes implicit in the ways criminologists describe each other: *she* does government consultancy (on the side of the devil); *you* are a campaigning criminologist (on the side of the angels); and *I* am an academic criminologist (i.e. objective and sitting on the fence). But, as Alvin Gouldner (1974), famously remarked, we are all also on our own side, and that means, for many of us, the desire to see our work endowed with a social value – from whatever angle we try to affect crime and justice issues. The problem then arises as to the present lack of any overarching ethic in professional academic criminology about the nature and purpose of an ideal criminal justice. Neither within criminology nor within the political and policy environments within which both professional criminology and penal politics are practised is there any agreement as to what criminology (or crime policy) is *for*. It appears, therefore, that critical academic criminologists have at least two peculiar and seemingly insuperable problems to confront when engaging in crime politics.

The first problem for academic criminologists consciously attempting to combine critique and politics inheres in the contradiction between the desire to call into question all known understandings of crime and justice at the same time as reconstructing those understandings in light of the deconstructive analysis. And the contradiction here is obvious: if the job of theorists is to call into question the known, how can academic criminologists at one and the same time maintain the theoretical distance necessary for critique *and* engage in the trimming that entry into penal politics entails? For when it comes to political action (as opposed to scientific agnosticism) the critic has to forego the luxury of critical distancing by engaging in a simplification (of findings, arguments and their implications) which exposes the new knowledge to a range of ideological interpretations and compromises which may well rob it of its radical power. Even worse, when, and if, any particular struggle over penal justice is won by academic criminologists, they are still professionally bound to be engaged in continuous critique of the ensuing policies. It is therefore difficult to see how criminologists could at one and the same time engage in reflexive critique *and* develop the institutional arrangements necessary to new policy implementation.

The second problem inheres in the lack of a professional ethic and a civic morals which might provide a unifying evaluative framework – a gold standard – for criminological debate. It has already been argued that different approaches to crime are incorporated into the criminologies of groups (e.g. civil servants, media professionals, campaigners) working under very different professional auspices or commercial or campaigning interests; and it is tempting at this point to imagine a standard (such as 'harm reduction' or 'inequality reduction') against which all proposals for policy changes could be evaluated . . . except one knows that there would be as many different definitions and interpretations of whatever 'gold standard' was chosen as there were interested parties! More fundamentally, however, and as Runciman (1966) and Rawls (1972) implied long ago, it is, in any case, difficult to imagine an ethic of justice to which all parties would subscribe in societies cross-cut with gross class, gender and ethnic inequalities.

Thus it seems to me that when talking about doing criminological critique and doing penal politics we have to make the discursive move from talking about 'academic criminology' to talking about the 'academic criminologists' who, though professionally constituted within the discourse of constant and altruistic critique, *as individuals*, have to make hard choices in academic environments increasingly less sympathetic to critical studies; and in political environments where critique is inimical to powerful interests.

Doing critique, doing politics: hard choices

Between long-term objectives and short-term objectives

One of the recurring dilemmas confronting theorists involved in the politics of social change (whether it be revolutionary whole-society change or merely revolutionary change of specific social arrangements) is to what extent the theory of change can be modified to accommodate short-term amelioration of social ills without thereby jettisoning the preconditions for the desired revolutionary change. For example, if one is an anti-prison campaigner should one go for the short-term objective of relieving some of the worst pains of imprisonment, thereby buttressing a foul system, or should one focus instead on the long-term abolition of imprisonment?

The short-term versus long-term debate was ongoing between participants in the UK campaigning group Women in Prison in the 1990s (see Carlen and Tchaikovsky 1996). And we oscillated between the two, sometimes basing our interventions on the short-term view, sometimes taking the long-term. For instance, whenever it was publicised that imprisoned women were giving birth in handcuffs, not being allowed to be present at the burial of their stillborn babies or being forcibly strip-searched by male officers we felt we had to make these foul practices public. But doing so took up an immense amount of time with often very short-term results, and such interventions became constant burdens on the resources of a very small and impecunious organisation. Yet, what was the alternative? Maynard Keynes (2007/1936) famously joked that in the long term we will all be dead; we thought that unless we confronted abuses of power in prisons wherever and whenever we witnessed them, we would all be so morally dead in the short term that life in the long term would not be worth living.

Between theoretical probity and political cunning in political and media debate

Or, in plain English, between either modifying new knowledge to make it more acceptable to politicians or maintaining its integrity at the cost of having it totally ignored. Basically, what I am talking about is the stance that an academic criminologist should maintain when engaged in debate in hostile media and policy arenas. For instance, whereas in an academic seminar one is professionally obliged to admit to ambiguities, contradictions and uncertainties about the likely outcomes of changes in policy, in media or policy debate, by contrast, in the interests of clarity of argument one has to come down firmly on one side or the other in interpreting or theorising data – even if one knows that such positive interpretations are actually quite dodgy. Is it justifiable for an academic to trim in this way? Is it ethical? It's certainly political. And several who advocate the development of a more public criminology seem to ignore this major dilemma confronting the simultaneous combining of critique and politics. Critique and politics are played to different rules and the critical campaigning criminologist or the critical criminologist engaging in the development of crime and justice policies is just as likely to be compromised by political strategies for securing particular objectives as is the administrative criminologist employed by the official agencies (see Carlen 2002). The alternative, of course, is that academics take arms against political cunning and engage in a political calculation involving a modification of their theoretical conclusions in a trade-off for some short-term political gain. This would not matter very much if one could argue that it is all a question of situational ethics – that in academic settings (e.g. teaching, academic writing, research) one is committed to scientific values, in the political arena to political strategy. And to a certain extent one *can* argue that . . . until one remembers that usually the only reason an academic has been invited into the political arena is because of claims to a knowledge based on scientific rigour. In short, the major danger when an academic attempts to meet oppositional political cunning by putting a more acceptable gloss on either an academic theory or set of research findings, is that critique and politics become conflated as political Truth (see Beck 1992). In my opinion, the main threats of such conflation are currently coming from governments via the universities in the forms of bureaucratised professionalism and the myth of social research relevance. Each manages to conflate critique and politics in ways that are not conducive to the successful pursuit of either new knowledge of crime or the realisation of a theoretically informed and democratic politics of crime.

Beware the search for truth

Beware bureaucratised professionalism

Although science is one of the oldest professions and was ideally pursued by practitioners licensed by professional associations, and according to their professional and craft principles, for centuries academics have also been what organisational sociologists call ascriptive professionals – meaning that our professional status is ascribed to us by the academic institutions in which we work. As such, the independence of the work in which academics can engage has constantly come under bureaucratic or political threat from within universities. I mention just two contemporary examples here: (i) the bureaucratisation of professional ethics and risk, and (ii) the bureau-quantification of quality.

The bureaucratisation of professional ethics and risk

In the last decade, many universities in the UK, Australia and the US, not content to allow professional associations to decide on ethical issues in relation to research, have applied a medical model of research ethics to assessment of social research proposals, and this widespread constraint upon social investigation has been inimical in particular to qualitative research and, together with risk assessments (for institutional insurance cover) presently poses a major threat to qualitative research. Such threat is amplified by the additional nonsense of the bureau-quantification of research quality.

The bureau-quantification of research quality

Reference has already been made to governmental research assessment exercises imposing extra-academic criteria in the assessment of research quality. However, there is another area of quantification which has been of concern over the last few years and one about which less has been written. I refer to the threat which citation analysis (known as 'impact factor' measurement) is posing to the integrity of peer–reviewed journals. Briefly: impact factor is a measure of a journal's 'impact' based on the number of citations to its articles during a specified period of time (usually two years). Because publishers argue that citation analysis is used by librarians in deciding which journals to take, by authors in deciding which journals to target, and by some research assessment exercises to assess the quality of a university's research output, journal editors have been put under pressure from publishers covertly to abandon anonymous peer review and instead commission top academics to write for a journal and also, in the selection of articles, to focus on fashionable topics. To this end, some publishers employ statisticians solely for the purpose of analysing citation stats, so that the information can be available to editors who are invited to make use of it in deciding which authors and articles they should publish in future.

The reason why academics should become more aware of this development is because it violates scientific ideals in the following ways: first, it is straightforwardly dishonest for a journal to claim that all articles are anonymously reviewed and then to commission and publish articles from so-called 'top authors'; second, because entirely focusing on high-impact authors is a threat to knowledge production as it would result in: no unknown theorists being published; no articles on new or unfashionable topics being published; and, given that well-known authors write as many dreadful articles as any one else, an overall decline in standards of academic writing. (For views from the physical sciences see Hall 2007; Lawrence 2007.)

Beware the pursuit of an imaginary relevance

An emphasis, by funding bodies, on an imaginary 'relevance' presently menaces criminologists from all sides: in the UK, for instance, research council grant application forms expect applicants to make claims about the potential usefulness of the research in question, as if the applicants should always already know what it is they are going to discover or produce; several criminologists who should know better often imply, when they are espousing 'partnerships' between academics and government departments, that all research can be made relevant to policymakers; public enquiries into the value of social science research have been known to insist that academic research reports be written up in easily understood language (e.g. Rothschild Report 1982) and so on. But it seems to me – and to return again to the desirability and/or possibility of academic forays into penal politics – that there is ample evidence that unless one can hold still the cultural, political and economic conditions in which new knowledge will be read and received, i.e. unless we know which publics are being referred to when we attempt to practise 'relevant criminology' and how those publics will interpret new research, there is little point in compromising either our research values or the conceptual language best suited to discovery and critique. In short, all research findings are interpreted within different constellations of political power and, like natural scientists, social scientists cannot ultimately be held to account for either the uses or the abuses to which new social scientific knowledge is put. For instance, criminologists may well convince the powers-that-be that some research indicates that imprisoning lawbreakers seems to make them more likely to commit crime in the future, but it is difficult to calculate the policy implications if the public hearing this are hearing it with different priorities in mind. If saving money is the political priority, steps may be taken to reduce prison populations. However, if maintaining employment rates is the priority, the prison population may well increase (see Carlen 2010 for an illustration of this point).

New directions for criminological knowledge

This chapter began by claiming that while all criminology is public, academic critique and penal politics are practised by people holding various, and often opposed religious, cultural and political beliefs about the causes of crime and the aims of criminal justice. Academic criminologists are distinct from other criminal justice professionals in working under a professional ethic which demands that they work to certain ethical, methodological and critical standards and observe certain professional protocols while doing investigative research and theoretical critique. None the less, the profession itself contains academics from the whole political spectrum and holding a wide range of views on crime and criminology. Consequently, when academic criminologists work in the public arena of penal politics, they cannot expect to invoke their professional organisations to support their interpretation of the relationships between their research findings and their policy recommendations. Instead they have to develop arguments which go beyond the methodological validity (or not) of their research findings or the logic (or not) of their theoretical perspective, and those arguments will depend not on any overarching altruistic professional values in relation to justice and punishment, but on the choices they make according to their own religious, political or ethical values. Furthermore, to have any success with those arguments, they will need to make them not only as professional academic criminologists, but also within campaigning groups or political parties, or with the help of sympathetic officials, or within segments of the criminology profession committed to the same policies and values. Thus, when criminologists enter the realm of penal politics, they leave in part their professional terrain and enter penal politics as academics in the service of some group with a particular political interest. They draw on their professional expertise, but only in the service of a politics of which they approve. The different protagonists in penal politics act within collectives, but they are usually not acting within a collective of academic criminologists. The *force* of critique and new knowledge depends upon the power of both the discourses and the collectives within which they are expressed. Accordingly, although it is important for a democratic penal politics that when criminologists do critique they adhere to the rules for research laid down by their professional associations, it is equally important that when they enter penal politics they do so explicitly as adherents to particular ideologies of justice. At the same time, it should be appreciated that the value of any academic knowledge that academics offer in service of a politics is always already diminished to the extent that the professional values of independence and altruism in research have been eroded, or even corrupted, by institutional environments more concerned with the quantity of the grant money coming in than with the quality of the research going out.

Finally, and in view of the threats to academic criminology which this chapter has identified, it might be timely for criminologists to act on the belief that criminology politics begin at home and, accordingly, to commence a collective struggle: first, *against* attempts from either within or outwith the academic profession to curb and corrupt the professional ideals of autonomy and altruism in research and critique; and, second, *for* a greater institutional encouragement of criminologists to engage both in more empirical and qualitative investigative research, and in more theoretical critique (see also Currie 2007). For although academic criminology as a profession is quite properly divided in regard to values, methodologies and politics, resistance to governmental attempts to erode the professional ideals of autonomy and independence in knowledge production is in the collective interests of criminology, criminologists and all their diverse publics.

Note

1 A very early version of this paper, entitled 'Doing Critique, Doing Politics' was presented as a keynote address at the Australian and New Zealand Critical Criminology Conference, 1 July 2010. I thank all the participants whose comments helped me to work out what it is I want to say. I thank Jacqueline Tombs for reading and commenting on the final version.

References

Beck, U. (1992) *Risk Society: Toward a New Modernity*. Cullompton: Willan.

Burawoy, M. (2005) 'For Public Sociology'. 2004 American Sociological Presidential Address in *American Sociological Review* 70: 4–28.

Carlen, P. (1998) 'Criminology Ltd: The Search for a Paradigm', in P. Walton and J. Young (eds) *The New Criminology Revisited*. London: Macmillan, pp. 64–75.

—— (2002) 'Controlling Measures: The Repackaging of Common Sense Opposition to Imprisonment in England and Canada', *Criminal Justice* 2(2): 155–72.

—— (2010) 'Against Evangelism in Academic Criminology: For Criminology as a Scientific Art', in Bosworth, M. and Hoyle, C. (eds) *What Is Criminology?* Oxford: Oxford University Press, pp. 95–110.

Carlen, P. and Tchaikovsky, C. (1996) 'Women's Imprisonment in England and Wales at the End of the Twentieth Century: Legitimacy, Realities and Utopias', in R. Matthews and P. Francis (eds) *Prisons 2000*. London: Macmillan, pp. 201–18.

Clawson, D., Zussman, R., Misra, J., Gerstel, N., Stokes, R., Anderton, A. and Burawoy, M. (eds) (2007) *Public Sociology*. Berkeley: University of California Press.

Currie, E. (2007) 'Against Marginality: Arguments for a Public Criminology', *Theoretical Criminology* 11: 175–90.

Ericson, R. (2005) 'Publicising Sociology', *British Journal of Sociology* 56(3): 365–72.

Gouldner, A. (1974) 'The Sociologist as Partisan', in A. Gouldner, *For Sociology: Renewal and Critique in Sociology Today*. New York: Basic Books, pp. 27–68.

Hall, P. (2007) 'Measuring Research Performance in the Mathematical Sciences in Australian Universities', *Australian Mathematical Society Gazette* 34: 26–30.

Hope, T. (2008) 'The First Casualty: Evidence and Governance in a War Against Crime', in P. Carlen (ed.) *Imaginary Penalities*. Cullompton: Willan, pp. 45–63.

Keynes, J. M. (2007) [1936] *The General Theory of Employment, Interest and Money*. Basingstoke: Palgrave Macmillan.

Lawrence, P. (2007) 'The Mismeasurement of Science', www.mrc-lmb.cam.ac.uk/PAL/pdf/mism_science.pdf

Lewis, D. (1997) *Hidden Agendas: Politics, Law and Disorder*. London: Hamish Hamilton.

Loader, I. and Sparks, R. (2010) *Public Criminology?* London: Routledge.

Lyman, S. and Scott, M. (1970) *A Sociology of the Absurd*. New York: Appleton, Century, Crofts.

Mathiesen, T. (1974) *The Politics of Abolition*. London: Martin Robertson.

—— (2004) *Silently Silenced: Essays on the Construction of Acquiescence in Modern Society*. Winchester: Waterside.

Ramsbotham, D. (2003) *Prisongate: The Shocking State of Britain's Prisons and the Need for Visionary Change*. London: Free Press.

Rawls, J. (1972) *A Theory of Justice*. Oxford: Clarendon Press.

Rothschild Report (1972) *A Framework for Government Research and Development*. Cmnd 5046, London: HMSO.

—— (1982) *An Enquiry into the Social Science Research Council*. Cmnd 8554, London: HMSO.

Runciman, W. G. (1966) *Relative Deprivation and Social Justice*. London: Routledge and Kegan Paul.

Smart, C. (1989) *Feminism and the Power of Law*. London: Routledge.

Uggen, C. and Inderbitzen, M. (2006) 'Public Criminologies'. Paper presented at the 2006 Annual meetings of the American Sociological Association, Montreal. www.soc.umn.edu/~uggen/uggen_inderbitzin_TC2006.pdf

Wacquant, L. (2002) 'The Curious Eclipse of Prison Ethnography in the Age of Mass Incarceration', *Ethnography* 3(4): 371–97.

Walters, R. (2003) *Deviant Knowledge: Criminology, Politics and Policy*. Cullompton: Willan.

2 Political economy and criminology

The return of the repressed

Robert Reiner

From political economy to policing – and back?

> There is relatively little the police can do about crime. We are not letting the public in on our era's dirty little secret; that those who commit the crime which worries citizens most – violent street crime – are, for the most part, the products of poverty, unemployment, broken homes, rotten education, drug addiction and alcoholism, and other social and economic ills about which the police can do little, if anything. Rather than speaking up, most of us stand silent and let politicians get away with law and order rhetoric that reinforces the mistaken notion that the police – in ever greater numbers and with ever more gadgetry – can alone control crime.
>
> (Di Grazia 1976: 24)

> Crime is down: blame the police.
>
> (Bratton 1998: 29)

Both the above quotes come from US big city police chiefs. The first is from an article by Boston Police Commissioner Robert Di Grazia, which appeared in the British Police Federation magazine. The second is from a chapter by New York City Police Commissioner William Bratton, published in an Institute of Economic Affairs book puffing the supposed achievements of 'zero-tolerance' policing. The two quotes are separated by much much more than just two decades in time; they are redolent of fundamentally different eras. They stand on either side of a remarkable global turnaround in political economy, culture, policing, penality and the politics of crime and criminal justice. Di Grazia evokes a discourse in which crime control and peace-keeping were seen as fundamentally problems of political economy not policing. Bratton embodies a born again can-do optimism in the powers of criminal justice: let off the leash, tough policing and punishment can provide public protection and security.

Di Grazia had it right, although his views have become hugely unfashionable. The replacement of political economy by policing as the prime social defence in the eyes of public and politicians alike has left us naked and vulnerable against a likely tsunami of crime and disorder in the wake of the economic collapse of recent years. There are some signs of a resurgence of political economy as a perspective in broader public debate, but with the exception of some recent discussions of punishment there are few indications of this in criminology as yet. This chapter will argue the need for political economy to underpin the analysis of crime and policing, as well as punishment. The next section will elaborate the significance of political economy as a perspective, and review its shifting fortunes in criminology. It will then be put to work as a framework for analysing contemporary trends in crime, disorder, punishment and policing. The conclusion will stress the urgency of a revival of social democracy as a basis for social justice and peace, whilst recognising the distance of this from current political trends.

Political economy and criminology

What is political economy?

The term 'political economy' usually implies a perspective that is distinct from 'economics', although they are also sometimes confusingly treated as synonymous. *The Journal of Political Economy*, for instance, is the title of the house journal of the Chicago School, most famously associated with Milton Friedman and other exponents of neo-classical economics. The application of this rational choice perspective to political behaviour and institutions is also referred to as political economy by many contemporary political scientists.

Generally, however, what is now taught and referred to as 'economics' is very different from the 'political economy' that was its origin. The most famous work of eighteenth-century political economy, Adam Smith's *The Wealth of Nations*, was part of a much wider exploration of social structure and relations, inextricably bound up with the moral philosophy that was the concern of Smith's other major work, *The Theory of Moral Sentiments* (Rothschild 2002; Haakonssen 2006). Marx saw himself as heir to this tradition, synthesising it with the dialectical philosophy of Hegel and with French Saint-Simonian socialism. Coming full circle, 'political economy' is sometimes used today as a virtual synonym for Marxism.

'Economics' cast off political economy in the late nineteenth century and presented itself as a distinct discipline focussing on the economic in abstraction from wider dimensions of ethics, politics, psychology or sociology. It now purports to be a supposedly apolitical, value-free, 'scientific' enterprise, analysing the 'economic' using primarily mathematical models based on highly abstract and simplified axioms about human motivation, decision-making processes and forms of social organisation. This scientistic aspiration, driven by physics envy, has caustically been dubbed 'autistic' economics by a growing movement of critical economists seeking a return to what they call 'real-world' economics, along the lines of the political economy out of which economics originally grew (Fullbrook 2007; www.paecon.net).

There was a parallel emergence in the late nineteenth century of other social science disciplines out of the broad 'predisciplinary' (Neocleous 2006: 19) discourses of political economy and philosophy: political science, sociology, psychology – and indeed criminology. This was interrelated with the growing separation between what were regarded as distinct social and institutional fields: 'private' and 'public'; 'civil society' and 'state'; 'the economy' and 'the polity'; 'criminal' and 'civil' law. Each came to be constituted and studied by an autonomous discipline (Neocleous 2000: 13–14; Lea 2002: chs 1–3). 'Political economy', by contrast, stresses the *embeddedness* of the 'economic' in wider networks of political, social and cultural processes and ethical concerns.

Political economy has been an important influence over the last three centuries in modern attempts to understand crime and its control (Reiner 2007a: 345–55). But its significance has been displaced, disputed or denied at times. In the late nineteenth century, when the term 'criminology' was first coined, it was used to refer to the emerging 'science of the criminal' pioneered by Lombroso and his associates. David Garland's influential historical analysis of the discipline argued that

> criminology is structured around two basic projects – the governmental and the Lombrosian. . . . oriented towards a scientific goal, but also towards an institutional field; towards a theoretical project, but also towards an administrative task. Whatever fragile unity the discipline achieves emerges from the belief that these two projects are mutually supportive rather than incompatible, that etiological research can be made useful for administrative purposes, and that the findings of operational research further the ends of theoretical enquiry.
>
> (Garland 2002: 16)

Whilst heuristically valuable, this distinction between the governmental and scientific projects of criminology is overdrawn. The term 'criminology' was specifically coined to describe the Lombrosian version of the quest for theoretical understanding of the aetiology of crime. But the project of developing such an analysis using the intellectual tools of social science, partly to further policy ends of achieving order and justice, long predated the label. The eighteenth century saw several versions of criminologies *avant la lettre*, notably the 'classical' school of criminal law and the 'science of police', which were closely linked to political economy. They were sidelined in the later nineteenth century by the rise of the positivist 'science of the criminal', with its aura of scientific rigour, objectivity and dispassionate expertise. More recently, in the late twentieth century, a similar downplaying of political economy in criminology was the result of the opposite one-sided repression: an attempt to marginalise theoretical questions for the sake of 'realism' – a pragmatic pursuit of policies that 'worked', denying the relevance of any consideration of deeper causes.

Political economy and the roots of criminology

The roots of criminology both as an analytic and a governmental project (although not as a word) lie in political economy. The standard account of the birth of criminology sees its origins in the 'classical' legal/administrative perspective associated with Beccaria's 1764 book *Dei Delitti e Delle Pene*, and its profound influence, via Blackstone, Bentham and others, on the Enlightenment movements for reform of criminal law and punishment. It has been argued that the 'classical' perspective is not fully criminological (apart from lacking the label) because it was not concerned with aetiological questions about the peculiarities of offenders, assuming a voluntaristic, rational economic actor model. Beirne has shown that this was certainly not true of Beccaria, who was strongly influenced by the emerging 'science of man' in the discussions of the philosophers and political economists of the Scottish Enlightenment, notably David Hume, Adam Ferguson and Adam Smith (Beirne 1991). This was a deterministic discourse concerned with explaining the causes of human conduct and society through the concepts of probabilism, sensationalism and associationism (Beirne 1993: 33–43). Histories of criminology often neglect the relationship between political economy and Enlightenment discussions of crime and criminal justice, reflected partly in the work of Beccaria (who was appointed to a chair of 'Political Economy and Science of Police' at Milan in 1768, where he delivered lectures on the 'Elements of Political Economy' (Pasquino 1978: 45)).

Political economy was associated more evidently with the 'science of police' that flourished in the eighteenth and early nineteenth centuries, which has been overlooked by criminologists until recently. Even now, it is seen as a source of the governmental project in criminology rather than the analytic. It is well known that the term 'police' originally had a much broader meaning, essentially coterminous with the internal policies of governments. What is less acknowledged is the intimate interdependence of 'police' and political economy. In his 1763 *Lectures on Justice, Police, Revenue and Arms* Adam Smith defined 'police' as

> the second general division of jurisprudence. The name is French, and is originally derived from the Greek 'politeia' which properly signified the policy of civil government, but now it only means the regulation of the inferior parts of government, viz: cleanliness, security and cheapness of plenty.
>
> (cited in Radzinowicz 1956: 421)

The eighteenth-century 'science of police' was a vast body of work that flourished across Europe. In England the leading exponent of the 'science of police' was the magistrate Patrick Colquhoun (Reiner 1988). Colquhoun is most commonly remembered as a pioneer of the modern British police in the narrow sense. However, he wrote extensively on political economy, crime and criminal justice, and his work can be seen as a precursor of criminology. To Colquhoun crime and criminal justice were not independent phenomena that could be considered in isolation from broader issues of social and economic structure. His proposals for the prevention and control of crime were rooted in empirical investigation of crime patterns. Colquhoun's analysis located the ultimate causes of crime in the overall structure of economy and society, but he was concerned to unravel the social and cultural mediations generating criminality and conformity.

Crime was 'the constant and never-failing attendant on the accumulation of wealth', providing the opportunities and temptations for misappropriation (*Treatise on the Commerce and Police of the River Thames*, 1800: 155–56). Crime (mainly theft) was attributable to the poor, but poverty did not *determine* crime. Crime had both structural and cultural sources. Structural factors included variations in the opportunities for training available to different ethnic groups, and downturns in the economic cycle. But cultural and informal moral controls (such as religion and the promotion of uplifting rather than 'bawdy' forms of popular pastimes) were also important to encourage 'manners' that were 'virtuous' rather than 'depraved'.

The reform of formal policing arrangements for which Colquhoun is best known was only a relatively minor aspect of the policies required to prevent crime. Effective deterrence by regular police patrol was important, and more effective than harsh punishment. But the operation of formal policing was primarily significant in symbolic and cultural rather than instrumental, utilitarian terms. The beneficial effects of police patrol were more to encourage moral discipline than to deter or catch perpetrators. Its terrain was to be 'upon the broad scale of General Prevention – mild in its operations – effective in its results; having justice and humanity for its basis, and the general security of the State and Individuals for its ultimate object' (Colquhoun 1800: 38).

Overall the analysis of security, order, crime and policing advanced by Colquhoun as the 'science of police' was more sensitive to the interplay of politics, law, and justice with criminality than the later nineteenth-century 'science of the criminal'. His pioneering attempts to chart social patterns and trends in crime statistically were developed with much greater depth and rigour by the early nineteenth-century 'moral statisticians' (Beirne 1993: chs 3, 4), before their eclipse by *soi-disant* criminology later in the century. Like the contemporaneous displacement of political economy by economics, the apparent gain in 'scientific' rigour by the Lombrosians was bought at a high price in terms of the obscuring of the political, economic and ethical dimensions of crime and welfare.

Twentieth-century sociological criminology

During the late nineteenth-century heyday of individualist positivism some macro-sociological analyses of crime, informed by political economy, continued. Above all, Durkheim's 1897 classic *Suicide* created a template for later theoretical analyses of fluctuating rates and patterns of deviance in terms of macro-social structure and culture, offering two seminal concepts, egoism and anomie.

In the early twentieth century there were scattered attempts to develop Marxist political economies of crime and punishment, notably the attempt to develop a systematic analysis of crime by Willem Bonger (Bonger 1916), and Rusche and Kirchheimer's political economy of punishment (Rusche and Kirchheimer 1939). To Bonger the main way in which capitalism was related to crime was through the stimulation of a moral climate of egoism, at all levels of society. In terms that anticipated Merton's analysis of anomie, Bonger talked of the stimulation of material desires by modern marketing, explaining not only proletarian crime but also crimes of the powerful.

Robert Merton's anomie theory remains the most influential formulation of a political economy of crime (Merton 1938). Most accounts portray it as 'strain' theory: a society that *culturally* encourages common material aspirations by a mythology of meritocracy, against a *structural* reality of unequal opportunities, generates anomic pressures and deviant reactions. More fundamentally, however, Merton suggested that anomie was related to the nature of aspirations in particular cultures. A highly materialistic culture – especially one that defines success almost exclusively in monetary terms – is prone to problems of moral regulation and crime, at *all* levels. This is not an economically determinist account; the cultural meaning of material factors like poverty or inequality is crucial. Despite its strengths, Merton's analysis fell out of fashion after the early 1960s. Its social democratic critique of unbridled capitalism was too cautious for 1970s radical criminology, too radical for post-1980s neoliberalism, and too structuralist for Foucauldians and postmodernists. It has, however, recently been influential in attempts to analyse variations in crime rates and patterns between different types of political economy (Currie 1997; Messner and Rosenfeld 2000, 2006; Reiner 2007b; *Theoretical Criminology* 2007; Hall *et al*. 2008; Hall and MacLean 2009).

The criminological perspective most explicitly rooted in political economy was the 'fully social theory of deviance' sketched in *The New Criminology* (Taylor *et al*. 1973: 268–80), the Bible of 1970s radical criminology. This stressed the interdependence of macro, meso, and micro structures, cultures, and processes. This was explicitly intended as 'a political economy of criminal action, and of the reaction it excites', together with 'a politically informed social psychology of these ongoing social dynamics' (ibid.: 279). It was an attempt 'to move criminology out of its imprisonment in artificially segregated specifics . . . to bring the parts together again in order to form the whole' (ibid.). The last few pages of *The New Criminology*, a quintessential statement of what its own authors later dubbed 'late idealism', sketched the possibility of a crime-free socialist society, a project whose utopianism in the light of the subsequent resurgence of 'free-market' capitalism has rather marginalised the book as a whole by its unfashionability. But the concluding chapter's first part, outlining the elements of a 'fully social theory' of crime that synthesises the still valid kernels of the earlier perspectives in the history of criminology which are reviewed in the bulk of the book, remains a model for criminological analysis applying the perspective of political economy.

Most research studies inevitably focus on a narrower range of phenomena, but the checklist of elements for a 'fully social theory' should be a reminder of the wider contexts that deviance and control are embedded in. The 1978 classic *Policing the Crisis* has been the most ambitious attempt to incorporate all these elements into the study of one specific phenomenon, a magisterial analysis of mugging and the reaction to it (Hall *et al*. 1978; Coleman *et al*. 2009). It moved out from an account of one robbery in Birmingham to a wide-ranging analysis of British economic, political, social and cultural history since World War II. It demonstrated the deeper concerns that 'mugging' condensed, and the impact of transformations in the political economy on black young men in particular. It remains an exemplar of how criminological analysis can interpret particular acts through a broader probing of the mediating institutional and cultural processes and pressures stretching between macro political and economic structures all the way down to specific interactions on the streets.

Realism, romanticism and root causes

Political economy has been sidelined in criminology during the last thirty years by a number of 'turns' in intellectual, cultural and political life. It has been caught in a pincer movement from right and left, denying the reality of 'society', or at any rate structural causes and grand narratives. In criminology this shift was announced stridently by the right-wing 'realist' critique initiated by James Q. Wilson's polemic against 'root cause' perspectives (Wilson 1975: xv). Shortly after that, a newly proclaimed left realism argued that rising crime in a more 'affluent society' constituted an 'aetiological crisis' for social democratic criminology (Young 1986). Mainstream empirical criminological research became ever more domin-ated by pragmatic concern with immediately practicable policies in the search for 'what works?' Causal explanation was limited almost entirely to individual and situational levels that are more amenable to policy interventions, and do not raise questions of wider social justice.

Whilst realism ousted political economy, it has been associated with a broader revival of neo-classical perspectives based on economic models, such as rational choice theory (Zedner 2006 offers a caustic critique). More recently, 'cultural criminologists' have claimed that political economy cannot comprehend the subjective seductions of crime and the romance of deviance (Katz 1988), although some have argued persuasively for a synthesis with structural perspectives (Young 2003; Hayward 2004; Hall and Winlow 2003, 2004, 2005, 2007; Hayward and Young 2007; Hall *et al.* 2008).

In the 1980s these critiques were buttressed by a belief that econometric evidence called into question any postulated relationships between crime and economic factors, such as unemployment or poverty (Box 1987). More recent studies, however, have shown that whilst economic factors are not automatically connected to crime, they help shape the cultures and meanings that do inform offending. Most recent econometric analyses do find that economic fluctuations and variations are related to crime trends and patterns (Reiner 2007b: 97–103). The difference from earlier studies is due to the quite distinct social meaning, extent and impact of unemployment, poverty and inequality during the post-war decades of Keynesian, welfare state compromise contrasted with the subsequent social tsunami of neoliberalism.

Political economy is not reducible, however, to the debates and research about the impact of specific economic variables such as unemployment, poverty or inequality on crime levels and trends. It constitutes a holistic approach, encompassing the dialectical complexity of interactions between macro structures and individual actions, and between structural and cultural processes. As Weber put it long ago, explanation has to be both 'causally adequate' *and* 'adequate at the level of meaning'. *Verstehen* and structural analysis are complementary not contradictory. This will be illustrated by a consideration of how crime and criminal justice trends and patterns in Britain can be understood.

Crime control and criminalisation: the long view

Between the mid-nineteenth and mid-twentieth century in Britain there developed a system of modern criminal justice that broadly sought to emphasise welfare, rehabilitation and re-incorporation, consensus and legitimacy. Like any criminal justice system it was based on the delivery of doses of pain, but compared with what came before and after there was an attempt, however imperfectly realised and often hypocritical, at minimising this and achieving a measure of consent. Welfarist social policy and amelioration, not exclusion and harsh sanctions, were seen as the basis of order and crime control, with policing and punishment as regrettably necessary stopgaps until root causes could be tackled.

The necessary condition for more consensual, welfarist criminal justice policies was that crime and disorder seemed to be contained, indeed reducing, as problems. National crime statistics began to be collected and published by the Home Office after the 1856 County and Borough Police Act, which established modern police forces throughout the country. From the 1850s until the 1920s crime levels recorded by the police remained on a plateau. Although there are no figures for crimes that were not prosecuted prior to 1856, on the basis of the judicial statistics historians generally believe that the mid-Victorian rates represent a decline from much higher levels in the early nineteenth century (Gatrell 1981). There is some debate about whether the flat trend from the 1850s to the 1920s is attributable to a low level of offending, or to supply-side rationing of measurement capacity, driven both by fiscal parsimony and the wish to present an appearance of success for the new police forces and other nineteenth-century criminal justice reforms (Taylor 1998, 1999; Morris 2001). But what is clear is that there was a steady state of criminalisation, and at any rate the appearance of success in crime control. Criminologists and policy-makers at the turn of the twentieth century (like their US counterparts in the 1990s and 2000s) were vexed about how to explain the great crime-drop (Radzinowicz and Hood 1986). Political and industrial disorder also seemed both less frequent, and less violent – a match rather than a battle – compared to the earlier nineteenth century or later twentieth (Geary 1985).

During the century between the 1850s and 1950s there also came to be embedded the system of policing celebrated as 'policing by consent' (Reiner 2010: chs 2, 3), and 'penal welfarism' (Garland 1985) became the prevailing response to apprehended offenders. Although these had complex conditions of existence, the underlying context was the gradual incorporation of the mass of the population into social as well as civil and political citizenship – what David Garland has called the 'solidarity project' (Garland 2001: 199). And it has been the reversal of the trend towards greater inclusion with the advent of neoliberalism over the last thirty years that has generated the crime and disorder explosions, and the harsher politics of law and order of recent times (Reiner 2007b; Hall *et al*. 2008).

The calculus of crime: charting recent trends

Criminal statistics are notoriously riddled with pitfalls: the huge extent of unrecorded crime, due to non-reporting by victims, non-recording by the police, and an incalculable volume of offending that victims and police never even become aware of, although these may encompass severe harms, including poverty or deaths, caused by corporations and states (Hillyard *et al*. 2004; Reiner 2007b: chs 2, 3; Green and Ward 2009; Pantazis and Pemberton 2009; Tombs and Whyte 2009). Changes in the recorded figures may be due not to changes in offence levels but to fluctuations in reporting or recording, or in the rules for counting crimes. Very substantial steps have been taken in recent decades to alleviate these problems by developing alternative measures, above all the regular British Crime Surveys (BCS) since the early 1980s. The availability of two alternative measures of trends gives greater confidence when they point in the same direction, as they did for the first decade of the BCS. However, in the 1990s the trends indicated by the police statistics and the BCS began to diverge, generating a politicised debate about their relative merits.

Putting together the different sorts of data available, what can be said about the trends in the last half century? The most apparent trend is the spectacular rise in recorded crime since the late 1950s. In the early 1950s the police recorded fewer than half a million offences per annum. By the mid-1970s this had risen to 2 million. The 1980s showed even more staggering rises, with recorded crime peaking in 1992 at over 5.5 million. By 1997 recorded crime had fallen back to 4.5 million. Major counting rule changes introduced in 1998 and 2002 make comparison of the subsequent figures especially fraught, but on the new rules (which undoubtedly exaggerate the increase) just under 6 million offences were recorded by the police for 2003/4. This has now fallen back again, to 4.3 million in 2009/10.

These statistics indicate a complex picture, but clearly pinpoint the reversal of the long march towards more inclusive citizenship, with the post-1970s neoliberal blitzkrieg as the accelerant behind a crime explosion in the 1980s heyday of Thatcherism (Reiner 2007a: chs 3, 4). Three distinct phases can be distinguished:

(i) *1955–83: Recorded Crime Rise*. Until the 1970s there was no other measurement of trends apart from the police statistics. But during the 1970s the General Household Survey (GHS) began to ask about burglary victimisation. Its data showed that most of the increase in recorded burglary was due to greater reporting by victims. Between 1972 and 1983 recorded burglaries doubled, but victimisation increased by only 20 per cent. Victims reported more burglaries mainly because of the spread of household contents insurance. This indicates that the increased rate in the 1970s for this highly significant crime was mainly a recording phenomenon. It is plausible that this was true of volume property crimes more generally, so that the rise of crime whilst the mixed economy, welfarist consensus survived was probably substantially less than the recorded statistics suggested.

(ii) *1983–1992: Crime Explosion.* The BCS in the 1980s showed the reverse: although recorded crime still increased more rapidly than BCS crime, the trends were similar. By both measures crime rose at an explosive rate during the 1980s and early 1990s, the Thatcher and early Major years. The decade and a half during which neoliberalism destroyed Britain's industrial base defined whole areas and generations out of the edifice of citizenship, creating a new excluded 'underclass' (Dahrendorf 1985; Young 1999; Hall *et al.* 2008). Neoliberal economics stimulated record growth for one industry: crime.

(iii) *1993– : Ambiguously Falling Crime.* From the early 1990s the trends indicated by the police statistics and the BCS began to diverge. The BCS continued to chart a rise until 1995, but the police-recorded data fell from 1992 to 1997. Insurance companies made claiming more onerous, thus discouraging reporting by victims, and more 'businesslike' managerial accountability for policing implicitly introduced incentives to keep crime recording down.

After New Labour came to power in 1997 the two measures continued to diverge – but in the opposite direction. BCS recorded crime has fallen continuously, and is now below the level of the first BCS conducted in 1981. The police recorded statistics, however, began to rise again from 1998 up to 2004, since when they have declined. The rise in the recorded rate was due overwhelmingly to two major changes in police procedures for counting crimes: new Home Office Counting Rules in 1998, and the 2002 National Crime Recording Standard (NCRS). These reforms boosted the recorded rate substantially compared to what would have been measured previously.

The BCS is free from the particular problems that make the police figures unreliable as a measure of trends. However, it is not (and has never claimed to be), a definitive count. It necessarily omits many offences: homicide, the supreme example of personal victimisation; crimes with individual victims who are unaware of what happened (such as successful frauds); crimes against organisations or the public at large; consensual offences such as drug-taking. Its sampling frame excludes certain highly victimised groups such as children under 16, and the homeless.

The dramatic overall fall in the BCS under New Labour also masked increases in some of the most alarming offences. Murder and other serious crimes of violence have increased in the last 30 years, and are now a higher proportion of all crimes, even though their overall incidence has fallen recently. During the 1960s and early 1970s the number of homicides recorded per year was 300–400, but has since roughly doubled. In 1976 just 5 per cent of recorded offences were classified as violent, but by 2007/8 this had increased to 19 per cent (partly because the counting rule changes lowered the threshold for recording violence). Recorded robberies rose sharply from the early 1990s, although they have been falling (erratically) in the last few years from a peak in 2001/2. So the trends are certainly not as rosy as the BCS total suggests, and the failure of public anxiety about crime to fall in line with the statistics is not merely due to an irrational 'reassurance gap'. The trends in crime during the last half-century indicate a clear overall pattern: the further the balance shifts away from social democracy and towards neoliberalism, the greater the growth in crime.

Serious violent crime in comparative perspective

There is also evidence that comparative differences in political economy underlie systematic variations in serious crime, especially homicide (Currie 1997, 1998, 2008; I. Taylor 1999; Messner and Rosenfeld 2000, 2006; Wilkinson 2005; Reiner 2007b: 103–10; Lacey 2008: 60; Hall and MacLean 2009; Wilkinson and Pickett 2009). These studies all show that homicide rates are higher in neoliberal than social democratic political economies. A heart of darkness pervades neoliberal as distinct from social democratic political economies: more serious violence and more cruel punishment. The immediate pain and symptom relief advocated by realists is vital, but only provided it does not become a diversionary and ultimately futile struggle to hold down the lid on what remain 'root causes' structured by different types of political economy.

Contemporary control: comparisons and trends

Punishment

There are also systematic variations in patterns of punishment in contemporary systems related to their political economies, as many recent studies have shown (Beckett and Western 2001; Downes 2001; Sutton 2004; Wacquant 2005, 2009; Cavadino and Dignan 2006; De Giorgi 2006; Downes and Hansen 2006; Reiner 2007a, b; Lacey 2008; Bell 2011). This association between types of political economy and punishment patterns at a macro level seems clear, although interpretation of the experience of specific societies requires more detailed and particularistic cultural analysis (Nelken 2009).

Policing

Compared to the now substantial literature on the impact of political economy on punishment, there has been relatively little discussion of how the advent of neoliberalism has impacted on policing. There are, however, two bodies of writing that celebrate transformations of policing in recent years as a key source of the crime fall. The first is a considerable corpus of work, mainly from the police themselves and their journalistic groupies, and is quintessentially represented by the boast from William Bratton, the former NYPD chief cited at the start of this chapter. Attributing the primary credit for declining crime to greater police numbers or effectiveness is both empirically and theoretically dubious, just as blaming them for the huge crime rise from the 1950s to the late 1990s would be (Reiner 2010: chs 5, 8).

The bottom-line point is that any conceivable level of police resources compared to the huge array of actual and potential crimes means that preventive and detective resources, even if deployed in the smartest possible ways, will be stretched so far that they can deliver only a small amount of deterrence. No doubt improvements in police strategy, especially intelligence-led prevention and investigation, have contributed to declining crime, but they are only a small part of the story. Policing is an element in shaping both the normal level of crime in a society, and temporary movements above or below that norm. But it is only one minor factor in the overall shaping of crime levels compared to broader issues of political economy, culture and social patterns (as indicated by the quote from former Boston police chief Di Grazia with which this chapter opened). The following diagram (Figure 2.1) suggests a theoretical model for analysing the contribution of policing to crime control.

The levels and patterns of crime in a society are shaped by a complex combination of interacting elements: how crime is conceptualised and labelled; motivating pressures and seductions; available means and opportunities; the potential informal and formal controls inhibiting offending (Reiner 2007b: ch. 4). Within this array, policing is only one element ('constables' in the diagram, borrowing Malinowski's depiction of modern criminal justice as 'codes, courts and constables'). Particularly ineffective policing may elevate crime levels higher than would be expected on the basis of all the other elements, and especially

SOURCES OF 'NORMAL' CRIME

- **Labelling**

(crime definitions, perceptions, reporting, recording measurement rules)

- **Motives**

(biology, psychology, political economy, culture, social patterns)

- **Means**

(technology, social routines, know-how)

- **Opportunities**

(target fluctuations: affluence/consumerism, economic cycles, social routines)

- **Controls**

(Informal: socialisation, culture, social bonds/stakes. Formal: codes, courts, constables)

↓

LONG-RUN EQUILIBRIUM 'NORMAL' CRIME RATE

Figure 2.1 Policing and crime control – a theoretical model

effective innovatory tactics may drive the rate down, at least for a time. But contrary to the 'police fetishism' that dominates popular culture and current political debate, policing must be put in its place – a small one.

A more sophisticated theoretical literature has also developed in the last 15 years, but which also implies an at least partly positive assessment of the impact of neoliberalism on policing. This is usually designated as 'the transformation thesis' (Reiner 2010: ch. 1). The core elements of change are seen as the end of the monopolisation of policing by the public police with the proliferation of a plurality of other policing bodies, and an internal transformation of the public police on more 'businesslike' lines under the impact of New Public Management and other neoliberal models. This is primarily presented as a description of trends, but with some exploration of their 'progressive' potential. Explanations of the changes are mainly derived from broader theorisations of late or post-modernity, risk society, and shifts in governmentality.

A key explanatory theme is that 'truth will out': the new policing trends have emerged because they solve manifest problems with the old, supposedly state-dominated policing arrangements, spearheaded in the Anglo-American world by Sir Robert Peel's 1829 creation of the London Metropolitan Police. This is summed up in the following passage:

> Peel's aspiration to ensure prevention through the certainty of detection and punishment has remained unrealised during the two centuries since the inception of the new police. There are a number of reasons for this, some of which relate to shortcomings within policing, others to problems within the wider criminal justice system. For example, during most of the post-war period, steadily rising rates of crime have exposed the limits of the Peelian project.
>
> (Johnston and Shearing 2003: 67)

These claims distort the history of policing in a number of ways. Crime rates fell steadily after the 1850s, as the Peelian police were rolled out across the country, remaining low until the First World War. Recent research has suggested that this decline may have been a statistical artefact conjured up by the police and Home Office to vindicate the new system, and to save Treasury resources (Taylor 1998, 1999). In any event, it is doubtful that the falling crime rates were primarily due to the policing changes. A much greater role was played by the long-term process of converting the 'dangerous classes' into the solid working class by incorporating them into the civil, political and economic rights of citizenship (Reiner 2010: chs 2, 3). But even if the falling crime rates were a political conjuring trick to promote the Bobbies, it worked. The myth of Scotland Yard's prowess ('always getting their man') became an international symbol of successful policing.

Although crime rates rose in the 1920s and 1930s, they declined again in the first post-war decade, and the myth of the Bobby as an important aspect of British national pride reached its zenith in the 1940s and 1950s. Recorded crime rates did begin to increase almost continuously after the mid-1950s, and the police certainly got some of the blame for this – but as unfairly as the credit they had received for the earlier fall. Faced with these huge crime increases, swamping their resources, the police were able to detect only a diminishing proportion of offences, undermining public confidence.

But neither the crime trends nor the changing public standing of the police were primarily due to failures of the Peelian model. The real driver of the problematic crime and criminal justice trends of recent years has been the dominance of neoliberalism. But in the new policing theories neoliberalism is discussed almost entirely as a rational set of programmes and ideas, curiously abstracted from its material effects and sources. (Harvey 2005 provides a succinct account of the economic and political sources and consequences of neoliberalism.) The rhetoric of neoliberal advocates is presented as if it was how it worked in practice, ignoring the disastrously deleterious effects. There is an acceptance of neoliberal claims about the possible pathologies of state institutions, but no recognition of the pathologies of the market that were understood even by neo-classical economists of earlier generations such as Alfred Marshall and Pigou.

The new theorists' critique of the state is presented as developing out of the radical criminologies that flourished in the 1960s and early 1970s.

> Three decades ago cutting-edge criminological theory grappled with 'the problem of the state'. . . . While the state – through the law – presented itself as an independent adjudicator between competing interests and claimed to ensure that all individuals had equal access to justice, formal legal equality was, in reality, a sham . . . Thirty years ago the state was considered to *be* 'the problem', its capitalist character rendering it structurally incapable of representing general 'public interests' over particular private ones.
>
> (Johnston and Shearing 2003: 33–34)

They then reflect on the 'strange paradox' that 'many of today's theorists' bemoan 'how neoliberalism has disaggregated the state apparatus' (ibid.). There is no paradox here. The nub of the critique of the state was that it was captured by the interests of capital, and the problem was how to make it deliver on its promise to represent the public good. As Tawney put it some 70 years ago, 'The question is not merely whether the State owns and controls the means of production. It is also who owns and controls the State.' (Tawney 1935: 165). 'The reality behind the decorous drapery of political democracy', he argued, is 'the economic power wielded by a few thousand – or . . . a few hundred thousand – bankers, industrialists, and landowners' (ibid.: 60).

To espouse neoliberalism, 'capitalism unleashed' (Glyn 2006) from behind the ideological veil of the state, is jumping from the frying pan into the fire. The claim that there are 'possibilities for disaggregating neoliberal strategies and practices, and rendering their often highly innovative developments available for appropriation and development by a "progressive" postwelfare politics' overlooks the inherent dysfunctional consequences of markets (O'Malley 1997). Markets have many unwelcome economic consequences unless states take countervailing measures: growing inequalities of power and wealth; allocation of resources tilted towards the desires of the rich (the democracy of the market is not one person one vote, but one pound one vote); insecurities caused by vicissitudes of health, age, natural disasters; and as we have re-learned painfully, wild macroeconomic fluctuations (Reiner 2007b: 1–11). Market dominated societies are associated with further social, ethical, political and cultural problems: the financialisation of all values, anomie produced by the stimulation of desires and aspirations beyond the possibility of achievement, egoism, corruption of democracy by the best politicians money can buy (Palast 2004; Jacobs and Skocpol 2005), authoritarianism as the 'strong state' wrestles to suppress resistance to the pathologies of the 'free market' (Polanyi 1944; Gamble 1994).

Analysing the historical roots of the recent policing transformations through the lens of political economy suggests a very different diagnosis to the new policing theorists. The pluralisation of policing and the application of New Public Management to the public police, are symptoms of, not solutions to, the current predicament. The Peelian police were established in Britain (and the US) in the early nineteenth century against wide and deep hostility especially from the then politically, socially and economically excluded masses. The police were established not because of technical failures of the previous forms of citizen policing, but because these were all clearly under the control of the gentry and made manifest the class nature of governance and law (Silver 1967).

The big job facing the early police leaders was to gain public consent, and somewhat different strategies were followed in Britain and the US (Miller 1977). The British route was a set of organisational policies seeking to represent the police as disciplined, apolitical, minimally armed, 'citizens in uniform' without special powers separating them from the public, enforcing an impartial law that benefited all classes as well as providing emergency social services to those in need (Reiner 2010: ch. 3). These ultimately succeeded in dispelling hostility and winning a fragile legitimation of the police, but only because the policies were developed in a benign context of the general march of social, political and economic citizenship (as classically spelled out by Marshall 1950). This reduced the extent of crime and disorder confronting the police, allowing them to consolidate the image of operating with minimum force and allowing room for the service role to be emphasised.

Police legitimacy was gradually undermined after the late 1960s but not because of defects in the policing model. The ultimate source was economic neoliberalism as initially heralded in the 'Selsdon Man' manifesto on which the Heath government was elected in 1970 before it was defeated by trade union opposition, then re-imposed on a reluctant Labour government by the IMF in 1976, enthusiastically espoused by the Thatcher Tories in 1979, and deeply embedded by New Labour's embrace of it in the 1990s. This set in train massive economic and social dislocation (especially large-scale long-term unemployment, inequality and social exclusion) and an increasingly anomic and egoistic culture, which in the 1980s generated a crime explosion and public disorder on a scale not seen for a century. Mediated by the unintended reversal of the policing policies that had achieved legitimation, the result was a decline in public confidence in the police.

How to deal with this was politically controversial in the 1970s and 1980s, and there appeared sharp politicisation of the issue of law and order (Downes and Morgan 2007; Reiner 2007b: ch. 5). The Tories espoused a tough new law and order rhetoric, whilst Labour clung to a social democratic analysis of the social roots of crime and disorder similar to the one suggested here. This fundamentally changed in 1992 when the then shadow home secretary Tony Blair's celebrated slogan 'tough on crime, tough on the causes of crime' heralded New Labour's conversion to the law and order approach, the first of several 'Clause 4' moments signifying its embrace of neoliberalism.

For the police this meant calling a bluff that had been successful for 150 years. The police had been symbolically acclaimed as the guardians of the public against threats of crime and disorder, but the real work achieving this was an array of economic, social and cultural processes that incorporated most sections of society into a common status of citizenship holding tensions and conflicts at bay. When neoliberalism unravelled this complex of subtle, hidden controls, the thin blue line turned out to be a Maginot line. The 'sovereign state' myth (Garland 1996) was unmasked, naked as Anderson's emperor in his new clothes. As researchers had suggested all along, the police alone could not have much impact on crime and disorder. But the newly ascendant and unquestioned politics of law and order demanded that they do just that, indicated most explicitly by the 1993 White Paper on *Police Reform* which declared bluntly that the police task was simply 'catching criminals'. This kick-started the NPM-inspired reforms of the 1990s and 2000s. Meanwhile a 'new feudalism' also gathered pace (Shearing and Stenning 1983), as those with the power to do so built exclusive bubbles of security. The transformation of policing stems neither from the inherent deficiencies of old, state policing nor the technical superiority of a new corporate mentality of pluralism embracing private security and a 'businesslike' re-invigorated public sector. It results from the destabilising and criminogenic effects of neoliberalism, which is the problem not the solution.

For a social democratic criminology

It is easy to espouse Gramsci's recommendation of pessimism of the intellect, much harder to follow his encouragement of optimism of the will. To many it appears that at present civilisation is fighting a losing battle with barbarism, as a centuries-long 'pseudo pacification process' unravels (Hall and Winlow 2004). But the same could have been said at almost any time since the lights went out over Europe in 1914 (apart perhaps from the post-war decades of social democratic consensus – and even then the shadow of nuclear Cold War was a serious threat). But hopefully criminology *can* interpret the world. And if Blatcherite neoliberalism changed it for the worse, it is perhaps possible to change it for the better.

There has been something of a *trahison de criminologists* (to paraphrase Benda) since the 1980s. This is found in the relative absence of critical attention given to wider social and political-economic sources of contemporary crime and criminal justice changes, at any rate until very recently. In the early stages of neoliberalism's rise, during the later 1970s and 1980s, conservative criminologists of course cheered it on. But *soi-disant* radical criminology also attenuated its critique of criminal justice in a variety of ways. For all their virtues, the various strands of the realist turn after the 1970s implied changing the subject, diverting attention from the large-scale social and cultural forces that were restructuring crime and criminal justice. 'Reformed' funding and career opportunities for academic criminologists encouraged this (Hillyard *et al.* 2004), but perhaps a deeper factor was an excessive intellectual modesty in the wake of the political defeats of Soviet communism and Western social democracy.

Nearly a quarter of a century ago, Zygmunt Bauman suggested that the role of intellectuals shifted from 'legislators' to 'interpreters' as modernity segued into postmodernity (Bauman 1989). They no longer enjoyed the respect or self-confidence to lay down laws from on high, mandating new values and directions, but could at best explain existing perspectives. In criminology as in other disciplines, a horror of judgmentalism served to eviscerate critique. Criminologists became either policy wonks or interpreters of the florid cultures of deviance. But there is an excluded middle in Bauman's dichotomy (paradoxically as he is a prime exemplar of it). This 'third way' is the intellectual (or criminologist) as prophet – in the meaning that prophesy had in the Old Testament, not its contemporary usage of Mystic Megs who purport to foresee the future. As Michael Walzer puts it,[1] the Old Testament prophet's message 'is not something radically new; the prophet is not the first to find, nor does he make, the morality he expounds. . . . The prophet need only show the people their own hearts' (Walzer 1993: 71–74). The prophet pointed out the way for people to realize values they *already* shared and accepted, but which their current practices frustrated. This was always a controversial intervention – as Max Weber suggested, the prophets were pioneering political pamphleteers (Weber 1952: 267). But their admonishments were compatible with Weber's strictures about value neutrality in the scientific, as distinct from political, vocation. The prophets based their critique of people's practices on invoking, not challenging, existing communal values. In this sense, prophecy was a paradoxical form of value-free preaching.

Many criminologists (like other social scientists, and as the Di Grazia quote I began with showed, even police chiefs) used to talk in this manner, presuming that a major source of crime and disorder was social injustice. For much of the twentieth century this social democratic perspective at least implicitly informed most sociological criminology, suggesting limited potential for criminal justice to control crime levels. Although intelligent policing and penal policy could more effectively relieve the symptoms of criminogenic political economic structures and cultures, this was what (in the context of the 'war on terror') Paul Rogers has dubbed 'liddism': an ultimately futile struggle to hold the lid down on the smouldering sources of crime. Social peace required getting tough on these causes. Whilst this perspective has for the time being lost the political battle (Reiner 2006), it has not lost the argument. There are still mysteries in explaining the sudden rise of neoliberalism to dominance in the 1970s, sweeping away so rapidly the post-World War II social democratic consensus that had delivered so much in terms of widely shared growth in material prosperity and security, as well as relatively low crime and benign control strategies by historical standards.

Even more important, and at least as mysterious: where are we going now? It is remarkable that so soon after the economic and financial crunch in late 2007 seemed to discredit the neoliberal model, its savagely deflationary prescriptions for dealing with the sovereign debt crisis (resulting from governmental support for banking) are the new orthodoxy. How can this zombie neoliberalism be explained? And what will it mean for criminal justice in Britain, in the hands of the new Conservative-led coalition?

Many liberals have been impressed and surprised by early signs of coalition willingness to reverse some of the trends to harsher punitiveness and the erosion of civil liberties under New Labour (and the Michael Howard regime at the Home Office before that). A landmark speech by justice secretary Kenneth Clarke on 30 June 2010 at the Centre for Crime and Justice Studies harked back to the philosophy articulated by the White Paper preceding the 1991 Criminal Justice Act, that prison was an expensive way of making bad people worse. For the first time in nearly 20 years, there was government questioning of Howard's mantra that prison works. This apparent conversion is welcome, even if it is largely prompted by economic considerations. But it is sadly predictable that these liberal ambitions will be frustrated in practice by increasing crime and disorder flowing from the financial cuts and downturn. As before, the 'freeing' of the economy will engender a strong state penal and policing response to the social dislocation it produces. The growth of demonstrations and protests against the coalition's cuts and the unjust burden placed on the relatively poor by the legal tax avoidance of the rich, spearheaded by heroic groups like UK Uncut, and the harsh policing tactics they have been met with, demonstrates this clearly. Neoliberalism fans social injustice and thus undermines liberal approaches to criminal justice (Reiner 2011). An alternative narrative to neoliberal instrumentalism and egoistic aspiration is needed, evoking the mutualism of Buber's ideal of 'I–thou' (as argued by Benjamin 2010 in relation to financial markets). This echoes the ethics of the Golden Rule that underpinned social democracy (Reiner 2006). A core criminological responsibility, I believe, is to chart a way forward to reviving the conditions for social security and peace, which social democracy had begun gradually to deliver.

Note

1 I am indebted to my son Toby's doctoral thesis on the political thought of Michael Walzer (T. Reiner 2011) for alerting me to this aspect of Walzer's arguments for preserving a social democratic voice in the face of the neoliberal tsunami of recent decades.

References

Bauman, Z. (1989) *Legislators and Interpreters*. Cambridge: Polity.

Beckett, K. and Western, B. (2001) 'Governing Social Marginality: Welfare, Incarceration and the Transformation of State Policy', *Punishment and Society* 3(1): 43–59.

Beirne, P. (1991) 'Inventing Criminology: The "Science of Man" in Cesare Beccaria's *Dei delitti e delle penne*', *Criminology* 29(4): 777–820.

—— (1993) *Inventing Criminology: Essays on the Rise of Homo Criminalis*. Albany: State University of New York Press.

Bell, M. (2011) *Criminal Justice and Neoliberalism*. London: Sage.

Benjamin, J. (2010) 'The Narratives of Financial Law', *Oxford Journal of Legal Studies* 30(4): 787–814.

Bonger, W. (1916) [1969] *Criminality and Economic Conditions*. Bloomington: Indiana University Press.

Box, S. (1987) *Recession, Crime and Punishment*. London: Macmillan.

Bratton, W. (1998) 'Crime is Down: Blame the Police', in N. Dennis (ed.) *Zero Tolerance: Policing A Free Society*, 2nd edn. London: Institute of Economic Affairs.

Cavadino, M. and Dignan, J. (2006) *Penal Systems: A Comparative Approach*. London: Sage.

Coleman, R., Sim, J., Tombs, S. and Whyte, D. (eds) (2009) *State, Power, Crime*. London: Sage.

Colquhoun, P. (1800) *Treatise on the Commerce and Police of the River Thames*. London: J. Mowman.

Currie, E. (1997) 'Market, Crime and Community: Toward a Mid-range Theory of Post-industrial Violence', *Theoretical Criminology* 1: 147–72.

—— (1998) 'Crime and Market Society: Lessons From the United States', in P. Walton and J. Young (eds) *The New Criminology Revisited*. London: Macmillan.

—— (2008) 'Pulling Apart: Notes On The Widening Gap In The Risks Of Violence', *Criminal Justice Matters* 70: 37–38.

Dahrendorf, R. (1985) *Law and Order*. London: Sweet and Maxwell.

De Giorgi, A. (2006) *Rethinking the Political Economy of Punishment*. Aldershot: Ashgate.

Di Grazia, R. (1976) 'What's Wrong with America's Police Leadership?', *Police*, May, p. 24.

Downes, D. (2001) 'The Macho Penal Economy', *Punishment and Society* 3(1): 61–80.

Downes, D. and Hansen, K. (2006) 'Welfare and Punishment in Comparative Perspective', in S. Armstrong and L. McAra (eds) *Perspectives on Punishment*. Oxford: Oxford University Press.

Downes, D. and Morgan, R. (2007) 'No Turning Back: The Politics of Law and Order into the Millennium', in M. Maguire, R. Morgan and R. Reiner (eds) *The Oxford Handbook of Criminology*, 4th edn. Oxford: Oxford University Press.

Fullbrook, E. (ed.) (2007) *Real World Economics: A Post-Autistic Economics Reader*. London: Anthem Press.

Gamble, A. (1994) *The Free Economy and the Strong State: Politics of Thatcherism*. Basingstoke: Palgrave Macmillan.

Garland, D. (1985) *Punishment and Welfare*. Aldershot: Gower.

—— (1996) 'The Limits of the Sovereign State: Strategies of Crime Control in Contemporary Societies', *British Journal of Criminology* 36(4): 1–27.

—— (2001) *The Culture of Control*. Oxford: Oxford University Press.

—— (2002) 'Of Crime and Criminals: The Development of Criminology in Britain', in M. Maguire, R. Morgan and R. Reiner (eds) *The Oxford Handbook of Criminology*, 3rd edn. Oxford: Oxford University Press.

Gatrell, V. (1981) 'The Decline of Theft and Violence in Victorian and Edwardian England', in V. Gatrell, B. Lenman, and G. Parker (eds) *Crime and the Law*. London: Europa.

Geary, R. (1985) *Policing Industrial Disputes*. Cambridge: Cambridge University Press.

Glyn, A. (2006) *Capitalism Unleashed*. Oxford: Oxford University Press.

Green, P. and Ward, T. (2009) 'Violence and the State', in R. Coleman, J. Sim, S. Tombs and D. Whyte (eds) *State, Power, Crime*. London: Sage.

Haakonssen, K. (ed.) (2006) *The Cambridge Companion to Adam Smith*. Cambridge: Cambridge University Press.

Hall, S., Critcher, C., Jefferson, T., Clarke, J. and Roberts, B. (1978) *Policing the Crisis*. London: Macmillan.

Hall, S. and MacLean, C. (2009) 'A Tale of Two Capitalisms: Preliminary Spatial and Historical Comparisons of Homicide', *Theoretical Criminology* 13(3): 313–39.

Hall, S. and Winlow, S. (2003) 'Rehabilitating Leviathan: Reflections on the State, Economic Regulation and Violence Reduction', *Theoretical Criminology* 7: 139–62.

—— (2004) 'Barbarians at the Gates: Crime and Violence in the Breakdown of the Pseudo-pacification Process', in J. Ferrell, K. Hayward, W. Morrison and M. Presdee (eds) *Cultural Criminology Unleashed*. London: Glasshouse.

—— (2005) 'Anti-Nirvana: Crime, Culture and Instrumentalism in an Age of Insecurity', *Crime, Media, Culture* 1(1): 31–48.

—— (2007) 'Cultural Criminology and Primitive Accumulation: A Formal Introduction for Two Strangers Who Should Really Become More Intimate', *Crime, Media, Culture* 3(1): 82–90.

Hall, S., Winlow, S. and Ancrum, C. (2008) *Criminal Identities and Consumer Culture: Crime, Exclusion and the New Culture of Narcissism*. Cullompton: Willan.

Harvey, D. (2005) *A Brief History of Neoliberalism*. Oxford: Oxford University Press.

Hayward, K. (2004) *City Limits: Crime, Consumer Culture and the Urban Experience*. London: Glasshouse.

Hayward, K. and Young, J. (2007) 'Cultural Criminology', in M. Maguire, R. Morgan and R. Reiner (eds) *The Oxford Handbook of Criminology*, 4th edn. Oxford: Oxford University Press.

Hillyard, P., Pantazis, C., Tombs, S. and Gordon, D. (eds) (2004) *Beyond Criminology*. London: Pluto.

Hillyard, P., Sim, J., Tombs, S. and Whyte, D. (2004) 'Leaving a "Stain upon the Silence"' *British Journal of Criminology* 44(3): 369–90.

Jacobs, L. and Skocpol, T. (eds) (2005) *Inequality and American Democracy*. New York: Russell Sage Foundation.

Johnston, L. and Shearing, C. (2003) *Governing Security*. London: Routledge.

Katz, J. (1988) *Seductions of Crime*. New York: Basic Books.

Lacey, N. (2008) *The Prisoners' Dilemma: Political Economy and Punishment in Contemporary Democracies*. Cambridge: Cambridge University Press.

Lea, J. (2002) *Crime and Modernity*. London: Sage.

Marshall, T. H. (1950) *Citizenship and Social Class*. Cambridge: Cambridge University Press.

Merton, R. (1938) 'Social Structure and Anomie', *American Sociological Review* 3: 672–82 (revised in R. Merton [1957] *Social Theory and Social Structure*, London: Free Press).

Messner, S. and Rosenfeld, R. (2000) 'Market Dominance, Crime and Globalisation', in S. Karstedt and K-D. Bussmann (eds) *Social Dynamics of Crime and Control*. Oxford: Hart.

—— (2006) *Crime and the American Dream*, 4th edn. Belmont, CA: Wadsworth.

Miller, W. (1977) *Cops and Bobbies*, Chicago: University of Chicago Press.

Morris, R. (2001) '"Lies, Damned Lies and Criminal Statistics": Reinterpreting the Criminal Statistics in England and Wales', *Crime, History and Societies* 5: 111–27.

Nelken, D. (2009) 'Comparative Criminal Justice: Beyond Ethnocentrism and Relativism', *European Journal of Criminology* 6(4): 291–311.

Neocleous, M. (2000) *The Fabrication of Social Order: A Critical Theory of Police Power*. London: Pluto Press.

—— (2006) 'Theoretical Foundations of the "New Police Science"', in M. Dubber and M. Valverde (eds) *The New Police Science*. Stanford, CA: Stanford University Press.

O'Malley, P. (1997) 'Policing, Post-Modernism and Political Rationality', *Social and Legal Studies* 6(3): 363–81.

Palast, G. (2004) *The Best Democracy Money Can Buy*. New York: Plume.

Pantazis, C. and Pemberton, S. (2009) 'Nation States and the Production of Harm: Resisting the Hegemony of "TINA"', in R. Coleman, J. Sim, S. Tombs and D. Whyte (eds) *State, Power, Crime*. London: Sage.

Pasquino, P. (1978) 'Theatrum Politicum: The Genealogy of Capital – Police and the State of Prosperity', *Ideology and Consciousness* 4(1): 41–54.

Polanyi, K. (1944 [2001]) *The Great Transformation*. Boston: Beacon.

Radzinowicz, L. (1956) *A History of the English Criminal Law and Its Administration from 1750, Vol. III*. London: Stevens.

Radzinowicz, L. and Hood, R. (1986) *A History of English Criminal Law and Its Administration, Vol. VI*. London: Stevens.

Reiner, R. (1988) 'British Criminology and the State', *British Journal of Criminology* 29(1): 138–58.

—— (2006) 'Beyond Risk: A Lament for Social Democratic Criminology', in T. Newburn and P. Rock (eds) *The Politics of Crime Control*. Oxford: Oxford University Press.

—— (2007a) 'Political Economy, Crime and Criminal Justice', in M. Maguire, R. Morgan and R. Reiner (eds) *The Oxford Handbook of Criminology*, 4th edn. Oxford: Oxford University Press.

—— (2007b) *Law and Order: An Honest Citizen's Guide to Crime and Control*. Cambridge: Polity.

—— (2010) *The Politics of the Police*, 4th edn. Oxford: Oxford University Press.

—— (2011) *Policing, Popular Culture and Political Economy: Towards A Social Democratic Criminology*, Farnham: Ashgate.

Reiner, T. (2011) 'Democracy, Community, Citizenship: The Political Thought of Michael Walzer', Ph.D. thesis, University of California–Berkeley.

Rothschild, E. (2002) *Economic Sentiments: Adam Smith, Condorcet and the Enlightenment*. Cambridge, MA: Harvard University Press.

Rusche, G. and Kirchheimer, O. (1939) *Punishment and Social Structure*. New York: Russell & Russell.

Shearing, C. and Stenning, P. (1983) 'Private Security: Implications for Social Control', *Social Problems* 30(5): 493–506.

Silver, A. (1967) 'The Demand for Order in Civil Society', in D. Bordua (ed.) *The Police*. New York: Wiley.

Sutton, J. R. (2004) 'The Political Economy of Imprisonment in Affluent Western Democracies, 1960–90', *American Sociological Review* 69(1): 170–89.

Tawney, R. H. (1935/1981) *The Attack and Other Papers*. Nottingham: Spokesman.

Taylor, H. (1998) 'Rising Crime: The Political Economy of Criminal Statistics Since the 1850s', *Economic History Review* LI: 569–90.

—— (1999) 'Forging the Job: A Crisis of "Modernisation" or Redundancy for the Police in England and Wales 1900–939', *British Journal of Criminology* 39: 113–35.

Taylor, I. (1999) *Crime in Context: A Critical Criminology of Market Societies*. Cambridge: Polity.

Taylor, I., Walton, P. and Young, J. (1973) *The New Criminology*. London: Routledge.

Theoretical Criminology (2007) Special issue on Robert K. Merton, February.

Tombs, S. and Whyte, D. (2009) 'The State and Corporate Crime', in R. Coleman, J. Sim, S. Tombs and D. Whyte (eds) *State, Power, Crime*. London: Sage.

Wacquant, L. (2005) 'The Great Penal Leap Backwards: Imprisonment in America from Nixon to Clinton', in J. Pratt, D. Brown, M. Brown, S. Hallsworth and W. Morrison (eds) *The New Punitiveness*. Cullompton: Willan.

—— (2009) *Punishing the Poor: The Neoliberal Government of Social Insecurity*. Durham, NC: Duke University Press.

Walzer, M. (1993) *Interpretation and Social Criticism*. Cambridge, MA: Harvard University Press.

Weber, M. (1952) *Ancient Judaism*. Glencoe: Free Press.

Wilkinson, R. (2005) *The Impact of Inequality*. New York: New Press.

Wilkinson, R. and Pickett, K. (2009) *The Spirit Level: Why More Equal Societies Almost Always Do Better*. London: Allen Lane.

Wilson, J. Q. (1975) *Thinking About Crime*. New York: Vintage.

Young, J. (1986) 'The Failure of Criminology: The Need for a Radical Realism', in R. Matthews and J. Young (eds) *Confronting Crime*. London: Sage.

—— (1999) *The Exclusive Society*. London: Sage.

—— (2003) 'Merton with Energy, Katz with Structure: The Sociology of Vindictiveness and the Criminology of Transgression', *Theoretical Criminology* 7(3): 389–414.

Zedner, L. (2006) 'Opportunity Makes the Thief-Taker: The Influence of Economic Analysis on Crime Control', in T. Newburn and P. Rock (eds) *The Politics of Crime Control*. Oxford: Oxford University Press.

3   Critical criminology, critical theory and social harm

Majid Yar

Introduction

Critical criminology emerged in the late 1960s from a convergence between social science and the wider spirit of oppositional political movements that characterised those turbulent times on both sides of the Atlantic. Committed to 'deconstructing' crime and crime control (Cohen 1998) so as to illuminate the manifold ways in which they reflect and reproduce patterns of power, inequality, exploitation and exclusion, the movement gained rapid momentum. In the intervening four decades, the critical orientation has expanded to include a wide range of over-lapping, intersecting (and sometimes competing) perspectives, variously identified as 'radical', 'feminist', 'abolitionist', 'conflict', 'peacemaking', 'constitutive', 'integrative', 'postmodern', 'green' and 'cultural' criminologies. However, despite the self-evident vigour of this critical propensity, it is notable that the tradition of critical theory (itself under constant development and revision since the 1920s) has found only a very limited purchase within critical criminology. In this paper (following some preliminary scene-setting) I sketch one way in which critical theory may make a decisive contribution to the development of critical criminology. Given the sheer diversity of perspectives that are encompassed within the 'broad church' of critical criminology, it is of course impossible to address the potential relevance of critical theory for even a handful of its specific formulations. Therefore, I have chosen here to focus on one important strand in recent critical criminology, namely the attempt to 'decriminalise' the discipline by shifting its object of analysis from the social construct of *crime*, and towards a focus upon the manifold *social harms* that are produced by patterns of inequality in advanced capitalism. While a harms-based conception of critical criminological inquiry is, I claim, one of its most promising avenues for development, it is nevertheless beset with problems in providing a coherent grounding for its key analytical–empirical category – that of harm itself. Turning to the recent development of critical theory based upon the concept of recognition, I attempt to show how such theory can resolve key problems facing harms-based perspectives, and so help shape critical criminology in a positive manner.

Critical criminology and critical theory

To speak of 'critical criminology' risks introducing confusion rather than clarification into any discussion of criminological theory. Many and diverse contributions to the field may be labelled as exercises in such a criminology, be it by the authors themselves or other readers who comment upon the works in question. What, if anything, unifies these efforts into a coherent 'critical' discourse remains an open question. As Gresham Sykes noted in an early discussion of critical criminology: 'what we are confronted with is not so much a body of precise, systematic theoretical propositions, as a viewpoint, a perspective, or an orientation' (Sykes 1974: 212). Despite the lack of 'systematic theoretical propositions', Sykes attempted to delineate some common characteristics that were shared across an emergent style of criminological enquiry in the 1960s and 1970s. These characteristics comprised a break with, and challenging of, assumptions that had supposedly organised the bulk of criminological inquiry until that point. The first facet of this critical stance was a rejection of method- ological and conceptual individualism in the development of aetiological accounts of crime. The second was a 'profound shift in the interpretation of motives behind the actions of the agencies that deal with crime' (ibid.: 208); defects and biases in the operation of criminal justice were not contingent imperfections but systemic features of an apparatus of social control directed by one class against another. Third, sociological functionalism's assumption that the law articulates a moral consensus across society was jettisoned in favour of the view that such laws are imposed by the powerful few upon the (relatively) powerless many. Fourth, official accounts of crime (its forms, frequencies, locations) were viewed not as measures but as constructs manufactured by the system in tandem with its organising purposes. If we take Sykes' characterisation of critical criminology's 'orientation' as reasonable, it becomes clear that it owes much of its organising assumptions to an earlier appropriation of Marxist ideas by analysts of crime. Broadly speaking, the aetiology of offending, the codification of criminal laws, law enforcement (from detection, through prosecution and punishment), and dominant cultural constructions of crime itself, are to be understood as the expressions of ruling class interests in a divided and conflict-ridden capitalist society. The criminological heirs of Marx borrowed and applied his ideas in a fairly *ad hoc* fashion,[1] resulting in a wide variety of propositions whose commonality amounted basically to a conviction that the dynamics of capitalist society were implicated in the genesis of 'crime problems' and that they conditioned the entire apparatus of crime control in decisive ways.[2] This orientation was evidently influential upon a range of criminological efforts, spanning not only so-called 'critical criminology', but also those variously styled as 'radical' and 'conflict' perspectives (Bernard 1981). Equally, it decisively shaped the development of the self-styled 'New Criminology' that emerged in the 1970s (Taylor *et al*. 1974), even as it sought to expand its gaze beyond the domain of class-based inequalities to include also those organised around gender, ethnicity and other categories of collective experience. Analytical categories (class, capital, ideology, hegemony, exploitation) derived from the Marxist tradition continued to feature (albeit in an attenuated form) in subsequent 'alternative' intellectual projects, including the likes of 'peacemaking criminology' and 'constitutive criminology', despite hostility to Marxism amongst some who seek a decisive break with its 'totalising' tendencies (Russell 2003). In particular, the 1970s and 1980s saw a decisive influence of neo-Marxism upon studies of crime that borrowed from Gramsci's analysis of hegemony (Hall *et al.* 1978) and Althusser's structuralist Marxism (Hirst 1975).

Given the manifold ways in which the legacy of Marxist thought has shaped the development of critical criminology, it is all the more surprising how little the neo-Marxism associated with critical theory has impacted upon the discipline. By critical theory I refer here specifically to the analysis of capitalist society developed by those associated with the Frankfurt Institute for Social Research from the 1920s onwards. The contours of the Frankfurt School's project were famously outlined by Max Horkheimer's opening address upon assuming the directorship of the Institute, entitled 'The Present Situation of Social Philosophy and the Tasks of an Institute for Social Research'. Here he presented the broad ambition of critical theory as:

> [T]he philosophical interpretation of the vicissitudes of human fate – the fate of humans not as mere individuals, however, but as members of a community. It is thus above all concerned with phenomena that can only be understood in the context of human social life: with the state, law, economy, religion.
>
> (Horkheimer 1993 [1931]: 1)

The first significant feature of critical theory, one that lends itself to informing a critical criminology, is its social ontology (adduced by Horkheimer above). For critical theory, individual action and experience can only be adequately grasped by situating it within the totality of social relations and institutions; such relations have ontological priority over the forms of subjectivity that they effectively call into being. A second important feature of the School's project relate specifically to its self-constitution as a *critical* discourse. Critical theory departs from a deeply ambivalent relation to Enlightenment thought, a stance that defines its overall orientation. At one level, it orients itself by the Enlightenment concern with human autonomy, freedom and self-realisation. However, unlike their predecessors (such as Kant), freedom is not conceived as a property of an individual will, but as something only possible in the dynamics of a social whole. While this view owes much of its inspiration to Hegel, the Frankfurt School dismissed any Hegelian proposition that human freedom is teleologically self-realising through some objective movement of history; rather, it is the product of a struggle for collective self-realisation in the face of social forces of domination that act to foreclose and limit humans' possibilities for being. Taken together, these commitments lead to the formulation of an intellectual and practical project that uses the Enlightenment's ideas against itself: the benchmarks of truth, autonomy, and freedom are used as a critical yardstick with which the failure to realise those aims in actual social, political and economic relations can be exposed and explained. Therefore, critical theory is *critical* foremost in that it seeks to generate knowledge that will inform and enable struggles for human freedom, and against all forms of institutionalised domination that curtail that freedom.

The Frankfurt School's critical diagnosis of the ways in which capitalist society limits human self-realisation and authenticity is pursued through a number of avenues, and with respect to a range of empirically evident phenomena that exemplify domination, deception and exploitation. For Adorno and Horkheimer (1997 [1947]), the domination of instrumental reason in capitalist modernity reduces humans to mere means, subjected to the ends of reproducing the dominant social system. Efficiency, technical control and rational planning become ends in themselves, and the original goal of Enlightenment reason (the liberation of human beings) is not only lost, but inverted: reason becomes the instrument of domination and subjugation. Across the spheres of politics, law, economy and culture, human existence becomes impoverished as a logic of domination takes hold. Likewise for Marcuse (2002 [1964]: 3) human existence is reduced to a 'one dimensional' conformity and drudgery: 'A comfortable, smooth, reasonable, democratic unfreedom prevails in advanced industrial civilisation'. The abrogation of genuine freedom is cemented through a satisfaction of 'false needs' which are themselves created by the system of mass consumption and popular culture. What this culturally induced myopia disguises is the 'waste and destruction ... exploitation and repression' upon which the 'progress' and material abundance of so-called 'advanced' societies are built (ibid.: xxx). In the subsequent development of critical theory by Habermas (1986), the ways in which power curtails human emancipation is made evident through its distortion of the inter-subjective conditions inherent in the process of moral–political discourse and decision making; where reason loses out to institutionalised patterns of power in the negotiation of our common public actions, the promise of genuine autonomy and self-realisation remains crucially unfulfilled.

It would be unfair to say that the critical project developed by the Frankfurt School, in its various iterations, has found no purchase whatsoever upon the development of criminology. However, Groves and Sampson (1986: 58) were largely justified in writing, a couple of decades ago, that: 'there have been very few attempts to apply critical theory to criminology' and that 'critical theory bears only a remote similarity to critical criminology'. Groves and Sampson themselves go on to suggest ways in which critical theory (as formulated variously by Horkheimer, Marcuse, and especially Habermas) might be mobilised to clarify a range of enduring criminological issues, including: the relationship between culture and social structure as it relates to crime; the incidence of crime as the outcome of social pathologies (or social 'irrationality' as they put it); and a conception of criminological knowledge that eschews positivism's pretensions to scientific neutrality in favour of an emancipatory commitment to the necessary links between theory and practice. While the authors elucidate the possible connections between critical theory and criminology with considerable subtlety and sensitivity, their efforts ultimately amount to a re-narration of a diverse body of extant criminological work, so as to show how that work already converges with those concerns elaborated by various critical theorists. In other words, they fall well short of proposing any fundamental and coherent reconceptualisation of criminology's empirical, analytic, or ontological categories in line with critical theory. Since Groves and Sampson first offered their reflections, elements of critical theory have made further headway into criminological theory and analysis. In particular, the rapid development of cultural criminology has found in the work, especially of Adorno and Horkheimer, resources for connecting issues of crime and deviance with the contours of contemporary consumerism and mass culture (see, for example, Hayward 2004). Yet again, however, ideas from critical theory are borrowed as a set of 'auxiliary assumptions' that can be appended to a range of other criminological and sociological theories, rather than serving as a means to revise the nature of criminological inquiry itself at a fundamental level.

In the remainder of this chapter, I will suggest one way in which just such a reorientation of critical criminology might be undertaken. I focus specifically upon the development of critical criminology as a 'zemiological' or social harms perspective, that which seeks to dispense with 'crime' as the fundamental empirical–analytic category for criminological inquiry, and instead seeks to formulate a critically and politically committed project centred around the manifold forms of harm that emerge from dominant patterns of social, economic, technological, and cultural practices (what amounts to a search for a 'replacement discourse' that transcends the discipline's focus upon 'crime' and provides it with an alternative object that is consistent with the broader pursuit of social justice – Henry and Milovanovic 1996). I suggest that while the harms perspective offers a fruitful way forward for critical criminology, it suffers from some basic problems with its conceptualisation of harm itself. By utilising the recent development of critical theory within the framework of *recognition* (most particularly by Axel Honneth), I suggest that this critical enterprise can be placed on a sounder theoretical, conceptual and analytic footing.

The critical theory of recognition: a brief overview

Before considering the potential contribution of contemporary critical theory to a harms-based critical criminology, it is necessary to briefly outline the contours of the recognition–theoretic version of critical theory. This has been developed in great part by Axel Honneth (a former student of Jürgen Habermas who succeeded his teacher as professor of philosophy at Frankfurt's Goethe University). Honneth's starting point is the common commitment of critical theory to diagnosing the ways in which Enlightenment ideals of freedom and autonomy are denied realisation by forms of domination that prevail in modern societies. Whereas his predecessors either (a) appealed to such ideals without providing any coherent definition what specifically they comprise (Adorno, Horkheimer, Marcuse), or (b) framed them purely in the terms of the ability to participate in procedural decision-making (Habermas), Honneth attempts to ground them in a coherent *philosophical anthropology*, a theory of human nature (one derived in large part from a re-reading of Hegel). Contrary to the assumptions of liberal–individualist thought, the individual is not viewed as a self-subsistent entity, 'always already' fully constituted as it enters the world. Against this 'monadic' ontology, Hegel argues that what he calls the 'independent consciousness' (equivalent to the sovereign individual of liberal theory) in fact exists in a paradoxical state of essential *dependence* upon others (Benjamin 1992: 189–90; also Gerson 2004). The individual comes to know himself, to recognise himself as a being with particular attributes or properties, through the acknowledgement conferred by an 'other'. An individual's sense of worth remains mere 'subjective self-certainty', and hence uncertain of itself, unless that sense of worth (or 'idea-of-self') is affirmed by others (Kojève 1969: 11; also discussion in Crossley 1996: 16–21). This position is exemplified in Hegel's famous exposition of the 'Master–Slave Dialectic' in the *Phenomenology of Spirit* (Hegel 1977). In the Dialectic Hegel hypothesises a scenario in which a seemingly autonomous subject (the Master) enjoys unrestricted acknowledgement of his freedom from the other. The other (the Slave) exists in order to answer the desires and affirm the authority of the Master. However, in the very moment of his 'triumph' (the apparent realisation of his self-conception as an autonomous, free individual) the Master is undone. First, because his autonomy is non-autonomous, insofar as he can only come to experience himself as such through a relation of dependence on the Slave; the Master is, in a reversal of positions, the Slave of the other because of this need, and the Slave is in fact the Master, in that he enjoys the power to arbitrate or mediate recognition. Second, and of crucial importance, is the 'incompleteness' or 'hollowness' in the self-affirmation that the Master experiences, in that the Slave is *compelled*, by virtue of his subordination, to recognise the Master. The Slave's recognition is *coerced*, forced from him through the basic asymmetry of his relationship of servitude to the Master. As Kojève (1969) notes, this is the essence of the Master's 'tragedy', that recognition of his value or worth can only be experienced as meaningful or 'real' if it is granted *freely* (rather than forced) from another who is simultaneously recognised as free in his own right. In other words, we only value recognition if it comes from those deemed worthy of granting it, and who can choose to do otherwise if they did not feel such esteem. The upshot of this analysis is twofold. First, it demonstrates that self-realisation cannot be anything other than an inter-subjective endeavour, and that the forging of a coherent sense of selfhood (self-esteem) is dependent upon recognition from others. Second, it shows that for recognition to work it must of necessity be a *mutual* relationship, one in which each recognises the other's autonomy, freedom and human value.[3] It is from this grounding that Honneth derives a moral–political vision for a just society, one in which public institutions mediate something akin to universal recognition of all by all, a mutually self-sustaining relationship of affirmation.

Honneth further develops his theory of recognition through a reading of Hegel's *Philosophy of Right* (Hegel 1991). In particular, Honneth (1996) discerns three distinctive social modes or levels of recognition, each corresponding to a different institutionalisation of social and political relations. At the level of formal political systems (coincidental with Hegel's notion of the state), we find the institutionalisation of *respect*, the universal recognition of value appropriate to membership of the human community as such. In practical terms, respect is mediated through *legal rights* in which are embedded fundamental principles of mutual regard. At the level of intra-group solidarity (continuous with Hegel's formulation of civil society), we find recognition in the form of *solidarity*, mechanisms of mutual esteem that acknowledge the value of shared cultural characteristics and social identities. At the level of intimate relations (corresponding to the Hegelian family) we find *love*, which is to be understood as 'referring to primary relationships insofar as they – on the model of friendships, parent–child relationships, as well as erotic relationships between lovers – are constituted by strong emotional attachments among a small number of people' (Honneth 1996: 95). In relations of love, one is recognised not as a rights-bearing subject equivalent to all others, nor as the holder of common traits shared with other members of a social group, but in one's *particularity*, by virtue of traits and characteristics that are *unique* to oneself.[4]

In sum, what Honneth attempts to provide is a theoretically coherent (and empirically informed) conceptualisation of the fundamental preconditions of human self-realisation. In other words, he gives a substantive content to the ideals of freedom and autonomy, demonstrating how they are practically realised in different spheres of social action and interaction. Conversely, these modes of realisation-through-recognition (as respect, esteem and love) serve as critical yardsticks (what Habermas calls *counter-factual normative ideals*) which can be used to identify existing social, political, economic and cultural arrangements that *deny* recognition to human beings (such as the refusal of political rights and liberties, the refusal to grant esteem for particular ways of life, and the refusal to meet people's basic needs for care and nurturing).

Social harm and recognition

There are manifold social actions, interactions and processes that generate harms for individuals and groups. Such harms span those located in the domain of the inter-personal, the sphere of institutionalised action, and also arise from the unintended consequences of macro-level processes. Recent critical criminology has devoted significant attention toward developing a 'social harms' approach to understanding and explaining social problems. Thus Hillyard and Tombs (2008: 14–16) advocate a harm-based conception of critical criminology that would embrace variously physical harms (assault, injury, death); financial/economic harms (impoverishment, fraud, theft); and emotional and psychological harms (the inducement of fear and insecurity amongst individuals and groups according to their social identities) (for other, similar attempts to define a 'harm approach' see *inter alia* Shearing 1989; van Swaaningen 1999; Muncie 2000; Hillyard *et al*. 2004).[5] The impetus for such developments has emerged from the critical criminological rejection of 'crime' as the most appropriate analytical category through which to grasp and define social problems. The current 'zemiologists' (those critical criminologists who advocate replacing the concept of crime with that of harm for the purposes of social inquiry) argue that the category of crime lacks any ontological integrity; it defines not a distinctive class of phenomena (i.e. is not a 'natural kind' – Wilkerson 1995), but is instead a socio-political construct that simply reflects the contingent ways in which political and economic power is formally actualised through law. Consequently, they argue that harm rather than crime is better suited to act as a critical conceptual anchor in documenting, explaining and challenging social problems.

While the aforementioned notion of social harms is indeed a promising orientation for critical criminology, it is nevertheless beset with conceptual problems and ambiguities. As its advocates themselves concede, social harm 'appears to be a generalised, amorphous term, covering an enormous range of quite heterogeneous phenomena' (Hillyard *et al.* 2004: 67). They go on to claim that this very capaciousness is one of the concept's great strengths, as compared to the category of crime that depends upon the formal *legal* recognition of a social problem before it enters the domain of analysis. Yet this lack of specificity leaves the concept of harm lacking the very same ontological reality that is postulated as grounds for rejecting the concept of crime. The appeal to social harm is sustained by its intuitive moral–political appeal and 'commonsense' purchase, but no more. Consequently, nowhere in the writings on social harm thus far discussed is there a concerted attempt to give the concept any analytical specificity, i.e. to define what makes something a 'harm' or 'harmful', or what distinguishes the harmful from the non-harmful. Below I shall argue that the concept of recognition is especially well suited to remedy this ontological deficit, providing firm conceptual ground upon which the critical criminological analysis of harms can proceed.

The theory of recognition can ground a theory of social harms, first, because it seeks to establish at a fundamental anthropological level the 'basic needs' that comprise the conditions of human integrity and well-being (what Aristotelians call 'flourishing'). The theory, as already noted, identifies a differentiated order of such needs through the categories of 'love', 'rights' and 'esteem' (Honneth 1996: 131–39). Each corresponds to a basic element that is required to secure the subject's integrity in its relation to self and others. Love satisfies the demand for 'emotional support' and a 'basic self-confidence' that one will be cared for by others; 'rights' mediate a demand for dignity and moral equality as an individual person amongst others; and 'esteem' grants a sense of one's value as a person with *particular* social and cultural traits and abilities. From this viewpoint, social harms can be understood to comprise nothing other than *the inter-subjective experience of being refused recognition with respect to any or all of these dimensions of need* (what Honneth calls 'disrespect'). The denial of love takes form most fundamentally as the 'violation of the body', in that the expectation that others will sustain one's basic ontological integrity is not met; the 'denial of rights' amounts to a refusal to accord one basic human dignity and equality; and the 'denigration of a way of life' amounts to the refusal to grant esteem on the basis of specific cultural traits and social identities (ibid.). If we understand harms in this way, as instances of 'disrespect' with reference to recognitive needs, then the 'range of quite heterogeneous phenomena' adduced by social harm theorists can find a coherent conceptual unity; each and all of these phenomena correspond to one order or other of non-recognition, and their 'ontological reality' *as* harms lies precisely in their nature as forms of 'disrespect'. To give some concrete examples, actions such as inter-personal physical, sexual and emotional violence within the family acquire their specifically *harmful* character because they violate the necessary conditions for a person to establish basic self-confidence through the experience of love. Public (including state sanctioned) practices of torture and abuse, theft and appropriation, amount to a denial of those rights that meet the need for dignity and equality amongst others as citizens. Practices such as market discrimination or symbolic denigration on the basis of gender, ethnicity, sexual orientation and suchlike are properly harms in that they deny those subject to them the experience of self-esteem or recognition of the distinctive worth of their identities and ways of life. Thus for each of the many forms of harm that may be adduced as social problems, we find a corresponding basis in the refusal of that recognition which is the basis of human self-realisation.

I have argued above that recognition can provide the much-needed ontological grounds for conceiving harms within critical criminological inquiry. Moreover, since the concept of recognition is 'multi-axial' (Yar 2001) it enables us to encompass within a single conceptual framework experiences that may at first sight appear profoundly dissimilar insofar as they occur across a wide range of institutional settings and/or at different socio-spatial scales. By using recognition as a theory of basic human needs and their violation, we can see that phenomena as diverse as the physical chastisement of a child by her parents to the impoverishment arising from the operation of global relations of capital share an underlying unity in that they are all forms of non-recognition. However, the multi-axial or differentiated character of the concept also enables us to avoid 'flattening' these diverse experiences of harm into a single *kind*; within its unifying parameters, recognition retains a crucial sensitivity to the different orders of forms of need that we experience as humans (love, respect, esteem) and we can allocate different harms to the appropriate order or kind of recognitive needs that are being violated. Recognition can thus perform the analytical work of describing and classifying social harms and problems according to the specific needs that they refuse. Moreover, it can perform the moral–evaluative work of assessing different social arrangements, actions, and institutionalised processes according to the extent to which they succeed or fail in satisfying those needs whose realisation is essential for human flourishing.

Recognition theory can not only help to resolve the ontological problems of social harm perspectives, but can also help to dissolve the juxtaposition of 'harm' and 'crime' into competing and non-compatible conceptual alternatives. As already noted, social harm theorists reject the use of crime as a foundational category for inquiry in that they view it as a socially and politically contingent category that does little more than reflect the interests of dominant social groups. For such theorists, crime (as a set of rules and corresponding sanctions formally institutionalised through law-making processes) amounts to a form of social control that (a) selectively prohibits and punishes behaviours that powerful interest groups view as a threat, and (b) leaves unprohibited and unpunished manifold more harmful behaviours perpetrated *by* and *on behalf of* the powerful, including those of environmental degradation, economic exploitation, and imperialist war-making. However, as I shall argue below, making recourse to recognition as the grounds of a theory of harms can help resolve this conflict by bringing 'crime' critically into the ambit of social inquiry.

Harm theorists' characterisation of law (both in its generality and in its specific criminal variant that defines 'crime') essentially conforms to the position adopted by the tradition of *legal positivism* within jurisprudence and the philosophy of law. Stated most crudely, the positivist perspective views law as an 'autonomous' domain that has no basis in morality, i.e. its provisions, postulates and prohibitions are not inferentially derived from, and do not represent, some underlying principle of morality or right (Conkin 2001; Kramer 2003). Rather, the validity of law is derived solely by reference to a social fact, such as the command of sovereign power (as proposed by Hobbes) or the contingent norms that take on an imperative form through the monopolisation of force by the state (as argued by Hans Kelsen and others) (Dyzenhaus 1999; Hobbes 2008). For positivists, we must exclude from our consideration of the validity of law any questions of its moral, social or political justifiability. Giving this positivism a Marxist gloss, criminal law becomes for harm theorists a coercive instrument legitimated by the power of the capitalist state, and thus irreducible to any valid principle of justice. However, if we start from a recognition theoretical standpoint, we can reconceive 'crime' (as constructed in law) as (at least in part) an articulation of a moral principle consistent with the preservation of subjects from harm. This is not to embrace, contra legal positivism, an unqualified legal naturalism that holds current legal principles to be justified by and consistent with moral principles that exist in the 'always and eternal' of universal imperatives (be it Kant's categorical or any other such variant). To do so would be to agree in essence with Voltaire's Dr Pangloss that we do indeed live 'in the best of all possible worlds', one in which the legal apparatus of bourgeois capitalist society (complete with deeply ingrained patriarchal and imperialist tendencies) serves to protect the needs and flourishing of all its citizens. However, we can from a recognition theoretical standpoint embrace what Sayer (2003) calls a 'qualified ethical naturalism' with respect to crime and criminalisation. For Sayer, such a position amounts to a realisation that our nature as social beings with defined and ineradicable needs and vulnerabilities necessarily grounds moral imperatives and social demands (without whose realisation we cannot sustain our existence *as social beings* in any meaningful sense – without such needs being met we cannot flourish – see also Sayer 2004). Using such naturalism as our starting point we can discern in criminal law an attempt (however partial, flawed or misguided) to enshrine in formal codes and prohibitions a principle of protection from harm *qua* recognition. Let us consider some concrete examples of crime. The legal sanctioning of acts of physical violence can be understood as a legitimate articulation of those needs associated with preserving the basic integrity of the self, i.e. the recognition of our need to be able to confront the world of others without fear of damage to our embodied selves, damage that would decisively undermine our basic self-confidence. Similarly, the legal guarantees of individual rights (equality before the law, the protection from the arbitrary use of power, rights of equal access to public goods), and the criminalisation of their violation, articulates an appreciation of those recognitive needs that Honneth identifies with the dignity of the person. Equally, recent legal measures to criminalise various forms of 'hateful' speech and representation can best be understood as concrete attempts to acknowledge the harm done to persons through the 'denigration of ways of life' and the impact this has upon persons' capacity to satisfy the need for social esteem. By using recognition as a benchmark or litmus test, we can evaluate the common categories of crime as legitimate (or illegitimate) with reference to the basic needs of social subjects. This enables us to discriminate between formally constituted categories of crime according to their consistency with the principle of promoting recognition, and whether they offer protection from social harm. To take one example, until 1994 there was no recognition in English criminal law of rape occurring within marriage; from a recognition-based understanding of social harms, this legal lacunae was illegitimate in that it failed to acknowledge that sexual coercion, occurring either inside or outside the context of any formally institutionalised relationships, violates the basic integrity of the self. Contrariwise, the introduction of criminal sanctions against such behaviour in the Criminal Justice and Public Order Act (1994) is legitimate from an ethically naturalistic standpoint because it enshrines protection from harm understood from a recognitive standpoint. We can similarly use harm as non-recognition to decisively establish the illegitimacy of laws such as those that criminalised consensual same-sex intercourse for long periods of British history, and which continue to do so in many states across the world. Given that such activities do not violate any harm principle, and that their criminalisation *does* violate the individual and collective realisation of dignity and self-esteem, their prohibition cannot be morally justified. By utilising recognition in this way as the conceptual basis for social scientific understanding of harms, we can decisively ground a critical analysis of crime and its consequences, and overcome some key analytical problems that have beset recent discussion in this area of inquiry.

Conclusion

In this paper I have reviewed the relationship between critical criminology and critical theory, suggesting that the latter has heretofore made extremely limited headway in terms of furnishing a coherent set of theoretical and conceptual underpinnings for criminology. This is all the more surprising given that critical criminology shares key features with critical theory, especially (1) an ontology that situates action and experience within wider social, political, economic and cultural processes; (2) a concern with the working of power and inequality, and the ways in which they systematically disadvantage some social constituencies; and (3) an epistemological commitment to eschew pretension to scientific neutrality in favour of a normatively oriented account of society that contributes to human emancipation. Taking one important strand within recent critical criminology, the development of a harms-based approach, I have sought to show how contemporary critical theory can in fact furnish ontological and empirical–analytic foundations for its inquiries. By utilising the critical theory of recognition, the concept of harm itself can be given a much-needed coherence and its unhelpful juxtaposition to 'law' can be transcended. While the enduring potential value of such a reformulation must be tested through the concrete analysis of social problems, I hope to have demonstrated that it is at least possible to lay sturdy foundations for critical criminology by drawing upon a heretofore largely ignored resource.

Notes

1 Hence they should not perhaps be identified as Marxist *per se*, but as enjoying a broader and looser *marxisant* orientation (Sparks 1980: 161).
2 For example, Bonger (1969 [1916]) argued that capitalism is criminogenic in that its cultivation of egoism and self-interest disposes people towards predation upon others, while simultaneously demoralising the poor whose unruly behaviour arises out a lack of 'civilisation and education' (ibid.: 168). Moving from crime causation to the legal construction of crime itself, Chambliss (1975) argues (amongst other things) that the system's disproportionate focus upon the working classes, and its neglect of offences by the rich and powerful, indicates how that system serves the interests of the ruling classes in capitalism. Looking at patterns of punishment, Rusche and Kirchheimer (1939) famously argued that historical variations in its severity could be explained by the relative scarcity of labour at different points in time; when labour power was scarce (and hence more valuable for the requirements of capitalist production), punishment tended to be attenuated in its severity so as to maximise the availability of labour power; conversely, a period of surplus labour power saw harsher punishment so as to suppress the threat from those excluded from the system.
3 The master–slave dialectic has been used to theorise the relationships of hierarchy within criminal groups; Hall *et al.* (2008: 105–5) combine the master–slave relation with Rousseau's analysis of self-love and pride (*amour-de-soi* and *amour propre*) so as to explicate the relations between the dominant and dominated in such groups.
4 Very similar arguments have been offered recently by Eagleton (2008) and Dews (2007).
5 We must distinguish here those harms that are properly *social*, which emanate from the actions and inactions of humans (individually and collectively) from those harms that arise ultimately from natural facts and processes that lie beyond the capacity for human intervention. Thus, for example, while differential mortality rates between the rich and poor are forms of social harm (since they could be alleviated through equality of access to nutrition, clean and safe living conditions, healthcare and so on) mortality as such (the inevitability of death) is a harm that lies beyond the social as it arises from our constitution as biological beings constrained by the life process.

References

Adorno, T. and Horkheimer, M. (1997 [1947]) *Dialectic of Enlightenment*. London: Verso.
Benjamin, J. (1992) 'Recognition and Destruction: An Outline of Intersubjectivity', in N. J. Skolnick and S. C. Warshaw (eds) *Relational Perspectives In Psychoanalysis*. Hillsdale, NJ and London: Analytic Press.

Bernard, T. J. (1981) 'The Distinction between Conflict and Radical Criminology', *The Journal of Criminal Law and Criminology*, 72(1): 362–79.

Bonger, W. (1969 [1916]) *Criminality and Economic Conditions*. Bloomington: Indiana University Press.

Chambliss, W. (1975) 'Toward a Political Economy of Crime', *Theory and Society*, 2: 149–70.

Conkin, W. E. (2001) *The Invisible Origins of Legal Positivism: A Re-Reading of a Tradition*. Dordrecht: Kluwer.

Cohen, S. (1998) 'Intellectual Scepticism and Political Commitment: The Case of Radical Criminology', in P. Walton and J. Young (eds) *The New Criminology Revisited*. London: Macmillan.

Crossley, N. (1996) *Intersubjectivity: The Fabric of Social Becoming*. London: Sage.

Dews, P. (2007) *The Idea of Evil*. Oxford: Wiley-Blackwell.

Dyzenhaus, D. (1999) *Legality and Legitimacy: Carl Schmitt, Hans Kelsen, and Hermann Heller in Weimar*. Oxford: Oxford University Press.

Eagleton, T. (2008) *Trouble with Strangers: A Study of Ethics*. Oxford: Wiley-Blackwell.

Gerson, G. (2004) 'Object Relations Psychoanalysis as Political Theory', *Political Psychology*, 25(4): 769–94.

Groves, W. and Sampson, R. (1986) 'Critical Theory and Criminology', *Social Problems*, 33(6): 56–80.

Habermas, J. (1986) *The Theory of Communicative Action: Reason and the Rationalization of Society*. Cambridge: Polity.

Hall, S., Critcher, C., Jefferson, T., Clarke, J. and Roberts, B. (1978) *Policing the Crisis: Mugging, the State and Law and Order*. London: Macmillan.

Hall, S., Winlow, S. and Ancrum, C. (2008) *Criminal Identities and Consumer Culture*. Cullompton: Willan.

Hayward, K. (2004) *City Limits: Crime, Consumer Culture and the Urban Experience*. London: Glasshouse/Routledge.

Hegel, G. W. F. (1977) *Phenomenology of Spirit*. Oxford: Oxford University Press.

—— (1991) *Elements of the Philosophy of Right*. Cambridge: Cambridge University Press.

Henry, S. and Milovanovic, D. (1996) *Constitutive Criminology: Beyond Postmodernism*. London: Sage.

Hillyard, P., Pantazis, C., Tombs, S. and Gordon, D. (eds) (2004) *Beyond Criminology: Taking Harms Seriously*. London: Pluto Press.

Hillyard, P. and Tombs, S. (2008) 'Beyond Criminology', in D. Dorling, D. Gordon, P. Hillyard, C. Pantazis, S. Pemberton and S. Tombs (eds) *Criminal Obsessions: Why Harm Matters than Crime*. King's College Centre for Crime and Justice Studies: London.

Hirst, P. Q. (1975) 'Marx and Engels on Law, Crime and Morality', in I. Taylor, P. Walton and J. Young (eds) *Critical Criminology*. London: Routledge.

Hobbes, T. (2008) *Human Nature* and *De Corpore Politico*. Oxford: Oxford University Press.

Honneth, A. (1996) *The Struggle for Recognition: The Moral Grammar of Social Conflicts*. Cambridge: Polity Press.

Horkheimer, M. (1993 [1931]) *Between Philosophy and Social Science. Selected Early Writings*. Cambridge, MA: MIT Press.

Kojève, A. (1969) *Introduction to the Reading of Hegel*, A. Bloom (ed.). New York: Basic Books.

Kramer, M. H. (2003) *In Defence of Legal Positivism: Law Without Trimmings*. Oxford: Oxford University Press.

Marcuse, H. (2002 [1964]) *One-Dimensional Man: Studies in the Ideology of Advanced Industrial Society*. London: Routledge.

Muncie, J. (2000) 'Decriminalising Criminology', in G. Lewis, S. Gerwitz and J. Clarke (eds) *Rethinking Social Policy*. London: Sage.

Rusche, G. and Kirchheimer, O. (1939) *Punishment and Social Stucture*. New York: Columbia University Press.

Russell, S. (2003) 'The Continuing Relevance of Marxism to Critical Criminology', *Critical Criminology*, 11: 113–35.

Sayer, A. (2003) 'Restoring the Moral Dimension in Social Scientific Accounts: A Qualified Ethical Naturalist Approach', paper presented at the International Association for Critical Realism Annual Conference, Amsterdam, online at: www.lancs.ac.uk/fass/sociology/papers/sayer-restoring-the-moral-dimension.pdf

—— (2004) 'Restoring the Moral Dimension: Acknowledging Lay Normativity', online at www.comp.lancs.ac.uk/sociology/papers/sayer-restoring-moral-dimension.pdf

Shearing, C. (1989) 'Decriminalising Criminology', *Canadian Journal of Criminology*, 31(2): 169–78.

Sparks, R. F. (1980) 'A Critique of Marxist Criminology', *Crime and Justice*, 2: 159–210.

Sykes, G. (1974) 'The Rise of Critical Criminology', *The Journal of Criminal Law and Criminology*, 65(2): 206–13.

Taylor, P., Walton, I. and Young, J. (1974) 'Advances Towards a Critical Criminology', *Theory and Society*, 1(4): 441–76.

van Swaaningen, R. (1999) 'Reclaiming Critical Criminology: Social Justice and the European Tradition', *Theoretical Criminology*, 3(1): 5–28.

Wilkerson, T. E. (1995) *Natural Kinds*. Aldershot: Avebury.

Yar, M. (2001) 'Beyond Nancy Fraser's "Perspectival Dualism"', *Economy and Society*, 30(3): 288–303.

4　The current condition of criminological theory in North America[1]

Walter S. DeKeseredy

A diverse range of theoretical work characterizes North American criminology. Yet, one would not know this if he or she only read *Criminology* and *Criminology and Public Policy*, which are the two official journals of the American Society of Criminology. Further, since their inception, very few Canadian scholars have published in these outlets, but theory construction and testing occurs north of the U.S. border. Certainly, what Jock Young (1988) stated over 20 years ago still holds true today: "American criminology is a powerhouse of ideas, research techniques and interventions which understandably dominate Western thinking about crime" (p. 293). Positivism continues to dominate the bulk of American criminology and the aforementioned journals are classic examples of this orthodox or mainstream way of thinking. The main objective of this chapter is not to carp about the hegemony of middle-of-the-road U.S. criminological thought. Nor is it to simply review theories recently constructed and tested in North America. Rather, the key goal is to document parallel and divergent theoretical trends in the U.S. and Canada. First, it is essential to examine the current political economic context of theoretical work now being done in North America.

North American criminological theories in political economic context

Frequent comparisons with the U.S. are facts of life in Canada (DeKeseredy, 2009; Grabb and Curtis, 2005). Moreover, in response to attempts by businesses, political agencies, and other formal organizations to adopt various U.S. policies and procedures, many Canadians passionately state, "We don't want to be American" (Hurtig, 1999; Marzolini, 2005). The same or similar statements are often stated in academic criminological circles. As Doyle and Moore (2011a) observe, "Canadian critical criminologists tend to look with disdain on much of the American criminological enterprise as blinkered, methodologically fetishistic, and compromised by its close alignment with the criminal justice system" (p. 6). Indeed, Canadian academic criminology is not monopolized by positivism, and social science departments that offer courses on deviance, crime, law, and social control are dominated by liberal scholars and researchers.

Since Canada's beginning, its economy, culture, criminal justice system, and scholarship have been heavily shaped by foreign influences (Donnermeyer *et al.*, 2011; Grabb, 2004). Canadian critical criminology, in particular, is profoundly guided by U.S., French, and British contributions dating back to the groundbreaking work of Taylor *et al.* (1973). One of the most powerful influences was Ian Taylor, who spent most of the 1980s (1982–89) at Carleton University in Ottawa. His impact on Canadian progressive sociological thought is still felt today and Canada is witnessing a growth in new criminology programs in this current era, some of which include a relatively large number of critical criminologists (DeKeseredy, 2011a). Alongside this expansion are the corporatization of Canadian universities and the emergence of administrative or applied criminology programs modeled after conservative criminal justice programs offered at U.S. institutions of higher learning (Cote and Allahar, 2011; Huey, 2011).

As is the case in the U.S., Canadian academic criminology, especially that which involves theorizing crime, law, and social control, is under siege and there is growing pressure to publish "so what? criminology" (Currie, 2007). Such work, referred to by Young (2004) as "voodoo criminology," involves a-theoretical, quantitative research on relatively minor issues and presenting the findings in an unintelligible fashion. Today, especially in the U.S., being labeled a theorist or referring to oneself as such can result in marginalization and difficulties landing a tenure-track position at a prestigious university or college. On the other hand, "so what?" criminologists are deemed as "good researchers," are more likely to be "in with the in crowd," and stand a better chance of getting an academic post at a large doctoral institution (DeKeseredy and Schwartz, 2010).

What Mills (1959) calls "abstracted empiricism" (e.g., research divorced from theory) is also necessary for getting increasingly limited external grants, and universities directly and indirectly compel faculties to get such money. Such pressure is partially fueled by government cuts to public education. For example, former Ontario premier Mike Harris is a strong advocate of free-market economic policies and he viewed post-secondary education as having "zero economic benefit." During his term in office (1994–2002), university/college funding dropped by 21 percent, while enrollment increased by 8 percent. Ontario's per capita university funding is now tenth out of 10 provinces and is not likely to improve in the near future. Nor will it do so across Canada (DeKeseredy and Schwartz, 2010; Martin, 2009).

Getting grants is difficult for North American scholars with a vested interest in theory construction. Most government agencies that fund criminological work have little money to begin with and those in charge of them call for research that evaluates the efficiency of mainstream policies, laws, and practices (DeKeseredy, 2011a; Savelsberg *et al.*, 2002; Walters, 2003). In Canada, the funding situation is worse than in the U.S. Under the Conservative federal government led by Stephen Harper, the Social Sciences and Humanities Research Council of Canada (SSHRC), which is the main Canadian funder of social scientific research, prioritizes business-related doctoral research (DeKeseredy and Schwartz, 2010; Fenwick, 2009). Hence, as Matthews (2009) puts it, "academic criminology appears to be becoming more marginalized and irrelevant" (p. 341).

Criminological theory development and critical thinking are also undermined in classrooms. For example, North American universities are pressuring criminology programs to prioritize teaching practical skills over theory (Huey, 2011). Sadly, there is much public support for this approach and for the marginalization and gutting of the humanities and social sciences. Related to this problem is that aggressively "lowering higher education" is one of the key reasons why people like Mike Harris, George W. Bush, and Stephen Harper get elected (Cote and Allahar, 2011; DeKeseredy, 2011a). Moreover, scores of people view criminological theories as impractical or irrelevant (Akers and Sellers, 2009), a view shared by many students and supported by conservative, corporate-oriented administrators. To make matters worse, given this disdain for theories, faculty who teach them, particularly if they are critical criminologists, are at great risk of receiving negative teaching evaluations, which, in turn, jeopardizes their tenure and promotion (Dupont, 2011).

In North America, as elsewhere, part-time faculty greatly outnumber tenured professors (Finder, 2007; Fordyce, 2011). Not only is this a stealth method of eliminating tenure (Unger, 1995), but it also precludes insecure instructors struggling to make ends meet from speaking out against corporatization and the assault on thinking theoretically about crime. As well, part-time or adjunct faculty have more to fear from students' teaching evaluations than their tenured counterparts, which is why many shy away from devoting much, if any, attention to theoretical concerns.

North American criminological theorists are targets of a "perfect storm," one that, in this post 9/11 world, is on the verge of turning into "academic McCarthyism" (Friedrichs, 2009). Nevertheless, theorists are not banding together to effectively challenge threats to their intellectual well-being (Huey, 2011; Israel, 2000), and the end result could be a type of academic apartheid or intellectual proletarianization. What, then, is to be done? It is beyond the scope of this chapter to provide detailed answers to this important question. Nevertheless, in a political economic context characterized by rabid conservative attacks on the liberal arts and humanities, "we need all the friends we can get," and should join forces with colleagues across the continent to ward off attempts to turn universities and colleges into non-academic training grounds for future agents of social control. Despite their ideological differences, it is time for mainstream and critical theorists to form a treaty to collectively struggle to ensure that theory remains a core part of the criminological curriculum.

Parallel and divergent theoretical trends in the U.S. and Canada: still mainly sociological after all these years

Much to the dismay of those who specialize in the "psychology of criminal conduct" (e.g., Andrews and Bonta, 2006), criminological theory on both sides of the North American border is still primarily sociological. Evidence for this observation is provided in virtually every theory text. Consider Lilly *et al.*'s (2010) widely used *Criminological Theory: Context and Consequences*, which is now in its fifth edition. This offering includes 15 chapters, 10 of which are sociological in nature and one that is an introduction to their text. And it appears that this intellectual state of affairs will continue well into the future, as indicated by Richard Rosenfeld's (2011) presidential address to the American Society of Criminology. He states that:

> The future of big-picture criminology and its policy relevance will not be secured with better crime data alone. As I have suggested, we need to build up the foundations of macrocriminology in other ways. Theories of the big picture based on systematic analyses of social institutions must be advanced. Empirical research to test and refine the theoretical developments must be conducted at the level of social systems and reveal the connections between system-level processes and the particulars of local milieux. Historical perspective is required to enlarge the explanatory scope of macrotheory and research, even in studies of the present.
>
> (p. 22)

Progressive cynics would not disagree with Rosenfeld's call; however, they are likely to assert that in the U.S., theory testing involving the use of highly unintelligible statistical procedures will take precedence over new sociological theory construction and the use of qualitative methods driven by theory. If the journal *Criminology* is any indication, then their prediction will come true. Note that not one of the articles in Volume 49, Number 1 that follow Rosenfeld's address is purely theoretical. Another thing to mull over is that given the devastating financial chain of events over the recent years, Rosenfeld does not mention Marxist analysis, and not one source that prioritizes gender is included in his bibliography.

Canadian criminological theory, too, is mainly sociological, but is not as strongly tied to positivism. As stated earlier, Canadian theoretical work is also influenced by a mixture of U.S. and European contributions, which is one of the key reasons why more Canadians publish in *The British Journal of Criminology* and *Theoretical Criminology* than in *Criminology*. Additionally, on top of being "resolutely sociological in orientation" (Carrington and Hogg, 2008: 5), critical criminological theorists are not as marginalized as they are in the U.S. (DeKeseredy, 2011a). The bulk of Canadian criminologists located in sociology departments across their country reject conservative perspectives, but many of them are, as is the case with most sociologists in the U.S., "liberal progressives." In other words, they: accept official definitions of crime (e.g., legal definitions); ignore concepts and theories offered by Marxist, feminist, critical race, and other "radical" scholars; call for fine-tuning state institutions' responses to social problems (e.g., expand the welfare state); pay little – if any – attention to the role of broader social forces; and primarily use quantitative methods to collect and analyze crime and criminal justice data (Ratner, 1985).

Despite its hegemony, sociological thinking about crime on both sides of the North American border faces many challenges, such as the negative impact of the growth in applied criminology programs described previously. Additionally, as Lilly *et al*. (2010) remind us, "the persistence of conservative politics and thinking has likely weakened the hold that theories with strong roots in the 1960s have on criminologists" (p. 296).

What's new?

There have been several new North American theoretical developments over the recent years. Canadian advances, though, have not kept pace with those crafted in the U.S. To the best of my knowledge, since the publication of power-control theory (Hagan, 1989; Hagan *et al*., 1987), the only new social scientific theories of criminal behavior to emerge out of Canada are a gendered left realist subcultural theory (DeKeseredy and Schwartz, 2010) and integrated accounts of woman abuse that prioritize the concept of male peer support.[2] Male peer support is defined as attachments to male peers and the resources they provide which encourage and legitimate woman abuse (DeKeseredy, 1990).

As well, to date, there are no criminological theory texts authored or co-authored by Canadian scholars. There are, of course, Canadian criminology texts, but increasingly we are seeing the "Canadianization" of U.S. contributions. This involves Canadian branches of large U.S. corporations, such as Pearson, contracting a Canadian criminologist to co-author a prominent U.S. book. The "Canadianized" texts are basically the same as the originals, but with relevant Canadian content scattered in each chapter. Canadian scholarly publishing is in a "precarious state," which "make[s] it difficult to communicate uniquely Canadian observations to a Canadian audience" (Doyle and Moore, 2011a: 7–8). On top of this and other challenges, the conspicuous absence of a vibrant Canadian criminology society or association indirectly contributes to the lack of uniquely Canadian theoretical work. People are more likely to find the bulk of Canadian criminologists milling around the halls of hotels hosting the American Society of Criminology (ASC) meetings, which is not necessarily a negative thing. Many rich international partnerships are created and nurtured at ASC conferences, and cultural criminology is a major example. Cultural criminology was born in the mid-1990s and its pioneers (e.g., Jeff Ferrell, Keith Hayward, and Jock Young) are based in the United States and the United Kingdom. There are also cultural criminologists in other parts of the world, including Canada, where Ryerson University scholar Stephen Muzzatti made several important contributions to the field and will continue to do so.[3]

Robert Park and Shaw and McKay are "long gone" (Sampson, 2002), but there is still a major interest in ecological perspectives on crime and deviance. Robert Sampson (2006, 2011), in particular, continues to play a key role in revitalizing the Chicago school of criminology by examining the relationship between neighborhood collective efficacy and crime. Collective efficacy is "mutual trust among neighbors combined with a willingness to intervene on behalf of the common good, specifically to supervise children and maintain public order" (Sampson *et al*., 1998: 1).

Collective efficacy theory is generally used to explain variations in U.S. urban crime and it has informed some Canadian inner-city public housing research (DeKeseredy *et al.*, 2003). Recently, it was applied to woman abuse in rural communities. For example, Donnermeyer *et al.* (2006) contend that social organization facilitates some types of crime even as it constrains others. Note that DeKeseredy and Schwartz (2008, 2009) found that many rural Ohio men can rely on their male friends and neighbors, including those who are police officers, to support a violent patriarchal status quo even while they count on these same individuals to help prevent public crimes (e.g., vandalism, burglary, etc.), which to them is acting on "behalf of the common good." Furthermore, in rural sections of Ohio and other states such as Kentucky, there is widespread acceptance of woman abuse and community norms prohibiting victims from publicly talking about their experiences and from seeking social support (Basile and Black, 2011; DeKeseredy *et al.*, 2007; Lewis, 2003).

The most popular theoretical frameworks to understand rural crime are place-based perspectives, such as social disorganization theory (DeKeseredy and Donnermeyer, 2011; Donnermeyer, 2007). As well, the ever expanding corpus of rural criminology is largely atheoretical and is mostly composed of either quantitative, statistical works or in-depth qualitative studies (Donnermeyer *et al.*, 2011). There are, though, some exceptions to this rule. For instance, a few critical criminologists developed integrated theories of separation/divorce sexual assault in rural areas and these offerings are heavily influenced by feminism, masculinities theories, and male peer support theory (DeKeseredy *et al.*, 2007; DeKeseredy *et al.*, 2004; DeKeseredy and Schwartz, 2009). Note, too, that there are some new attempts to advance left realist perspectives on rural crime and social control (DeKeseredy and Donnermeyer, 2011; Donnermeyer and DeKeseredy, 2008). There is growing evidence that crime is common in rural communities and thus it is time for theoretical work of all kinds to take more frequent "departures from criminological and sociological urbanism" (Hogg and Carrington, 2006).

Contrary to what some anti-feminist scholars and right-wing fathers' rights advocates claim (e.g., Dutton, 2006, 2010), some feminists theorize women's use of violence and societal reactions to such behavior (e.g., Jones, 2010). Additionally, Stanley Cohen's (1980) concept of moral panic is an integral part of much recent North American feminist theoretical work on negative media images of teenage girls, such as those involving relational aggression in Hollywood movies like *Mean Girls* (Chesney-Lind and Jones, 2010). Chesney-Lind and Irwin (2008), among others (e.g., DeKeseredy, 2010), assert that the media, together with some social scientists (e.g., Garbarino, 2006), lawyers, agents of social control, and other "experts," have jumped on the bandwagon to transform girls who violate myriad patriarchal gender norms in the U.S. and Canada into folk devils. A folk devil is a "socially constructed, stereotypical carrier of significant social harm" (Ellis, 1987: 199). As vividly pointed out by contributors to Chesney-Lind and Jones' (2010) anthology, many girls are labeled as being made up of "sugar and spice and everything evil" (Schissel, 1997: 51).

North American feminists continue to theorize male-to-female violence and such work now includes a strong emphasis on intersectionality, especially perspectives on intimate violence in the lives of African-American women (e.g., Potter, 2008). Intersectionality "addresses the manner in which racism, patriarchy, class oppression, and other discriminatory systems create background inequalities that structure the relative positions of women, races, ethnicities, classes and the like" (Crenshaw, 2000, p. 8). Intersectionality also garners much attention in the masculinities and crime theoretical literature (DeKeseredy, 2011b).

Many criminological theories have been applied to the issue of race/ethnicity and crime (Gabbidon, 2010), but until recently, as Unnever and Gabbidon (2011) note, "Inexplicably, however, no criminological theory exists that fully articulates the nuances of the African American experience and how they relate to their offending" (p. x). Similarly, in Canada, where aboriginal people's issues are of major concern to many social scientists, there is no theory that fully explains the complexities associated with this cultural group's involvement in crime. Unnever and Gabbidon now offer a theory of African-American offending, and while there is no distinct theory of aboriginal offending, there is a large Canadian literature on the criminalization and systematic oppression of aboriginals. No publication on these issues is complete without an in-depth section on colonialist practices, many which are still in place in Canada (Restoule, 2009; Woolford, 2011). Colonialism is also examined in Canadian theoretical work on violence in the lives of immigrant girls and women of color (Jiwani, 2006; Rajiva and Batacharya, 2010).

Mainstream life-course theories, such as those offered by Laub and Sampson (2003), are more popular in the U.S. than in Canada. Nevertheless, feminist criminologists in both countries share a keen interest in gendered pathways in and out of crime, which is similar to life-course analysis (Lilly *et al.*, 2010; Miller and Mullins, 2006). One recent example is Canadian Judith Grant's (2008) work on marginalized rural Ohio women's pathways to recovery from substance abuse. Theorizing corrections personnel's use of male-based actuarial risk and need assessment instruments for female offenders, such as the Level of Service Inventory (LSI) (Andrews and Bonta, 2000), is another thing that some Canadian and U.S. feminist criminologists have in common (Balfour, 2011; Davidson and Chesney-Lind, 2009; Hannah-Moffat, 2004).

With origins mainly in France and Germany, postmodern thought, especially the writings of Michel Foucault, has had a stronger impact on Canadian criminologists than on their U.S. counterparts (Doyle and Moore, 2011a). Still, the U.S. is home to some of the world's leading postmodernists, including Dragan Milovanovic (2011), who continue to generate new ways of thinking critically about crime. However, as is the case with most variants of critical criminology, postmodernism has had little, if any, influence on criminal justice and social policy in both Canada and the U.S.

Canada is officially a bilingual country. Thus, it is not surprising that Michel Foucault's work is more widely read and cited in that country than in the U.S. Still, an ongoing Canadian problem is the marginalization of francophone criminology, regardless of whether it is mainstream or critical. Much, if not most, of French theoretical work (based mainly out of the province of Quebec) is consumed only by francophone researchers, instructors, and practitioners (Doyle and Moore, 2011a; Dupont, 2011). Note, too, that Quebec universities attract many international francophone scholars, but, ironically, those visiting Montreal from France and Belgium devote much time and energy to gathering English-language publications that are unavailable in their home countries (Doyle and More, 2011b).

It is unclear whether Francis T. Cullen (2009) still holds this belief, but at the end of the last decade he stated in the preface to Walsh and Beaver's (2009) anthology *Biosocial Criminology: New Directions in Theory and Research*, "I am equally persuaded that sociological criminology has exhausted itself as a guide for future study on the origins of crime. It is a paradigm for the previous century, not the current one" (p. xvi). It is highly doubtful that biosocial theories will ever completely replace sociological perspectives. Yet, they are becoming more popular in certain academic groups, but more so in the U.S. than Canada.

Conclusion

Lilly *et al.*'s (2010) observation is directly relevant to any attempt to describe the current condition of criminological theory in North America:

> At this stage in its development, criminology might be said to suffer from an embarrassment of riches. The field is filled with an array of competing theoretical paradigms. Part of the richness in theorizing stems from attempts to revitalize old models in new ways, to integrate traditional approaches into fresh perspectives, and to elaborate ideas that heretofore were underdeveloped within an existing perspective. Part of this richness reflects the efforts of scholars coming into the discipline with different ideologies and with different scholarly training (e.g., economics, psychology). Part of it manifests truly fresh ideas and ways of illuminating the world that redirect theoretical inquiry and empirical investigation. . . .
>
> (p. 415)

Many readers will disagree with my interpretation of the current state of North American criminological theory and contend that some important theories were omitted, such as institutional-anomie and general strain theories (Agnew, 2006, 2011; Rosenfeld and Messner, 2011). This is all to the good, and as Ellis (1987) notes in his commentary on the categorization of deviance theories, "Here, as elsewhere, there is a lot of room for differences in judgement" (p. xiii). To be sure, what makes criminology so exciting are the ongoing and ever changing theoretical debates, and there will be many more, despite social scientific theories being under siege in numerous institutions of higher learning. One more example of the attack on the "soft sciences" is this statement made by Member of Provincial Parliament John Milloy, Ontario's minister of training, colleges and universities, in his announcement about funding 6,000 more M.A. and Ph.D. students in the next six years:

We're not saying 'no' to any more master's programs in history or the humanities, but we want to look at high-demand programs that make sense – engineering, health, environmental studies are examples – and programs that mesh with our research priorities as a province.

(cited in Brown, 2011: A10)

What will the future bring? Perhaps, given funding schemes like the one announced by Milloy, theory construction will become more conservative and positivistic in nature. Undeniably, broader political economic forces help shape theoretical development, and many scholars will "go where the money is" to preserve their jobs and/or to get external support for their research. This was always the case in the academy, regardless of who was in charge of educational funding and government research agencies. Also, criminological thought has, for a very long time, been dominated by orthodox views.

Nonetheless, more progressive academic ways of thinking about crime persist and the American Society of Criminology's Division on Critical Criminology (DCC) offers critical thinkers much support and shelter from the neo-liberal storm. Even so, conspicuously absent from the DCC is a critical mass of scholars who engage with political economy perspectives. In the UK, such work was "pursued with renewed vigour" during the Tony Blair years in response to New Labour crime control policies (Carlen, 2007/08). As Steve Hall and Simon Winlow note in their introduction to this book, there is a need for new directions in criminological theory. Hopefully, North American scholars will be motivated to revisit Marxist analyses of crime and social control in light of major global economic crises and the continued use of mass incarceration. Those interested in doing this work will find Robert Reiner's contribution to this volume most valuable.

While pursuing new directions in theory, theorists should also engage in a form of "newsmaking criminology" (Barak, 1988, 2007), one that entails using mainstream media and new electronic technologies (e.g., Facebook) to sensitize cynical students, policy makers, and members of the general public to the importance of theorizing crime, law, and social control. As stated by Kurt Lewin (1951), the founder of modern social psychology, "There is nothing so practical as a good theory" (p. 169) and this message needs to be spread far and wide. Ian Taylor, in a 1986 presentation given at the Canadian Sociology and Anthropology Association meeting in Winnipeg, Manitoba, stated that criminologists should strive to achieve the highest level of theorizing. There is no disagreement here, but in this current political economic climate it is equally important to demonstrate that criminological theories are not just academic products of "impractical mental gymnastics" or "fanciful ideas that have little to do with what truly motivates people" (Akers, 1997: 1).

Notes

1 I would like to thank J. Robert Lilly, Steve Hall, Stephen Muzzatti, Martin D. Schwartz, and Simon Winlow for their helpful comments and guidance.
2 For more information on these perspectives, see DeKeseredy *et al.* (2007); DeKeseredy *et al.* (2004); DeKeseredy and Schwartz (2002, 2009), DeKeseredy *et al.* (2008), and Schwartz and DeKeseredy (1997).
3 See, for example, his (2012) chapter in DeKeseredy and Dragiewicz's (2012) *Handbook of Critical Criminology*.

References

Agnew, R. (2006) *Pressured into crime: An overview of general strain theory*. Los Angeles: Roxbury.

—— (2011) 'Revitalizing Merton: General strain theory.' In F. T. Cullen, C. L. Johnson, A. J. Myer, and F. Adler (Eds.), *The origins of American criminology* (Advances in Criminological Theory, Vol. 16, pp. 137–58). New Brunswick, NJ: Transaction.

Akers, R. L. (1997) *Criminological theories: Introduction and evaluation*. 2nd ed. Los Angeles: Roxbury.

Akers, R. L. and Sellers, C. S. (2009) *Criminological theories: Introduction, evaluation, and application*. New York: Oxford University Press.

Andrews, D. A. and Bonta, J. (2000) *The level of service inventory-revised: User's manual*. Ottawa: Multi-Health Systems.

—— (2006) *The psychology of criminal conduct*. 4th ed. Cincinnati: LexisNexis.

Balfour, G. (2011) 'Reimagining a feminist criminology.' In A. Doyle and D. Moore (Eds.), *Critical criminology in Canada: New voices, new directions* (pp. 227–42). Vancouver: University of British Columbia Press.

Barak, G. (1988) 'Newsmaking criminology: Reflections on the media, intellectuals, and crime.' *Justice Quarterly*, 5, 565–88.

—— (2007) 'Doing newsmaking criminology from within the academy.' *Theoretical Criminology*, 11, 191–207.

Basile, K. C. and Black, M. C. (2011) 'Intimate partner violence against women.' In C. M. Renzetti, J. L. Edleson, and R. Kennedy Bergen (Eds.), *Sourcebook on violence against women* (pp. 111–32). Thousand Oaks, CA: Sage.

Brown, L. (2011, June 8) 'Ontario to fund 6,000 more post-grad degrees: Focus will be on fields in high demand, such as engineering, health.' *Toronto Star*, A10.

Carlen, P. (2007/08) 'Editorial: Politics, economy and crime.' *Criminal Justice Matters*, 70, 3–4.

Carrington, K. and Hogg, R. (2008) 'Critical criminologies: An introduction.' In K. Carrington and R. Hogg (Eds.), *Critical criminology: Issues, debates, challenges* (pp. 1–12). Portland, OR: Willan.

Chesney-Lind, M. and Irwin, K. (2008) *Beyond bad girls: Gender, violence and hype*. New York: Routledge.

Chesney-Lind, M. and Jones, N. (Eds.) (2010) 'Fighting for girls: New perspectives on gender and violence.' Albany, NY: SUNY Press.

Cohen, S. (1980) *Folk devils and moral panics*. Oxford: Basil Blackwell.

Cote, J. E. and Allahar, A. L. (2011) *Lowering higher education: The rise of corporate universities and the fall of liberal education*. Toronto: University of Toronto Press.

Crenshaw, K. (2000) 'The intersectionality of race and gender discrimination.' Retrieved

June 10, 2011, from www.isiswomen.org/womenet/lists/apgr-list/archive/msg00013. html

Cullen, F. T. (2009) 'Preface.' In A. Walsh and K. M. Beaver (Eds.), *Biosocial criminology: New directions in theory and research* (pp. xv–xvii). London: Routledge.

Currie, E. (2007) 'Against marginality: Arguments for a public criminology.' *Theoretical Criminology*, 11, 175–90.

Davidson, J. T. and Chesney-Lind, M. (2009) 'Discounting women: Context matters in risk and need assessment.' *Critical Criminology*, 17, 221–46.

DeKeseredy, W. S. (1990) 'Male peer support and woman abuse: The current stake of knowledge.' *Sociological Focus*, 23, 129–39.

—— (2009) 'Canadian crime control in the new millennium: The influence of neo-conservative US policies and practices.' *Police Practice and Research*, 10, 305–16.

—— (2010) 'Moral panics, violence, and the policing of girls: Reasserting patriarchal control in the new millennium.' In M. Chesney-Lind and N. Jones (Eds.), *Fighting for girls: New perspectives on gender and violence* (pp. 241–54). Albany, NY: SUNY Press.

—— (2011) *Contemporary critical criminology*. London: Routledge.

—— (2012) 'History of critical criminology in Canada.' In W. S. DeKeseredy and M. Dragiewicz (Eds.), *Handbook of critical criminology* (pp. 61–69). London: Routledge.

DeKeseredy, W. S., Alvi, S. Schwartz, M. D. and Tomaszewski, E. A. (2003) *Under siege: Poverty and crime in a public housing community*. Lanham, MD: Lexington Books.

DeKeseredy, W. S. and Donnermeyer, J. F. (2011) 'Thinking critically about rural crime: Toward the development of a new left realist perspective.' Paper presented at the 2001 York Deviancy Conference, University of York, Heslington, York.

DeKeseredy, W. S., Donnermeyer, J. F., Schwartz, M. D., Tunnell, K. D. and Hall, M. (2007) 'Thinking critically about rural gender relations: Toward a rural masculinity crisis/male peer support model of separation/divorce sexual assault.' *Critical Criminology*, 15, 295–311.

DeKeseredy, W. S. and Dragiewicz, M. (Eds.) (2011) *Handbook of critical criminology*. London: Routledge.

DeKeseredy, W. S., Rogness, M. and Schwartz, M. D. (2004) 'Separation/divorce sexual assault: The current state of social scientific knowledge.' *Aggression and Violent Behavior*, 9, 675–91.

DeKeseredy, W. S. and Schwartz, M. D. (2002) 'Theorizing public housing woman abuse as a function of economic exclusion and male peer support.' *Women's Health and Urban Life*, 1, 26–45.

—— (2008) 'Separation/divorce sexual assault in rural Ohio: Survivors' perceptions.' *Journal of Preventions and Interventions in the Community*, 36, 105–20.

—— (2009) *Dangerous exits: Escaping abusive relationships in rural America*. New Brunswick, NJ: Rutgers University Press.

—— (2010) 'Friedman economic policies, social exclusion, and crime: Toward a gendered left realist subcultural theory.' *Crime, Law and Social Change*, 54, 159–70.

DeKeseredy, W. S., Schwartz, M. D. and Alvi, S. (2008) 'Which women are more likely to be abused? Public Housing, Cohabitation and Separated/Divorced Women.' *Criminal Justice Studies: A Critical Journal of Crime, Law, and Society*, 21, 283–93.

Donnermeyer, J. F. (2007) 'Locating rural crime: The role of theory.' In E. Barclay, J. F. Donnermeyer, J. Scott and R. Hogg (Eds.), *Crime in rural Australia* (pp. 15–26). Sydney: Federation Press.

Donnermeyer, J. F. and DeKeseredy, W. S. (2008) 'Toward a rural critical criminology.' *Southern Rural Sociology*, 23, 4–28.

Donnermeyer, J. F., DeKeseredy, W. S. and Dragiewicz, M. (2011) 'Policing rural Canada and the United States.' In R. I. Mawby and R. Yarwood (Eds.), *Rural policing and policing the rural: A constable countryside?* (pp. 23–33). Surrey: Ashgate.

Donnermeyer, J. F., Jobes, P. and Barclay, E. (2006) 'Rural crime, poverty, and community.' In W. S. DeKeseredy and B. Perry (Eds.), *Advancing critical criminology: Theory and application* (pp. 199–218). Lanham, MD: Lexington Books.

Doyle, A. and Moore, D. (2011a) 'Introduction: Questions for a new generation of criminologists.' In A. Doyle and D. Moore (Eds.), *Critical criminology in Canada: New voices, new directions* (pp. 1–24). Vancouver: University of British Columbia Press.

—— (2011b) 'Part 1: Canadian criminology in the twenty-first century.' In A. Doyle and D. Moore (Eds.), *Critical criminology in Canada: New voices, new directions* (pp. 25–30). Vancouver: University of British Columbia Press.

Dupont, B. (2011) 'The dilemmas of "doing" criminology in Quebec: Curse or opportunity.' In A. Doyle and D. Moore (Eds.), *Critical criminology in Canada: New voices, new directions* (pp. 55–74). Vancouver: University of British Columbia Press.

Dutton, D. G. (2006) *Rethinking domestic violence*. Vancouver: University of British Columbia Press.

—— (2010) 'The gender paradigm and the architecture of antiscience.' *Partner Abuse*, 1, 5–25.

Ellis, D. (1987) *The wrong stuff: An introduction to the sociological study of deviance*. Toronto: Macmillan.

Fenwick, S. (2009, March 9) 'Business focused fix for SSHRC.' *The Gateway*, 1.

Finder, A. (2007, November 20) 'Adjuncts outnumber tenured professors on U.S. campuses.' Retrieved June 16, 2011 from www.nytimes.com/2007/11/20/world/americas/20iht-college.1.8401446.html

Fordyce, L. R. (2011) 'Predictions and realities of distance education.' In C. P. Ho (Ed.), *Technology, colleges and community 2011 conference proceedings* (pp. 71–78). Honolulu: University of Hawai'i Press.

Friedrichs, D. O. (2009) 'Critical criminology.' In J. M. Miller (Ed.), *21st century criminology: A reference handbook*, Vol. 1 (pp. 210–18). Thousand Oaks, CA: Sage.

Gabbidon, S. L. (2010) *Criminological perspectives on race and crime*. 2nd ed. London: Routledge.

Garbarino, J. (2006) *See Jane hit: Why girls are growing more violent and what we can do about it*. New York: Penguin Press.

Grabb, E. (2004) 'Economic power in Canada: Corporate concentration, foreign ownership, and state involvement.' In J. Curtis, E. Grabb, and N. Guppy (Eds.), *Social inequality in Canada* (pp. 20–30). Toronto: Pearson Prentice Hall.

Grabb, E. and Curtis, J. (2005). *Regions apart: The four societies of Canada and the United States*. Toronto: Oxford University Press.

Grant, J. (2008) *Charting women's journeys: From addiction to recovery*. Lanham, MD: Lexington.

Hagan, J. (1989) *Structural criminology*. New Brunswick, NJ: Rutgers University Press.

Hagan, J., Gillis, A. and Simpson, J. (1987) 'Class in the household: A Power-control theory of gender and delinquency.' *American Journal of Sociology*, 92, 788–816.

Hannah-Moffat, K. (2004) 'Criminality, need and the transformative risk subject: Hybridizations of risk/need in penalty.' *Punishment and Society*, 7, 29–51.

Hogg, R. and Carrington, K. (2006) *Policing the rural crisis*. Sydney: Federation Press.

Huey, L. (2011) 'Commodifying Canadian criminology: Applied criminology programs and the future of the discipline.' In A. Doyle and D. Moore (Eds.), *Critical criminology in Canada: New voices, new directions* (pp. 75–98). Vancouver: University of British Columbia Press.

Hurtig, M. (1999) *Pay the rent or feed the kids: The tragedy and disgrace of poverty in Canada*. Toronto: McClelland and Stewart.

Israel, M. (2000) 'The commercialization of university-based criminological research in Australia.' *Australian and New Zealand Journal of Criminology*, 33, 1–20.

Jiwani, Y. (2006) *Discourses of denial: Mediations of race, gender, and violence*. Vancouver: University of British Columbia Press.

Jones, N. (2010) *Between good and ghetto: African-American girls and inner-city violence*. New Brunswick, NJ: Rutgers University Press.

Laub, J. H. and Sampson, R. J. (2003) *Shared beginnings, divergent lives: Delinquent boys to age 70*. Cambridge, MA: Harvard University Press.

Lewin, K. (1951) *Field theory in social science: Selected theoretical papers*. New York: Harper and Row.

Lewis, S. H. (2003) *Unspoken crimes: Sexual assault in rural America*. Enola, PA: National Sexual Violence Resource Center.

Lilly, J. R., Cullen, F. T. and Ball, R. A. (2010) *Criminological theory: Context and consequences*. 5th ed. Thousand Oaks, CA: Sage.

Martin, R. (2009, October 20) 'What happened to Canada's education advantage?' *Toronto Star*, A19.

Marzolini, M. (2005) *Canadian–U.S. relations*. Toronto: Pollara.

Matthews, R. (2009) 'Beyond "so what?" criminology: Rediscovering realism.' *Theoretical Criminology*, 13, 341–62.

Miller, J. and Mullins, C. W. (2006) 'The status of feminist theories in criminology.' In F. T. Cullen, J. P. Wright and R. K. Blevins (Eds.), *Taking stock: The status of criminological theory* (Advances in Criminological Theory, Vol. 15) (pp. 217–49). New Brunswick, NJ: Transaction.

Mills, C. W. (1959) *The sociological imagination*. New York: Oxford University Press.

Milovanovic, D. (2011) 'Postmodern criminology.' In W. S. DeKeseredy and M. Dragiewicz (Eds.), *Handbook of critical criminology* (pp. 150–59). London: Routledge.

Muzzatti, S. L. (2011) 'Cultural criminology: Burning up capitalism, consumer culture and crime.' In W. S. DeKeseredy and M. Dragiewicz (Eds.), *Handbook of critical criminology* (pp. 138–49). London: Routledge.

Potter, H. (2008) *Battle cries: Black women and intimate partner abuse*. New York: New York University Press.

Rajiva, M. and Batacharya, S. (Eds.) (2010) *Reena Virk: Critical perspectives on a Canadian murder*. Toronto: University of Toronto Press.

Ratner, R. S. (1985) 'Inside the liberal boot: The criminological enterprise in Canada.' In T. Fleming (Ed.), *The new criminologies in Canada: State, crime, and control* (pp. 13–26). Toronto: Oxford University Press.

Restoule, B. M. (2009) 'Aboriginal women and the criminal justice system.' In J. Barker (Ed.), *Women and the criminal justice system: A Canadian perspective* (pp. 257–88). Toronto: Emond Montgomery.

Rosenfeld, R. (2011) 'The big picture: 2010 presidential address to the American Society of Criminology.' *Criminology*, 49, 1–26.

Rosenfeld, R. and Messner, S. F. (2011) 'The intellectual origins of institutional-anomie theory.' In F. T. Cullen, C. L. Johnson, A. J. Myer and F. Adler (Eds.), *The origins of*

American criminology (Advances in Criminological Theory, Vol. 16) (pp. 121–35). New Brunswick, NJ: Transaction.

Sampson, R. J. (2002) 'Transcending tradition: New directions in community research, Chicago style – The American Society of Criminology 2001 Sutherland address.' *Criminology*, 40, 213–30.

—— (2006) 'Collective efficacy: Lessons learned and directions for future inquiry.' In F. T. Cullen, J. P. Wright and K. R. Blevins (Eds.), *Taking stock: The status of criminological theory* (Advances in Criminological Theory, Vol. 15) (pp. 149–67). New Brunswick, NJ: Transaction.

—— (2011) 'Communities and crime revisited: Intellectual trajectory of a Chicago school education.' In F. T. Cullen, C. L. Jonson, A. J. Myer and F. Adler (Eds.), *The origins of American criminology* (Advances in Criminological Theory, Vol. 16) (pp. 63–85). New Brunswick, NJ: Transaction.

Sampson, R. J., Raudenbush, S. W. and Earls, F. (1998) *Neighborhood collective efficacy: Does it help reduce violence?* Washington, D.C.: U.S. Department of Justice.

Savelsberg, J. J., King, R. and Cleveland, L. (2002) 'Politicized scholarship: Science on crime and the state.' *Social Problems*, 49, 327–48.

Schissel, B. (1997) *Blaming children: Youth crime, moral panics and the politics of hate.* Halifax, Nova Scotia: Fernwood.

Schwartz, M. D. and DeKeseredy, W. S. (1997) *Sexual assault on the college campus: The role of male peer support.* Thousand Oaks, CA: Sage.

Taylor, I., Walton, P. and Young, J. (1973) *The new criminology: For a social theory of deviance.* London: Routledge and Kegan Paul.

Unger, D. N. S. (1995) 'Academic apartheid: The predicament of part-time faculty.' *The NEA Higher Education Journal*, Spring, 61–64.

Unnever, J. D. and Gabbidon, S. L. (2011) *A theory of African American offending: Race, racism, and crime.* London: Routledge.

Walsh, A. and Beaver, K. M. (Eds.) (2009) *Biosocial criminology: New directions in theory and research.* London: Routledge.

Walters, R. (2003) 'New modes of governance and the commodification of criminological knowledge.' *Social and legal studies* 12, 5–26.

Woolford, A. (2011) 'Criminological nightmares: A Canadian criminology of genocide.' In A. Doyle and D. Moore (Eds.), *Critical criminology in Canada: New voices, new directions* (pp. 136–61). Vancouver: University of British Columbia Press.

Young, J. (1988) 'Radical criminology in Britain: The emergence of a competing paradigm.' *British Journal of Criminology*, 28, 289–313.

—— (2004) 'Voodoo criminology and the numbers game.' In J. Ferrell, K. Hayward, W. Morrison and M. Presdee (Eds.), *Cultural criminology unleashed* (pp. 13–28). London: The Glasshouse Press.

Part II
Criminological theory, culture and the subject

5 The biological and the social in criminological theory

Tim Owen

Introduction

This chapter is a contribution towards meta-theoretical development as part of the post-postmodern return to sociological theory and method associated with Archer (1995), Layder (1997, 2007), Mouzelis (1995, 2007), Owen (2009a, 2009b) and Sibeon (2004, 2007), in tandem with a cautious attempt to build bridges between criminological theory and selected insights from evolutionary psychology and behavioural genetics. In the pages that follow I will suggest a way that criminological theory might move beyond its four main theoretical obstacles. These obstacles are the nihilistic relativism of the postmodern and post-structuralist cultural turn; the oversocialised gaze and harshly environmentalist conceptions of the person; genetic fatalism or the equation of genetic predisposition with inevitability (Owen 2009b) and bio-phobia (Freese *et al.*, 2003) that appear to dominate mainstream criminology; and the sociological weaknesses of many so-called biosocial explanations of crime and criminal behaviour (see for instance Walsh and Beaver, 2009; Walsh and Ellis, 2003), which, although dealing adequately with biological variables, appear to neglect or make insufficient use of meta-concepts such as agency–structure, micro–macro and time–space in their accounts of the person. I will suggest that a way forward lies in the form of an ontologically flexible, meta-theoretical sensitising device, alternatively referred to by Owen (2009b) as *post-postmodern* or *genetic-social* in order to distance the framework from hard-line sociobiology.

My starting point is to modify Sibeon's (ibid.) original anti-reductionist framework to include a new focus upon the biological variable (the evidence from evolutionary psychology and behavioural genetics for a partial genetic basis for human behaviour in relation to sexuality, language, reactions to stress, etc.), genetic fatalism, the oversocialised gaze and psychobiography. This new framework is capable of making a contribution towards a return to sociologically based theory and method and suggesting a way forward for criminological theory, and also towards a cautious marriage between the biological and social sciences that is balanced and does adequate justice to the mutuality between genes and environment. Here, the evidence that genes play a role alongside environment in terms of causality in relation to human behaviour is considered (Cosmides and

Tooby, 1997; Hamer and Copeland, 1999; and Pinker, 1994). My contention is that there is sufficient evidence to warrant the incorporation of a focus upon the biological variable into the new meta-theoretical framework, alongside meta-concepts, notions of dualism – as opposed to a Giddensian duality of structure – and notions of psychobiography (Layder, 1997, 1998; Owen, 2009a) that describe the asocial and dispositional aspects of the person, and modified notions of Foucauldian power. The latter notion of modified Foucauldian power entails a recognition of the dialectical relationship between agentic and systemic forms of power; the relational, contingent and emergent dimensions of power; and the concept that *contra* Foucault, power can be stored in *roles*, such as those played by police officers, and in *systems*, the most obvious of which, for criminologists, is the criminal justice system. It is important to keep in mind here the idea of mutuality when focusing upon biological variables in criminological analysis, what we might call the 'feedback loop' which embraces genes and environment, acknowledging the mutuality and plasticity between them. The framework I am attempting to develop posits that 'nurture' depends upon genes, and genes require 'nurture'. Genes predetermine the broad structure of the brain of Homo sapiens, but they also absorb formative experiences, react to social cues or, as Hamer and Copeland (1999) suggest, can be switched on by free-willed behaviour and environmental stimuli. For example, stress can be caused by the outside world, by impending events, bereavements and so on. Short-term stressors cause an immediate increase in the production of norepinephrine and epinephrine hormones responsible for increasing the heartbeat and preparing the human body for 'fight or flight' in emergency situations. Stressors that have a longer duration may activate a pathway that results in a slower but more persistent increase in cortisol. Cortisol can suppress the working of the immune system. Thus, those who have shown symptoms of stress are more likely to catch infections because an effect of cortisol is to reduce the activity and number of white blood cells or lymphocytes (Becker *et al*, 1992). As Martin (1997) shows, cortisol does this by switching on genes, and it only switches on genes in cells that possess cortisol receptors, which have in turn been switched on by environmental stimuli such as stress caused by bereavement. The cortisol was made in the first instance because a series of genes, such as CYP17, was switched on in the adrenal cortex to manufacture the enzymes necessary for making cortisol. There are important implications here which inform my attempt to construct *genetic-social* criminological theory. For example, elevated levels of norepinephrine have been linked with aggressive criminal behaviour by Filley *et al*. (2001). Hostile behaviour can be induced in humans by increasing plasma levels of norepinephrine, whereas agents that block norepinephrine receptor cells can reduce violent behaviour (ibid.). The enzyme monoamine oxidase is involved in the reduction of norepinephrine, and low levels of the enzyme correlate with violent criminal behaviour as low levels of monoamine oxidase allow norepinephrine levels to increase (Klinteberg, 1996).

My approach to criminological theorising acknowledges that crime may be socially constructed, in the sense that human actors ascribe meaning to the world, but that there is still a reality 'out there' in the sense that environmental conditions are potential triggers of genetic or physiological predispositions towards behaviour that may be labelled criminal. However, that does not mean that behaviour should be viewed as reflecting an inherited, pre-written script that is beyond individual control. For example, reflexive agents possess the agency to choose not to engage in criminal activities where they believe that their actions will harm others and offend ethico-social codes, or where the rewards are outweighed by negative consequences. Agency, in turn, is influenced not only by morality or reason but also by inherited, constitutional variables. An inherited impulsive disposition may predispose an actor to formulate and act upon potentially criminal decisions. In *genetic-social* theorising, the biological variable must be considered as one element within multifactorial explanations for crime and criminal behaviour, alongside critique of agency–structure, micro–macro, time–space and so on.

This *genetic-social* (Owen, 2009a) framework arises in response to what I consider to be the following illegitimate forms of theoretical reasoning: reification, essentialism, duality of structure, relativism, genetic fatalism and the over-socialised gaze. The framework offers a flexible ontology and relies upon a multi-factorial analysis. It is capable of identifying a way forward beyond the anti-foundational relativism of postmodernism and Foucauldian post-structuralism, aspects of our intellectual life that are complicit in the stagnation of critical criminology. An approach which sidesteps the 'nature versus nurture' divide which still haunts mainstream criminology, and emphasises instead the mutuality between genes and environment is essential if we are to advance upon Shilling's (1993) starting point for a biological sociology, and supersede the biologically top-heavy, largely American attempts at biosocial analysis (Herrnstein and Murray, 1994; Mednick *et al.*, 1987; Mednick and Volavka, 1980; Walsh and Beaver, 2009; Walsh and Ellis, 2003; Wilson and Herrnstein, 1985), which appear to lack a sufficiently sophisticated appreciation of sociological theory that would make them truly 'biosocial'. These elements combined make a framework that can contribute towards a new direction for criminological theory as part of a return to sociological theory and method in the age of the human genome. Its methodological generalisations, as opposed to substantive generalisations, its lack of 'bio-phobia' and its realist social ontology make it a sensitising device with the potential for future theoretical and explanatory use best expressed in terms of large-scale synthesis.

Genetic fatalism and the oversocialised gaze

In what follows, we consider the arguments for the inclusion of the terms genetic fatalism and the over-socialised gaze in the framework for studying crime and criminal behaviour. Genetic fatalism refers to 'a widespread tendency within social science to equate genetic predisposition with inevitability' (Owen, 2009a: 116). The over-socialised gaze refers to harshly environmentalist accounts which deny biological or partially biological causality in relation to human behaviour altogether. The greatest error in the work of many of the authors who have attempted to bridge the social science and biological science divide (Benton,

1991, 2003; Newton, 2003; and Shilling, 1993) lies in the tendency to equate predisposition not with genes but with inevitability.

In the 1970s, after the publication of E. O. Wilson's book *Sociobiology*, there was a counter-attack against the idea of genetic influences upon human behaviour, led by Richard Lewontin and Stephen J. Gould, Wilson's Harvard colleague. Their dogmatic slogan 'not in our genes!' may have been a plausible hypothesis at the time, but now, in the face of around 30 years of evidence from behavioural genetics, it is impossible to deny that genes certainly do influence behaviour. It is now vital to move beyond Shilling's (ibid.) suggestion that the human body is simultaneously biological and social by acknowledging the mutuality of genes and environment. In the light of Newton's (ibid.) call for a more sophisticated understanding of biology and psychology, perhaps we should strive to avoid sociological and criminological accounts which deny the possibility that the physical can be at the mercy of the social.

Another illicit form of theoretical reasoning which we should avoid is the oversocialised gaze. If genetic fatalism is the equation of biological determinism with inevitability, the oversocialised gaze refers to strongly environmentalist accounts of the person which seek to deny biological variables, instincts and so on altogether. Surprisingly, in the age of the Human Genome Project, many such accounts can be found within sociology and criminology. For example, Giddens's (1993: 57) suggestion that 'human beings have no instincts in the sense of complex patterns of unlearned behaviour' appears to be a case in point. Foucault's (1980) argument that sexuality is a socio-cultural creation, that sexuality as we know it is the production of a particular set of historical circumstances and obtains only within the terms of a discourse developed since the seventeenth century, is another example of the oversocialised gaze. Foucault's position is similar to that of the symbolic interactionist writers Gagnon and Simon (1973), who adopted a radical form of social constructionist theory which is extremely oversocialised, essentially arguing that there is no natural sexual drive in human biological make-up, and addressing human sexuality entirely as a cultural and historical construction. As far as Gagnon and Simon were concerned, not only do we learn what sex means, and what is sexually arousing to us, we also learn to want sex. The authors acknowledge that the human body has a repertoire of gratifications, but this does not mean that we instinctively want to engage in them. Certain gratifications will be selected as sexual as we learn 'sexual scripts'. From this perspective, social-isation is not concerned with controlling innate sexual drive so that it is expressed in civilised, acceptable ways, but the learning of complicated sexual scripts which serve to specify circumstances that elicit the sexual drive itself. From this standpoint, similar to the Foucauldian conceptualisations of sexuality, the sexual drive is a learnt social goal. Contradictory evidence can be found in the work of Hamer and Copeland (1999: 163), who have shown clearly how genes influence our sexual drive and 'help make us receptive to the social interactions and signs of mutual attraction that we feel instinctively and now call love'. Importantly, Hamer and Copeland (ibid.) provide not only cogent evidence for emotional and sexual instincts, but also evidence that genes are not fixed instructions; rather, they take their cue from the environment. I want to argue strongly for the mutuality between genes and environment, rather than oversocialised or genetically fatalistic accounts of the person. In what follows, I will examine selected examples of evidence for a genetic basis for some human behaviour, and for the inclusion of the meta-concept of the biological variable in the new framework.

Incorporating the biological variable

Evidence for the idea that human beings evolved complex behaviour by adding instincts to those of their ancestors, rather than replacing instincts with learned patterns of behaviour, can be found in the work of the psycho-linguist Pinker (1994). Pinker's argument is that the intention of most social scientists has been, and still is, to examine and trace the ways in which behaviour is influenced by the social environment. We should perhaps also examine the ways in which the social environment is produced by our innate social instincts. Barkow *et al.* (1992) suggest that culture is the product of individual human psychology rather than vice-versa. According to these authors, it has been a major mistake to oppose nature to nurture, because learning is dependent upon innate, instinctive capacities to learn and there are innate constraints upon what can be learned. Biological organs can be 'reverse engineered to discern what they are "designed" to do' (ibid.: 2) in the same way as machines can be studied. Pinker (1994) emphasises that machines are meaningless except when described in terms of their functions. In the same way, it is meaningless to describe the human or animal eye without mentioning that it is designed for the making of images. Barkow *et al.* (1992: 2) argue that the same principles apply to the human brain, and its modules are likely to have been designed for particular functions. For instance, the evidence that the human sense of grammar is innate is particularly strong.

However, many social scientists appear to be firmly resistant to the idea of human instincts, despite the strength of the evidence for their existence. It seems to be the case that many social scientists prefer to think, contrary to the abundance of biological evidence, that genetic influences upon human behaviour are merely side-effects of the ability of the brain to understand speech. The twentieth-century paradigm that claims only non-human animals possess instincts begins to develop cracks in the foundations once we consider the Jamesian idea that some instincts cannot develop without learnt, outside effects. William James (1890) believed that the complexity of human behaviour suggested that humans have more rather than fewer instincts than animals. Yet, the belief that human beings possess no innate characteristics outside of, 'a set of simple reflexes plus a range of organic needs' (Giddens, 1993) appears to be firmly entrenched within the disciplines of criminology and sociology in particular. One line of evidence comes from 'the fact that language is so specific to our species' (Hamer and Copeland, 1999: 231). Just as human beings possess the greatest cognitive ability of all the species, so they have the greatest ability to communicate thoughts. There is no animal parallel to the complex human language that is able to distinguish past, present and future, and express concepts pitched at a high plane of abstraction. It is not unreasonable, then, for Hamer and Copeland (ibid.: 232) to further suggest that 'there must be something about the human genetic blueprint that makes us especially capable of language'.

Hamer and Copeland (ibid.: 233) also acknowledge that human languages possess very complicated rules. All languages have their own precise grammar, syntax and pronunciation. This is what prompted Noam Chomsky to theorise that a newborn baby's brain is 'prewired' with the basic ability to recognise sounds and to learn the rules of grammar and syntax. Chomsky postulated an 'innate language acquisition device'. According to Chomsky's theories, the specific language an infant learns depends completely upon the environment, but 'the basic ability to learn the rules and apply them to the billions of different combinations is genetically preprogrammed' (Hamer and Copeland, 1999: 233).

Hamer and Copeland suggest that one way to isolate the specific genes involved may be to study what happens when the language acquisition device goes awry, as in the case of a family sharing a specific language impairment (SLI) which 'mangles' language. In such cases, the authors suggest, children start talking late, and then have great problems articulating words, and make grammatical errors that may persist throughout adulthood. Such people can have normal intelligence and possess skills in many dimensions other than language. Specific language impairment, as Hamer and Copeland (ibid.: 233) make clear, runs in families, and this suggests the distinct possibility of a genetic basis. Pinker (1994) describes a family in which the grandmother has the impairment, as do four of her five children, and they in turn have twenty-three children, of whom eleven have the 'language problem'. However, as Pinker (ibid.) notes, one of the grandmother's daughters speaks normally, and so do all their children, as if this side of the family had escaped the gene. According to Hamer and Copeland (1993: 233), '[t]his is just the sort of pattern expected for a condition caused by a single dominant gene, although the gene itself has not yet been identified'.

Regarding dyslexia and biological causality, more progress has been made in locating the genetic roots. Once called 'word blindness', dyslexia is characterised by difficulty in learning to read 'despite adequate intelligence and character' (Hamer and Copeland, ibid.: 233). As the authors suggest, it appears to be caused by a 'fundamental brain disconnect between different words and their meaning' (ibid.: 233). The malfunction is specific to reading, and, as the authors show, dyslexics can be highly intelligent; they just cannot read adequately. As many as 8 per cent of children in the USA are reading-disabled by standard school system criteria, and children with dyslexia also constitute the largest group of students in receipt of special education services (ibid.). Dyslexia was first recognised in 1896, and within a decade it was known to run in families. Since then, family and twin studies have shown a substantial genetic effect, with most dyslexics having at least one other person in the family who has reading problems, and the rate in identical twins is 40 per cent.

Hamer and Copeland acknowledge that a reading disability is clearly a very complex disorder with many different causes, inherited and environmental. Even so, there appear to be some families in which one major gene is involved. As the authors show, scientists at the University of Colorado and at the Boys Town National Research Hospital started a 'gene hunt' in families with at least two dyslexics. They found evidence 'linking reading scores to chromosome six and found similar results in fraternal twins' (ibid.: 233), and '[m]ore recently, a different group of scientists at Yale University, found linkage to the same chromosome in yet another group of dyslexic families' (ibid.: 233–34). As Hamer and Copeland suggest, these appear to be solid results, but it is not yet known which gene is involved or how it works. What does appear to be evident is that:

> The gene has a major effect on the ability to break down long words into syllables, but not on comprehension of short words. That suggests something quite specific – a breakdown in the brain circuit used to segment words – rather than a more general problem. So when the actual gene is found it may tell us something about that particular part of intelligence dealing with language.
>
> (Hamer and Copeland, 1993: 234)

Although the authors claim that the gene for grammar has yet to be isolated, more recent work by Enard *et al.* (2002) and Lai *et al.* (2001) suggests that a genetic mutation may be responsible for Severe Language Impairment (SLI). There is indeed a gene on chromosome 7 responsible for this disorder in one large pedigree and in another smaller one. The gene is known as Forkhead box P2, or FOXP2 for short, and according to Lai *et al.* (ibid.) it is a gene whose job is to 'switch on' other genes – a transcription factor. When it is damaged, the person never develops full language.

Robin Dunbar (1996) has argued that language took over the role that grooming occupies in ape and monkey communities in the natural world; the maintenance and development of social bonds. When human beings began to live in large groups, it became necessary to invent a form of social grooming that could be done by several people at once: language. Dunbar has noted that human beings do not use language simply to communicate useful information, but in the main for social gossip. Walker and Shipman (1996) make the point that modern humans need a broad cord to supply the nerves to the chest for close control of breathing during speech. It is worthy of note that other still later skeletons of Homo erectus have high ape-like larynxes that might be incompatible with elaborate speech. Indeed, it might even be the case that since the attributes of speech appear so late in human evolution, language may well have been a recent invention, appearing as late as 70,000 years ago. Language is not the same thing as speech, and syntax, grammar, recursion and inflection may be ancient, but they may have been done with hands, not voices, and it may be possible that the FOXCP2 mutation of less than 200,000 years ago represents not the moment that language itself was invented, but rather the actual moment that language could be expressed through the human mouth as well as through the hands.

In the light of this mounting evidence that genetic problems can disrupt an important social tool such as language, and by extension impact on social relations, my argument is that we need to modify Sibeon's (2004) original anti-reductionist framework (see Owen, 2007b, 2009a) to include a focus on the biological variable, and to include evidence from evolutionary psychology and behavioural genetics for a partial genetic basis for some human behaviour. There appears to be strong evidence that genes do play a role alongside that of environmental influences (Bogaert and Fisher, 1995; Cosmides and Tooby, 1997; Enard *et al.*, 2002; Hamer and Copeland, 1999; Harris, 1998; Lai *et al.*, 2001; and Pinker, 1994). In line with the work of other anti-reductionist thinkers such as Sibeon (2004) and Layder (1997, 2007), the framework focuses upon dualism rather than the duality of structure favoured by sociologists of the body. This is to avoid what Archer (1995: 167–68) calls 'central conflation'. Sometimes in the course of an analysis it may be necessary to examine the biological and the social separately, whilst acknowledging the fact that genes take their cue from nature. Approaches which favour a duality of structure make the separation of the two variables virtually impossible. This mirrors the conflation of agency and structure to be found in Giddensian structuration theory. In what follows, we will consider the argument for including the meta-concept of psychobiography into the new framework.

Psychobiography

There are close links between the concept of the biological variable and Derek Layder's (1997) concept of psychobiography; the largely unique, asocial components of an actor's disposition, behaviour and self-identity. These aspects are regarded by Layder as relatively independent of face-to-face interaction and the macro-social. For Layder, human beings are composed of unique elements of cognition, emotion and behaviour that are, in some sense, separable from the social world, while at the same time related in various ways to social conditions and social experiences. He appears to be advocating a renewal of sociological theory and method beyond the modern and the premature notion of the postmodern, favouring a flexible ontology which avoids both the absolutist knowledge-claims of meta-narratives and the reductionism and essentialism of modernist paradigms. He favours a cogent, modest approach to social explanation which retains a distinct epistemological commitment to realism, recognising that society is multiform, relatively indeterminate and difficult to predict. This meta-theoretical approach is similar to Sibeon's (2004) original framework, in that it avoids unitary, reductionist explanations and opposes the idea of duality of structure. It is also against attempts to collapse distinctions between agency and structure, micro and macro and time–space. Layder (1998) criticises symbolic interactionism, Giddensian structuration theory and Foucauldian insights for having 'flattened' ontologies which serve to ignore vertical differentiation of the various spheres (or domains) of social reality. In Layder's view, differing forms of social reality cannot be reduced to reductionist explanations such as 'intersubjectivity' or 'social systems'. As is the case with Owen (2007b) and Sibeon (2004), Layder appears to favour flexible, multifactorial explanations as opposed to the relativism of postmodern/post-structuralist accounts. He is critical, in particular, of postmodernist attempts to decentre the subject. His emphasis upon psycho-biography's relative autonomy leads him to repudiate this decentring and the idea that social actors are the effects of discourse. Layder's stratified ontology and theory of domains suggests that social reality constitutes four social domains, and they relate to the subjective and objective realms. The subjective part of social life is conceived of as having two domains: the individual-subjective referred to as psychobiography, and the intersubjective labelled as situated activity, with the objective–systemic dimension consisting of social settings and contextual resources. The latter term refers to cultural phenomena, and the distribution of resources relating to, for example, social class, ethnicity and other sources of inequalities and power relations. Layder maintains that objective and systemic variables may influence but do not determine the subjective dimension, the latter consisting of psychobiography and situated activity. On the other hand, psychobiography and situated activity shape, in part, but do not actually determine social settings and contextual resources (the objective dimension of the social). There is clearly justification for including the meta-concept of psychobiography in the framework, and for reformulating the term so that it includes biological variables such as predisposition and instinct.

As I suggested above, the task here has been to establish whether there is sufficient evidence from evolutionary psychology and behavioural genetics to justify modifying Sibeon's (2004) original anti-reductionist framework to include such new meta-concepts as the biological variable, psychobiography, the oversocialised gaze, and genetic fatalism, in an attempt to point a possible way forward towards a *genetic-social* criminological theory in which there is a proper balance between the social and the biological. In what follows, the new framework is codified and its explanatory potential more fully revealed.

The genetic-social framework and its application

To recap, the ontologically flexible framework is an example of meta-theory. It relies upon methodological generalisations as opposed to substantive general-isations, and multifactorial analysis, preparing the ground for further theoretical and empirical investigation involving large-scale synthesis. The sensitising device arises out of a critique of the following cardinal sins: essentialism; relativism; reification; the oversocialised gaze; and genetic fatalism. The intention now is to show how the framework may be applied and how it may inform criminological theorising, and first we must turn to what criminological theorising must avoid. Essentialism should be avoided, and is regarded here as a form of theorising that, in aprioristic fashion, presupposes a unity or homogeneity of social phenomena. This can include social institutions, or taxonomic collectives such as 'white men' or Charles Murray's 'underclass'. Reification is regarded here as the illicit attribution of agency to entities that are not actors or agents. An actor is an entity that in principle has the cognitive means of formulating, taking and acting upon decisions. Therefore, 'the state', 'the Metropolitan Police', 'society' and so on are not regarded as actors. This approach, particularly with regard to conceptualisations of the state as a non-actor, places the framework very much at odds with conceptions favoured within much of leftist idealism. It is also at odds with Garland's (2001) over-reliance upon the Foucauldian concept of discourse, which appears to rest upon a reified notion of agency. Like Foucault, Garland appears to presume that discourses are themselves social actors in the sense of a 'crime consciousness' diffused through the media. Arguably, however, discourses are a form of material that needs to be manipulated by social actors (Owen, 2007b). In *genetic-social* theorising, we may conceptualise discourse as a potential influence upon social actors, but to regard discourse as an agent is to engage in illicit reification. When Garland (2001: 120) suggests that the punishment of criminals is 'the business of the state', which he regards as symbolic of 'state power', and that 'the state' is responsible for the care of offenders, he is engaging in reification. As has been hopefully made clear, the state cannot be regarded as an actor in the sense that Garland appears to imply, although its functionaries may be individual social actors. The framework also entails an avoidance of relativism, the philosophical stance associated with postmodernism (Lyotard, 1984; Milovanovic, 1996, 1997, 1999) and post-structuralism (Foucault, 1980; Smart, 1995; Young, 1995). Relativists reject foundationalism, from which future criminological theory can be generated, in tandem with failing to provide acceptable epistemologies and viable theories. For example, the most basic criticism of Foucault's relativistic position is that he never applies it to his own theories and conceptual frameworks. Foucault is open, that is to say, to 'the self-referential objection' (Blackledge and Hunt, 1993) which posits that, if all theories are the product of a particular situation, then so too is that theory, and it therefore has no universal validity. To put it another way, if truth and falsity do not exist in an absolute sense, then Foucault's thesis about the relativity of all knowledge cannot be 'true' in this sense. In arguing the way he does, Foucault is surely employing the very criteria of truth and validity which he claims are culturally relative. He is employing reason to try to prove the inadequacy of reason. Put simply, the relativist statement that there can be no general theory is itself a general theory (Sibeon, 2004).

The oversocialised gaze refers to harshly 'environmentalist' accounts which are characterised by a strong antipathy towards genetic, or partially genetic, explanations; for example, the theories of the Chicagoans, Shaw and McKay (1942), which imply that individual action can be explained solely by the larger environment in which the individual resides, and Sutherland's (1947) view that criminal behaviour is entirely learned. Genetic fatalism refers to a widespread tendency within criminology and other social sciences to equate genetic determinism with inevitability. It is a mistake to view the genes involved in human behaviour as immutable. Genes can be switched on, and both external events and free-willed behaviour can switch on genes. This is quite a different concept from the Lombrosian idea that individuals are 'born to be criminal'.

In addition to these 'cardinal sins', the *genetic-social* framework focuses upon the following meta-theoretical formulations which can be utilised to inform criminological theorising. Here a non-reified conception of agency is favoured, in which actors/agents are strictly defined as entities that are, in principle, capable of formulating and acting upon decisions. Structure here is regarded as the 'social conditions' (Hindess, 1986: 120–21) or the circumstances in which actors operate, including the resources that actors may draw upon. Structure, may then refer to discourses, institutions, social practices and individual/social actors. In this form of criminological theorising, micro–macro should be viewed as distinct and autonomous levels of social process. Additionally, dualism is favoured as a meta-concept as opposed to a Giddensian duality of structure, because, in criminological analysis, agency–structure, micro–macro and biology–social should be employed as dualisms that refer to distinct, autonomous phenomena. The intention of this is to avoid what Shilling (1993) argues for in his analysis of the human body as simultaneously biological and social. Shilling has collapsed both terms into an amalgamated whole within which elements cannot be separated, resulting in 'central conflation' (Archer, 1995). We need to acknowledge that genes and environment both play a role in human behaviours, and dualism if correctly employed is a useful concept which enables the separation of elements like agency, structure, biology, the social and so on, enabling us to examine the links between them, and to assess the relative influence of each element in any social context. Classical theorists drawn upon in criminological theorising such as Durkheim, have tended to regard time as social time, distinct from a natural essence. Here time–space as a meta-concept refers to how differing time frames, including those associated with the macro-social order and those with the micro-social order, interweave. *Genetic-social* criminology acknowledges what is referred to here as the biological variable; the evidence from evolutionary psychology and behavioural genetics for a, at least in part, biological basis for some human behaviours. This acknowledgment might, for example, inform the study of masculinities associated with Collier (1998), Connell (2000), Jefferson (2007), MacInnes (1998) and Messerschmidt (1993). All these scholars provide interesting evidence for the social construction of masculinities, and for gender inequalities based upon the dominance of 'hegemonic masculinity' (Connell, ibid.). However, they neglect to acknowledge biological variables in their analyses and their work contains theoretical deficits and shortcomings in relation to the role of male sexuality in crime, which lies beyond social construction in the realm of genes. Modified notions of Foucauldian power are employed in *genetic-social* criminological analysis, and the multiple nature of power is acknowledged. As I have shown elsewhere (Owen, 2007b), power exists in more than one form, and in particular there are objective, structural, systemic and agentic forms of power. The latter term refers to the partly systemic, partly relational and partly variable capacity of agents to shape events in a preferred direction. This modified notion of Foucauldian power (Owen, 2007b; Sibeon, 2004) recognises the dialectical relationship between agentic and systemic forms of power; the relational, contingent and emergent dimensions of power, and the concept that, *contra* Foucault, aspects of power can be 'stored' in positions/roles and as social systems/ networks. As Owen (2007b) has shown, Garland's (2001) Foucauldian conception of power requires some necessary modifications. His 'culture of control' thesis would be strengthened by utilising Foucauldian concepts in a more critical, selective fashion informed by critique of agency–structure, micro–macro and time–space. Foucault and actor-network theorists such as Callon and Latour (1981) tend to push relational and processual concepts of power to the point of denying that power can be stored. It is quite probable some social agents possess more power than others because certain elements of power can be stored in roles such as those of police officers and magistrates, and in dominant networks of social systems. Garland's argument for criminal offenders to be treated as 'individuals' (2001) would also be strengthened by an acknowledgement of psychobiography, the largely unique, asocial aspects of an individual's disposition, behaviour and self-identity (Layder, 1997; Owen, 2007b, 2009a). An emphasis upon flexible, multifactorial explanation as opposed to anti-foundational relativism, coupled with the inclusion of psychobiography's relative autonomy in combination with an acknowledgement of biological variables, would act as a corrective to the Foucauldian decentring of the subject and the spurious idea that actors are the effects of discourse.

Concluding observations

To reiterate, it is the contention here that a genetic–social, meta-theoretical framework, which entails a flexible ontology, relying upon multifactorial analysis rather than reified and essentialist analysis, is best equipped to cautiously point a possible 'way forward' for criminological theory, beyond anti-foundational relativism and the environmentalist rejection of biology. This is an approach which sidesteps the nature versus nurture divide, and which emphasises instead a balanced account of the mutuality between genes and environment. It is my view that crime may be socially constructed, but there is still a reality 'out there' in which criminologists need to acknowledge that biological factors may 'switch on' genetic impulses to generate behaviour that can be labelled criminal when they interact with other social and psychological factors. However, human beings are reflexive agents with the agency to choose not to engage in criminal activities where they believe that the rewards are outweighed by negative outcomes or actions offend moral prohibitions. Agency, in turn, is certainly influenced by inherited constitutional variables. These are early days, but hopefully these elements combined make the framework a useful, conceptual toolkit. Its methodological generalisations, as opposed to substantive generalisations, its rejection of biophobia and its adoption of a realist social ontology make it a sensitising device with some potential for future theoretical and explanatory use (Owen, 2009b; 2012).

References

Archer, M. (1995) *Realist Social Theory: The Morphogenetic Approach*. Cambridge: Cambridge University Press.

Barkow, J., Cosmides, L. and Tooby, J. (1992) *The Adapted Mind*. Oxford: Oxford University Press.

Becker, J.B., Breedlove, S.M., Crews, D. and McCarthy, M.M. (1992) *Behavioural Endocrinology*. Cambridge, MA: MIT Press.

Benton, T. (1991) 'Biology and social science: why the return of the repressed should be given a (cautious) welcome', *Sociology*, 25, 1: 1–29.

—— (2003) 'Ecology, health and society: a red-green perspective', in S.J. Williams, L. Birke and G. Bendelow (eds) *Debating Biology: Sociological Reflections on Health, Medicine and Society*. London: Routledge.

Blackledge, D. and Hunt, B. (1993) *Sociological Interpretations of Education*. London: Routledge.

Bogaert, A.F. and Fisher, W.A. (1995) 'Predictors of university men's number of sexual partners', *The Journal of Sex Research*, 32, 119–20.

Callon, M. and Latour, B. (1981) 'Unscrewing the big Leviathan: how actors macro-structure reality and how sociologists help them to do so', in K. Knorr-Cetina and A.V. Cicourel (eds) *Advances in Social Theory and Methodology: Towards an Integration of Micro-and Macro-Sociologies*. London; Routledge.

Collier, R. (1998) *Masculinities, Crime and Criminology*. London: Sage.

Connell, R.W. (2000) *The Men and the Boys*. Berkeley: University of California Press.

Cosmides, L. and Tooby, J. (1997) *Evolutionary Psychology: A Primer*. www.psych.ucsb.edu/research/cep/primer.html

Dunbar, R. (1996) *Grooming, Gossip and the Evolution of Language*. London: Faber and Faber.

Enard, W., Przeworski, M., Fisher, S.E., Lai, C.S.L., Wiebe, V., Kitano, T., Monaco, A.P. and Pääbo, S. (2002) 'Molecular evolution of FOXP2, a gene involved in speech and language', *Nature*, 418: 869–72.

Filley, C.M., Price, B.H., Nell, V., Antoinette, T., Morgan, A.S., Bresnahan, J.F., Pincus, J.H., Gelbort, M.M., Weissberg, M. and Kelly, J.P. (2001) 'Towards an understanding of violence: neurobehavioural aspects of unwarranted physical aggression: Aspen neurobehavioural conference consensus statement', *Neuropsychiatry, Neuropsychology and Behavioural Neurology*, 14: 1–14.

Foucault, M. (1980) *The History of Sexuality*. New York: Vintage Books.

Freese, J., Li, J-C.A. and Wade, L. (2003) 'The potential relevances of biology to social inquiry', *Annual Review of Sociology*, 29: 233–56.

Gagnon, J.H. and Simon, W. (1973) *Sexual Conduct*. London: Hutchinson.

Garland, D. (2001) *The Culture of Control: Crime and Social Order in Contemporary Society*. Oxford: Oxford University Press.

Giddens, A. (1993) *Sociology*. Cambridge: Polity Press.

Hall, S. (1985) 'Authoritarian populism: a reply to Jessop *et al.*', *New Left Review*, 151, pp.115–24.

Hamer, D. and Copeland, P. (1999) *Living With Our Genes: Why They Matter More Than You Think*. London: Macmillan.

Harris, J.R. (1998) *The Nurture Assumption*. London: Bloomsbury.

Herrnstein, R.J. and Murray, C. (1994) *The Bell Curve*. New York: Basic Books.

Hindess, B. (1986) 'Actors and social relations', in M.L.Wardell and S.P.Turner (eds) *Sociological Theory in Transition*. London: Allen and Unwin.

James, W. (1890) *Principles of Psychology*. New York: Holt.

Jefferson, T. (2007) 'Masculinities', in E. McLaughlin and J. Muncie (eds) *The Sage Dictionary of Criminology*. London: Sage, pp. 245–47.

Klinteberg, B. (1996) 'Biology, norms, and personality: a developmental perspective', *Neuropsychobiology*, 34: 146–54.

Lai, C.S., Fisher, S.E., Hurst, J.A., Vargha-Khadem, F. and Monaco, A.P. (2001) 'A forkhead domain gene is mutated in a severe speech and language disorder', *Nature*, 413: 519–23.

Layder, D. (1997) *Modern Social Theory: Key Debates and New Directions*. London: UCL Press.

—— (1998) *Sociological Practice: Linking Theory and Social Research*. London: Sage.

—— (2007) 'Self-identity and personhood in social analysis: the inadequacies of postmodernism and social constructionism', in J.L. Powell and T. Owen (eds) *Reconstructing Postmodernism: Critical Debates*. New York: Nova Science Publishers.

Lyotard, J.F. (1984) *The Postmodern Condition:A Report on Knowledge*. Trans. G. Bennington and B. Massumi. Manchester: Manchester University Press.

MacInnes, J. (1998) *The End of Masculinity*. Buckingham: Open University Press.

Martin, P. (1997) *The Sickening Mind: Brain, Behaviour, Immunity and Disease*. London: HarperCollins.

Mednick, S.A., Moffit, T. and Stack, S. (eds) (1987) *The Causes of Crime: New Biological Approaches*. Cambridge: Cambridge University Press.

Mednick, S.A. and Volavka, J. (1980) 'Biology and crime', in N. Morris and M. Tonry (eds) *Crime and Justice, Vol. 2*. Chicago: University of Chicago Press.

Messerschmidt, J.W. (1993) *Masculinities and Crime*. Lanham, MD: Rowman and Littlefield.

Milovanovic, D. (1996) 'Postmodern criminology', *Justice Quarterly*, 13(4): 567–609.

—— (1997) *Chaos, Criminology and Social Justice*. New York: Praeger.

—— (1999) 'Catastrophe theory, discourse, and conflict resolution', in B. Arrigo (ed.) *Social Justice/Criminal Justice*. Belmont, CA: Wadsworth.

Mouzelis, N. (1991) *Back to Sociological Theory: The Construction of Social Order*. London: Macmillan.

—— (1995) *Sociological Theory: What Went Wrong? Diagnosis and Remedies*. London: Routledge.

—— (2007) 'Cognitive relativism: between positivistic and relativistic thinking in the social sciences', in J.L. Powell and T. Owen (eds) *Reconstructing Postmodernism: Critical Debates*. New York: Nova Science Publishers.

Newton, T. (2003) 'Truly embodied sociology: marrying the social and the biological?', *Sociological Review*, 51(1): 20–41.

Owen, T. (2006) 'Genetic-social science and the study of human biotechnology', *Current Sociology*, 54(6): 897–917.

—— (2007a) 'After postmodernism: towards an evolutionary sociology', in J.L. Powell and T. Owen (eds) *Reconstructing Postmodernism: Critical Debates*. New York: Nova Science Publishers.

—— (2007b) 'Culture of crime control: through a post-Foucauldian lens', *The Internet Journal of Criminology* (www.internetjournalofcriminology.com).

—— (2009a) *Social Theory and Human Biotechnology: With a Foreword by Professor Derek Layder (University of Leicester)*. New York: Nova Science Publishers.

—— (2009b) 'England and Wales: the criminal justice system in "post-industrial" society', in J.L. Powell and J. Hendricks (eds) *The Welfare State in Post-Industrial Society: A Global Perspective*. New York: Springer.

—— (2012) *Criminological Theory: Beyond Postmodernism*. London: Palgrave Macmillan.

Pinker, S. (1994) *The Language Instinct*. London: Penguin.

Pollock, K. (1988) 'On the nature of social stress: production of a modern mythology', *Social Science and Medicine*, 26(3): 381–90.

Shaw, C.R. and McKay, H.D. (1942) *Juvenile Delinquency and Urban Areas*. Chicago: University of Chicago Press.

Shilling, C. (1993) *The Body and Social Theory*. London: Sage.

Sibeon, R. (2004) *Rethinking Social Theory*. London: Sage.

—— (2007) 'An excursus in post-postmodern social science', in J.L. Powell and T. Owen (eds) *Reconstructing Postmodernism: Critical Debates*. New York: Nova Science Publishers.

Smart, C. (1995) *Law, Crime and Sexuality*. London: Sage.

Sutherland, E.H. (1947) *Principles of Criminology*. Philadelphia, PA: J.B. Lippincott.

Walker, A. and Shipman, P. (1996) *The Wisdom of the Bones: In Search of the Human Origins*. London: Weidenfeld and Nicolson.

Walsh, A. and Beaver, K.M. (eds) (2009) *Biosocial Criminology: New Directions in Theory and Research*. New York: Routledge.

Walsh, A. and Ellis, L. (eds) (2003) *Biosocial Criminology: Challenging Environmentalism's Supremacy*. New York: Nova Science Publishers.

Wilson, J.Q. and Herrnstein, R.J. (1985) *Crime and Human Nature*. New York: Simon and Schuster.

Young, A. (1995) *Imagining Crime*. London: Sage.

6 From social order to the personal subject

A major reversal

Michel Wieviorka

Sociology can shed light, if not on criminology itself – a subject of which sociologists (Mucchielli 2010)[1] tend to be somewhat critical – at least on thinking about crime. This has been the case since Emile Durkheim's well-known propositions, followed by those of his pupil, Paul Fauconnet, less well-known but a stimulating addition. To recall briefly, Emile Durkheim considered that crime has a function in society; it is normal because a society without crime is impossible. For Durkheim crime is necessary, and even useful, the generator of changes; crime is 'a factor in public health, an integral part of all healthy societies' and the 'conditions of which it (crime) is part are themselves indispensable to the normal evolution of morality and law' (Durkheim 1947: book I, p. 70). For Fauconnet, it was the crime that was important and not the criminal or their victim; the ideal would be to be able to punish the crime itself, but as this is not possible, the criminal takes the place of the crime – the criminal serves as a scapegoat (Fauconnet 1920).

The sociological analysis of crime is not a one-best-way procedure and, as for any important social phenomenon, approaches and orientations can vary. While there has long been a consensus amongst sociologists to reject approaches which explain crime as an inherent trait of human nature using concepts drawn from the physical, biological, congenital or racial attributes of the criminal, as did the Italian criminologist, Cesare Lombroso, it is not difficult to perceive a strong opposition between those for whom, in the direct line of Durkheim's propositions and those of his school, the appropriate starting point for considering crime is society or the system and those for whom the starting point is the individual and his or her personal responsibility in the criminal act. Holism versus methodological individualism – this tension which is at the core of the most central debates in the social sciences today is also operational in dealing with crime. This will be the main theme of the remarks below: present-day developments are in many respects more favourable to the point of view of the individual, and more specifically to the individual subject, than to the whole constituted by society.

Prior to theoretical concepts, if sociology can contribute to a better understanding of crime today, it is primarily by emphasising the major present-day developments which result in our no longer considering this phenomenon as we used to in the past, at the time of Durkheim for example. We have to take into consideration the major changes which weigh heavily on the reality of crime but also on our perception and our representations. These changes are countless; they owe a lot to new technologies, in particular in communication, or those which enable us to provide demonstrations or proofs (for example the DNA techniques of identification) but also, and mainly, to the work of societies on themselves, which result in some crimes impelling recognition in novel fashion in the collective consciousness, whereas others cease to be considered as such. Thus, as we shall see, the violence to which women or children are subjected have become crimes, whereas in the past they were ignored, or practically ignored. Racism, as Jean-Paul Sartre said in describing one specific form, anti-Semitism, has, since the encounter with Nazism, ceased to be an opinion and has become a crime (Sartre 1946). But also, to take an example which goes in the opposite direction, abortion in Western societies has ceased to be overwhelmingly considered as a crime to become, on the contrary, a source of progress and control of their own experience for very many women.

The era of the victim

In traditional societies, but also until the mid-twentieth century, and including the most advanced industrial countries, little attention was paid to the victim of the crime, or only as an afterthought. Their suffering, the challenge to their physical or moral integrity, even their destruction, was not at the centre of thinking or action in the face of crime. What is important – and we find this point in Durkheim's sociology – is the offence to which society itself has been subjected as a result of the crime, the threat or the risk which it implies for social order. Here the scapegoat mechanism is particularly significant: avoiding, compensating and punishing crime then involves the imposition of sanctions which may, ultimately, transform a person or a group into innocent victims paying for a crime which they have not committed in order to maintain social bonds intact.

But today it is no longer possible to deal with crime without taking an interest in its victims, without considering what has happened to them. Not only is it a question of ensuring the protection and the smooth running of social order, the state, or society as a whole by punishing crime; the victim also has to be considered. Even if, by punishing the crime, society in its entirety takes the place of the victim, this no longer suffices. The state no longer has full and entire authorisation to take the place of the victim. The latter is no longer satisfied with knowing that the criminal who committed an offence has been punished by the legal system on behalf of the collective. The victim is no longer willing to be displaced in the course of the procedure which will end in punishment.

Historically, it is impossible to locate the most important sources of this evolutionary movement which ushers us into the era of the victim. Some stem from international life and wars, the others are internal to certain societies, beginning with those known as the 'Western' democracies.

On one hand, the present-day victim emerges onto the international scene in the nineteenth century, when the Swiss citizen, Henri Dunant, on seeing the battlefield of Solferino in 1859, imagined the Red Cross with the idea of organising aid to the military victims of the war. This project had a basic dimension: it implied that the point of view of states be transcended and that a law to authorise this transcendence be implemented. At this stage it also had limits because it only applied to military personnel and not to civilians. It should be noted that at the time war damage affected far fewer civilians than today: during World War I, 5 per cent of the victims were civilians, as compared with 50 per cent during World War II and 90 per cent in the wars of the 1980s and 1990s (Cheterman 2001: 1–6). Today the protection of civilians has become a constant preoccupation, whereas at the outset it was a question of protecting the belligerents.

Towards the end of the nineteenth century, the point of view of war victims was strengthened by the arrival on the scene of psychiatry, with Jean-Martin Charcot, then, with Sigmund Freud, of psychoanalysis: war also produces traumatisms and neuroses and wreaks havoc on minds and not only on bodies. On the other hand, the present-day victim also appeared, once again as from the mid-nineteenth century, when the violence, both physical and moral, to which women and children were subjected, was discovered especially in the industries developing in Western Europe. Doctors, lawyers and members of parliament were to play a decisive role in this movement along with writers, including novelists like Victor Hugo, or militants, in particular feminists. The victim appeared once again at the time of the anti-slavery struggle, as well as towards the end of the nineteenth century in industrial societies when the welfare state, social security or yet again the first laws on industrial accidents were taking shape, since the state then recognised that certain types of injury incurred must be anticipated and recognised socially and possibly be prevented or compensated.

A second phase in this long process of recognition of victims was inaugurated in the twentieth century, in the 1960s, and was the real indicator of entry into the era of the victim. On one hand, humanitarian organisations were developing in matters of war and international relations; theories were being developed about the right to intervention and humanitarian interventions were bypassing the principle of state sovereignty which theoretically regulated international life. On the other hand, in the most modern societies, the women's movements were denouncing violence in the private sphere; rape, including conjugal rape, was genuinely becoming a criminal offence, whereas until then the police, the courts and politicians had usually been indifferent, or even hostile, to the victims. The discovery by public opinion, but also by public authorities, of the violence sustained by women was extended further by the increasing coverage given to violence sustained by children and by intense awareness of the ravages of paedophilia which, till then, had usually been contained and covered by institutions. The scandals which in recent years have shaken the Catholic Church are a perfect illustration of this point.

Whether it be a question of women and children, but also of victims of racism, older people and the disabled, the victim's point of view has now entered the public sphere; crime has become visible and perceived as such, and the studies and research referred to by the term victimology confirm this evolution, with the collection of data about the crime on the basis of what the victims say. The movement in this direction was so strong that it gave rise to discussions and criticisms: should we not be wary of what the 'victims' say, particularly when it is a question of children who are easy to manipulate and liable to tell stories? Do movements in support of the victims not contribute to the weakening and undermining of institutions? The fact remains that a decisive turning point had been reached; crime is no longer, or is not uniquely, a challenge to the social order or the state, nor can it be reduced to what society considers as such and finds it necessary to punish. Instead, and on a very different plane, it also and primarily constitutes an invasion of the integrity of its victims.

Furthermore, throughout the world there has been increasing sensitivity to the need to denounce crimes against humanity, a concept which updates the classical norms of crime definition. This rise in power of victims denouncing genocide, mass killings, the African slave trade and other historical crimes was inaugurated in the form of mobilisations of which we find examples in numerous societies. In the United States for example, Native American movements put an end to the images dominant at the time according to which immigrants from Europe, in their advance towards the West, brought progress and civilisation, which the barbarians, who were only good at getting drunk and killing, resisted – the 'Western', as a type of film that displayed this ideology on screen, disappeared in the 1970s. At the same time, the 1950s movement for civil rights, then the Black movement in the 1960s, recalled the brutality of the conditions of arrival, then of the existence of Black people in the past, and stressed the continuity which existed with the injustices and racism to which they are still subjected today.

In France, to take another country, regionalist movements denounced the destruction of the languages and cultures which they were reclaiming as a result of Jacobin centralism concerned with eradicating regional specificities; the Jews demanded that the French state recognise its responsibility in the destruction of the European Jews by Nazism; Armenians took action to ensure recognition by the law of the genocide committed by the Turkish state in 1915, etc. In several countries, such as South Africa and Latin America, commissions of the 'truth and reconciliation' type have endeavoured, not simply to punish crimes, but to set up new procedures in which the memory of the victims is taken into consideration where, as a result, remembrance affords space for mourning, the recognition of crimes and forgiveness.

All these changes, the main features of which are outlined here, weigh heavily on the definition of the crime and on its punishment. They open up new discussions, bring onto the scene the crime victims who were almost non-existent, allowing them the possibility of requesting an explanation for the recent past, but also for distant crimes of which they are not themselves personally direct victims, and by turning to those in power who did not personally participate in these crimes, challenging states which, in the last resort, may not be concerned, as is the case with the Armenian organisations who demand world-wide recognition of the 1915 Armenian genocide, including that of states which had nothing to do with it.

These changes also have an influence on criminology itself. Some, since the victims are alive today, intend to examine the relations between victims and guilty, in the extension of a viewpoint which owes a lot to Hans von Hentig. He argues that there is a relation and genuine, shared features between the victim and the torturer. Others endeavour to show that some individuals, for reasons inherent to their personality and their own story, are more likely than others to become victims, with the idea, for example, that today's criminal was yesterday's victim of the same type of crime; a rape for example. This is never very far from a process aimed at making the victim of the crime the person who is guilty of it.

The state and crime

Traditionally, society is the framework within which crime is judged and punished, in more or less close conjunction with a state and a nation. When a crime includes dimensions which extend beyond this framework it becomes the concern of inter-state relations, their accords, and their participation in international organisations. But since the 1970s this traditional framework has been challenged, in the first instance as a result of globalisation. This weakens the capacity of states to regulate their economic and financial matters, and it promotes the emergence or the increase of forms of violence which are defined as criminal at levels other than in the context of the state. Organised criminality is spreading at an increasingly 'global' level, whether it be trafficking in drugs, arms, human organs or, yet again, prostitution; terrorism is changing and also becoming 'global', in particular with radical Islamism and some of the attacks made in its name, the most spectacular being that of 11 September 2001 in the United States. Cultural and social changes are taking place in arenas other than those restricted to the 'society', itself located in a nation-state; this can be seen in particular with the importance which is now assumed by the phenomena of diasporas which, according to some researchers, are possibly becoming transnational.

In this context, political violence can change and become so close to organised crime that it is almost the same thing. We observe this each time guerrilla organ-isations, like FARC in Columbia, move from political demands – the concern to take state power or to arouse a people or a nation in revolutionary mode – to the most banal forms of criminality: looting, drug trafficking, villainous kidnappings, etc. I have suggested the use here of the term infra-political violence. We also observe that the state seems to be unable to cope, or appears out of its depth when the violence becomes meta-political, with a self-ascribed religious dimension, as is the case of radical Islamism.

Crime is transformed, or, in any event, experienced and treated differ-ently when contemporary developments include strong tendencies to dis-institutionalisation and when the institutions which are the guardians of the social fabric, order and security, but also of the socialisation of children (schools) or the welfare state experience increasing difficulties, seem less and less able to fulfil their mission, making the state look like an actor incapable of assuming its fundamental responsibilities, while at the same time modern individualism seems to be heightened, including its appeals to individual persons. Traditionally, when confronted with crime, the state is expected to assume its vocation of monopoly of the legitimate use of physical force, which Max Weber expressed well in his celebrated lecture in 1919:

> Ultimately, one can define the modern state sociologically only in terms of the specific *means* peculiar to it, as to every political association, namely, the use of physical force. [. . .] Today the relation between the state and violence is an especially intimate one [. . .] Today, however, we have to say that a state is a human community that [successfully] claims the *monopoly of the legitimate use of physical force* within a given territory [. . .] The state is considered the sole source of the 'right' to use violence.
>
> (Weber 1963 [1919])

But, apparently unable to cope with world-level economic processes, and with their domestic implications, the present day state seems less capable than yesterday's of constituting the territorial, administrative, legal and perhaps symbolic framework of collective life. It retreats when faced with criminal activities, whether they be organised or not, and, while the economy is being privatised, at the same time the state is abandoning a part of its monopoly of legitimate use of physical force to private actors. For example, private companies carry out tasks of security, guarding, surveillance and protection of people and property which normally is the concern of public authorities and the police.

More generally speaking, the rise in importance of themes dealing with human rights leads to the subjectivity and integrity of the victims taking precedence over social order or the higher interests of state. This cannot fail to have repercussions on the definition of crime and its treatment. In this context, new proposals are appearing to ensure the response to crime. Thus, important currents of opinion insist on the importance of reparation, and attempt to invent forms of punishment other than the most common one of imprisonment. Making legal reparation means listening to victims while at the same time believing in the possibility of perpetrators of crimes to mend their ways.

Moreover, when the concept of crime against humanity can be advanced, the definition of the crime is beyond the control of societies and states. The first concrete demonstrations of this only date back to the end of World War II with the Nuremberg Trials. Here crime can no longer be reduced to a challenge to the social order, the state or the normal working of society; it concerns another level and other norms, and its punishment can no longer be entrusted to the justice of one state. From this point on, new discussions have been initiated, for example concerning supra-national or international justice when a criminal is being judged for crimes against humanity: is it really a question of a higher justice? Is it not simply the justice of the strongest or the conquerors? Similar types of questions are posed when states, backed up by the legitimacy conferred on them by the international community, or a part of it, attack a dictatorship or a particularly brutal power, flouting the principle which traditionally organises the relations between states, and according to which each state is free to deal with domestic issues as it thinks best.

All this does not mean that present-day developments are one-dimensional and of necessity lead to the demise of the state or the decline of the nation. In fact, it is preferable to speak of a change, in which the functions and capacities of the state, or the symbolic and cultural strength of the nation, are being transformed.

In conclusion

This change may at least in part be understood as the entry into a historical period in which the point of view of the personal subject can and must be taken into consideration if the intention is to tackle the major questions associated with crime. Henceforth, the criminal is not, or is not uniquely, the product of social, cultural, political and economic determinants; nor can the criminal be reduced to a natural disposition. Criminals, as individual subjects, are responsible for their acts, except if they can demonstrate, as Adolf Eichmann for example attempted to do, that they acted in obedience to a legitimate power, in this instance state power as exercised by Hitler. This subjectivity of the criminal refers to their capacity to do evil, which is to say to destroy the subject, both in themselves and in others.

The point of view of the subject also refers us back to the victim, who is increasingly defined as affected or destroyed as a subject, and liable, if the need arises, to make demands on these grounds; this impacts considerably on the meaning of the punishment. The point of view of the subject is also increasingly clearly asserted when it is a question of deciding whether or not certain practices or decisions are criminal, for example in medical matters, when it is a question of deciding on life or death, of medically assisted procreation, or euthanasia. Here, in certain instances, only ethics can decide, often beyond the law and norms, on an individual basis, which is obliged to involve the intervention of the subjectivity of the person concerned if they are capable of so doing, or, if not, ways of taking their place – for example when it is a question of an embryo or of a person in a deep, long-term coma – by setting up committees or commissions for clinical ethics, as we see in some hospitals.

In the last resort, the most critical factor in the changes affecting criminology is the reversal of perspectives: we have moved from a viewpoint which for long focused on order, the state, social ties and collective awareness to one in which the focus is on the individual subject. This is why sociological knowledge, but also philosophical consideration of this concept of the subject, are now so important.

Note

1 Cf. for example in France the work of Laurent Mucchielli, who develops a critical approach to criminology in its pretensions to becoming a fundamental science. For example, Mucchielli (2010).

References

Cheterman, Simon, 'Introduction: Global Norms, Local Contexts', in Simon Cheterman (ed.) *Civilians in War*, Boulder, CO: Lynne Rienner, 2001, pp. 1–6.

Durkheim, Emile, *Les Règles de la méthode sociologique*, Paris: Presses Universitaires de France, 1947 [1894].

Fauconnet, Paul, *La Responsabilité. Étude de sociologie*, Paris: Alcan, 1928 [1920].

Mucchielli, Laurent, 'De la criminologie comme science appliquée et des discours mythiques sur la "multidisciplinarité" et "l'exception française"', *Champ pénal [Penal field], nouvelle revue internationale de criminologie* (online), vol. VII, 2010, put online 6 February 2010, accessed 8 May 2011. http://champpenal.revues.org/7728

Sartre, Jean-Paul, *Réflexions sur la question juive*, Paris: Gallimard, 1946.

Weber, Max, *Le savant et le politique,* Paris, Plon "10–18", 1963 [1919], pp. 124–25.

7 The discourse on 'race' in criminological theory

Colin Webster

The native's muscles are always tensed. You can't say that he is terrorized, or even apprehensive. He is in fact ready at a moment's notice to exchange the role of quarry for that of hunter. The native is an oppressed person whose permanent dream is to become the persecutor.

(Frantz Fanon, *Concerning Violence*, 1965)

. . . systematic comparative analysis is essential: it is necessary to demonstrate that 'black' people collectively are treated in a certain manner or experience a particular disadvantage, and that the same treatment and disadvantage are not experienced by any other group.

(Robert Miles and Malcolm Brown, *Racism*, 2003)

These contrasting quotes – one an imaginary of a reversal of power, the other an injunction to avoid *a priori* assumptions about the influence of 'race' – are connected in going to the heart of some difficult theoretical questions about 'race', ethnicity and crime. A cursory glance at criminological theory textbooks suggests mainstream theory takes a 'colour-blind' approach. Accordingly, the same theories used to explain 'white' crime equally apply to 'black' crime because there is little difference in their conditions and causes. Leaving aside the fact that when majorities define minorities as having 'ethnicity' they define themselves as having this also, and discounting the remnants of a discredited biological criminology that still believes 'races' exist, this seems odd. Among other things this chapter asks whether there are grounds to justify a distinct theory of ethnicity, race and crime rather than being subsumed into general criminological theories of crime and justice.

The structure of this chapter is first, to assess whether evidence supports the case for a distinct theory and suggest that the measurement of disproportionality is partly tautological and partly politically expedient, but mostly futile. There are, though, reasons to be worried about geographical variation and disproportion of minority involvement in predatory and violent crime. Second, to suggest that individual freedom from discrimination conferred by the discourse of human rights, anti-discrimination and anti-racism has been disconnected from substantive social and racial justice. Third, to argue that connections between ethnicity and crime are inherently spatial. Fourth, the chapter reviews different broad theoretical approaches and perspectives as to their adequacy and coherence, and how theory might be improved by close-up, micro, urban ethnographic study. The chapter concludes that recurring themes in theoretical considerations of ethnicity, race and crime should not divert our attention from the increasingly opaque ways ethnicity is culturally constructed in capitalist neoliberal societies.

Obsessive measurement: individualism, 'human rights' and discrimination

The field of ethnicity, race and crime is marked by an obsessive, deracinated measurement of proportionality and discrimination. Empiricist measurement of differences in minority and white offending levels and patterns, treatment by the police and criminal justice processes and outcomes has occurred over many years to little avail in effecting these levels, treatment, patterns and outcomes. Seemingly pointless, a legitimate question is what are the real interests and purposes served by this monitoring?

Begun in Britain since the 1976 Race Relations Act, expanded by Home Office studies and surveys since the 1980s and 1990s, ethnic statistics have grown in inverse proportion to any serious attempt to address disproportional treatment of minorities by the police or the criminal justice system. Despite the last Labour government's commitment to tackling this problem, the over-representation of black and mixed race people has *increased* on all of the key indicators; and Asians also now have started to be over-represented. Given that there is little evidence that minority offending or discrimination has increased, might it be that the persistence of this statistical picture may lend itself to reinforcing negative stereotypes, and that keeping account of disproportion encourages the very discrimination that monitoring is supposed to dispel because it racialises crime while offering little explanation why disproportion occurs (FitzGerald, 2009)? That the socio-demographic profile of those who come into contact with criminal justice isn't monitored raises more questions, not least that this omission exaggerates the role of ethnicity and cuts off alternative perceptions of the crime problem. Rather, bureaucratically defined ethnic categories offer a confused, fixed and narrow picture, repeatedly presented, of unchanging ethnic groups that confuse visible 'race' with cultural ethnicity, conflate the variation of ethnic identity, and take little account of the new complexity of Britain's ethnic landscape. The largest single ethnic minority in Britain is 'White Other' – a group that has very significantly grown since its enumeration in the 2001 Census (FitzGerald, 2009). If this empiricist bias is to be overcome theory will have to face the sociological and criminological redundancy of the official data upon which it often relies. Overwhelmed by such data, the ways criminological theories address ethnicity, race and crime is decidedly underwhelming.

The British political context of obsessive ethnic monitoring is that 'From the mid-1970s onwards . . . traditional class allegiances were weakened, while local, gender and ethnic identities grew more insistent. Politics became increasingly managed and manipulated'(Eagleton, 2011: 4). While ethnic monitoring appears concerned with prohibiting discrimination, this concern comes at little political cost for UK or US governments because it doesn't address growing social and racial inequality and injustice (Irvin, 2008; Toynbee and Walker, 2010). This growing inequality is not only between rich and poor but affects the middle class too, creating a generalised anxious insecurity (Frank, 2007). Given the legal regime of equality before the law or of government protected civil and human rights in the US and Britain, the state can no longer be seen to engage in or license racially discriminatory acts with respect to its own citizens or legitimate residents. To do so would undermine its legitimacy as the defender of both freedom and formal equality. Formal equality is expressed as 'equality of opportunity', ignoring structural and substantive inequality that if addressed would mean an equal *start* in life for all regardless of background. Instead, 'opportunity' is aligned with social mobility for meritorious individuals, i.e. the recruitment of already advantaged groups and elites, not opportunity for all (Barry, 2005; Dorling, 2010).

Disproportionate 'risk', discrimination and outcomes

Recent reviews and discussions of ethnicity, race and crime all share a concern with alleged disproportionate offending, different and discriminatory treatment, and their relationship, cause and remedy (Bhui, 2009; Gabbidon and Green, 2005; Patel and Tyrer, 2011; Phillips and Bowling, 2007; Unnever and Gabbidon, 2011; Webster, 2007). Various criminogenic factors and discriminatory activities are proffered to explain that although many different individuals and groups can suffer disadvantage and criminogenic conditions, visible minorities most suffer these conditions compounded by discrimination. Minorities tend to be younger and of lower-class background, live in lone parent families, have more often been in care, lack education and/or are unemployed, live in urban areas of high crime and social deprivation, have an active street life and consequently form a core component of the population available for policing. These conditions form the basis on which visible minorities are likely to be associated with crime, gang membership and disorder. Young black men in particular, and to an increasing extent Asian young men, suffer ascriptions of aggressive hyper-masculinity, are said to lack social controls of parenting and schooling, and of becoming involved in the sorts of crime which may bring them to the attention of the police. In any case the police disproportionately target young urban males – black, Asian and white – who having come to the attention of the police, are sucked into a spiral of amplified contact and conflict (FitzGerald, 2009; McAra and McVie, 2005). If the certainties of racial stratification, disadvantage and discrimination are in and of themselves responsible for racial disparities and disproportion in offending, then the question of how this circle might be broken becomes a moot point. If, however, offending in and of itself drives disproportionate treatment and outcomes, the circle is repeated only in the other direction. None of this, as it stands, is particularly useful to theoretical formulations.

Particularities of ethnicity and crime: robbery, violence and homicide

Desiccated and deracinated as they may be, some criminological measures suggest worrying underlying trends in both Britain and the US of very real concern to criminological theory (Bowling and Phillips, 2007; FitzGerald, 2009; Miller, 2010; Ministry of Justice, 2010; Shiner, 2010; Smith, 2003; Unnever and Gabbidon, 2011). African American men are 6 per cent of the population of the United States yet account for nearly 60 per cent of the robbery arrests in the US and half of all those arrested for murder and non-negligent manslaughter. Although only 16 per cent of the 10–17 year old population, young black people accounted for 52 per cent of juvenile violent crime arrests, 58.5 per cent of the youth-related arrests for homicide and 67 per cent of the arrests for robbery. Commenting on these proportions, Unnever and Gabbidon (2011: 3–4) state that 'Given these indisputable racial disparities, we are perplexed why so few scholars have devoted time to pursuing theoretical formulations exclusively devoted to African American offending.' The same can be said for the situation in Britain in respect of African and African Caribbean offending.

Black young people made up 27 per cent of robbery offences dealt with by the Youth Justice Service for England and Wales in 2004, but were only 3 per cent of the 10–17 year old population. Approaching a third of all 'muggings' are committed by black offenders and only half by white, a third of 'muggings' and 43 per cent of police recorded robberies were in London, and over half of those arrested for robbery in London were judged by officers to be black (Clancey *et al.* 2001). This is twice the rate for *all* police recorded crime and violent offences in London and three times the rate of recorded 'mugging' elsewhere in the country. These figures cannot be explained by the concentration of the black and Asian population in London, and in any case in some predominantly black areas 86 per cent of suspects are identified as black, according to police records and victims' reports.

Even more striking, in London between 1999 and 2006, 64 per cent of all homicide victims were young black men aged 10–17 and 58 per cent aged 18–20, yet black men make up only 7 per cent of London's population. Nationally, between 2007 and 2010, 12 per cent of homicide victims were black and 8 per cent were Asian. Black victims were much more likely to be children and young people, and homicide by sharp instrument and shooting was much more likely within this group. Black victims were concentrated in London, the West Midlands and Manchester, with 63 per cent of all victims in London, and killings tended to be intra-ethnic with 78 per cent of black victims killed by someone from the same ethnic group (Smith *et al.*, 2011). Explanations why black young people living in particular places are more likely to rob or be killed than other groups are found in the individual and group dynamics of particular neighbourhoods and geographies.

Particularities of ethnicity race and place

It should not be surprising that strong spatial patterns are found within the particularities of ethnicity and crime. And these are clearest in relation to homicide. Murder rates have increased in particular places, and for a particular group of people living there, and this rise was particularly noticeable among young men living in a poor area from the early 1980s recession (Dorling, 2005). The rise in murders in the rest of the 1980s and 1990s was also geographically concentrated. Most worryingly, in the most recent years the rates for the youngest men have reached unprecedented levels. These men carry these rates with them as they age, and overall murder rates in Britain may continue to rise despite still falling for the majority of the population in most places. There is a strong correlation between homicide rates and levels of poverty and social inequality, and the risk of murder became more concentrated spatially, socially and ethnically (Dorling, 2008). In the US, Karen Parker (2008) has shown that changes in the local urban economy influenced homicide rates over time and for specific groups. Local processes of deindustrialisation between 1980 and 1990 directly affected African American men first, then whites and blacks throughout the 1990s. As the 'new' service economy took hold and joblessness, job stability and inequality reduced, so too did urban violence in the late 1990s. Equally important were the nature of the work available and the segregation of the labour market along racial and gender lines, degrees of housing segregation and competition for jobs, immigration and ethnic diversity. It is to these contexts we must look to understand the dynamic processes by which crime and homicide rates rise and fall over time.

Other dimensions of the construction of ethnicity and crime through spatial boundaries and borders are also found in British research about the existence, structure and operation of 'gangs'. Whether they are the main source of cultures of violent criminality in some British cities, or whether they are linked to ethnicity, is controversial and the evidence contradictory. Studies have grappled with whether territoriality might be an escalator to more violent forms of crime, mostly involving illegal drugs that connect young people to organised adult criminal networks. Some studies suggest that escalation varies with area and city, but ethnicity appears not to be a strong factor in whether this happens or not, as territoriality exists within and between groups from similar ethnic backgrounds even if accentuated where neighbourhood boundaries coincide with ethnic divisions. Some accounts question whether gangs exist in any meaningful sense, while other accounts make a strong case for the existence of gang-affected neighbourhoods, especially in London and South Manchester, and their association with serious criminality and visceral violence,[1] often connected to ethnically influenced violent struggles for particular forms of financial, social or cultural capital by monopolising violence within a given neighbourhood (see the debates in Goldson, 2011).

The peculiarities of race, space and crime are also found in policing and justice by geography and place. London seems in some respects quite different to many provincial cities in respect of the policing and court disposals of minority and marginalised groups. Discrimination by the police and the courts may be closely tied with variation in the social class and ethnic makeup of areas and neighbourhoods, which in turn influences local police and court cultures (Feilzer and Hood, 2004; Hood, 1992; Newburn and Reiner, 2007). Stop and search, arrest rates and robbery are related to areas of residence, disadvantage and deprivation, street availability of certain populations, the transience of the white population and housing tenure, all of which are known to be associated with ethnic and class origin (Bowling and Phillips 2007). Whites living in 'blacker' areas have a higher stop and search arrest rate than blacks and blacks living in 'whiter' areas have higher rates than whites. 'Being out of place' seems more important in Leeds than in London (Jefferson *et al.*, 1992; Walker, 1988). The policing of working-class areas can be disproportionate to local crime levels, particularly in relation to robbery offences, and particularly in London (MVA and Miller, 2000). The astonishing geographical concentration of robbery in London may in part be because it is one of the most unequal cities in western neoliberal societies, offering opportunity and vulnerability in a place where consumer culture is often at the centre of young black lives (Hallsworth, 2005). These same factors – of course – turn out to explain rates of street crime in other areas also, where the majority of robbers are white (FitzGerald *et al.*, 2003).

The discourse of 'race' in criminological theory: the black ghetto, American 'exceptionalism' and 'cultures of violence'

Theoretical perspectives about the association of race, ethnicity and crime may be organised into five sorts of overlapping explanation. Already discussed, the first argues that membership of a black and minority group disproportionately exposes individuals to criminogenic risks and conditions that at least in part are explained as inherent in socially and racially stratified societies. The second, again already discussed, and which dominates the literature, posits that members of black and minority groups tend to suffer racial discrimination and disparity at the hands of the police and the criminal justice system. A weaker version of this perspective is that the police and criminal justice system are 'institutionally racist'; a stronger version that the wider society is 'structurally racist', that racism is systemic and endemic, and that criminal justice-based discrimination is symptomatic of structural racial inequality. The third is that enduring historical legacies of racial injustice remain in the 'collective memory' of indigenous and immigrant minorities resulting from slavery and colonialism. As a consequence the capacity of people to form stable relationships and bonds with white institutions is undermined and their social integration into post-slavery and post-colonial societies made difficult or denied, leading to alienation. A fourth perspective argues that the creation of marginalised and functionally redundant black and minority urban populations in neoliberal societies is strongly associated with neoliberal political economy that 'seeks to bring all human action into the domain of the market' (Harvey, 2005: 3). The disappearance of secure work, dismantling of welfare and the 'warehousing' of the poor into segregated and racially stigmatised ghettoes and prisons, are all strongly associated with ethnic origin. Finally, and previously argued by this author, is a perspective emphasising the changing, contingent, situated and varied forms of ethnic relations, of which crime is a part, and where culturally and spatially constructed ethnicity is strongly interwoven with status and class (Webster, 2007, 2008).

Now follows a closer consideration of these perspectives in an attempt to derive some recurring themes and arguments, ascertain their coherence and adequacy, and lead to some sort of conclusion about the discourse of 'race' in contemporary criminological theory in light of this and the preceding discussions. The processes by which African Americans migrated from the Southern rural to Northern urban industrial states, and those previously colonised emigrated to metropolitan European societies are well known. Their reception by their 'hosts' was often hostile and sometimes violent but they had little choice through chain migration about settling in what were, or were soon to become, or later became, peripheral declining urban areas marked by poor jobs, poor housing, poor schools and increasingly transient populations. From the 1970s onwards many migrants and especially their children became (and remain) vulnerable to changes in the economy – from industrial to service industries – and recession, accompanied by changes in the class composition of inner-city American neighbourhoods. The collapse and disruption of traditional employment and marriage opportunities in neighbourhoods saw an expansion of the 'underground economy of the urban poor' (Venkatesh, 2006). Social and economic change – particularly deindustrial-isation – were directly implicated in the decline of the black ghetto, creating marked differences and conflict between generations, and older residents remarked on the loss of cohesion that had resulted (Liebow, 1967; Venkatesh, 2000).

All these places exhibited the emerging classic twentieth-century American urban pattern of race relations which links ethnically based changed fortunes, residential and workplace segregation, white flight and suburbanisation. Close-up urban ethnographic studies showed how the arrival of African American immi-grants in Northern cities between 1900 and 1930 was met with white violence, then white flight to the suburbs helped by racially discriminatory employment policy, home loans and public housing policy, that ethnically divided and seg-regated work, leisure and residence. These processes were repeated across the US urban landscape, eventually resulting in 'American Apartheid', which consolidated and ethnically concentrated the black ghetto (Linkon and Russo, 2002; Massey and Denton, 1993;). Studies also found that black neighbourhoods in the 1940s and 1950s were more cohesive and stable; there were plentiful jobs, tolerable housing and much greater class mixing and integration in the black community than is the case today. Ghettoes then experienced stable populations, less con-centrated poverty or crime, and the overwhelming majority of black men were working and the majority were not poor (Drake and Cayton, 1993; Frazier, 2001). Existing colour lines were less significant than distinctions within neighbourhoods based more on perceptions and stereotypes of black middle-class and lower-class life within the ghetto than they were about race.

Some of the implications for debates in the US about ethnicity, race and crime are that the deterioration and decline of the black ghetto is relatively recent and must be put in the context of US economic and urban public policy since the 1970s, not the long-term collective memory of the ritualised humiliations of post-slavery society or, more immediately, the behaviourally different or discrete characteristics assigned to black ghetto members. It is to the *recent* history of American Apartheid that that we should look for explanations of the negative features of ghetto life. The stymieing of the gains from black legal and civil rights and relatively well paid, secure and unionised jobs in places like Detroit by job flight, the persistence of workplace discrimination; and intractable racial seg-regation in housing are relatively recent (Sugrue, 2005). And yet it was still the case that white *and* black living in the ghetto or contiguous white enclaves, in places like Detroit, Chicago, Philadelphia, Harlem and Baltimore, were more fearful and anxious about proximity to, and the presence of, growing black and white poverty and crime than they were of racial difference. This was as much about hanging on to 'respectability', avoiding 'downfall' into poverty, and in some cases whites resisting white flight to the suburbs, as it was about race (Hartigan, 1999; Kefalas, 2003). Neighbourhoods are not neatly bounded areas whose residents are said to be of one mind but are highly internally segmented and ordered (Suttles, 1968, 1972). Without underplaying racial fears that associate ethnicity with crime and violence in the United States, fears over status, class and respectability can be just as important, while a singular focus on black ghetto crime ignores these nuances (Massey and Denton, 1993; Patterson, 1997). What are ignored are the aspirations of the majority of ghetto members – the black working poor – struggling to protect 'decent' or 'respectable' values against criminal 'street' values; supplementing and supplanting the collapsed or aban-doned work of law enforcement in the ghetto, not only in respect of street-gang violence, but across a range of criminality and violent abuse found there (Venkatesh, 2000). Besides, ghettoes aren't closed systems and ghetto members constantly cross and negotiate ghetto 'boundaries' to carry out poor work in the wider economy, and this makes it difficult to argue that behaviourally isolated class- and race-based, homogenised groups and places actually exist in any meaningful way (Anderson, 1999; Duneier, 1992, 1999; Jackson, 2001).

The internal dynamics of the black ghetto have been said to work through its isolation, impoverishment and then criminalisation, particularly through the emergence of an underground economy largely based on the political economy of crack cocaine and heroin markets – trafficking, distribution, middle-men, dealers and users. Criminalisation largely through the effects of the 'war on drugs' from the 1970s to the present precipitated highly aggressive and corrupt policing and was mediated by cultural processes. Style, music, dress, argot and nomenclature, expressive of subculture, identity and consumer culture are said to explain how symbolic and real violence, and poverty, are mediated by cultural values and the perverse moral rules of the 'code of the street' (Moskos, 2008; Simon and Burns, 1997). This cultural reading of race and crime – made popular by the epic TV drama *The Wire* – can be compared to the approach taken by writers such as Bourgois (1995), Nightingale (1993) and Young (1999, 2002). They argue that black criminality is paradoxical because like 'respectable' ghetto dwellers, ghetto criminals share the consumerist values and aspirations of the wider society. The difference is that core ghetto criminals share hyper-consumerist values, exaggerate and over-identify with these values, search for insatiable but unavailable consumer status and recognition, while feeling humiliation and anger about their thwarted desires. Nightingale's (1993: 11) study of inner city black young people in Philadelphia concluded, '[it] is the increasing presence of mainstream American cultural forms in inner-city life that offers the best explanation for why urban African Americans' experience of poverty, joblessness, and racial exclusion has become so filled with violence'. Bourgois' (1995) study of the underground crack cocaine economy in East Harlem (now 'outsourced' to Mexican border towns, with even more viscerally violent consequences, see Vulliamy, 2010), found that this economy provided financial means to *engage* with the American Dream, not *oppose* mainstream cultural values. The damaging and destructive social psychological self-entrapment in criminal ghetto life and what we might understand about criminal identities as a consequence deserves further inquiry (Hall *et al.*, 2008). It should be noted, however, that the conflation of 'hyper-ghetto', 'hyper-masculinity' and 'hyper-consumerism' may be hyperbole when actual experiences of living and surviving in the ghetto may be more mundane. The legitimate or illegitimate pursuit of the American Dream has soured, as once again economic crisis and recession has disproportionately fallen on the poor. Today, Detroit and Baltimore have the highest (mostly black) homicide rates in the US after years of reduction of these rates, facing their worst economic crisis in living memory centred on foreclosures on housing loans. The consequences have been the further abandonment of whole districts, left empty as the credit crunch has cost 33,000 householders in Baltimore their properties, in a city where the population has fallen in recent decades from a million to 300,000, and where 50,000 homes were already unoccupied, leaving urban devastation, homelessness and a renewal of criminality (Lanchester, 2010).

In an influential macro analysis of the effects of neoliberal economic, urban and housing policy and cultural changes from the mid-1970s that punishes poverty in the black ghetto, Loic Wacquant (2008, 2009a, 2009b) has implicated these changes with an explosion of black criminality. For Wacquant (2008) the rapid growth of the informal and criminal subsistence economy is closely linked to a retrenchment and shortening of welfare coverage, joblessness, and stopgap criminal alternatives to low-waged, dead-end and insecure jobs. The criminal economy requires routine predatory crime and violence using the ghetto's few remaining residual assets of physical prowess and street knowledge that offer a modicum of financial security. Polarised labour markets and housing policies segregated and concentrated black poverty into 'hyper-ghettoes' structured according to a core of jobless and a periphery of the working poor. In these places, insecurity and precariousness have become permanent features of life, uncoupled from the fortunes of the wider economy. The ghetto has become a repository and relegation of a redundant black working class, many of whom may never work again. Ghetto members are doubly regulated through a cyclical contraction or shortening of welfare and the runaway expansion of the prison by means of workfare *and* 'prisonfare', policing *and* the market, two integral components of the neoliberal state in the modern era in Anglo-American societies (Wacquant, 2009a). As a consequence punishment has mushroomed as a way of governing racial division and poverty and the prison has become a 'surrogate ghetto': '*the penal system has partly supplanted and partly supplemented the ghetto* as a mechanism of racial control' (Wacquant, 2009b: 155–56). The appreciation of this 'new governance of social insecurity' requires criminological theory to relinquish its obsessive focus on crime to refocus attention on the new politics and policy of poverty, particularly its double regulation. In a functionalist twist, Wacquant (2008) argues that the material purpose of re-linking social welfare and penal policies is to force problem populations off welfare, lock them up when necessary, and eventually push them into the peripheral sectors of the secondary labour market. The symbolic purpose is to respond to, and channel, diffuse class anxiety and simmering ethnic resentment found across all but the most privileged groups in society, toward the street criminal and profligate welfare recipient.

Wacquant's (2002) scorn for urban ethnography's emphasis on the subjective resilience and fortitude of ghetto dwellers is evidenced in his claim that ethnography seems ignorant of the objective exploitation in degraded labour markets and the visceral and violent nature of ghetto life. In reply, ethnographers point to his overwrought and over-general portrayal of ghetto life that hides variation and nuance – of conflict and cooperation – in social and race relations. Wacquant finds differences between the ghettoes of different societies but not within ghettoes. His portrayal of hardened, embittered, unremitting and seemingly inevitable poverty and racism and their punishment seems too total, too general and too reliant on a functional view of neoliberal economic and urban policy. Wacquant knows his Marx but has forgotten his Weber in a portrayal of social life in the black ghetto reduced to the 'need' for a functional repository of surplus labour. Weber (1968: LXXXVII) linked status groups to ethnicity so that groups based on positive or negative social honour express this through cultural values, style of life and consumption, often against class interests which are rooted in the sphere of production and acquisition, not social life. Status involves relations of power, allegiance and competition within a social, not only an economic order. Members are obliged to maintain social order, uphold status and social honour. Ethnic honour is a specific honour of the status group entered through allegiance, conflict and cooperation within neighbourhoods. Kevin Stenson's (2012: 11) critical assessment of Wacquant's work argues against the tendency to reduce global, ubiquitous and shifting cultural constructions of racial identities to narrowly national ones simply of economics and social control, and suggests that just as dominant groups – ethnic or others – attempt to monopolise social honour and resources 'from above', so too do groups at neighbourhood level 'from below', which may sometimes reverse power relations through cultural processes and meanings.

Distinctive theories of ethnic offending and victimisation

The third perspective mentioned above most qualifies in claiming to be a distinctive theory of race, ethnicity and crime. According to this perspective an enduring legacy of historical injustices and racial domination continues to influence and alienate black people today. Linked to the 'colonial model' and 'critical race theory' this perspective remains undeveloped in criminological theory (Gabbidon, 2010; Ross, 2010). Emphasising the 'unique' experiences and legacies of black and previously colonised groups, it postulates that the 'psychological damage' done by these memories is carried across generations and can be renewed as immigrants and their children meet the hostility of their host country. While first-generation immigrants are law-abiding, have low expectations for themselves and accept their lowly positions, their children do not. Their children develop higher expectations of assimilation that are thwarted, disappointed and unfulfilled as they meet discrimination, experience reduced self-esteem and alienation, and social isolation reduces self-control, thus shaping disproportionate criminality (Tonry, 1997). Smith (2005) argues that in the case of the second generation, the divergence to greater criminality among African Caribbean groups in the UK compared to Asian groups cannot be explained by disadvantage as this equally affects black and Asian groups. For British African Caribbeans, the legacy of slavery and inferiority and unfulfilled cultural expectations of British life disrupted family formation and led to sometimes violent rebellion against authority, and general lawlessness, just as it had done in the US. The nature of these psychological effects caused by the negative experiences of colonisation and inferiority are captured by Fanon (1986, 2001), showing how these feelings were strongly associated with aggressive syndromes because of racist stereotyping and criminalising by the colonisers. This dynamic of inferiority – its internalisation in the 'the black man's' emulation of 'the white man' – might in part be overcome through a sort of cathartic violence, which would only feed the colonisers racist stereotypes.

Drawing on some of these arguments, Unnever and Gabbidon's (2011) distinct theory of African American offending provides a model of how criminological theory might develop and extend towards a general understanding of ethnicity and crime. The theory's distinctiveness is predicated on the exceptional or 'unique' nature of the experiences and worldview of African Americans. Born of a long history of 'public dishonour and ritualised humiliation', a worldview deeply socialised within families and neighbourhoods, this worldview offers resilience, a means to to fend off the negative effects of racial injustice, while these effects can also induce feelings of disrespect, loss of prestige and status. In some instances they lead to oscillating feelings of hopelessness, depression, shame, anger, aggression and defiance, and offending. This is particularly likely when the law is distrusted and lacks legitimacy, and is perceived to apply unequally. Distancing themselves from the shame of being treated unfairly by whites, African Americans' externalised feelings are sometimes displaced onto more vulnerable, more available people within their own community. That only a minority of blacks engage in crime is explained by variations in experiences of racial injustice and racial socialisation. For some, discrimination increases the probability of offending according to *the degree* to which discrimination is experienced. If internalisation of negative depictions and racist stereotypes debilitates and depletes esteem and status, then the role of friends, peer networks, and especially family members and parents is also important in attenuating the negative effects of discrimination, encouraging resilience and promoting egalitarian values rather than mistrust of white-dominated institutions. It is difficult, however, to see how legacies of slavery and colonialism might inform black young people's responses to marginalisation in modern urban societies, as many are unlikely to be aware of or know about such depredations. The theory would need to account for the well documented periodic cohesion found in black family and neighbourhood life, disrupted by changed fortunes in the here and now rather than the possession of a cursory awareness and knowledge of the past, preoccupied with survival in the here and now rather than inherited legacies or worldviews. Having much to commend it, notably the notion of socially supported resilience and degree of exposure to discrimination, Unnever and Gabbidon's (2011) criminological theory of the distinctiveness of African *American* offending, despite drawing on a wide range of criminological theories, remains limited to a particular experience and it would be mistaken to apply it elsewhere.

As we have already seen in the discussion of British gang research, we should be extremely sceptical of transferring theories from an American context to a British one. Britain does not possess ethnically based ghettoes in any meaningful sense. Spatial segregation is based on housing tenure in general and rental tenure in particular as well as other proxies for social class and status, rather than race (Dorling, 2010; Finney and Simpson, 2009; Keith, 2005; MacDonald *et al.*, 2005; Webster, 2008). Similarities with the US are found in underlying status anxiety about being too close, socially and spatially, to concentrated poverty and desires to maintain 'respectability' (Watt, 2006: 788). Solidities and solidarities of ethnic identity are looser, more transient and temporary, and shared friendships and aspirations occur across ethnicity (Gunter, 2010; Gunter and Watt, 2009). As one study showed, black young people's responses to permanent school exclusion were to draw on family, community and friendship networks in forging alternative notions of success to overcome and transform earlier school 'failure', to return to further education and build resilience and aspiration (Wright *et al.*, 2010). There remain however, classed trajectories produced economically, as well as culturally, and social networks and local reputations that combine at the level of neighbourhood to create 'cultures of violence' and 'street capital' as a backdrop to alternative 'personal social mobility' and status (Henderson *et al.*, 2007; Sandberg and Pedersen, 2009).

Conclusion

We have seen how racism is linked to economics (especially labour markets and housing), and therefore inextricably to class, and that race *and* class are mutually compounding, not exclusive, sources of discrimination. This complex, compounding interrelationship is revealed in close-up studies of urban multi-ethnic life, but the meaning of race is fluid and it has many determinants. Garner (2010) is surely right in arguing that racialisation – the cultural making of racial subjects – is linked to post-colonial nomenclatures and is closely bound up with labour markets: in particular with both internal and international migration of workers and the ensuing imbalance of the power relations characterising modern capitalism. As Rattansi (2005: 296) argues, the interpretations and contexts that can be afforded to 'race' suggest that 'a dismantling of racism also requires, simultaneously as well as in the long run, a strategy to reduce relevant class inequalities, forms of masculinity, nationalisms and other social features, whereby racisms are reproduced in particular sites'. Racism cannot be understood in a model where only 'race' matters in the construction of identities. Class or gender are unlikely either, to take causal pre-eminence and, like race, are likely to combine across different places and time. The problem is the dominance of frameworks that reject class as a useful point of focus in criminological theory, in part it would seem, because it is rare that individuals embrace class identity unequivocally, at least subjectively and therefore meaningfully. Class analysis should, where appropriate, balance status analysis, particularly in respect of ethnicity, with more amorphous cultural and consumption values and identities. There has, nevertheless, been confusion or conflation of class, ethnicity and status, seen in contemporary popular culture's value judgements about cultural and consumption tastes.

Segregation on grounds of race or ethnicity rather than class in Britain hardly exists in any significant way, unlike the US, where it does at all levels of the African American class structure, and the ghetto really does exist for the black working poor. That does not mean that race is absent from British society, on the contrary. Through notions of 'ethnic monitoring', 'citizenship' and 'social cohesion' black and minority ethnic people have been the subjects of intense state scrutiny, intervention and governance, while this is claimed not to be racialised. Patel and Tyrer (2011) correctly identify the almost wholly empiricist terms of the race and crime debate, and how this obscures analytical and theoretical questions about power, particularly how racial boundaries are reproduced. As Wacquant argues, there has been a conflation and complementing of the functions of prison and ghetto culture, punishment and welfare, in the US in particular. Goldberg's (2009) prescient delineation of 'racial neoliberalism' warns that racism and its causes have become diluted, obfuscated, opaque, amorphous and therefore made invisible, predicated on racial denial and cosmetic masking. This warning should be taken seriously. At the same time, in neoliberal societies obfuscation of 'race' and racism partly reflects social polarisation within ethnic groups, 'normalising' or making the minority structure more like the majority white class structure. Claims about the demise of the category race and public racism in the contemporary period, first featured amid optimism that racial exclusion would decline alongside state welfare, are today more likely to be made on grounds of the incompatibility of significant racism with neoliberal capitalism. An increasing stress on individualised merit and ability and the growth of 'colour-blind' free markets where only these qualities are rewarded means that racism is seen at most as personal preference and racial expression is made private, mostly beyond state delimitation. But neither is the state any longer committed to ameliorating structural inequalities while still concerned above all with issues of crime, security and immigration. The shift from charges of institutional or systemic racism to personalising and individualising racism is mirrored in attitudes to poverty and inequality in a relinquishing of responsibility for what have become the undeserving poor as a group without individual merit.

Note

1 Citing Bullock and Tilley's (2002) study, Pitts (2011) states that between April 2001 and March 2002, South Manchester gangs were responsible for 11 fatal shootings, 84 serious woundings and 639 other incidents of violence involving firearms, and that many victims and perpetrators were in their early teens.

References

Anderson, E. (1999) *Code of the Street: Decency, Violence, and Moral Life of the Inner City*, New York: W. W. Norton.

Barry, B. (2005) *Why Social Justice Matters*, Cambridge: Polity.

Bhui, H. S. (2009) *Race and Criminal Justice*, London: Sage.

Bourgois, P. (1995) *In Search of Respect: Selling Crack in El Barrio*, Cambridge: Cambridge University Press.

Bowling, B. and Phillips, C. (2007) 'Disproportionate and Discriminatory: Reviewing the Evidence on Police Stop and Search', *Modern Law Review*, 70(6): 936–61.

Bullock, K. and Tilley, N. (2002) *Shooting, Gangs and Violent Incidents in Manchester: Developing a Crime Reduction Strategy*, London: Home Office.

Clancy, N., Hough, M., Aust, R. and Kershaw, C. (2001) *Crime, Policing and Justice: the Experience of Ethnic Minorities. Findings from the 2000 British Crime Survey*, Home Office Research Study 223, London: Home Office.

Dorling, D. (2005) 'Murder in Britain', *Prison Service Journal*, no. 166.

—— (2008) 'Commentary', *Environment and Planning A*, vol. 40: 255–57.

—— (2010) *Injustice: Why Social Inequality Persists*, Bristol: The Policy Press.

Drake, St. C. and Cayton, H. R. (1993 [1945]) *Black Metropolis: A Study of Negro Life in a Northern City*, Chicago: University of Chicago Press.

Duneier, M. (1992) *Slim's Table: Race, Respectability and Masculinity*, Chicago: University of Chicago Press.

—— (1999) *Sidewalk*, New York: Farrar, Straus and Giroux.

Eagleton, T. (2011) *Why Marx Was Right*, London: Yale University Press.

Fanon, F. (1965) *Concerning Violence*, Harmondsworth: Penguin.

—— (1986) *Black Skin, White Masks*, London: Pluto Press.

—— (2001) *The Wretched of the Earth*, London: Penguin Books.

Feilzer, M. and Hood, R. (2004) *Difference or Discrimination? Minority Ethnic People in the Youth Justice System*, London: Youth Justice Board.

Finney, N. and Simpson, L. (2009) *'Sleepwalking to Segregation'? Challenging Myths about Race and Migration*, Bristol: The Policy Press.

FitzGerald, M. (2009) '"Race", Ethnicity and Crime', in Hale, C., Hayward, K., Wahidin, A. and Wincup, E. (eds) *Criminology*, 2nd edn, Oxford: Oxford University Press.

FitzGerald, M., Stockdale, J. and Hale, C. (2003) *Young People and Street Crime*, London: Youth Justice Board.

Frank, R. H. (2007) *Falling Behind: How Rising Inequality Harms the Middle Class*, London: University of California Press.

Frazier, F. E. (2001) *The Negro Family in the United States*, Notre Dame, IN: University of Notre Dame Press.

Gabbidon, S. L. (2007) *Criminological Perspectives on Race and Crime*, London: Routledge.

—— (2010) *Race, Ethnicity, Crime and Justice: An International Dilemma*, London: Sage.

Gabbidon, S. L. and Green, H.T. (2005) *Race, Crime and Justice*, London: Routledge.

Garner, S. (2010) *Racisms: An Introduction*, London: Sage.

Goldberg, D. T. (2009) *The Threat of Race: Reflections on Racial Neoliberalism*, Oxford: Blackwell.

Goldson, B. (ed.) (2011) *Youth in Crisis? 'Gangs', Territoriality and Violence*, London: Routledge.

Gunter, A. (2010) *Growing Up Bad: Black Youth, Road Culture and Badness in an East London Neighbourhood*, London: Tufnell Press.

Gunter, A. and Watt, P. (2009) 'Grafting, Going to College and Working on the Road: Youth Transitions and Cultures in an East London Neighbourhood', *Journal of Youth Studies*, 12(5): 515–29.

Hall, S., Winlow, S. and Ancrum, C. (2008) *Criminal Identities and Consumer Culture: Crime, Exclusion and the New Culture of Narcissism*, Cullompton: Willan.

Hallsworth, S. (2005) *Street Crime*, Cullompton: Willan.

Hartigan, J. (1999) *Racial Situations: Class Predicaments of Whiteness in Detroit*, Princeton, NJ: Princeton University Press.

Harvey, D. (2005) *A Brief History of Neoliberalism*, Oxford: Oxford University Press.

Henderson, S., Holland, J., McGrellis, S., Sharpe, S. and Thomson, R. (2007) *Inventing Adulthoods: A Biographical Approach to Youth Transitions*, London: Sage.

Hood, R. (1992) *Race and Sentencing*, Oxford: Clarendon Press.

Irvin, G. (2008) *Super Rich: The Rise of Inequality in Britain and the United States*, Cambridge: Polity Press.

Jackson, J. L. (2001) *Harlem World: Doing Race and Class in Contemporary Black America*, Chicago: University of Chicago Press.

Jefferson, T., Walker, M. and Seneviratne, M. (1992) 'Ethnic Minorities, Crime and Criminal Justice: A Study in a Provincial City', in Spalek, B. (ed.) (2008) *Ethnicity and Crime: A Reader*, Maidenhead: Open University Press.

Kefalas, M. (2003) *Working-Class Heroes: Protecting Home, Community, and Nation in a Chicago Neighborhood*, Berkeley: University of California Press.

Keith, M. (2005) *After the Cosmopolitan: Multicultural Cities and the Future of Racism*, London: Routledge.

Lanchester, J. (2010) *Whoops! Why Everyone Owes Everyone and No One Can Pay*, London: Allen Lane.

Liebow, E. (1967) *Tally's Corner: A Study of Negro Street Corner Men*, Boston: Little, Brown.

Linkon, S. L and Russo, J. (2002) *Steeltown U.S.A.: Work and Memory in Youngstown*, Lawrence, KS: University Press of Kansas.

MacDonald, R., Shildrick, T., Webster, C. and Simpson, D. (2005) 'Growing up in Poor

Neighbourhoods: The Significance of Class and Place in the Extended Transitions of "Socially Excluded" Young Adults', *Sociology*, 39(5): 873–91.

Massey, D. S. and Denton, N. A. (1993) *American Apartheid: Segregation and the Making of the Underclass*, Cambridge, MA: Harvard University Press.

McAra, L. and McVie, S. (2005) 'The Usual Suspects? Street-life, Young People and the Police', *Criminal Justice*, 5(1): 5–36.

Miles, R. and Brown, M. (2003) *Racism* 2nd Edition, London: Routledge.

Miller, J. (2010) 'Stop and Search in England: A Reformed Tactic or Business as Usual?' *British Journal of Criminology*, 50: 954–74.

Ministry of Justice (2010) *Statistics on Race and the Criminal Justice System 2008/09*, London: Ministry of Justice.

Moskos, P. (2008) *Cop in The Hood: My Year Policing Baltimore's Eastern District*, revised ed, Princeton, NJ: Princeton University Press.

MVA and Miller, J. (2000) *Profiling Populations Available for Stops and Searches*, Police Research Series Paper 131, London: Home Office.

Newburn, T. and Reiner, R. (2007) 'Policing and the Police', in Maguire, M., Morgan., R. and Reiner, R. (eds) *The Oxford Handbook of Criminology*, 4th edn, Oxford: Oxford University Press.

Nightingale, C. (1993) *On the Edge*, New York: Basic Books.

Parker, K. F. (2008) *Unequal Crime Decline: Theorizing Race, Urban Inequality, and Criminal Violence*, London: New York University Press.

Patel, T. G. and Tyrer, D. (2011) *Race, Crime and Resistance*, London: Sage.

Patterson, O. (1997) *The Ordeal of Integration: Progress and Resentment in America's 'Racial' Crisis*, Washington, DC: Civitas/Counterpoint.

Phillips, C. and Bowling, B. (2007) 'Ethnicities, Racism, Crime and Criminal Justice', in Maguire, M., Morgan., R. and Reiner, R. (eds) *The Oxford Handbook of Criminology*, 4th edn, Oxford: Oxford University Press.

Pitts, J. (2011) 'Mercenary Territory: Are Youth Gangs Really a Problem?' in Goldson, B. (ed.) (2011) *Youth in Crisis? 'Gangs', Territoriality and Violence*, London: Routledge.

Rattansi, A. (2005) 'The Uses of Racialisation: The Time-Spaces and Subject-Objects of the Raced Body', in Murji, K. and Solomos, J. (eds) *Racialisation: Studies in Theory and Practice*, Oxford: Oxford University Press.

Ross, L. E. (2010) 'A Vision of Race, Crime, and Justice Through the Lens of Critical Race Theory', in McLaughlin, E. and Newburn, T. (eds) *The Sage Handbook of Criminological Theory*, London: Sage.

Sandberg, S. and Pedersen, W. (2009) *Street Capital: Black Cannabis Dealers in a White Welfare State*, Bristol: The Policy Press.

Shiner, M. (2010) 'Post-Lawrence Policing in England and Wales: Guilt, Innocence and the Defence of Organizational Ego', *British Journal of Criminology*, 50: 954–74.

Simon, D. and Burns, E. (1997) *The Corner: A Year in the Life of an Inner-city Neighbourhood*, London: Canongate.

Smith, D. J. (2005) 'Ethnic Differences in Intergenerational Crime Patterns', in Tonry, M. (ed.) *Crime and Justice: A Review of Research*, vol. 32, Chicago: University of Chicago Press.

Smith, J. (2003) *The Nature of Personal Robbery*, Home Office Research Study 254, London: Home Office.

Smith, K., Coleman, K., Eder, S. and Hall, P. (2011) *Homicides, Firearm Offences and Intimate Violence 2009/10*, London: Home Office.

Stenson, K. (2012) 'The State, Sovereignty and Advanced Marginality in the City', in

Squires, P. and Lea, J. (eds) *Criminalisation and Advanced Marginality: Critically Exploring the Work of Loïc Wacquant*, Bristol: The Policy Press.

Sugrue, T. J. (2005) *The Origins of the Urban Crisis: Race and Inequality in Postwar Detroit*, Classic Edition, Princeton, NJ: Princeton University Press.

Suttles, G. (1968) *The Social Order of the Slum: Ethnicity and Territory in the Inner City*, Chicago: University of Chicago Press.

—— (1972) *The Social Construction of Communities*, Chicago: University of Chicago Press.

Tonry, M. (ed.) (1997) *Ethnicity, Crime and Immigration: Comparative and Cross-National Perspectives*, Chicago: University of Chicago Press.

Toynbee, P. and Walker, D. (2010) *The Verdict: Did Labour Change Britain?* London: Granta Books.

Unnever, J. D. and Gabbidon, S. L. (2011) *A Theory of African American Offending: Race, Racism, and Crime*, London: Routledge.

Venkatesh, S. (2000) *American Project: The Rise and Fall of a Modern American Ghetto*, London: Harvard University Press.

—— (2006) *Off the Books: The Underground Economy of the Urban Poor*, London: Harvard University Press.

Vulliamy, E. (2010) *Amexica: War Along The Borderline*, London: The Bodley Head.

Wacquant, L. (2002) 'Scrutinizing the Street: Poverty, Morality, and the Pitfalls of Urban Ethnography', *American Journal of Sociology*, 107(6): 1468–1532.

—— (2008) *Urban Outcasts: A Comparative Sociology of Advanced Marginality*, Cambridge: Polity.

—— (2009a) *Prisons of Poverty*, London: University of Minnesota Press.

—— (2009b) *Punishing the Poor: The Neoliberal Government of Social Insecurity*, London: Duke University Press.

Walker, M. (1988) 'The Court Disposal of Young Males by Race, in London in 1983', *British Journal of Criminology*, 28: 442–60.

Watt, P. (2006) 'Respectability, Roughness and "Race": Neighbourhood Place Images and the Making of Working-class Social Distinctions in London', *International Journal of Urban and Regional Research*, 30(4): 776–97.

Weber, M. (1968) *Economy and Society*, vol. 1, London: University of California Press.

Webster, C. (2007) *Understanding Race and Crime*, Maidenhead: Open University Press.

—— (2008) 'Marginalised White Ethnicity, Race and Crime', *Theoretical Criminology*, 12(3): 293–312.

Wright, C., Standen, P. and Patel, T. (2010) *Black Youth Matters: Transitions from School to Success*, London: Routledge.

Young, J. (1999) *The Exclusive Society: Social Exclusion, Crime and Difference in Late Modernity*, London: Sage.

—— (2002) 'Crossing the Borderline: Globalisation and Social Exclusion: The Sociology of Vindictiveness and the Criminology of Transgression', accessed 25/02/2005. www.malcolmread.co.uk/JockYoung/crossing.htm

8 Using cultural geography to think differently about space and crime

Keith J. Hayward

Introduction

The story of criminology's fascination with space is a long and Byzantine one, encompassing everything from the early nineteenth-century *cartes thématiques* of Adolphe de Quételet, to the very latest developments in global information systems and computer-aided crime mapping. However, as the history of criminology is told, when it comes to criminology's relationship with ('criminogenic') space, one moment stands out above all others. Such is the influence of the work of the Chicago School of sociology that few criminological scholars working today will not be familiar, at least to some extent, with the School's various theoretical and empirical analyses of the link between crime and 'the environment'. The specific details of the Chicago School approach have been well rehearsed elsewhere and thus need no further exposition here. Instead, I start this essay with recourse to the Chicago School by way of a provocation. My opening position here is that, for all its numerous theoretical insights and undeniable disciplinary impact, the Chicago School's legacy within criminology is not without its problems. Specifically, the School's interpretation and utilization of 'space' set the geography of crime down a very particular and in my opinion rather narrow conceptual path, from which it has rarely deviated. This chapter is an attempt to plot some possible alternative routes; the ultimate goal being to challenge contemporary criminologists to think differently about the role and the nature of space within our discipline.

1925: a tale of two essays

Things were buzzing on Chicago's Midway in 1925. Not only was the University of Chicago home to the world's pre-eminent sociology department, but it was also the year that Robert Park, Ernest Burgess and their student Roderick McKenzie published the seminal collection *The City* (1925). The concept of ecology had been doing the rounds of American sociology since the 1880s (see Small and Vincent 1894), but it was this volume, and one essay in particular, Burgess' 'The Growth of the City' (1925), that solidified Chicago-style (urban) sociology by linking the notion of human ecology and competition for space to what Kimball

Young described as Robert Park's 'zone thing' (Lindstrom and Hardert 1988: 270). Burgess' famous five-ring map of the city stands as perhaps the ultimate paradigmatic expression of the city in modernity. Certainly within criminology, it triggered a longstanding fascination with ecological grids, areal models and other subsequent diagrammatic efforts to further establish causal links between the environment and deviance/social action (the most famous, of course, being the abstracted plotting of juvenile delinquency court statistics onto Burgess' concentric circle model by Chicagoans Clifford Shaw and Henry McKay).

Park and Burgess may have been on the same page theoretically but by all accounts when it came to their respective personalities they were chalk and cheese. As is well-documented, Park was a former hard-bitten newspaper man, and as such was known for his plain speaking, charismatic teaching style, and an easy manner that enabled him to mix well in social groups of all types. Already independently wealthy, he married into serious money and thus had the means to travel extensively and indulge his interests. Burgess on the other hand was 'an affection-starved soul' (Bogue 1974), who 'looked like a preacher' (Lindstrom and Hardert 1988: 284), never married, and as the years went by became increasingly introverted. Of the two, it was Burgess who was the criminologist. Both were unapologetic urbanists. The social effects of rapid industrialization and urban population expansion were central to how they understood urban space and theorized the link between crime and the environment. Accordingly, their work encapsulated the dynamism and air of progress that was such a feature of Chicago's brief but frenetic history. This story, of course, is well known within criminology – to a greater or lesser degree it features in every criminology textbook ever written. However, at this point we deviate from the standard account of 'Chicago-style sociology'. As the subheading suggests, this is a tale of *two* essays, and elsewhere another story was unfolding – albeit one entirely unfamiliar to the vast majority of criminologists.

A long way from the tenement houses and Louis Sullivan-designed sky-scrapers of Chicago, a very different America was under observation. In the dusty canyons of northwest Mexico and on the fecund glades of Missouri's Ozark Highlands, a University of Chicago-trained geographer named Carl O. Sauer was undertaking fieldwork that would later become the foundation stone of American cultural geography. The contrast between Sauer and Park could not be starker. While photographs of Park depict him as the classic Chicago academic, all steel-rimmed glasses and Brooks Brothers suits, Sauer was the quintessential field geographer. The photo on the inside of *Land and Life*, the definitive collection of his most important works, is typical. Covered in dust, dressed in khakis, sporting knee-length leather gaiters, and with tobacco pipe clenched resolutely between his teeth, Sauer was no dapper urbanist. His laboratory was 'the landscape' and his passion was the mores and norms of indigenous people. Given that criminology, with very few exceptions, has steadfastly ignored matters rural perhaps it's no surprise, then, that Sauer is entirely absent from the criminological canon. Yet, there is much of value for criminologists in Sauer's work and its legacy, and where better to start than with his classic article published in the very same year as Burgess' 'The Growth of the City'.

It would be both unfair and incorrect to suggest that Park and the early figures of the Chicago School were crude environmental determinists in the tradition of Friedrich Ratzer and Ellen Churchill Semple. Indeed, in many ways their theory of human ecology was an attempt to go beyond simple neo-Lamarckism. Yet, it is hard to deny the extent to which they ascribed *causal influence to the environment*, as R. D. McKenzie makes clear when he defined social ecology as: 'the study of the spatial and temporal relations of human beings affected by the selective, distributive and accommodative forces of the environment' (1924: 288). Likewise Park was happy for Chicago's diverse social and cultural features to be understood not as something of woman's making, but rather as the product of a geographic 'super organism'. Sauer's position was very different. His was an attempt to eschew what he described as 'causal geography'; his simple starting premise being that man shaped the environment, not vice versa. In this sense his work is an explicit rejection of what he saw as the fundamental errors of geographic environmental determinism. For Sauer the qualities and activities of man are not 'products' of a 'narrowly rationalistic thesis [that] conceives environment as process' (1925 [1963]: 349), rather:

> [W]hat man does in an area because of tabu or totemism or because of his own will involves use of environment rather than the active agency of the environment. It would, therefore, appear that environmentalism has been shooting neither at cause nor effect, but rather that it is bagging its own decoys.
>
> (Ibid.)

Sauer's understanding of space differed sharply, then, from the one proposed by the Chicago School; it was a notion that attempted to appreciate and comprehend how individuals and groups lived in place and in turn shaped *it*, not the other way round. Indeed, although his principal target was ethnocentric environmental determinism with its 'rigorous dogma of materialistic cosmology', Sauer opened out his critique at various points to cover concepts that at the time were the stock-in-trade of Park and his adherents. Citing Park *et al.*'s *The City* in a footnote, Sauer states that 'Sociologists have been swarming all over the precincts of human ecology' (ibid.: 353); a concept that earlier in his essay he dismissed in the following passage (that also hints at his general dislike of quantitative analysis):

> It is better not to force into geography too much biological nomenclature. The name ecology is not needed . . . Since we waive the claim for the measurement of environmental influences, we may use, in preference to ecology, the term morphology to apply to cultural study, since it describes perfectly the method.
>
> (Ibid.: 342)

The method to which Sauer refers is a critical system of material/spatial phenomenology known as 'the morphology of the cultural landscape'. Central to this method is an understanding of culture. Hence Sauer's famous statement that: 'The cultural landscape is fashioned from a natural landscape by a culture group. Culture is the agent, the natural area is the medium, the cultural landscape the result' (ibid.: 343). With such statements, groundbreaking for the time, Carl O. Sauer laid the foundations for cultural geography. A focus on 'cultural areas', cultural particularism and human geographic activity, the importance of reading spaces in terms of their history and chorology, anti-ethnocentrism, and an underlying interest in cultural anthropology, are all central concerns of Sauer's long and distinguished career, and all axiomatic concepts within the field of cultural geography.

Two different essays, two very different stories. Each highly influential in their own way, for as we will now see, each set the tone for their respective discipline's approach to the study of space.

Space in criminology and cultural geography: a short historical review/comparison

Promoted as an introductory guide to the 'new and innovative' science of crime mapping and aimed largely at 'crime analysts and other practitioners interested in visualizing crime data through the medium of maps', the US National Institute of Justice publication *Mapping Crime: Principle and Practice* (Harries 1999) reveals the full extent of criminology's current fascination with 'scientific' method. Perhaps the most explicit criminological example to date of ecological and environmental abstraction, *Mapping Crime* offers us a somewhat disconcerting glimpse of a future that has already arrived: a world of 'global satellite orientation', 'scatter diagrams', 'crime moments', 'stick streets', and 'choropleth maps'. Abstraction, of course, is fully acknowledged. Harries even poses the question 'how much abstraction can we tolerate?' The logic of his answer is enlightening. While initially he accepts that 'more abstraction equals less information', he sidesteps the problem by claiming later that one can view this trade-off another way: 'More abstraction equals greater simplicity and legibility (more effective visual communication). [While] Less abstraction equals greater complexity, less legibility (less effective visual communication)' (ibid.: 10). So goes the thinking behind the very latest development in spatial criminology. It is a logic that too often pervades the geography of crime.

Conceptually, of course, there is little new here. Consider, the late fifteenth-century painting, *Ideal City (with Circular Temple)*, by the circle of Pierro della Francesca. At one level, this celebrated work of art can be read as a simple Renaissance civic vista, all classical columns and architectural detail. However, at another level, the picture tells a very different story about the relationship between technological development and urban space. If today we are witnessing remarkable transformations in the technical representation of space via the combination of computer-aided map making and ortho-rectified imagery (both from satellite and aerial sources), a similar revolution was underway during Pierro della Francesca's time. Not only had Brunelleschi invented and introduced the use of geometric linear perspective in painting, but also the development of the 'iconographic plan' had greatly enhanced the architect's power of representation. These developments, along with the increasing accuracy and sophistication of Renaissance drawing and surveying instrumentation, contributed to the pronounced distancing of architect from his subject. This 'distance' is exemplified by Francesca's *Ideal City (with Circular Temple)*, a painting not only bereft of all people, but of any sense of the muddiness and complexity of urban life. This form of representation is interesting for two reasons. First, because of the way these new commissions, designed to absolute standards, overtly reflected the dominant economic and political order of idealized Renaissance society. Second, as Ruth Eaton states, they highlight 'the progressive objectification of the city and the detached and intellectual approach adopted by the planner' (2001: 41):

> The fact that the buildings themselves have become the main actors in these scenes bears testimony to the fact that the city is considered in an increasingly objective manner. Above all, space – no longer just an environment to which the individual is subjugated – has become rationalised, the human mind has expressed its superiority over natural circumstances, and matters of consequence have become irrelevant.
>
> (Ibid.: 50)

My point here, of course, is that, whether it's fifteenth-century developments in technocratic representation, or the newest modes of 'visual communication' associated with contemporary crime mapping, fascination with technology has frequently triumphed over other more humanistic approaches. This is certainly true when it comes to criminology's longstanding relationship with space. The result, as I have stated elsewhere (Hayward 2004), is a 'flight from reality' whereby criminology too often distills human lived experience and the inherently pluralistic fabric of life to leave only the discourse of demographics, statistics and multi-factorialism. To illustrate this point more fully, let us return to the Chicago School.

Contrary to most mainstream criminological accounts, the Chicago School of sociology did not start with Park, Burgess and a map of concentric circles – far from it. Originally the University of Chicago was most noted for its association with American pragmatism and the works of Dewey, Mead and Tufts. On occasion the influence of these 'first generation' Chicagoans on the subsequent work of the School is acknowledged (see Sumner 1994, for a rare example). However, what is almost never acknowledged is the extent to which these pragmatists influenced groundbreaking spatial analyses of Chicago that predated the work of Park and his followers by several decades. The social reformer and pioneering feminist sociologist Jane Addams had close working relationships with most of the leading Chicago pragmatists, and as such was committed to social progress through the 'liberation' of education and other forms of radical emancipatory practice. Addams' 'critical pragmatism' led her to found the Hull-House settlement and ultimately to publish *Hull-House Maps and Papers* (1895), a collection of essays and micro street maps (compiled by residents) detailing the slum spaces of Chicago east of Hull-House. Addams' work was so far ahead of its time, it's hard to do it justice (see commentary on Addams – and W. E. B. DuBois – in Sibley 1985). Not only was she a progressive social reformer and political activist, but she also fused critical pragmatism with what Mary Jo Deegan (1988: ch. 9) has called 'cultural feminism'; the belief (70 years ahead of second generation feminists) that a world organized around feminine values would be more pro-ductive, peaceful and just. Given that Addams' body of work often contained a strong spatial component, including the mapping of social and demographic characteristics of populations within a geographic area, why do Addams and Hull-House feature so rarely in the criminological canon? Again, the answer lies in criminology's fascination with technology, in this case the scientism associated with the statistical methods of demography and human ecology as applied to the 'city as a social laboratory' (Park 1925a).

As Deegan makes clear in her fascinating book *Jane Addams and the Men of the Chicago School*, for all their undeniable achievements Park, Burgess and the other key figures of the Chicago School have a stain on their collective reputation in the form of their systematic marginalization of the work of Addams and her fellow Hull-House sociologists. This marginalization took a number of forms. Desperate to create a respectable area of specialized expertise, Park and Burgess did all they could to legitimize the 'new field' of sociology. Thus, the 'Settlement' was soon rejected in favour of the 'laboratory of the city', where, as Park stated in 1919, 'civilization and social progress have assumed ... something of the character of a *controlled experiment*' (Park quoted in Deegan 1988: 34, emphasis added). This type of thinking was anathema to the Hull-House sociologists, whose humanism meant they flatly rejected such scientism, as Addams makes clear in the following passage:

> I have always objected to the phrase 'sociological laboratory' applied to us, because Settlements should be something much more human and spontaneous than such a phrase connotes, and yet it is inevitable that the residents should know their own neighborhoods more than any other, and that their experience should affect their convictions.
>
> (Addams 1910, cited in Deegan 1988: 35)

Addams, it would seem, was not only the progenitor of cultural feminism, she was also cultural criminologist *avant la lettre*!

The tension over scientific method that existed between the University of Chicago sociologists and the Hull-House researchers should not be underestimated; not least because it masked other reasons for the ostracism of Jane Addams – not just by the Chicago School, but by succeeding generations of American soci-ologists. There is no doubt that both Park and Burgess were greatly influenced by Addams and *Hull-House Maps and Papers* – Burgess especially. Prior to his faculty post at Chicago, he had stayed at Hull-House, cited its work in congratulatory tones, and was himself something of a would-be social reformer, a position he would later overtly distance himself from.[1] However, as time wore on Park's influence took hold and Burgess began to downplay Hull-House, dismissing it as 'social work' aimed at 'reporting' to the public 'the feelings and sentiments of those living in the ethnic slums' (Burgess quoted in Deegan 1988: 63). At the same time, in a bid to promote the 'scientific and objective' approach of University of Chicago sociology, Burgess rushed to take credit for the first official juvenile delinquency maps, even though Hull-House researchers had produced these maps much earlier. Park's role in the marginalization of Addams was even more pronounced. Despite a personal history of advocacy and critical muckraking, it is fair to say that, when it came to empirical sociology, Park was keen to adopt a much safer, 'value free' position, as Deegan makes clear: 'Park profoundly embodied the conflicts of the new sociology. He legitimized a conservative political role for sociologists and left a legacy for future sociologists who worked to maintain the status quo while mildly condemning it' (ibid.: 158). In short, radical politics and substantive social change were not on the agenda for 1920s University of Chicago sociologists.[2] Consequently, Addams was ostracized and her 'status as a sociologist diminished drastically' (ibid.: 144). Add to this the fact that Addams and her female Hull-House sociologists were further undermined by the anti-feminism that was symptomatic of 1920s Chicago sociology (Deegan 1988) and it is clear that, just as Francesca's *Ideal City* was emblematic of Renaissance power, Burgess' concentric circle map was equally an expression of the dominant ideological and political order of idealized early twentieth-century American capitalist society (see Smith 1988).

But what of that other aspect of Chicago School sociology: their ethnographic focus on the 'the private world of the deviant', and the mundane and innovative social processes that constituted the urban way of life? Despite the School's groundbreaking role in systematizing new research methods like participant-observation and the life history, the 'appreciative' legacy of the school (see Matza 1969), as oriented to the urban environment, increasingly fell victim to outside policy influence and rational abstraction (see relatedly, Platt 1994); processes that in turn placed a strong emphasis on various forms of 'correctionalism'. Matza makes this point clear in his comments on Nels Anderson's seminal naturalist ('appreciative') study, *The Hobo*:

> Anderson's study, like most emanating from the Chicago school, was supported and partly financed by municipal agencies and commissions that were interested in ameliorating the grievous conditions associated with vice, alcohol, wandering, vagrancy and begging. Thus, the mixture of naturalist and correctional sentiments was institutionally based as well as existing as an intellectual tension in the work of the Chicago school.
>
> (Matza 1969: 26)

Thus the street is co-opted 'from above' in the sense of city planners and governmental and civic agencies inviting in the perspective of the rational policy-oriented ideal – a road that led ultimately to the creation of disciplinary variants such as environmental and administrative criminology.³ The advantage of this approach, of course, is that it produces *readily quantifiable results*, typically in the form of computer-processed police statistics or surveys. These statistics in turn contribute to a wider framework of government networks based around an actuarial and calculative approach to the control and ('risk') management of social problems. Under such a system, urban space – like the school, the courtroom, and the prison – becomes a focus solely of statistical analysis, at once a place of audit and a testing ground for new initiatives and policy implementation. In other words, the identification of 'criminogenic spaces' simply:

> constitutes a new site of intervention for government practices, a new practicable object, quite distinct from the individual offenders and legal subjects that previously formed the targets for crime control. Moreover, the criminogenic situation is like 'the economy' or 'the population' in being a domain with its own internal dynamics and processes.
>
> (Garland 1997: 187)

Such an approach represents nothing less than the deformation of public space, the *hollowing out* of the urban environment. Complex urban social dynamics are not easily integrated into the type of managerialistic, postcode-specific framework that underpins the new space of crime intervention/prevention/mapping (see Burrows 2008; Burrows and Gane 2006), and as a result, the various micro processes and cultural *particularities* that manifest themselves at street level are stripped of their inherent specificity, meaning, and serendipity.

What can criminology do, then, to overcome this rigid, formalized geography of crime? In my opinion, one answer can be found in the cultural geographic tradition originated by Carl Sauer and subsequently developed at the University of Berkeley, and more latterly at other West Coast geography departments. Let us now turn to the way space is conceptualized within this field.

For all Sauer's insights his research was more geographic than cultural. What was needed was for someone to shift the focus from landscape to lifeworld and put the 'cultural' firmly into cultural geography. The first notable attempt to do this was by one of Sauer's students, Wilbur Zelinsky. In his 1973 classic *The Cultural Geography of the United States*, the arch American assimilationist Zelinsky celebrated culture – but culture of a particular form. For all its idiosyncrasies, Zelinsky believed that American culture could still be understood as a totality, a 'superorganism' – not in the earlier Parkian sense of an environmentally causal superorganism, but in the sense of shared, holistic culture that:

> is something both of *and beyond* the participating members. Its totality is palpably greater than the sum of its parts, for it is superorganic and supra-individual in nature, an entity with a structure, set of processes, and momentum of its own, though clearly not untouched by historical events and socio-economic conditions.
>
> (Zelinsky 1973: 41)

Like Sauer, Zelinsky was a vehement champion of diverse groups and marginalized ethnicities. The problem, however, was that he was trying to flesh out an assimilationist theory of culture and space at the very moment – 1973 – that the 'American Dream' was being assailed from all sides. In sum, Zelinsky's cultural geography was at root singular. What was needed at that time was an assemblage of cultural geographies capable of theorizing dissent and spatial heterogeneity as much as consent and mutual experience. And thanks to the 'cultural turn' this is exactly what happened.

A case could be made that no discipline was more affected by the cultural turn of the 1970s than geography. If one could characterize the Sauer–Zelinsky debate as a small firefight on the edge of the empire, by the mid-1980s geography's hinterland had been overrun by something resembling total disciplinary war. At this point, our potted history of cultural geography will become familiar to criminologists. Some of the key influences that transformed human and cultural geography in the 1980s – Foucault, Gramsci, and Stuart Hall and the Birmingham School of cultural studies – also greatly influenced criminology, or at least parts of it, most notably sub-cultural and feminist criminology. And this is the difference. While mainstream criminology remained largely unaffected by the social theoretical revolution ushered in by the cultural turn, geography's relationship was substantive and enduring (Matless 1995); a point Don Mitchell makes clear: '[t]he "cultural turn" is not limited to the subfield of cultural geography. Rather, in all manner of human geographies – from economic to political, from urban to regional, from feminist to Marxist – "culture" has become a primary focal point of study' (2000: 63). No surprise, then, that one of the defining books of post-modernism was by a geographer – David Harvey's *The Condition of Postmodernity*; a brilliant text that eruditely documents how the trajectories of the political, the spatial, the temporal, and the economic, crosscut with the cultural. But what of cultural geography specifically? How did it emerge from the disciplinary turf wars brought on by the cultural and spatial turns? The answer to this question is foreshadowed in earlier critiques of Sauer and Zelinsky.

If, in many disciplines, the cultural turn is seen as an apolitical moment, this was not the case with human and social geography. The debates over space and the cultural–political nature of pluralism and opposition provoked a more pronounced political stance amongst many geographers, resulting ultimately in the development of more radical forms of spatial and cultural analysis. Nowhere was this more apparent than in cultural geography (Cosgrove 1983). Three figures stand out: Denis Cosgrove, James Duncan and Peter Jackson, all of whom in their own way had been early critics of Sauerian landscape-oriented cultural geography. Significantly, Duncan believed that Sauer and Zelinsky had failed to grasp the role that *power* played in shaping culture. As a corrective, he proposed a conception of culture that prioritized 'the many problematic social, political, and economic relationships' that dictate the conditions in which we live our lives (Duncan 1980: 198). Jackson (1989) agreed, weighing in later to critique early cultural geography's rural/ecological bias, the legacy, he claimed, of Sauer's traditional geographic fieldwork sensibility. If cultural geography was to remain vital in challenging and changing times, it needed to eschew its fascination with barns, allotments, and indigenous outposts, and train its attention instead on the more pressing problems of civic unrest and the material and spatial consequences of economic recession. Thus, thanks in large part to the efforts of Cosgrove, Duncan and Jackson, 'the new cultural geography' was born, a more diverse, politically charged variant than its older country cousin.

It is this latter variant that can be of considerable use to criminology generally, and environmental and cultural criminology specifically (Hayward 2004). My position here can be expressed in the following terms:

1   If contemporary areal/environmental criminology and its attendant abstract spatial practices such as crime mapping and 'hot spot' policing is haunted by a failure to consider the intricate nature of space and the diversity and complexity of human actions within space, the new cultural geography, with its emphasis on the relationship between culture and space, can provide a useful corrective.

2   Even though criminology has a long and productive tradition of considering key issues such as power and meaning, too often these analyses have only peripherally engaged with issues relating to spatiality. With its emphasis on the spatial nature of political and economic power, and how landscapes function as systems of social reproduction (including the cultural geographies of race, gender and resistance), the new cultural geography can greatly improve existing criminological enquiry into meaning, power, and political economy.

3   In its mainstream variant, criminology has fallen some way short of a meaningful engagement with the social theoretical debates that seek to explain the various socio-economic and cultural transformations that one might describe here as 'late modernity'. Certainly, a great deal of empirical/ statistical criminology proceeds as if oblivious to the complexities associated with the late modern condition – whether these complexities relate to the thematics of space, culture or identity. If criminology is to continue to develop as a well-rounded, vital social scientific discipline attuned both to the current times and to the social theoretical discourse that surrounds these times, it can no longer proceed in this isolated intellectual state. With its aim of using contemporary social theory and inter-disciplinarity to celebrate complexity and understand cultural acquiescence and resistance, the new cultural geography could help criminology address this shortcoming.

To be sure, these are lofty statements, and such aims will not be achieved easily – but this should not deter us from trying. In a bid to kick-start the process, the final section of this chapter offers some tentative potential ways of achieving at least aspects of these statements. The examples that follow are not meant to be exhaustive; just some thoughts to provoke further discussion on how we might develop an understanding of 'criminogenic space' that, like cultural geography, is infused with a strong inter-disciplinary approach and an ability to think beyond superficial interpretations – whether theoretical, structural or spatial.

Thinking differently about space and crime

In this final section I want to use some prominent examples of ongoing work within the field of cultural geography that would seem appropriate to criminological research, be it of a theoretical or empirical nature. For shorthand purposes I have allied each subtheme of cultural geography with one of three spheres or registers – the 'conceptual/theoretical', the 'material/physical', and the 'virtual/networked'. Various other areas of cultural geography are equally applicable (see Hayward, 2012 for an elaboration of this argument).

Conceptual/theoretical: Let us start with ongoing developments in so-called non-representational theory (NRT). Although complex, at bottom NRT can be understood as an attempt to move beyond static or fixed geographic accounts of landscape in a bid to create instead an alternative approach that actively incorporates the experiential, affective, and inter-material aspects of space that rarely feature in traditional representational geography (or for that matter in most criminology). Expressed differently, the key idea here is that there is an affective wash that soaks everyday spatiality. In NRT the talk is thus of 'relational and engaging spaces', 'complexity', 'event sensations' and of the importance of inter-disciplinarity and the need for a 'multiplicity of theoretical voices' (Thrift 1996). Such terms confirm the openly acknowledged influence of post-structuralism, and in particular 'the avenues for thought opened up by the translation of the work of Deleuze and Latour' (Anderson and Harrison 2010: 3). However, the relationship between NRT and post-structuralism needs clarification if NRT is not to be dismissed as just another slice of highfalutin postmodern spatial theory. The first thing to state is that, while NRT is clearly indebted to the aforementioned 'new cultural geography' (ibid.: 5–6), it should not be viewed simply as an extension of the type of geographic social constructivism that characterized much cultural geography in the 1980s and 1990s. Admittedly, NRT is interested in symbolic meaning and cultural representation, but it also prioritizes the material (see below), something exemplified in a question posed by Anderson and Harrison in their thoughtful introduction to NRT: 'if life is constructed, how come it appears so immutable?' To put it another way, despite its name, *(critical) representation actually matters to NRT*. This tension is nicely encapsulated by Hayden Lorimer, who in a review of NRT makes the point that by using the word 'non' in its name, NRT is shortchanging itself: 'An alteration to the chosen title might help for starters. I prefer to think of "more-than-representational" geography, the teleology of the original "non-" title having proven an unfortunate hindrance' (2005: 84). Lorimer goes on to offer his own explanation of NRT that is worth quoting here in full. NRT, he opines, is about

> [e]xpanding our once comfortable understanding of 'the social' and how it can be regarded as something researchable. This often means thinking

through locally formative interventions in the world. At first, the phenomena in question may seem remarkable only by their apparent *in*significance. The focus [of NRT] falls on how life takes shape and gains expression in shared experiences, everyday routines, fleeting encounters, embodied movements, precognitive triggers, practical skills, affective intensities, enduring urges, unexceptional interactions and sensuous dispositions. Attention to these kinds of expression, it is contended, offers an escape from the established academic habit of striving to uncover meanings and values that apparently await our discovery, interpretation, judgement and ultimately representation. In short, so much ordinary action gives no advance notice of what it will become. Yet, it still makes critical differences to our experiences of space and place.

(Ibid.)

Lorimer's language is refreshingly clear – something not always the case with NRT. This tendency towards unnecessarily dense conceptualization is clearly a product of the aforementioned post-structural influence. It is something that needs to be addressed if NRT is to have value in fields other than cultural and human geography (Lorimer 2007: 97). It is my contention that criminology, with its more practical application, can be of use here, not just in terms of tightening up the worst excesses of post-structural discourse, but in providing a tangible outlet for some of the spatial principles associated with NRT. Let us explore this point further by looking at the potentiality of NRT within one specific branch of contemporary criminological theory – cultural criminology (e.g. Ferrell *et al.* 2008).

The possibility of exploiting the broader utility of NRT within cultural criminology has recently been explored by Campbell in an interesting article that investigates the performative practices of stalking. Campbell highlights the 'considerable resonance' between developments in NRT and

a cultural criminological approach [that] emphasizes the subjective, affective, embodied, aesthetic, material, performative, textual, symbolic and visual relations of space, as well as recognizing that the settings of crime are neither fixed nor inevitable but are relational, improvised, contingent, constructed and contested through an array of creative and dynamic cultural practices, made meaningful within and mediated by wider processes of social transformation.

(Campbell 2012: 2)

Campbell has alighted on something important, a relationship that could indeed prove 'wholly reciprocal and mutually beneficial'. With its accessible and deliberately provocative prose style, coupled with its enduring focus on the excesses of capitalism and the exclusionary strategies associated with consumer culture, cultural criminology could potentially demystify the 'tantalizing language' associated with too much NRT, whilst at the same time adding a more robust materialist spine to NRT's putative political aspirations. In turn, NRT could aid cultural criminology in its ongoing attempt to counter sanitizing criminal justice logics such as 'hot spots', 'secure zones', and the other postcode-specific actuarial frameworks that constitute much of today's formalized geography of crime. So what aspects of NRT are most immediately applicable to (cultural) criminology? Three areas stand out.

First, NRT's focus on affective landscapes or experiential spaces where feelings of, *inter alia*, fear, danger, ennui, disgust, boredom, isolation, hedonism or excitement pervade.[4] To an extent this approach has been foreshadowed by feminist criminologists in earlier work that utilized psycho-geography and cognitive mapping to articulate women's fear(s) of public spaces. However, rather than plotting an emotion like fear on a map, NRT seeks to show how emotions actually influence or shape space more than they arise *in* space (see Anderson 2004 on the spatiality of boredom, an emotion much discussed by cultural criminologists, see Ferrell 2004).[5] What is being sought here is the territorialization of affect (affect in the sense of Pile's (2005: 48) notion of 'the social relations of emotion'), a geography of sensation that can be materially represented. This is important for any number of reasons, but by way of example consider how emotions prefigure physical exclusion and oppression; a point the criminologist Leo Cheliotis makes clearly when critiquing the lack of attention to empirical reality in Zygmunt Bauman's sociology/dichotomy of space:

> If nothing else, to conclude that the roots of physical exclusion ultimately lie within physical exclusion is to preclude the questions thereby raised: how is it that victims find themselves separated from victimizers in the first instance? Does not prior separation occur under conditions of spatial proximity and optical interpersonal visibility?
>
> (Cheliotis 2010: 132)

Second, an interest in the multisensual landscape inevitably results in NRT adherents training attention on embodied actions and 'performances'. Here, once again, many of the more interesting aspects of NRT are shrouded in unfathomable post-structural semantics. However, it is possible to discern some useful insights for broadening criminology's homogeneous reading of modernist space. The emphasis placed on 'events', for example, is useful both in terms of mapping performative protest (a representational undertaking), and for understanding how local actions and practices can be incorporated into forms of community activism or 'cosmopolitics' (a more non-representational endeavour). In the words of Anderson and Harrison, non-representational theories (and they do prefer the plural expression) '*are marked by an attention to events and the new potentialities for being, doing and thinking that events may bring forth*' (2010: 19, emphasis as in original). In less abstract terms, consider how this focus on events could be applied to cultural criminology's interest in street resistance, environmental and political social movements, or alternative community justice actions around issues like policing, gangs or surveillance/sousveillance. Interestingly, NRT's preoccupation with this subject can be traced all the way back to early Sauerian cultural geography, and specifically the idea that geographers need to study man's intimate and material relationship with the soil/terrain. Consequently, a lot of non-representational work has focused on such areas as urban horticulture, gardening and allotment communities. However, more recently, NRT has come out of the 'potting shed' and adopted a more stridently political stance. Here the emphasis is on the participative, transformative and emancipatory potential of performative landscapes, and the potential of a 'suppler form of politics, born of experimental connections in the constant proliferation of events' (Lorimer 2007: 91).

Third, NRT's focus on so-called 'relational materialities' and 'non-human associations' offers the potential for establishing a long overdue link between criminology and 'actor-network theory'. Simply stated, actor-network theory is an anti-essentialist social theoretical framework emerging from science and technology studies that seeks to understand the networked relations between human and non-human phenomena (see Murdoch 1998; Whatmore 2003 for examples of actor-network theory as applied to space). It rejects technical and social determinism and presents instead a 'socio-technical' account in which neither the social nor the technical is prioritized. One obvious example would be the rise of smart phones (i.e. while smart phones would seem to be the product of purely technical developments, in fact they are (in part) designed by software engineers who are informed by the human needs of social networks. Correspondingly, social networks are themselves the product of technological innovation). NRT is keen to develop a 'relational–material' or 'associative' account of 'the social' that seeks to understand place/landscape in terms of the interaction between humans, objects, machines technology and even animals: 'These entities do not exist independently from one another, neatly separated into discrete ontological domains; rather all co-exist on the same "plane of immanence"' (Anderson and Harrison 2010: 14). Such a statement may appear abstract, but consider if you will how this approach might be useful when it comes to understanding how humans relate and interact with criminological phenomena such as public and private forms of decentralized surveillance (both in terms of traditional camera technology and more recent developments in aural surveillance) or the type of physical 'target hardening' practices advocated by situational crime preventionists.

Physical/material: Despite the strides made by proponents of NRT in terms of understanding place as if it were a living thing, a multi-layered congress of emotional, embodied, relational, cultural, political and spatial dynamics, the obvious critique exists that it lacks a tangible physical dimension. To some extent this critique can be countered by other developments within contemporary cultural geography – most notably the notion of 'parafunctional space'.

As we have seen, crime mapping rests on a morphology of form and function ('form dictates function; function follows form'). The result is a gapless, utilitarian, purposive and semiotically unambiguous grid that maps onto socio-demographic and economic hierarchies. Parafunctional spaces/maps are very different. My starting point here is a collaborative essay by the sociologist Nikos Papastergiadis and the photographer Heather Rogers (1996). Drawing on the work of Michel de Certeau, Papastergiadis and Rogers deploy the term *parafunctional space* to refer to city spaces that appear to have 'given up' the struggle of shaping time and space, or where the most fundamental of modernist linkages is severed – the (functional) link between use and space as operationalized by names. Consider the following interpretation of parafunctional space, as glossed by the teaching team at the School of Architecture and Design, University of South Australia:

> Liminal spaces exist in-between – perhaps they've been abandoned or ruined, perhaps they are a set or constellation of surfaces, perhaps they are named 'waste', perhaps they are 'condemned'. These spaces do not 'function' as we might think 'function' functions – as meaning. These spaces do not do as they are told. (This is a sentence to imagine with: place an emphasis on 'do' and 'told', for example.) That is, they do not serve or operate 'the kind of action or activity proper' to their form, shape, (original) intention. While they function, the functional cannot have an exact relation to design as these spaces are marked by the yet-to-be . . .[6]

These functionless, evidently non-modernist, parafunctional spaces represent the exact opposite of discipline (see Figure 8.1). Not only do they typically lack any formal surveillance mechanisms, they represent the abandoned, anonymous, and seemingly meaningless spaces within our midst – the places on the (metaphorical) edge of society (see relatedly Franck and Stevens 2006 on 'loose space').

From a criminological perspective, it is problematic parafunctional spaces – the run-down playground, the badly lit side street, the unofficial homeless sleep space – that typically preoccupy administrative criminologists, crime mappers and crime preventionists. For example, Papastergiadis describes:

> how state and council authorities try to keep specific spaces to their specificity: seating is changed in railway waiting rooms and on platforms to discourage sleeping by the homeless (UK, USA), just so they do not 'sink' into a parafunctional state of ambiguity and contamination.
>
> (2002: 45)

In this sense, situational crime preventionists are essentially seeking to return spaces that have lost their function back *within* the ordered planner's fold of the modernist grid. To re-link 'space' and 'use' in one unequivocal functionality is thus a project of semiotic disambiguation – the attempt to close down an object/ place's spatial reference so that it has only one unique meaning. Seats are *only* for sitting on – not for sleeping, skateboarding, partying or busking on. Under this rubric, controlling crime becomes as simple as mapping place, function and meaning so that the rational utility-seeking subject no longer has to deal with any form of complexity whatsoever. However, as anyone who takes the time to walk or cycle through the city will surely tell you, streets and city spaces are rarely, if ever, unequivocal.

Figure 8.1 Parafunctional space: the implosion of the Spanish property boom has
        resulted in the alternative use of unfinished holiday homes by Tenerife
        fishermen.
Source: Photo credit: Keith Hayward.

To sum up, the concept of parafunctional space can help criminologists understand places in terms of hidden micro-cultural practices, distinct spatial bio-
graphies, relationships (or non-relationships) with surrounding spaces/structures,
intrication with different temporalities, intrinsic social role(s) – both perceived
and actual – and networks of feelings and semiotic significance. Categories of
knowledge that do not feature in the types of computer-aided map making and
ortho-rectified imagery that drives contemporary digital crime mapping.

Virtual/networked: From the physical to the virtual. As the internet and digital
communication technology have transformed society, criminology has been
employed to explain and counter the myriad forms of crime, danger, and deviance
that quickly appeared in the wake of the 'digital revolution'. Some excellent work
has emerged in the burgeoning field of internet crime (see Jewkes and Yar, 2010
for an overview). However, whilst 'cyber crime' is now an established area of
criminological attention, most research has tended to focus either on explaining
and identifying various forms of online crime, or developing ways to combat it,
either through regulation and internet law or by policing the internet and computer
forensics. This is understandable as there are major problems to solve, and
moreover these problems are fluid, mutable, and constantly evolving, reflecting

the 'fast twitch' nature of the internet and its attendant forms of digital technology. What other tools, then, might help criminologists in their understanding of internet crime? In what follows I will suggest that ongoing developments in cultural geography and associated spatial theory could prove useful allies for criminology as it seeks to make sense of cyber space and how human beings use and abuse it.

At the conceptual level, one might say that ongoing criminological and legal work on cyber crime is primarily concerned with *diffusion*, whether in terms of the increased criminal opportunities afforded by decentralized networks, or the potential diffusion of victimhood associated with digital crimes such as phishing email scams or identity theft. Consider, for example, the legal/preventionist response to the compression and sharing of digital music files. The initial music industry panic was followed by expensive litigation and a subsequent flurry of excessive governmental legislation/prohibition that not only missed the target, but ultimately missed the point: that despite claims to the contrary, media conglomerates continue to grow and profit, largely because of the way they have adopted new business models that work with and not against 'the download generation'. From a spatial perspective one might say that rather than emphasizing models of diffusion, a better way of thinking about digital/online (criminal) activities is as *process*, i.e. as phenomena in constant dialogue and transformation with other phenomena/technologies. Here we enter the familiar territory of Manuel Castells' networked 'space of flows' (in contrast to the fixed geography of 'space of place'), and the less familiar, more esoteric social theory of Deleuze and Guattari's acentered rhizome, a metaphorical subterranean stem that connects any point to any other point. From a spatial perspective: 'The rhizome pertains to a map that must be produced, constructed, a map that is always detachable, connectable, reversible, modifiable, and has multiple entryways and exits and its own lines of flight' (Deleuze and Guattari 1988: 23). Such thinking allows sociologists of the internet to think differently about online space and digital culture, developing concepts such as 'virtuality', 'telepresence', 'convergence' and 'presence', all of which I believe have potential criminological application.

The term 'convergence' will be well known to many cyber crime experts, for at one level it describes the straightforward convergence of the technological (the networkable, compressible, and manipulable features of the digital format) and regulatory processes associated with the digital media experience. Here talk is of 'weightless money' (e.g. cash transfers), 'weightless products' (e.g. e-books, and 'virtual goods' in online gaming platforms) and the 'weightless economy' (e.g. 'intellectual property laws' and 'information colonialism'). Such areas interest criminologists, of course, because they spawn criminogenic counter-phenomena such as 'weightless money launderers', 'weightless counterfeiters', and 'weightless IP and biopirates'. At another level, however, convergence is a more complex process, especially when considered in relation to the theoretical discourse surrounding virtuality and the blurring distinction between the virtual and the actual. Consider online crimes perpetrated against cyber profiles/identities such as game avatars. Courts in various jurisdictions have already heard a number of cases involving online theft, fraud, and even cyber bullying and assault in multi-player online role-playing games such as *Second Life* and *World of Warcraft*. Although much-hyped, this blurring of the virtual and the actual is typically limited to monetary matters, as players find themselves out of real money as a result of the theft of, for example, virtual 'goods' or 'land'. However, on occasion this blurring process is more complex and spatially interesting. Recently, Linden Lab, the company that developed and operates *Second Life*, found itself at the center of a media storm after the German TV station ARD claimed that a *Second Life* player paid for sex with underage players or players posing as (digital) minors. Ultimately it transpired that the players involved in the incident were a 54-year-old man and a 27-year-old-woman who used their online avatars to depict a virtual sex act between a man and a child avatar. At a practical level, this incident highlights issues of jurisdiction – the player involved was German, and in Germany 'simulated' sex with children is punishable by up to 5 years in prison (in other countries it is not an offence). However, what is arguably more interesting is how this incident highlighted the nature and role of intentionality within virtual space. For some time now, intentionality has been a sufficient cause for prosecution in real-life cases involving the online 'grooming' of minors by paedophiles. However, the *Second Life* case illustrates that virtual actions/intentions can also lead to *actual* consequences. ARD passed the images to a state attorney in Halle; while Linden Lab contacted the German authorities, and subsequently made it abundantly clear that they would not tolerate 'erotic ageplay' on their site and would do all they could in the future to bring virtual and real-life paedophiles to justice.

Moving beyond legal questions of intentionality, these incidents raise other interesting questions about how online space is navigated and conceived by individuals. Key here is the notion of 'telepresence' that has been used to describe the immersive experience associated with certain aspects of digital culture. Simply stated, communication technologies have the potential to alter the way we experience the sense of *being* in an environment:

> Presence is relatively unproblematic in unmediated situations, we *are* where we 'are' ... However, when mediated communication or long distance interaction is introduced into the equation, things begin to change. In this situation we gain the ability to simultaneously exist in two different environments at the same time: the physical environment in which our body is located and the conceptual or interactional 'space' we are presented with through the use of the medium.
>
> (Miller 2011: 31)

The 'interactional space' associated with telepresence has interesting crimin-ological connotations. Most obviously, digital technology creates what one might describe as porous *spaces of subjectivity* in which moves made via the rhizomic, hyperlinked internet appear materially or spatially insignificant, but in reality have tangible consequences. Obvious examples here include surfing for sub rosa sexual imagery (see Jenkins 2001, for example, on the online subcultural practices associated with child pornography), and the type of hate-speech that is now such a common feature of 'comment' and 'message' boards. Indeed, the 'a-spatial' nature of online 'communities' actually lends itself to 'emotion dumping' and other outpourings of personal self-expression that would never be tolerated in physical space, from 'virtual revenge talk' and 'online vigilantism' (see Cottee 2010), to 'cyber bullying' and 'online stalking'.

Telepresence has been much discussed by cultural geographers interested in digital culture. However, what is of even more relevance to criminologists (especially those concerned with diffusion of victimization) is the more recent interest in digital 'presence' (Licoppe 2004). Of most significance here is Vince Miller's recent work on how the online self is uploaded and presented via both network profiles, active and non-active forum and chatroom registrations, abandoned blogs and online shopping accounts, and what he describes as 'phatic' communication such as status updates, informationless gestures ('pokes'), microblog 'shout outs', and other forms of digital interaction that prioritize 'connection and acknowledgement over content and dialogue' (Miller 2011: 205). Such information, Miller argues, constitutes our digital 'presence', a quasi-private disembodied virtual 'persona' that exists at various points across the spatial architecture of the internet. If historically, privacy revolved around secrecy, anonymity, and solitude, today there is a vast online reservoir of personal information about each and every one of us, from uploaded tagged photographs, to our consumer preferences and surfing habits. In virtual space we never sleep, we are always out there, 'alive' so to speak. What's more, digital 'personal traces', unlike 'hard copy' information, have a permanent life span. As Miller suggests, there is no more 'social forgetfulness', our virtual 'presence' is there to be trawled, data-mined, and profiled by everyone from credit and consumer agencies, to anonymous dataveillance and surveillance organizations. Miller's concept of presence has obvious criminological application; not just in terms of specific cyber crimes like identity theft, but in other areas such as the rehabilitation of offenders and how post-release/prosecution identity might be affected by one's residual online presence, or in relation to other areas of digital research such as Mark Poster's notion of the digital panopticon and connected questions about the legal dimensions of privacy and data collection.

Conclusion

This chapter offered up for discussion some alternative, even imaginative new ways of thinking about space and crime. My starting point was a straightforward one: that too much areal criminology (both historical and contemporary) tends to mathematize the issue of environment, prioritizing abstract space over and above phenomenological place. In doing so it abandons any attempt at a (fully) appreciative cultural analysis of the internal dynamics of space, emphasizing instead rational abstractions and rigid multi-factorial analyses that, although useful for short-term crime reduction, do little to aid our understanding of wider spatial and structural problems. Although at times my argument has been provocative, my intention was not to undermine all aspects of environmental and spatial criminology – on the contrary much of this work – from Burgess to Bottoms, from Herbert to Harries – is of considerable insight. Instead, my overarching aim is simply to try and improve existing research into the relationship between space and crime. It is my opinion that cultural geography can help in this process. I am not naïve enough to suggest that cultural geography and attendant concepts such as non-representational theory will subsume existing criminological methods, but that maybe these more experimental approaches might be useful as a 'background hum, asking questions of style, form, technique and method' (Lorimer 2008: 556) – after all criminology is always in need of new directions.

Notes

1 The putative title of Burgess' uncompleted autobiography was *I Renounce Reform and the Reformer: The Story of a Conflict of Social Roles*. One can almost feel Park standing over Burgess' shoulder, nodding approvingly.
2 This point is backed up by the unwritten restrictions imposed on critical writing and faculty activism by University of Chicago administrators. The controversial dismissals of W. I. Small and Edward Bemis are testimony to this atmosphere of control.
3 Interestingly, this process of abstraction also occurred in sociological as well as statistical ways. As Henry and Milovanovic (1996: 22) point out in their analysis of the Chicago School, as time passed the street became conceptualized in ever more abstract environmental terms via such notions as the 'subculture' of the street gang, the 'identity' of the neighbourhood, the 'social norms' of prostitution, truancy or vagrancy, and the 'order' of structural class relations.
4 Importantly in NRT, 'affect' and 'emotion' are not the same thing. So for example, while the geography journal *Emotion, Space and Society* focuses on emotional geographies, NRT considers emotions to be cognitive and hence less important than pre-cognitive or non-representational considerations.
5 Although humanistic, NRT (unlike feminism) has a fairly pronounced 'anti-biographical' streak (Thrift 2008: 7).
6 http://ensemble.va.com.au/home/prjct_nts.html. The School's particular interpretation of parafunctional space is based primarily on Papastergiadis' (2002) article 'Traces Left in Cities'.

References

Anderson, B. (2004) 'Time-stilled space-slowed: how boredom matters', *Geoforum*, 35 739–54.

Anderson, B. and Harrison, P. (2010) *Taking-Place: Non-Representational Theories and Geography*, Farnham: Ashgate.

Bogue, D. J. (1974) *The Basic Writings of Ernest W. Burgess*, Chicago: Community and Family Study Center.

Burgess, E. W. (1925) 'The growth of the city', in R. E. Park, E. W. Burgess and R. D. McKenzie (eds) *The City*, Chicago: University of Chicago Press.

Burrows, R. (2008) 'Geodemographics and the construction of differentiated neighbourhoods', in J. Flint and D. Robinson (eds) *Cohesion in Crisis?* Bristol: Policy Press.

Burrows, R. and Gane, N. (2006) 'Geodemographics, software and class', *Sociology*, 40 (5) 793–812.

Campbell, E. (2012) 'Landscapes of performance: stalking as choreography', *Environment and Planning D*, forthcoming.

Cheliotis, L. (2010) 'The sociospatial mechanics of domination: transcending the "exclusion/inclusion" dualism', *Law Critique*, 21 131–45.

Cosgrove, D. (1983) 'Towards a radical cultural geography', *Antipode*, 15 1–11.

Cottee, S. (2010) 'A grammar of everyday justice talk', paper presented at the annual meeting of the Law and Society Association, Renaissance Chicago Hotel, Chicago, IL, 27 May.

Deegan, M. J. (1988) *Jane Addams and the Men of the Chicago School*, New York: Transaction.

Deleuze, G. and Guattari, F. (1988) *A Thousand Plateaus*, London: Athlone.

Duncan, J. (1980) 'The Superorganic in American cultural geography', *Annals of the Association of American Geographers*, 70 181–98.

Eaton, R. (2001) *Ideal City: Utopianism and the (Un)Built Environment*, London: Thames and Hudson.

Ferrell, J. (2004) 'Boredom, Crime, and Criminology', *Theoretical Criminology*, 8 (3) 287–302.

Ferrell, J., Hayward, K. and Young, J. (2008) *Cultural Criminology*, London: Sage.

Franck, K. and Stevens, Q. (eds) (2006) *Loose Space*, London: Routledge.

Garland, D. (1997) '"Governmentality" and the problem of crime: Foucault, criminology and sociology', *Theoretical Criminology*, 1 (2) 173–214.

Harries, K. (1999) *Mapping Crime: Principles and Practice*, Washington, DC: National Institute of Justice.

Hayward, K. J. (2004) *City Limits: Crime, Consumer Culture and the Urban Experience*, London: Glasshouse.

—— (2012) 'Five spaces of cultural criminology', *British Journal of Criminology*, 52 (3), May.

Henry, S. and Milovanovic, D. (1996) *Constitutive Criminology*, London: Sage.

Jackson, P. (1989) *Maps of Meaning: An Introduction to Cultural Geography*, London: Unwin Hyman.

Jenkins, P. (2001) *Beyond Tolerance: Child Pornography on the Internet*, New York: New York University Press.

Jewkes, Y. and Yar, M. (2010) *Handbook of Internet Crime*, London: Sage.

Licoppe, C. (2004) '"Connected" presence: the emergence if a new repertoire for managing social relationships in a changing communication technoscape', *Environment and Planning D*, 22 (1) 135–56.

Lindstrom, F. B. and Hardert, R. A. (eds) (1988) 'Kimball Young on the founders of the Chicago School', *Sociological Perspectives*, 31 (3) 269–97.

Lorimer, H. (2005) 'Cultural geography: the busyness of being "more-than-representational"', *Progress in Human Geography*, 29 (1) 83–94.

—— (2007) 'Cultural geography: worldly shapes, differently arranged', *Progress in Human Geography*, 31 (1) 89–100.

—— (2008) 'Cultural geography: non-representational conditions and concerns', *Progress in Human Geography*, 32 (4) 551–59.

McKenzie, R. D. (1924) 'The ecological approach to the study of the human community', *American Journal of Sociology*, 30 (3) 287–301.

—— (1925) 'The ecological approach to the study of the human community', in R. E.

Park, E. W. Burgess and R. D. McKenzie (eds) *The City*, Chicago: University of Chicago Press.

Matless, D. (1995) 'Culture run riot? Work in social and cultural geography, 1994', *Progress in Human Geography*, 19: 395–403.

Matza, D. (1969) *Becoming Deviant*, Englewood Cliffs, NJ: Prentice Hall.

Miller, V. (2011) *Understanding Digital Culture*, London: Sage.

Mitchell, D. (2000) *Cultural Geography*, Oxford: Blackwell.

Murdoch, J. (1998) 'The spaces of actor-network theory', *Geoforum*, 29 357–74.

Papastergiadis, N. (2002) 'Traces left in cities' in Leon Van Schaik (ed.) *Poetics in Architecture*, London: Architectural Design, Wiley Academy.

Papastergiadis, N. and Rogers, H. (1996) 'Parafunctional spaces', in J. Stathatos (ed.) *Art and the City*, London: Academy Group.

Park, R. E. (1925a) 'The city as a social laboratory', in T. V. Smith and L. White (eds) *Chicago: An Experiment in Social Science Research*, Chicago: University of Chicago Press.

—— (1925b) 'The city: suggestions for the investigation of human behaviour in the urban environment', in R. E. Park, E. W. Burgess and R. D. McKenzie (eds) *The City*, Chicago: University of Chicago Press.

Park, R. E., Burgess, E. W. and McKenzie, R. D. (eds) (1925) *The City*, Chicago: University of Chicago Press.

Pile, S. (2005) *Real Cities*, London: Sage.

Platt, J. (1994) 'The Chicago School and first hand data', *History of Human Sciences* 7 57–80.

Sauer, C. O. (1925 [1963]) 'The morphology of landscape', in Leighly, J. (ed.) *Land and Life: A Selection of the Writings of Carl Ortwin Sauer*, Berkeley: University of California Press.

Sibley, D. (1985) *Geographies of Exclusion*, London: Routledge.

Small, A. and Vincent, G. (1894) *Introduction to the Study of Society*, New York: American Book Co.

Smith, D. (1988) *The Chicago School: A Liberal Critique of Capitalism*, New York: St. Martin's Press.

Sumner, C. (1994) *Sociology of Deviance: An Obituary*, Buckingham: Open University Press.

Thrift, N. (1996) *Spatial Formations*, London: Sage.

—— (2008) *Non-Representational Theory: Space, Politics, Affect*, London: Routledge.

Whatmore, S. (2003) 'Generating materials', in M. Pryke, G. Rose and S. Whatmore (eds) *Using Social Theory: Thinking Through Research*, London: Sage.

Zelinsky, C. (1973) *The Cultural Geography of the United States*, Englewood Cliffs, NJ: Prentice-Hall.

9 Consumer culture and the meaning of the urban riots in England

Steve Hall

This is what 'back to basics' was really about: the unleashing of the barbarian who lurked beneath our apparently civilised, bourgeois society, through the satisfying of the barbarian's 'basic instincts'. . . . On British streets during the unrest, what we saw was not men reduced to 'beasts', but the stripped-down form of the 'beast' produced by capitalist ideology.

(Slavoj Žižek, 2011)

Following earlier disturbances in the banlieues of Paris in 2005, the English riots occurred in August 2011 in similar locales of permanent recession that bordered centres of opulence and consumer chic. Both were triggered by the deaths of young people in confrontations with police; two in Paris electrocuted and one in London shot. Although the common trigger seemed to be an affront to the community's sense of justice, neither set of riots made the transition from the initial reaction to personal injustice to an articulate call for broader social justice and political change. Rather, both were characterised by a rapid transition from fleeting protests to vandalism and looting. French rioters complained about policing and exclusion from the rewards of the consumer economy, whilst in London and other urban centres in England the rioters targeted police, shops, 'the rich', and unfortunate bystanders, some taking advantage of the opportunity to acquire 'free stuff' in a series of raids and assaults whose organisation was aided by encrypted mobile phone messages. Small protests against injustice quickly descended into large incoherent melées that showed all the signs of depoliticisation, objectless dissatisfaction and absorption into an anti-social and apolitical world of consumer signs.

In the torrent of commentary that flooded the news media and the blogosphere in the wake of the English riots, the argument rapidly polarised. In the midst of conservative platitudes about feral youth and moral decline and liberal-leftist platitudes about poverty and disenfranchisement, some of the more astute commentators were quick to coin phrases such as the 'consumer riots' or 'the riots at the end of history' (see Goodhart, 2011), indications of the gradual breakdown of the neoliberal system of deregulated economics, cultural liberalism and social risk management that has been with us since the early 1980s. Perhaps there was a faint, repressed political energy underneath these riots, but, apart from a brief upsurge of micro-politics in the initial protest, it remained submerged and inarticulate; in the macro-political sense, one thing did *not* lead to another. In the wake of the riots many young people seemed agitated yet hesitant and confused, unsure of the sentiments and reasons behind their participation, apart from simply having been caught up in the excitement caused by the surrounding commotion.

No doubt the usual 'evidence-based policy research' that will be conducted over the next few years will throw up lots of 'nuances' and suggest a few ways to keep the lid on things without getting excessively punitive. However, social scientists have been conducting such research since the first politically inarticulate riots occurred in the USA in the late 1960s (see Flamm, 2005). Despite our expanding knowledge base, further riots occurred in Britain in the 1980s and early 1990s alongside political protests and strikes, and, in terms of theory or macro-policymaking, we did not seem to be much further forward. Once again, in 2011, the same predictable debate sprang up in popular culture, politics and academia. Where the liberal-left blamed poverty, inequality, lack of opportunity and confrontational policing, the neoliberal right conjured up the usual demons of evil individuals, poor parenting, feral youth, soft criminal justice and – to refer to the coalition government's official term – 'sheer criminality'. The British prime minister, David Cameron, kept his explanation as simple, individualistic, condemnatory and emotive as possible. This seemed to set the tone of the debate, and the liberal-left were co-opted into a slugging match where they found it impossible to compete unless they adopted a similarly simplistic position. The riots became yet another excuse to continue the epic boxing match between the concepts of 'moral decline' and 'poverty and inequality'; a battle that is interminable because neither side has the intellectual strength to knock out its opponent.

Despite the establishment of the simplicity principle in the political game, the riots yet again followed the eruption into public view of advanced capitalism's deepening global economic crisis. The basic politico-economic process behind the current crisis is a story too familiar to repeat here, except to say that the neoliberal restructuring of the British economy according to the logic of global finance capital produced some quite calamitous sociological and criminological effects in the 1980s, which included an explosion in criminality that accompanied the reduction of working people from empowered political actors to statistics in mathematical equations (see Crouch, 2011; Reiner, 2007; Winlow and Hall, 2006). Crime rates did begin to decline in the mid-1990s, but during this period neither the authoritarian state nor the liberation of the individual from modernity's discourses of domination was the prime mover in the maintenance of public order. Crime fell as various economic sectors were expanded to compensate for the decline of tenured jobs and the corrosion of community, identity, politics and the security that had been promised and to a significant extent delivered by social democracy to the post-war generations. Increased consumption was enabled by an unprecedented expansion of credit on the back of an inflated housing market, which expanded low-grade employment in service industries and welfare payments and allowed access to remarkably cheap goods, lurid entertainment, alcohol and soft drugs, the essential pharmacological accoutrements in consumer capitalism's libidinal drive-based economy and its attendant culture of anhedonic nihilism (see Fisher, 2009; Stiegler, 2011). As techniques of pacification and ideological enrolment, the stick of an expanding surveillance state and prison population and the carrot of personal freedom were complementary – perhaps even secondary – to the expansion of cheap, available opportunities for hedonistic consumption.

As the neoliberal project is driven along by an unforgiving economic and financial logic, politics, culture and moral agency no longer function as drivers for human activity but fragile compensations, conciliators and stabilisers in capitalism's historical pseudo-pacification process (see Hall, 2000; 2007; Hall *et al.*, 2008). The strategy of maintaining public order by appeasing depoliticised populations built up large deficits and debts in Western nations. The ability of governments and populations to reduce the deficits and pay back loans became dependent on the recirculation through these nations of the profits made by constant global economic growth; this growth is now reaching its concrete, objective limit (Heinberg, 2011). The current unnerving proximity to this limit and the initial effect of mass unemployment amongst largely depoliticised populations whose symbolic lives are dependent on consumption are the fundamental conditions for the outbreaks of politically inarticulate street crime, public disorder and punitive responses that look set to become fixtures in the advanced capitalist era. The aetiological focus on street crime is not intended to detract from the criminological motif that organised crime and 'crimes of the powerful' cause more social harm than the crimes of the powerless, but to bring to the criminological debate the issue of the recent suffocation of the Big Other of oppositional politics (see Winlow and Hall, 2011) – which once sought to confront the ruling elite and their exempted crimes – by the hands of neoliberalism and postmodern left-liberalism.

Despite the increasing polarisation of wealth in the neoliberal era, resentment is not caused simply by relative poverty and sentiments of social injustice; the working class had been living with relative poverty and indeed collectively struggling against social injustice throughout the era of high industrial capitalism. The extreme objectless anxiety, cynicism and loss of faith that afflicted the unemployed and those in precarious forms of unemployment from the 1980s onwards were the products of life in a socioeconomic milieu in which atomised and depoliticised individuals and sociocultural groups were set against each other in an unforgiving competition. The failure of the dominant left-liberal opposition to articulate an intellectual explanation and a political response has deepened the resentment and turned it into active hostility and loss of faith (see Flamm, 2005). As young people experienced a sharp decline in socioeconomic prospects the possibility of a futile existence became the norm, trapping them in the inertia of an endless dismal present separated from the past and the future. Youth employment in Europe is now reaching unprecedented statistical heights, from 10–20 per cent in northwestern Europe to around 50 per cent in some parts of southern Europe and the Balkans (ILO, 2010), and most of the jobs available to young people across the neoliberal West are precarious, low-paid and unsatisfying 'Mcjobs' (Ritzer, 1993). This time, however, neoliberalism and postmodern left-liberalism have combined to ensure that they face this difficulty in the absence of explanatory and unifying political symbolism.

The virtual erasure of the invaluable intellectual poles of working-class history and high culture from school curricula has left many young people politically illiterate, and migrants only dimly aware of the historical and politico-economic process they have recently joined. The grants system for higher education was withdrawn, and even in the humanities and social sciences most politically and historically embedded discourses were dismissed by a new wave of liberal-postmodern catastrophists as illegitimate 'grand narratives'. Most disciplines focused almost exclusively on identity politics and made plaintive appeals to the individual's moral agency, producing a cornucopia of structurally disconnected analyses of discrimination and hostility between different ethnic and sub-cultural groups. This replaced political economy and dialectics, which were given constant critical treatment by censorious and vigilant liberal-postmodernists until they were all but discarded, allowing normalising and subjectifying processes to be disconnected from economy, class, ideology and the unconscious. Depth thinking in general was dismissed as essentialist, reductionist and cynical (see for instance Sibeon, 2004; Turner, 2010). All that remained was the unpredictable but benign moral agent making choices in the constant 'grassroots' cumulative process of reconstituting society's relations and institutions. The fundamental question of why society's major institutions – government, banking, corporations, work, media, education and so on – were most emphatically *not* being reconstituted or brought under democratic control by the will of the people was removed from the agenda.

Popular culture – the inter-generational transmitter of skills, meaning, unifying myths and politics and a potential hothouse of creativity – was thoroughly depoliticised and emptied of any unifying potential as it was displaced by the revolving carousel of corporate fashions and lifestyles. Even the master signifier of rebelliousness was captured and put to work by a psychosocially sophisticated advertising industry that took advantage of the human being's underlying sense of Lacanian 'lack' and anxiety to create insatiable desires for consumer items (Frank, 1997). As part of their overall efforts the mass media also propagated celebrity culture, using celebrities as mannequins for expensive bling, thus lowering the value of ordinariness and keeping the population constantly looking upwards. This further fuelled individual anxiety whilst dislocating the ethical connection between work, parenthood and citizenship to create a post-social melée in which conformist ambition and self-promotion with the aid of consumer accessories became essential for the individual's psychic survival. One can almost see in the mind's eye Alan Sugar's or Donald Trump's self-satisfied grin as apolitical and anxious yet highly ambitious and stylish young people struggle to reform their very souls in the image of the ruthless uncultured entrepreneur that these two represent. For the 'losers', the unfortunately less ambitious and presentable at the other end of the scale, the rules governing entitlement to welfare benefits were constantly changed, whilst increases were kept below inflation and the benefits available to the 16–24 age group cut to the bone. Many young people were forced into work schemes that offered few long-term job prospects; they could see quite clearly that they were being used as sources of cheap labour by unscrupulous employees. However, they now inhabit an incoherent liberal-postmodern world where the deceased Big Other has been replaced by a panoply of bureaucratic 'little others' that try to manage the sceptical postmodern subject and the 'risks' it encounters (Žižek, 1997; 2002; see also Winlow and Hall, 2011). Thus they have no class narrative or trustworthy political institutions to which they can turn, only a corporately manufactured youth culture of simulated differences orchestrating variations in cool scepticism and cynicism.

Greed and corruption were exposed amongst our elected representatives and the corporate elite, brought into stark relief between 2008 and 2011 by the British MPs expenses scandal, the phone-hacking activities of newspaper staff and the immediate return of vast bonuses to bankers and financial traders after their irresponsible lending had triggered the Credit Crunch. Here neoliberalism's spectacular plutocratic elite, who seemed immune from the law whilst the powerless were regularly punished to its very limits, were caught in the full glare of the headlights. Corruption and the macro-political manoeuvres made in the service of the plutocrats' project of economic and cultural restructuring became ever more transparent, spectacular and crude (Jameson, 2010), and their role in the impoverishment and disenfranchisement of so many young people became more obvious. Quite soon after the riots a minority of politically aware young people in a number of Western cities organised vociferous protests against the current order. Yet, amongst the English rioters there were no signs of clear and articulate political opposition to the capitalist system, its plutocratic elite or its state machine. Despite their apparent role as the perpetrators of the original injustice, the police were targeted mainly when they stood between the rioters and their objectives, which seemed to be limited to looting, vandalism and intimidation. This does not negate the possibility that some inarticulate political sensibility underpinned the riots and other forms of late modern crime and unrest, but it does suggest that, despite over 150 years of organised working-class politics, during the past 30 years a chasm has been reopened between unconscious political drives/ reactions and conscious thought and coherent political opposition. Whilst the current urban 'occupations' indicate the return of at least the possibility of unifying politics amongst a minority of the middle classes, what was up to the 1970s a politically articulate and volatile English working class has been thoroughly depoliticised.

If the English riots are to be theorised in today's context, the first move is to transcend yesterday's explanations, or at least to stop swallowing them whole. It is too easy to say that the riots and the coalition's authoritarian response vindicate the left-idealist thinking of the 1970s, to be found in works such as *Policing the Crisis* (Hall *et al.*, 1978). This was written during a time when articulate, organised political opposition and the culturally communicated and reproduced hope for a fundamentally transformed socioeconomic system were in abundance. The basic argument was that the petty criminality of the more marginalised and desperate elements of the poor was seized upon and blown out of all proportion by the predominantly conservative mass media. This, so the story goes, tapped into a tradition of authoritarian populism to create a 'moral panic' – whatever that over-used term actually means – thus helping the increasingly neoliberalised conservative party into government on a law and order ticket in 1979 by manufacturing consent and maintaining the legitimacy of its core ideological principles during a time of politico-economic crisis. This analysis is the bedrock of current left-liberal thinking, which has mutated into the broader and more systematic claim that the constant demonisation of socioeconomic outcasts as the constituents of a 'dangerous class' has fed a hegemonic current of 'crime-consciousness' that helps to sustain an underlying 'culture of control' (Garland, 2001).

However, after 30 years of neoliberal governance, and in the midst of gathering economic instability, there are few signs of the phenomena that might indicate a general 'moral panic' and a mass upsurge of authoritarian populism. The recent riots brought out the worst of the fringe racist-nationalists in the blogosphere, especially on the rather robust comment sites attached to national newspapers. However, that is their new natural habitat; their opinionated excess does not represent a mass sentiment, and, contra Goodwin's (2011a; 2011b) analysis, neither do very rare actions such as that of the spree-killer Anders Breivik. There is of course an ugly undercurrent in European and Anglo-American culture, and it can be stirred up, but so far it has not resulted in a swing to the far right anywhere near large enough to be electorally significant; the British and US electorates continue to vote primarily on the state of the economy. The potential authoritarian political response has been successfully repressed in the same box of political incoherence that contains the inarticulate ire of the disenfranchised. The political unconscious of the right also seems to be separated from its consciousness and organisation to the extent that it remains impotent as a practical force. We can be forgiven for a double value-judgement here; it's without doubt a good thing that we see this separation as a good thing, especially as it marginalises and represses the far right, but the existence of this separation across the whole political spectrum does suggest that neoliberalism is a true post-political force whose target for total destruction is not just extremism but the possibility of politics in general.

What we *did* see after the riots, however, was the surveillance state bursting into action. In stark contrast to its preventative impotence, it identified and arrested many rioters with breathtaking speed and efficiency, bringing them before extended courts to receive swift and largely disproportionate punishments. The condensation of events usually performed by media producers to increase dramatic effect occurred in reality and was thus unnecessary. Just as the shopkeepers did not know what had hit them at the hands of the rioters, the rioters were equally shocked by their treatment at the hands of the state. This pre-condensed mass-mediated 'crime and punishment' spectacle, broadcast without respite by 24-hour news channels, performed its placatory task very well; no need for a 'moral panic' and no chance of such a reaction as the population were drawn into this fast-moving narrative, where the simulacrum of disorder erupts only for order to be swiftly restored by the authorities. CCTV, broadcast television, cameras, cellphones and social media combined to increase the speed and the diffusion of images, creating spectacular theatre from the system's inherent dromological efficiency (Baudrillard, 1994; Virilio, 1986). Such was the impact of the riots and the criminal justice system's response that the whole event appeared before the viewers as if it were an episode of a TV drama: criminal eruption, dramatic complications, moral frisson and speedy resolution when the cops and the lawyers, after initially being caught on the hop, come good to balance the scales of justice and comfort us all before we get off to bed. This is just as we have been taught to like it; the real processes, structures, causes, perpetrators and victims are quickly forgotten, as is the presence of the shadowy surveillance state. In the post-political simulacrum there is always a happy ending to comfort us and a brand new show ready to keep us entertained. Should similar events occur, even in the near future, the *thread*, the vital connection between the events that constitute the historical process and contain the potential energy to drive it towards some greater event – and the emergence of an *ideological opposition* that brings itself into being to defy inevitability and divert the course of history before the point of no return is reached – will both be lost. And so it goes; a sequence of 'presents', one damned thing after another, propels us to an unpredictable end. In the absence of articulate politics and a sense of narrative the world passes us by, its punctuated eruptions and swift resolutions functioning only to maintain our comfort and complacency.

There was no 'moral panic'. This threadbare concept is based on a notion of objectified fear, the ideological selection of scapegoats on whom blame can be laid for unknown sources of anxiety. However, it is impossible to turn prior and clearly objectified fear onto numerous and ideologically selected scapegoats; only objectless anxiety has the phenomenological flexibility required for this task (see Wilkinson, 1999). Historically, the underlying condition in which riots tend to occur has been serious economic instability and the (very) objective fear of descending into extreme poverty and social chaos. Caught in the fallout from Wall Street and exacerbated by the strain of reparations demanded in the Treaty of Versailles, the economic crash and the social disintegration that followed the failure of the liberal Weimar government between 1929 and 1933 is the classic example. The Nazis' response was to turn anxiety onto traditional scapegoats already adumbrated by the deep prejudices of the residual nationalist–racist currents that existed in society at the time. However, this culturo-political tactic requires the initial negation of what should be the real object of fear in order to construct fearsome imaginary agents – immigrants, criminals, terrorists and so on – as substitutes for the underlying structural processes and their real active and ministerial agents, the current corporate and political elite. The initial negation allows ideological forces to tap into the primal source of objectless anxiety, which is, according to Lacan (2004), the pre-Oedipal narcissistic individual, who lacks the coherent order of symbols required to objectify and explain the disturbing irruptions of the Real on the emotional and undeveloped cognitive aspects of the psyche. Every society has the ability to point out and symbolise the *real* external source of the experiential proto-symbolic irruptions that are creating anxiety and turn it into objectified fear. However, the Weimar Republic was the site of an institutionalised class struggle over the meaning of the source of anxiety. The left pointed to the inherently unstable capitalist market economy and the ruling class in whose benefit it operated, whilst the far right constructed from their own deep prejudice internal agents of ethico-cultural decay (Jews, Romanies, Slavs and so on). However, the neoliberal era is the first in which an underlying left–right consensus has developed. These former adversaries in what was once a great ideological struggle – or at least a site of institutionalised argument and bargaining between capital and labour (Wieviorka, 2009) – now agree that to objectify the unstable capitalist economy and its attendant culture of competitive individualism as the true external source of permanent anxiety and unrest, thus turning the unidentified source of anxiety into a legitimate objectified source of fear, is not only pointless but dangerous, the first step on the road to totalitarianism as the sheer magnitude of what needs to be done to reform these underlying processes and structures is brought into relief.

Thus right and left no longer struggle against each other for the mandate to govern political economy. Even though the liberal-postmodernist left will not broadcast it too loudly; it has joined the right in the decision to carry on acting as if Thatcher's 'no alternative' dictum is correct and Fukuyama's (1993) 'end of history' has really arrived (Žižek, 2010). Liberal democracy and global capitalist markets are now officially permanent features of humanity's future, and whatever plutocratic and disintegrative tendencies exist within them must be addressed by ethical civic and administrative agents working within the system. Whatever we do, we must do it within the system's parameters; we can no longer talk in mainstream academic life or popular culture about the real source of anxiety on which the real objects of fear can be symbolised by a new ideological truth-project (see Badiou, 2006a). The ontological bedrock of our politics and our thinking has been reset; the capitalist system no longer exists as an official object of analysis, and, to be part of the liberal–postmodern social-scientific community, we must instead turn our attention to moral agents, minimal human rights, micro-power relations, single-issue social movements and policies, risks and situational crime-prevention measures.

We are no longer encouraged to delve underneath these new social 'fundamentals' to symbolise what we find there. The strength of the left-idealist argument in older works such as *Policing the Crisis* was that at least to some extent it supplemented the weak 'politics of fear' argument with the stronger 'politics of distraction', positing the economy as the real problem from which attention was being diverted by the law-and-order politics of the time. However, it did so from a Gramscian perspective, which posited hegemony as the principal means of ideological reproduction. Hegemony is the cultural method of 'manufacturing consent', by which individuals are ideologically incorporated into the capitalist system to accept its social order as timeless and natural. To function, it requires a constant supportive bias in mass media productions, the education system and popular culture in general. Hegemony is essentially a mechanism for reproducing orders of symbols and their associated emotional attachments, rather like a genetic code passed down through each new generation of species. Thus the existence of 'black muggers' as part of a demonic underclass can be portrayed as an unwanted and corrosive part of that natural order, the uncivilised or 'feral' underbelly that has avoided incorporation and socialisation into the system's eternally righteous values, a demonic threat or 'folk devil' (Tannenbaum, 1938) that demands the attention of the system's disciplinary and corrective apparatus. However, used in this way hegemony is a rather one-dimensional concept in the sense that hegemonic meaning is seen to manufacture consent, or impose meaning on the majority of the population; the population itself plays little more than a passive role in the production of the sort of sentiments, knowledge and ideas that accord with and affirm those of the ruling elite. We must re-examine these notions of 'ideology as knowledge' and passivity, but also question liberal-pluralism's standard 'dominant ideology thesis' (see Abercrombie *et al.*, 1981), which suggests that a dominant ideology cannot be imposed by such inefficient means on a population with diverse views.

The liberal-pluralist establishment that tends to dominate Anglo-American social thought was quite scathing about Louis Althusser's (1969) notion that individuals are 'interpellated' or 'hailed' by ideological state apparatuses that operate on behalf of ruling ideas to become subjects of an ideology that always pre-exists them. Althusser had used Lacan's concept of the mirror-stage to theorise the human subject. Originally conceived as a stage in child development, Lacan revised the concept to mean a permanent social process of identification and subjectification, but, as the result of a rather hasty reading of Lacan's complex oeuvre, Althusser had misinterpreted the position. Žižek (2000; 2006) offers an appealing alternative to the concepts of hegemony and ideology used by Hall *et al.* (1978) and Althusser (1969), one that results from a more sophisticated reading of Lacan. Where hegemony relies on the manufacture of consent by the imposition of meaning on individuals and their ensuing incorporation, and interpellation relies on the active hailing and subsequent 'turning round' of the potential subject towards ruling ideas, Žižek recognises that Lacan's whole system of thought is based on the anxious, premature subject's *active solicitation* of a system of coherent symbolic meanings, without which the world is an incomprehensible and terrifying magma of unknown irruptions on the uneducated senses. If such a system exists and appears dominant and potent, individuals, in order to save their own sanity as they grow from infants into symbol-reading adults, are driven to seek their own subjectification within its structure of meanings because they have no choice but to seek and find structured meaning in general (Hall, 2012a; 2012b; Johnston, 2008). The rational, private individual choice of meanings posited by liberals (see Thomas, 2009), and Derrida's (1967) and Foucault's (1970) endlessly metamorphosing phantasmagoria of post-structural texts and discourses, are not only myths but precisely what individuals cannot bear to live with, their very nemesis, the portal to permanent anxiety, private eccentricity and political inertia. To convince individuals that they are the subjects of either free choice or the unpredictable dance of the mutating discourses is to convince them that their eventual accommodation with a strict order of symbols is something other than what it is.

Over and above the recognition of the subject's unavoidable need to solicit that which can entrap it (Hall 2012b; Johnston, 2008), criminology also needs to work with an updated understanding of how postmodern ideology actually works. As we have seen, Gramsci's theory of hegemony, as used by post-war theorists, showed us how 'ruling ideas' are diffused and transformed into broadly accepted knowledge; they saw ideology principally as *a problem of knowledge*. The claim that ideology 'covers up' actuality with illusion rests on the premise that *we don't know it, but we are doing it* (Žižek, 1997; 2002), which carries with it the implication that if we 'sus' it we might pluck up the courage to stop doing it. However, now that the combined forces of neoliberalism and postmodern left-liberalism have persuaded us to move beyond truth and 'grand narratives', the postmodern subject likes to think that it cannot be conned or cajoled into anything. We are now fully rational, sceptical individuals *beyond ideology* and capable of seeing the world as it truly is. However, despite knowing all about it, we continue to act as if we don't know about it; postmodern life has opened up a sceptical distance between the subject and her social action. The conceit that we can't be fooled by the system's ideology is today's passive-narcissistic substitute for the redundant political passion to change it. This self-satisfied delusion does not prevent but actually encourages our active participation in both the legal and illegal dimensions of the capitalist project. We still believe, but our *active* belief is now unconscious and pragmatic whilst our once potent and often oppositional conscious beliefs are parodied into obsolescence (Winlow and Hall, 2011). Thus postmodern capitalism is not threatened by the subject's knowledge that its own activities are environmentally destructive, socially corrosive and economically exploitative. The 'diversity' extolled and analytically centralised by liberal plural-ists is the product of different modes of pragmatic and micro-political participation in the system decorated by redundant cultural symbolism. The structure and modus operandi of ideology has moved beyond a totalising system of knowledge- and thought-control towards the encouragement of the marked distinction between belief and social activity; we are free to mock capitalism from our different standpoints as long as we keep on 'doing' it, which is why we end up mocking ourselves. The role of postmodern hegemony is to *maintain that separation*.

The upshot of this revived Hegelian, Marxist and Lacanian thinking coming from a new breed of radical Continental philosophers such as Žižek (2010) and Badiou (2006b) is that there can be no alternative political thought and action without the construction of an alternative ideology that offers the subject a permanent home of structured and coherent yet amendable meaning that exists in direct opposition to neoliberalism. Criminological theorists must now confront the possibility that postmodernism liberalism's endless diversification, deconstruction and reconstruction of meaning is an active part of neoliberalism's depoliticisation and desubjectification processes. Operating in a space once occupied by the relatively coherent discourse of the oppositional left – which itself eventually degenerated into comical factionalism at the hands of narcissistic would-be leaders – it increases the objectless anxiety that allows the prevailing ideology to construct its imaginary objects and maintain its narrative as an explanation of the thread that connects real events. Put very simply, even though our sceptical postmodern heroes might not believe this narrative in its entirety, it offers no alternative way of thinking and therefore confuses things more and makes things worse by prolonging objectless anxiety, which is now not the product of what we don't know but of what we do 'know' as active participants but daren't think or talk about because we are convinced that there is no alternative.

The true danger of liberal–postmodernist capitalism is that its culture is rapidly transforming diverse forms of scepticism into totalising nihilism. As we continue to 'do capitalism' with the diverse means at our disposal, urban crime and sporadic apolitical forms of unrest will be permanent features of the capitalist system as it approaches its objective limit. Conversely, there will be no sea-change in hostile and punitive public attitudes unless an alternative ideology becomes sufficiently dominant to act as the order of symbolic meaning for the majority of the population. Anglo-American culture is at the forefront of this epochal shift in the operation of ideology, and this is at the root of the fundamental distinction between the global political protestors and the English 'consumer rioters' in 2011. The English riots threw into question the common assumption in cultural criminology that criminality might be a misdirected form of vitalism, transgression and resistance, the struggle of the naturally creative and rebellious sovereign individual against oppressive authority and the quest for Deleuzean escape routes. The more mainstream social democratic notion that the urban area is the site where we can see multicultural individuals settling into Beck's benign *cosmopolis* (see Boyne, 2001) could also appear to be a little premature. What we saw was an eruption of enraged conformity and intra-class hostility, a spectacular illustration of the incorporation into the surrogate world of consumer capitalism of systematically depoliticised individuals unable to locate themselves in the socioeconomic and political structure and recognise their enemy. Shops and shopkeepers represented proximate and concrete barriers to the 'stuff' they craved, and that is precisely as far as their collective imagination could stretch. The striking scene of a young person looting another one who had been injured in the riot, although not representative of all the other rioters, illustrates the extremity of an atomised, nihilistic, depoliticised competitive–individualist culture given its only coherent symbolic form by consumer goods (Hall *et al.*, 2008).

This was a culture turning in on itself, an outbreak of the historically unique eviscerated and sporadic form of late-capitalist barbarism predicted in earlier research (Hall, 2000; Hall and Winlow, 2004; Horne and Hall, 1995) and later developed as the concept of *pseudo-pacification*. This is a long-term historical process in which capitalism stimulates acquisitive–aggressive drives and desires in a culture of atomised insecurity and competitive individualism and simultane-ously relocates morality from its position as a source of inspiration and ethical realist desire to an instrument of restraint, sublimation and insulation. Thus these stimulated drives and desires can be harnessed to the economy whilst the system establishes and reproduces the degree of pacification and public order necessary for the maintenance of the circulatory economic processes required for it to function (Hall, 2007; 2012a).

In a culture defined by the pseudo-pacification process, the constant over-stimulation of drives transposed into desires for consumer objects and hedonistic freedom is the cultural norm accepted by the majority, but the riots demonstrated significant differences in the acceptance of the sensibilities and rules that structure the insulating normative order. A small band of protestors and a small heterogeneous band of rioters were outnumbered by a majority who looked upon them with disgust, condemnation and punitive intent. The current divisions within the disintegrated, factionalised and depoliticised former working class (see Žižek 2010) were revealed in stark relief. The rioters displayed no conception of the system in which they live or their plutocratic structural enemy. A few saw the police, the functionaries of the structural elite, as the principal enemy, a mis-recognition created by the displacement of the traditional dialectical class struggle by liberalism's flattened, undialectical tension between the individual and the state (Bosteels, 2010). Others, unconnected with the incident that triggered the riots, misrecognised the 'rich' as local shopkeepers and other fellow citizens who had businesses or jobs, or even backpacks, electronic gadgets or scooters. Infuriated by this misrecognition and the explosive nature of the attacks, the mainstream of shopkeepers, technocrats and insecure workers duly rounded on the outcasts, who were defended largely by middle-class social liberals whose function it is to 'manage' and pacify the population by representing their idealised image of it. Solidarity in adversity, the core working-class value and the beating heart of its politics, was notable only by its absence, replaced only by brief flurries of vigilantism.

Social–liberal researchers such as MacDonald *et al.* (2010) seem to confuse traditional values *peculiar* to the working class – such as solidarity, camaraderie, anti-utilitarianism and political opposition – with *general* values such as family cohesion, the work ethic, occasional neighbourliness and civic community. They project these general values, only sporadically practised amongst their own lower middle class, onto the factional remnants of a working class that was fragmented by neoliberalism's restructuring of British life. The sense of historical continuity at the heart of this analysis is untroubled by a more appropriate sense of discontinuity, loss and absence, largely the products of the failure to oppose transatlantic consumer culture and neoliberalism with sufficient vigour and help the traditional working class to survive and develop as a political force. An imaginary romanticised 'multitude' in a simulated 'community' is substituted for the reality of a disintegrated and internally hostile culture in political disarray, and thus it is possible to avoid an intellectual encounter with the magnitude of the 'problem' itself and the political and cultural reconstruction required to recover a sense of solidarity and begin a process of renewal.

Theoretical criminology's avoidance of this intellectual encounter precludes any discussion of what – over and above the standard concepts of poverty and disenfranchisement or lack of socialisation and self-control – might have been driving the rioters. We could argue that the most pressing criminological question in the late-modern age is why outcasts consistently choose criminal enterprise, looting, vandalism and the furtherance of personal consumer interests over solidarity and politics (see Hall, 2012a). It's not enough to keep repeating the fact that most poor people do not commit actual crime as symbolised and managed by the criminal justice system, as most social–liberal researchers do (see Clement, 2010; MacDonald *et al.*, 2010). This avoids the crucial distinction between the *latent* and the *manifest* and the underlying political question that might address the issue of latency; very few of those who resist the criminal opportunities that abound in areas of permanent recession express genuine sentiments of political solidarity, in some cases displaying sentiments of pride in disunity and active hostility to each other (see Hall *et al.*, 2008). The naïve idea that crime is 'non-conformist' or 'proto-political' (Taylor *et al.*, 1973) is belied by the looters' conformity to raw Mandevillean vices, and the equally naïve idea that organic political opposition is rife amongst the working classes in general is belied by the conformity of the majority to the moral insulation – emphasised by Adam Smith (1984) as the vital ethical brake on the potentially runaway capitalist system – that keeps these vices in check, which produced the fearful and punitive reaction of the majority to its brief and localised disintegration at the hands of the rioters.

However, whilst these researchers are right that many amongst the politically disunited working class are *driven* but *not driven to distraction* by these vices, it's difficult to detect the presence of either traditional or renewed forms of political opposition. What our previous research has suggested (Hall *et al.*, 2008; Winlow and Hall, 2006) is that relatively successful individuals in most socioeconomic locations, from corporate boardrooms to sink estates, achieve their success by practising Thatcherite drives, desires and techniques of gratification (see also Dodge, 2007; Punch, 1996); we might hesitate to call them values. These are basically stimulated and harnessed vices in the Mandevillean sense, later regurgitated by the libertarian guru Friedrich von Hayek (1948), and predicated on the core assumption that the systematic stimulation of vices such as greed and envy can, if harnessed through the mechanism of the market, produce mutual benefits in the form of economic growth and individual freedom. Let's remind ourselves what Baroness Thatcher said when she was prime minister:

> They're casting their problem on society. And, you know, there is no such thing as society. There are individual men and women, and there are families. And no government can do anything except through people, and people must look to themselves first. It's our duty to look after ourselves and then also to look after our neighbour . . . No one would remember the Good Samaritan if he only had good intentions. He had money as well.

The key notions are that people should look *to* themselves and look *after* themselves before they consider others, and that looking after oneself is first and foremost an economic activity. It appears that Thatcher was not purely

Mandevillean, but she placed Mandeville's vices *before* Smith's moral restraints, in fact as the vital precursor without which practical ethics and sociability would be impossible. Economic benefits can never be the result of a moral community acting on behalf of mutual interests and demanding equality at the point of ownership and production. Here personal responsibility – no bad thing in itself – is conflated with self-interest, which in turn is economised and understood in terms of personal enrichment. In the hurly-burly of everyday life it is very easy to mistake the mutual economic benefits that in boom times stem from the application of vices to market economies as the product of a moral community whose members are looking after each other's interests. Therefore, it is also very easy for those who orchestrate and take central roles in the application of these vices and the subsequent production of economic benefits to present themselves as great benefactors, and very easy for the beneficiaries to believe them. This is a public image cultivated by corporate capitalists and bankers offering cheap goods and easy credit and governments offering security and protection, as well as criminals operating in sink estates who offer home-grown variants of all these goods and services (Hobbs, 1989; 1998).

In a chorus of synchronised knee-jerks that could not be bettered by the Tiller Girls, social-liberal critics of our work seemed to think that by pointing out the influential presence of criminal entrepreneurs and the lack of political opposition amongst the majority we were tarring the whole working class with the same brush. These critics, it must be said, either misunderstood or for some reason decided not to engage with the finer theoretical points that were vital to the argument (see for instance Clement, 2010; Ilan, 2011; MacDonald *et al.*, 2010; Shildrick, 2011). In fact, what we actually said was that criminogenic competitive–individualist and economised drives – a condensed and raw form of the drives at the Mandevillean heart of Thatcherism – were:

> taken up first by *a pro-entrepreneurial minority among the working class* who continued to reproduce them across their own history as the disorganised 'casual poor', whose precarious condition was more conducive to egotism and demoralisation than political solidarity . . . Yet, among many working-class cultures, especially those in the industrial heartlands, *traditional non-utilitarian values were still quite strongly reproduced.* Consumerism's move was to *depoliticise and individualise these values and encourage them to mutate into regulatory value/norm hybrids* that would sublimate the competitive individualist ethos that was to be re-established in the country by consumer capitalism and its attendant neo-liberal political project. When this occurred during the 1980s, large numbers of the 'rough' section quite rapidly became heavily involved in shadow-enterprise, much of it semi-legal or criminal, while the regulatory norms of the 'respectable' section held, creaking and groaning, to ward off predatory behaviour and supply the service industry with workers and the expanding higher education sector with students.
>
> (Hall *et al.*, 2008: 129, italics added)

Quite simply, we argued that what social-liberal researchers mistake as 'traditional values' are actually relocated values acting as the functional insulating norms that prevent the whole system erupting into violence and criminality. These value/ norm hybrids are to some extent holding out, but, first weakened by post-war consumer culture, finding themselves further corroded by neoliberalism's renewed competitive–individualist imperatives. This relocation renders the value system more fragile, because of course restraints are more irksome than inspiring, and the process is criminogenic because individual criminal entrepreneurs can become very influential and find far more easily both recruits and markets in areas of permanent economic recession where the mechanisms of cultural reproduction have been disrupted. Many of the individual criminals we interviewed consistently displayed sentiments that were distinctly Thatcherite in that they put their own interests first and the interests of others second by a long way, and understood their main interest to be personal enrichment. Absent was the personal responsibility to nurture others – which Thatcher had posited as a secondary and dependent obligation, or perhaps a choice, this is unclear – made possible only after personal enrichment had been achieved. In his work on youth gangs in impoverished locales Pitts (2008) has since corroborated the thesis that in locales of permanent recession successful criminal entrepreneurs wield significant cultural influence, backed up by intimidation and violence, to incorporate young people, whose work prospects are very poor and whose fragile identities are reliant on consumer symbolism, into hierarchically structured gangs, from which disengagement is often very difficult. The easy drift-in/drift-out process posited by Matza (1964) – another crumbling mainstay of criminological thinking since the 1960s – is too time-bound, naturalistic and simplistic to explain today's processes of assimilation and escape.

Neoliberal political economy, its underlying competitive individualism, its new ideological mode, its climate of objectless anxiety and its attendant consumer symbolism, have had a profound effect on subjectivity, social processes and social relations in England over the past 30 years. Current social theory is predicated on the assumptions that capitalism's institutions are constituted and reconstituted by reflexive moral agents and that its historical momentum is irreversible and progressive; thus social cohesion and justice can be established by ensuring rights to participatory inclusion (Gane, 2004). Yet, despite the revelation of plutocratic class dominance of almost feudal proportions, the reaction of large sections of the political and popular classes in Britain and the USA has been regressive and moralistic, a return to fundamental Protestant condemnation of the immoral, undeserving individual. The liberal-left's counter-move, the claim that the riots were an expression of an underlying political sentiment precipitated amongst the economically marginalised by a sense of social justice, was belied by the nature of the riots themselves, little more than nihilistic vandalism and aggravated shopping with a bit of intra-class bullying added in for good measure; no articulate political demands were made.

Languishing in the shadow of the Gulag and the Holocaust, post-war liberal discourses have, at their ethical and ontological core, not been driven by visions of a better future but by the fear of fear; the fear of the barbarism of order that might follow public reaction to the barbarism of disorder. The neoliberal solution has been to maintain pacification by dissolving politics. However, in today's very different situation, where global capitalism is fast approaching its objective limit and threatening unruly consequences, this discourse is self-defeating. To deny the rationality and functionality of objective fear is to enable the reproduction of complacency, the depoliticised substitute that is prone to shock, breakdown and extreme reactions as the pool of latent objectless anxiety in which the subject swims is agitated by external events, whilst the subject itself can discover no plausible external objects on which to focus its ethico-political energy. Thus the subject is driven inwards to the obscene Real, the congealed ideology that is harboured by each individual in the deep core of the psyche and the neurological system, the way that we have come to feel about the world that we have been forced to live and act in for many generations. Objectless anxiety, the unavoidable product of the depoliticisation that was normalised from the 1980s onwards, is the psychosocial energy source that drives and shapes the tendency of this subject to eschew politics in favour of various permutations of criminal, defensively complacent and moralistic–punitive modes of existence. Orientations to criminality and punitiveness can exist inside the same apolitical individual, which is understandable when one considers their shared root in the anxious reaction to everyday life in a fragmented, incoherent and unstable socioeconomic system that has strategically dispensed with its political objects.

The renewal of ideology and politics has been resisted by right and left, who are in the thrall of catastrophism, the fear of the return of totalitarianism should the masses choose to disrupt the capitalist order as a politically organised collective. Many amongst the left regard resistance to capitalist authority as organically pre-existent, but recent research is finding very little evidence to support this standard left-idealist notion; there is resistance to authority, but not specifically capitalist authority, only the temporary authority of lifestyle symbols, the transgression of which energises the incremental dynamic of consumer culture (Frank, 1997; Hall *et al.*, 2008). Since the 1980s the direct ideological struggle against capitalism, its subjective drives, its dominant neoliberal ideology and its ruling corporate–political class has been restricted to a small band of activists on the fringe, whilst the majority of the former working class have sunk into a state of anhedonic nihilism (Fisher, 2009) or have allowed themselves to be transported into consumer culture's surrogate socio-symbolic world, where the only struggle is against the next-door neighbour over the amount of bling the individual is able to display (Naylor, 2011; Smart, 2010).

Recent events and reactions suggest that criminological theorists should not simply regurgitate the theories of the pre-neoliberal 1960s and 1970s but start thinking again with a clear mind, perhaps reviving selected classical theories and synthesising them with new ideas appropriate to today's world. This is a complex task that requires collective effort, but this brief analysis of the recent urban riots brings two important problems into relief. First, as we have seen, we need to revise and refine the 'politics of fear' principle on which much post-war criminological thought was founded. Second, we must consider the probability that the riots were not political or even proto-political, but representative of the absence of politics, which tells us that we must reinvestigate the relation between ideology, experience and the subject's drives and desires (see Burdis and Tombs, this volume; Hall, 2012b; Johnston, 2008). The rioters were not organised proletarians, and, after the initial trigger, neither did they prove themselves to be members of an organic moral community responding to injustice. They seemed to exist outside of social space and politics; or we might say that politics has narrowed to cast them outside where they express their discontent as an 'abstract negativity', a Hegelian 'rabble' (Žižek, 2011). In the dark and anxious world of no hope and no realistic alternative – described in earlier work as a state of *anelpis* (Horne and Hall, 1995) – visions of a better future punctuate the gloom only in eccentric individual and tribal forms that have little in common with each other. At the root of depoliticisation is the absence of a world view, an order of symbols that individuals can use to explain themselves, their sentiments, their circumstances and the events that irrupt on their senses in the context of the late capitalist world, its structures and its processes.

In the noisy commotion of the riots we could hear the echo of Marcuse's (1991) 'repressive desublimation', as free rein is given to drives and desires manufactured by consumer-capitalist processes of stimulation, commercialisation and control. What we get from the liberal-left's 'evidence based policy research' is simply an expanding list of objective external conditions – relative poverty, disenfranchisement, state brutality and so on – in a grand proliferation of atheoretical 'whataboutery' that offers no analysis of the subject as it forges and reproduces itself in their midst. The liberal-left preach equality in the absence of an alternative ideology or political mechanism for re-organising socioeconomic relations and subjects in a way that equality can become an ethical goal or a practical possibility (see Flamm, 2005). This reluctance leaves a huge vacuum into which the right pour, advocating personal responsibility, discipline and punishment of the disenfranchised whilst explaining away as 'necessary to economic growth' the venality, exploitation and corruption practised every day by those who inhabit the top strata. The conflict we saw on the streets of urban England was neither social nor political, but an atomised intra-class fracas between those with a stake in capitalism and those with no stake in anything at all, happy only in the brief moment when others could be seen to be sharing their unsymbolised torment. In neoliberalism's divided social world, the pseudo-pacification process begins to break down and the internal ideological kernel of greed, envy and latent anxiety can no longer be evenly and efficiently harnessed to the economy. This powerful energy is become increasingly untethered and free-ranging, and in the absence of politics and a shared symbolic order, we must resign ourselves to the continuation of the situation as described, the latent objectless anxiety of a slowly disintegrating pseudo-pacification process punctuated by unpredictable eruptions of the barbarism of disorder, automatically triggering the barbarism of order in a downward spiral towards a fractious society of enemies.

References

Abercrombie, N., Hill, S. and Turner, B. (1981) *The Dominant Ideology Thesis*. London: Allen & Unwin.

Althusser, L. (1969) *For Marx*, trans. B. Brewster. London: Verso.

Badiou, A. (2006a) *Being and Event*. London: Continuum.

—— (2006b) *Metapolitics*. London: Verso.

Baudrillard, J. (1994) *Simulacra and Simulation*, trans. S. F. Glaser. Ann Arbor: University of Michigan Press.

Bosteels, B. (2010) 'The Leftist Hypothesis: Communism in the Age of Terror', in C. Douzinas, and S. Žižek (eds) *The Idea of Communism*. London: Verso.

Boyne, R. (2001) 'Cosmopolis and Risk: A Conversation with Ulrich Beck', *Theory, Culture and Society,* 18(4): 47–64.

Clement, M. (2010) 'Teenagers Under the Knife: A Decivilizing Process', *Journal of Youth Studies*, 13(4): 439–51

Crouch, C. (2011) *The Strange Non-Death of Neo-Liberalism*. Cambridge: Polity.

Derrida, J. (1967) *Of Grammatology*, trans. Gayatri Chakravorty Spivak. London: Johns Hopkins University Press.

Dodge, M. (2007) 'From Pink to White with Various Shades of Embezzlement: Women Who Commit White-collar Crimes', in H. Pontell and G. Geis (eds) *International Handbook of White-Collar and Corporate Crime*. New York: Springer Hall, 2012.

Fisher, M. (2009) *Capitalist Realism: Is There No Alternative?* Alresford: O Books.

Flamm, M. (2005) *Law and Order: Street Crime, Civil Disorder, and the Crisis of Liberalism*. New York: Columbia University Press.

Foucault, M. (1970) *The Order of Things: An Archaeology of the Human Sciences*. London: Tavistock.

Frank, T. (1997) *The Conquest of Cool: Business Culture, Counterculture and the Rise of Hip Consumerism*. Chicago: University of Chicago Press.

Fukuyama, F. (1993) *The End of History and the Last Man*. London: Penguin.

Gane, N. (2004) *The Future of Social Theory*. London: Continuum.

Garland, D. (2001) *The Culture of Control*. Oxford: Oxford University Press.

Giddens, A. (1984) *The Constitution of Society: Outline of the Theory of Structuration*. Berkeley: University of California Press.

Goodhart, D. (2011) 'The Riots at the End of History', *Prospect*, 9 August, www.prospectmagazine.co.uk/2011/08/the-riots-at-the-end-of-history/

Goodwin, M. (2011a) *New British Fascism: The Rise of the British National Party*. London: Routledge.

—— (2011b) 'Norway Attacks: We Can No Longer Ignore the Far-right Threat', *Guardian*, 24 July, www.guardian.co.uk/commentisfree/2011/jul/24/norway-bombing-attack-far-right

Hall, S. (2000) 'Paths to Anelpis: Dimorphic Violence and the Pseudo-pacification Process', *Parallax*, 6(2): 36–53.

—— (2007) 'The Emergence and Breakdown of the Pseudo-Pacification Process', in Watson, K. (ed.) *Assaulting the Past*. Newcastle upon Tyne: Cambridge Scholars Press.

—— (2012a) *Theorizing Crime and Deviance: A New Perspective*. London: Sage.

—— (2012b) 'The Solicitation of the Trap: On Transcendence and Transcendental Materialism in Advanced Consumer-capitalism', *Human Studies* (forthcoming).

Hall, S., Critcher, C., Jefferson, T. and Clarke, J. (1978) *Policing the Crisis: Mugging, the State and Law and Order*. London: Macmillan.

Hall, S. and Winlow, S. (2004) 'Barbarians at the Gates: Crime and Violence in the Breakdown of the Pseudo-Pacification Process', in J. Ferrell, K. Hayward, W. Morrison and M. Presdee (eds) *Cultural Criminology Unleashed*. London: Cavendish.

Hall, S., Winlow, S. and Ancrum, C. (2008) *Criminal Identities and Consumer Culture: Crime, Exclusion and the New Culture of Narcissism*. London: Willan/Routledge.

Hayek, F. (1948) *Individualism and Economic Order*. Chicago: University of Chicago Press.

Heinberg, R. (2011) *The End of Growth: Adapting to our New Economic Reality*. Forest Row: Clairview.

Hobbs, D. (1989) *Doing the Business: Entrepreneurship, the Working Class, and Detectives in the East End of London*. Oxford: Oxford University Press.

—— (1998). 'Going Down the Glocal: The Local Context of Organised Crime', *The Howard Journal*, 37(4): 407–22.

Horne, R. and Hall, S. (1995) 'Anelpis: A Preliminary Expedition into a World without Hope or Potential', *Parallax*, 1(1): 81–92.

Ilan, J. (2011) 'Reclaiming Respectability: The Class-cultural Dynamics of Crime, Community and Governance in Inner-city Dublin', *Urban Studies*, 48(6): 1137–55.

ILO (International Labour Office) (2010) *Global Employment Trends for Youth*. Geneva: ILO Publications.

Jameson, F. (2010) *The Valences of the Dialectic*. London: Verso.

Johnston, A. (2008) *Zizek's Ontology: A Transcendental Materialist Theory of Subjectivity*. Evanston, IL: Northwestern University Press.

Lacan, J. (2004) *The Seminar, Book 10: Anxiety, 1962–3*, ed. J. A. Miller. Paris: Seuil.

MacDonald, R., Webster, C., Shildrick, T. and Simpson, M. (2010) 'Paths of Exclusion, Inclusion and Desistance: Understanding Marginalized Young People's Criminal Careers', in S. Farrall, S. Maruna, R. Sparks and M. Hough (eds) *Escape Routes: Contemporary Perspectives on Life After Punishment*. London: Routledge.

Mandeville, B. (1970) *Fable of the Bees: Or Private Vices, Publick Benefits*. London: Penguin.

Marcuse, H. (1991) *One-Dimensional Man: Studies in the Ideology of Advanced Industrial Society*, 2nd edn. London: Routledge.

Matza, D. (1964) *Delinquency and Drift*. New York: Wiley.

Naylor, R.T. (2011) *Crass Struggle: Greed, Glitz and Gluttony in a Wanna-have World*. Montreal and Kingston: McGill-Queen's University Press.

Pitts, J. (2008) *Reluctant Gangsters: The Changing Face of Youth Crime*. London: Willan/Routledge.

Punch, M. (1996) *Dirty Business: Exploring Corporate Misconduct*. London: Sage.

Reiner, R. (2007) *Law and Order: An Honest Citizen's Guide to Crime and Control*. Cambridge: Polity.

Ritzer, G. (1993) *The McDonaldization of Society*. Thousand Oaks, CA: Pine Forge Press.

Shildrick, T. (2011) 'Hardship in the Land of Plenty: Poverty and Inequality in Britain and the United States', *Sociology*, 45(2): 343–48.

Sibeon, R. (2004) *Rethinking Social Theory*. London: Sage.

Smart, B. (2010) *Consumer Society*. London: Sage.

Smith, A. (1984) *The Theory of Moral Sentiments*. Indianapolis: Liberty Fund.

Stiegler, B. (2011) 'The Pharmacology of Desire: Drive-Based Capitalism and the Libidinal Dis-Economy', *New Formations*, 72: 150–61.

Tannenbaum, F. (1938) *Crime and Community*. New York: Ginn.

Taylor, I., Walton, P. and Young, J. (1973) *The New Criminology: For a Social Theory of Deviance*. London: Routledge.

Thomas, K. (2009) *The Ends of Life: Roads to Fulfilment in Early Modern England*. Oxford: Oxford University Press.

Turner, C. (2010) *Investigating Social Theory*. London: Sage.

Virilio, P. (1986) *Speed and Politics: An Essay on Dromology*. New York: Semiotext(e).

Wieviorka, M. (2009) *Violence: A New Approach*, trans. David Macey. London: Sage.

Wilkinson, I. (1999) 'Where Is the Novelty in our Current "Age of Anxiety"?', *European Journal of Social Theory*, 2(4): 455–67.

Winlow, S. and Hall, S. (2006) *Violent Night: Urban Leisure and Contemporary Culture*. Oxford: Berg.

—— (2009) 'Living for the Weekend: Youth Identities in North-East England', *Ethnography*, 10(1): 91–113.

—— (2011) 'What is an "Ethics Committee"?: Academic Governance in an Epoch of Belief and Incredulity', *British Journal of Criminology*, http://bjc.oxfordjournals.org/content/early/2011/10/20/bjc.azr082.abstract

Žižek, S. (1997) *The Abyss of Freedom*. Ann Arbor: University of Michigan Press.

—— (2000) *The Ticklish Subject: The Absent Centre of Political Ontology*. London: Verso.

—— (2002) *Welcome to the Desert of the Real*. London: Verso.

—— (2006) *The Parallax View*. Cambridge, MA: MIT Press.

—— (2010) *Living in the End Times*. London: Verso.

—— (2011) 'Shoplifters of the World Unite', *London Review of Books*, 19 August.

10 Censure, culture and political economy

Beyond the death of deviance debate

Colin Sumner

In *The Sociology of Deviance: An Obituary* (1994), I concluded that the concept of deviance as behaviour breaching social norms had been superseded. This was widely accepted (e.g. Bendle 1999, Mitchell Miller *et al.* 2001, Best 2004, Moxon 2010) and the reviews were very positive (e.g. Loader 1995, Venkatesh 1995, O'Connell 1995, Roberts 1996, and Lemert 1995). But some American sociologists claim to have spotted deviance, like Elvis, re-entering the building. Scorning my work and tying their claims to a Republican neo-conservatism, they have called for the resurrection of the idea of deviant behaviour as an antidote to what they see as contemporary amoral relativism and cultural decline (Goode 1995, 2002, 2003, 2004a, 2004b; Hendershott 2002; see also Marshall *et al.* 2007).

Nevertheless, deviance remains lifeless and its recent autopsy was unnecessary. The concept of social censure has considerably more descriptive and explanatory power, is research-generative and can be deployed irrespective of politics. Out there, censure is ubiquitous. In this essay, I want to illustrate this, and draw out its sociological significance, by commenting on the recent UK riots (see also Sumner 2011a, 2011b). Our societies have undergone a shift in the way they operate. If the 1960s were a time of deviance, in thought and in action, this new century is a time of censure both in thought and in action.

The dying of the light

Even Goode admitted that 'work in the field of deviance today is less bountiful, less abundant, less plentiful, and if we are to trust citation figures, theoretically and conceptually less creative, innovative, influential and vital than it was in the 1970s and 1980s' (2004b: 52). Its twin, the concept of social control, has also declined in energy and utility (see Bergalli and Sumner 1997: 25–33). Any dynamism left in the idea of deviance by the 1990s was confined to the sardonic and positive deployment of stigma as a badge of pride and parody within identity politics, for example the recent 'Slutwalks'.

Words are meaningless outside of a language structure, and scientific concepts only have vitality within a theory combining logic and evidence. That theory is lodged within an historical period and societal conditions that feed its plausibility. The idea of the free movement of labour did not have much comprehension within slave societies, and only developed within economic theory inside the capitalist mode of production. Similarly, as the post-war consensus broke down in Western democracies, the idea of social deviation from agreed norms gradually evaporated as an incisive notion in social science and in popular morality – it became quite obviously what it had always been in principle, namely a social censure.

As Joel Best pointed out: '[b]y the mid-1970's, there was no consensus about how deviance ought to be defined, what phenomena it ought to encompass, or how these disagreements might be resolved' (2004: 486). Such a conceptual dis-appearance is akin to that of dark with the coming of light. It can arrive gradually but is always total when complete. 'That time and its discourse have passed: our vision is too politically aware to slip back' (Sumner 1994: 311).

The death metaphor itself is, Best says, a red herring; deviance simply did not turn out to be that useful a concept (2004: 489). It was, he said rightly, a generalizing concept that blurred too many differences and similarities between censured behaviours; sociologists found it more precise to talk about the specificities of, say, prostitution or homicide. Indeed, mental illness only shared the same bed as political dissidence under the Madame of a particular political ideology.

My own critique took a stronger form, namely that 'deviance' was actually a social censure, albeit a liberal one closely linked with the New Deal social administration in the USA (see Sumner 1994: ch. 3 but also 1983a, 1990a, 1990b, 1997, 2004, 2006). During that period and until the 1970s, the concept had some truth-value or purchase within social reality. With its need for moral conformity, social order and population management, American society of the Great Depression flirted with the notion of a 'clinical' sociology, a science of the social, the idea that we Ph.D.s could treat deviants scientifically on the basis that society was a sick 'patient'. 'Rebels without a cause', the physically challenged, the 'badly brought up', juvenile delinquents, members of other cultures, sexual and cultural explorers, 'socially inadequate', and even professional criminals were analysed by administrators and academics in the 1930s, influenced by psychiatry and psychoanalysis, as a group that evidenced system issues or 'social problems'. The category of social deviance actually had little purchase in the UK and Europe, even in the 1960s, perhaps reflecting our post-war humanism, the limited nature of our immigration conflicts and the embedded nature of our class system. European sociologists rarely questioned who had the right to define normality, and were more concerned with social defence and reconstruction, erecting legal, political and bureaucratic barriers to the possibility of fascism ever returning – with the behaviour of the state and its political and legal constitution.

Social deviance in the USA comprised a set of negative categories designed to warrant and fit the agreed punishment and regulation of people generally seen as deviant from general community norms (Goffman 1968a: 334; also Sumner 2006). A broad moral consensus was assumed so these were not defined by being enemies of the state. For example, the sociology of deviance did not study the Rosenbergs or McCarthyism, whereas European sociology would have. Generally, to paraphrase Goffman, US sociology targeted those perceived to be in some sort of collective denial of the post-war consensual social order (see 1968b: 170–71); the rebels without a cause, hippies rather than communists, or, in Foucault's terms, those adjudged as needing tutelage and therapy before they could slot into the conveyor belt of 'mildness–production–profit' (1977: 219). This was its uniqueness. European sociology was always much more concerned with what the state defined as right and wrong, with legal rights, and with the moral, ideological and political authority of the state.

Like Foucault (1967: ix–x), and trying to absorb and move beyond the gains made in American deviancy theory, I depicted the censure of deviance as constituted by a series of normative judgments, or ideological cuts in the fabric of thought, made in the heat of social conflicts of all kinds and embedded with interest in subsequent practice; the dominant judgments being those made by the rich, powerful and authoritative by means of the state. These dominant moral judgments shaped the distinction between deviance and normality; they were the foundations of custom, law and science as a 'morality beyond the expertise of common sense and the commoner – a people divorced from its practical reflections, practical reflections divorced from the people' (ibid.).

So, today, I would assume from the outset that riot is not a descriptive neutral term that formed and survived through agreement, but a selective and partisan ideological category based on the perception of 'disorder' from the top. I would expect research to confirm that historically it was a censure by the rich and powerful of the resistance and mischief of the poor and powerless. I would also expect that when we take the long view of history, we would find that (a) the censured activity is actually very common or not abnormal, and (b) that many famous or established people engaged in it. As historian of London, Peter Ackroyd said of the recent riots:

> [T]hey simply show a pattern of activity in the city that will endure as long as the city itself . . . Rioting has always been a London tradition. . . . since the early Middle Ages. There's hardly a spate of years that goes by without violent rioting of one kind or another. They happen so frequently that they are almost part of London's texture. The difference is that in the past the violence was more ferocious, and the penalties were more ferocious – in most cases, death.
>
> (Ackroyd and McSmith 2011, also Sumner 2011b)

In short, my work re-defined the concept of deviance and its status, it did not just dismiss it. The censure of deviance was revealed as part of the heat of the battle not the lens of a neutral observer. The concept thus died of natural causes, reworked in the course of scientific activity, and had no life-support from current social conditions.

The death of deviance and the rise of culture

Goode was alarmed to find that other sociologists saw deviance in severe decline within US universities (see 2003: 511) and pursued the matter obsessively, creating a 'death of deviance debate'. This 'debate' never took off, even in the USA, and was a damp squib. Even if many US universities had continued to teach the field, it would not have proved anything anyway given the communitarian tendencies there arising from the great melting pot of immigration.

Goode correctly argued that the field of deviance develops out of, and emphasises, diversity and multiculturalism. The idea of deviance was not born out of moral absolutism but from the pragmatic tolerance needed in composing the New Deal; from attempts by sociologists, politicians, psychiatrists and social administrators to defuse structurally profound social divisions, at very much the same time that anthropologists were 'discovering' that the social practices of 'natives' in developing countries were not the 'mindless' rituals of 'alien savages' but the expressions of a different culture. The concept of deviance was part of the very discovery of the concept of culture itself (see Bauman 1973 and Sumner 1979). The post-war systems-managers pragmatically wrote off persistent social conflicts by saying that deviants need to be re-socialized into 'our culture' – the censure of deviance was not initially morally relativistic and certainly not politically agnostic, but merely pragmatic in search of peace, stability and prosperity.

After 1945, liberal versions of deviancy theory questioned whether re-socialization could work, given structural inequalities, and held that variance, diversity and resistance to conformity were actually positive human attributes of any healthy society and to be celebrated as features of any democracy. Finestone's elegant elegy (1964) to the 'cool cats' of 'color' remains a classic statement of the culturally specific character of supposedly deviant behaviour and was about 50 years before *The Wire*. Lemert (1972) liked the term 'human deviance' and produced studies demonstrating how human beings are aware of and respond to the social censure of deviance. Radical deviancy theory went even further, claiming that much deviance was authentic human resistance to inhuman or oppressive social conditions (Taylor *et al.* 1973).

Today's UK Tory politicians, in contrast, are returning to the Victorian period in portraying this summer's looting and public disorder as purely criminal activity entirely disconnected from its surrounding culture. It is as if the American experience of the twentieth century, and all the intellectual gains of the sociology of deviance, never happened. Like Goode and Hendershott, however, they want to stamp out anything that challenges their world. Theirs is the opposite of an understanding of the humanity of 'the riots' and an outright denial of any possible such character. Inevitably the punishments that were to follow would be disproportionately severe, unlike the almost saintly tolerance shown to the greater asset destruction caused by the bankers, who were also their friends, relatives, colleagues and peers. This inconsistency is not only venal and amoral; it destroys any potential common ground upon which to base an idea of deviance, leaving only opposed censures. Many people would condemn the riots as wrong of course, but are even angrier that the politicians (a) cannot see that they were less damaging than the deregulated banks failing to protect savings from speculative trading, and (b) cannot understand that the two are connected, if only because the latter, amongst many examples recently, set a very bad example.

Modern capitalist cultures cannot permit the full range of human variance, diversity or resistance, although they do better than the old feudal world or the closed Stalinist societies. Goffman commented: 'mental hospitals are found because there is a market for them' (1968a: 334). Social censure and regulation exist because human societies need them, but their strength and form varies with the type of society: market societies will generate different censures and forms of regulation from those societies where the state allocates goods. 'Riot' in modern capitalist societies is a censure of chaotic, public, free, collective movement, whether or not it destroys shops and liberates commodities or is anti-authority or just drunken; it is punished by deprivation of freedom, and both the event and its censure happen mainly in the market society which generates them. Riots, whether as the censure or the censured actions, do not tend to occur in a satrapy or a Soviet Union. In societies of that type, it is best to be organized, armed and popular if you want to revolt or have a drunken brawl because you are more likely to be censured as dissidents or saboteurs and shot.

Sociologists like Goffman saw the recurrent need to stigmatize or brand individuals as a social system-need, not as a necessary indication of individual defects; however, they never linked the cultural patterns of censure to the particularities of social structure (Sumner 1994: 225 ff.). For Goffman, in a multicultural, divided world, anyone could become a deviant in a lottery of 'fateful actions' where some were praised and others censured. In my view, neither the selectivity of social censure nor the form and character of human variance are both cultural forms tightly reflecting the economic and political worlds they inhabit. Riots are as much part of capitalism as boom and bust.

If we compare investment bankers with rioters, we can see that the rich and powerful often engage in anti-social behaviour but are rarely censured as anti-social for it in the popular media or in popular culture. Indeed, the word 'society' has that 'other' meaning as the cultural habitat of the rich and powerful. Their frequent serious anti-sociality is overlooked in our fascination with their lifestyle peccadilloes and the privacy battles that ensue. They can send thousands to their deaths in war, ensure their friends and relatives obtain lucrative government contracts, or destroy the life-savings of ordinary workers but none of that would ever be classified as social deviance. That tells you all you need to know about deviance. It has a very specific meaning in Western cultures, one that most certainly does not include the nasty habits of 'high society'.

The rich and powerful, as authorities, ensure the 'correct' cultural assignment of censures to the 'appropriate' categories of the population, and therefore do not usually receive them themselves: turkeys do not vote for Christmas. It ensures that those connected to riots and looting, however remotely, are sentenced heavily and that those whose behaviour brings the country's and the world economy to its knees are rewarded with huge bonuses, pay-offs, pensions, peace and quiet, and of course full state honours or titles. In the moral economy of modernity, riot and authority are opposites. Nothing much has changed on this score since the eighteenth century (Thompson 1975). The very censure of riot speaks first and foremost of lack of authority. Authority without fairness or integrity provokes mischief, theft, damage, protest and rebellion; this is duly censured as 'rioting', and the cycle continues.

For Goode, deviance is an appropriate generic term to describe 'behavior that calls forth' negative social reactions and therefore the death of deviance is an impossibility because we always have to call censured behaviour something (2002: 108). He is wrong. It may not be the behaviour that elicits the stigma – there is smoke without fire – branding may occur because of vested interests or cultural prejudice; also the same behaviour can elicit very different responses from authority depending on who is involved and the context of the relationship. The behaviour is not the key to the censure; it is not its secret and becomes less so every decade we live in the information society of spin, spying, surveillance and gossip. Therefore it is misleading to refer to 'deviant behaviour' when any behaviour could be censured as deviant depending on the context and when there are many moralities in an amoral world. If we use the neutral term censured behaviours, it reserves all possibilities for the court of evidence. The censure might turn out to be fair or agreeable but it might turn out to be arbitrary, inappropriate or even fascistic.

The power to publicize the meaning of behaviour in today's world, notably the power to censure, is a massive capacity owned by the few, yet even their tabloid naming and shaming does not determine popular perception and often feeds off it. *Contra* Goode's view of deviance as trans-historical, we live in a world in the twenty-first century that is quite distinct in that its forms of political domination and authority are very dependent on the power to censure. Of course, in medieval times, the ecclesiastical courts regulated the petty improprieties of the villeins, but never has there been so much social censure, nor in so many places in the system, nor so much branding power in the hands of so few; and villain is the word for naughty, rude or criminal today in so many languages. This is such a difference in size, degree and reach that it amounts to a very different modus operandi in social relations. In the information age, the epoch of blogging, spin, sound-bites, and the sponsored speech, social censure is king.

Behaviours do not speak for themselves; and less today than ever. Killing can be many things other than murder: euthanasia, accident, negligence, recklessness, heroism, collateral damage, suicide, assisted suicide, abortion or disaster. Asset-stripping or stock shorting can be forms of destroying value in the corporate world; in the unincorporated world we have malicious damage and rioting. These different activities have little in common yet are perversely related in casino capitalism. Calling them both behavioural deviations creates confusion, explains nothing, is misleading, and generates nothing of scientific interest. A censure analysis, devoid of moral absolutism and distinguishing rigorously the behaviour from the social reaction and from the meaning of both to their agents, raises interesting research questions immediately.

For example, is destroying value by throwing bricks through the windows of closed shops in a national chain so much worse than destroying value by leveraged shorting of an un-owned stock or insurance policy? Both are attacks on the inflated asset values of others at the end of an asset price boom. What really is the difference? Both are value corrections. What is worse to whom and why? Is apparent proximity to core dominant values of our society what explains the muted and variable reaction to stock shorting and apparent distance from those values that accounts for the relentlessly negative response to 'rioting'? But what if the investment bankers who oppose the Glass–Steagal Act and the separation of retail from investment banking, care nothing for the social consequences of their actions, for moral values, for domination or for anything other than making money? And what if the rioters dearly love the commodities they steal from the shops they loot? Are the bankers then the deviants and the looters loyal supporters of capitalism? Or were the English looters of 2011 sent to prison as criminals with such long sentences, despite their love of commodities, ultimately because they exposed the lack of control of the authorities? Is that why there was little 'rioting' in Wales and Scotland, countries with their own parliaments and clear national identities?

The sociological concept of deviance was not some great transcendental truth striding through history. It was not even used until the twentieth century, nor does it serve us well to understand forms or categories of censured practices in previous epochs. 'Deviance' as an idea is on a par with 'degeneracy' from the nineteenth century: both are censures reflecting the ideological and historical character of thinking about blame and transgression during their time. Censure is the general, trans-historical concept, the idea that is workable in all periods, the term that appears in Shakespeare, Sellin and Becker.

The call for the resurrection of deviance

Goode's view of the residual vitality of deviance was confronted with the evidence of his own survey (2003), the survey of Mitchell Miller *et al.* (2001), and the views of many sociologists (e.g. Bendle 1999, Best 2004), so Hendershott's Catholic fundamentalist *The Politics of Deviance* (2002), demanding the resurrection of a concept of deviance, could be expected to please him. It did the opposite (Goode 2004b). Goode read it 'in horror', and then radically re-worked his position, to become a kind of conflict theorist, arguing (2004b: 47) that the story of deviance is a battle to control the ways people think, feel and behave – where the winners classify themselves as normal and the losers are excluded beyond the boundaries of society.

Goode objected to Hendershott's book absolutism: as if 'deviance *is* preordained, *does* drop down from the skies, should *not* be thought of as constructed or relative to time and place', 'I was hurled back into the nineteenth century, into a Platonic or Manichean absolutistic world of light and darkness' (2004b: 47). His trans-historical, universal, concept of deviance had become a historically specific social censure! He later changes his mind again in the hope that the 2004 US presidential election, in bringing back the Republicans, might return 'deviant behaviour' to centre stage politically. Hendershott was now transformed from a 'crackbrained lunatic, spouting silly ideas'[1] to a 'flagbearer' for that section of the US population wanting a return to traditional morality and 'family values' (ibid.). He then wonders whether deviance can be said to be dead or unimportant, given the rise of the Republican, absolutist, right.

Goode declared that the sociology of deviance is not dead, just less 'creative and vital' (2004b: 52). It had, he claims, evolved into a series of ethnographies of cultural sub-worlds such as those of 'Rodeo groupies. Strip club bouncers. Men who intentionally spread HIV. Female-to-male transsexuals'. Anyone smell a cultural agenda here? A resurrection of deviancy theory driven by the absolutist right is a timely reminder that 'new directions' need not be progressive and can be nostalgic. Indeed, Goode's examples raise questions for the fashionable 'cultural criminology'. Documenting the minutiae of subcultural eccentricity is interesting but, sociologically, in itself does it move us forwards? Describing what rioters wear or the music they like, noting their use of smartphones, etc., is relevant and important but is no substitute for answers to key analytic questions such as were the riots a subcultural expression, or a 'flash mob' orchestrated by the criminal underground, or a moment of aggravated shopping during an under-consumption crisis.

Resisting the temptation to speculate on the significance of 'rodeo groupies', we note that Goode believed that the 'Hendershotts of the world' influenced academia through their control of budgets for universities and research funding. If he were right, there would be more social deviance classes and original research. Recent experience in both the US and UK, however, suggests an increased caution on university research ethics committees and institutional review boards and therefore on what fieldwork on deviance universities will permit.

We leave Goode to his confusion and turn to the religious absolutism driving the resurrection fantasy. Hendershott had noted that 'few sociologists teach about deviance and even fewer write about it' (2002: 7–8). She believed they were scared to face facts about the dissolution of traditional morality: to 'even speak of the concept of deviance any more' would mean them reluctantly discussing 'homosexuality, teenage promiscuity, adultery and addiction in relation to standards of "acceptable conduct"' (ibid.: 8). She added that for Foucault and myself, 'madness, murder, incest, prostitution, homosexuality, illegal drug use and robbery were not "deviance" [but] "categories of censure" mapping out new systems and territories of domination' (p. 5).

Today, Hendershott complained, landlords are accused of causing homelessness and an unfair economy blamed for causing economic crime. We hear the familiar Christian refrain, applied of course only to the poor and vulnerable: people must take responsibility for their actions. 'Behavior that is socially and personally destructive' is 'on the rise' (p. 7); '[N]obody was stamped as deviant' (p. 6). She concluded that '[m]ost social scientists became convinced that the sociology of deviance was more about the imposition of selective censure by the dominant elements of society – the 'construction' of deviance – than it was about deviant behaviour itself' (p. 3).

In this fantasy of a resurrection denied, Hendershott completely ignores the rise of 'left realism' in criminology in the 1980s, which recognized the shabby reality of being in 'the underclass' and the harsh reality of being a victim of street crime, rape or domestic violence. Both of these demanded a renewal in Labour policies to recognize victims and rein in crime, and both obtained large-grant survey work. Hendershott also seems unaware of Marx's comments on the criminal 'scum' amongst the 'rotting masses' and the reactionary role they play in political struggles. She would, however, be aware of radical Catholic orders, that do so much to foster development in developing countries, countering the effects of global capitalism, but she says nothing of their views on what is socially deviant.

Hendershott wanted the concept of deviance to be resurrected: 'reports of its death were greatly exaggerated – particularly as we watched an escalation in behaviours that would have been declared deviant in the past' (2002: 7). So, the eternity of riots and underclass crime prove that the concept of deviance is a good way of understanding what's happening? Confusing the thing in itself with the thing for itself, its intellectual concept, and invoking the contemporary cultures of dependency in our inner cities, Hendershott bemoaned the fact that these were once called deviance and that in itself would have been the basis for doing something about them. She said there were 'no deviants left, only victims'. Yet deviance for her was a useful concept in 'helping us understand social order'; more likely, in enforcing the present social order (see ibid.: 156).

Like other US conservatives J. Q. Wilson and Daniel Moynihan, Hendershott wants a world where social stability is based on a consensual moral order, integral to which would be 'a shared concept of deviance', the contests around which would function as a progressive boundary-maintenance system (ibid.). But wouldn't it be even better, more democratic, if we had social stability based on cultural diversity? Given the cultural diversity of US society, doesn't her position mean that the only way her favoured politics can succeed is through the suppression of other cultures, for a 'shared moral order' is not likely to be voluntary? And would she accept that bad banking and politicians milking office are a much bigger threat to order than the underclass? She regrets that deviance today has become the battlefield for single-issue campaigners, grinding their axes for their members, and calls for a re-moralization of society (ibid.: 163); not apparently aware that so did I (in Bergalli and Sumner 1997: 149; also in Sumner 1990a: 49–52), to protect people against business, the capitalist state, and multinationals. That's the problem with a return to moral absolutism: there are no moral absolutes, and there never were.

Reflecting US neo-conservatives' ideological inability to accept disagreement, and their zealous, fanatical assertion of a single set of moral values to unite the universe under the rule of the stars and stripes, Hendershott recalls Senator Moynihan addressing the ASA in 1992 and asserting an increase in 'the amount of deviant behavior' (quoted Hendershott 2002: 7). Even in a forum of US sociologists like himself, a man so 'supportive of social science research' only received 'subdued applause'. Moynihan apparently argued that we had been de-stigmatizing previously deviant acts and needed to be more intolerant. Even those conservatives who would dig up the grave for an attempt at resurrection know that the corpse is six feet under. One day perhaps they will grasp the reasons for that, and see that it is only their Cold War delusion that leftist politicos killed it. The behavioural concept of deviance died of natural causes. Their arguments for its resurrection are right-wing political ideology from a bygone age linked to a desired resurrection of that bygone age.

There is certainly a need for a critical re-moralization of society, and for a major review and restatement of the criminal law – to reverse the influence of the amoral culture of the rich and powerful at all points. The concept of social censure does not imply a critique of all censuring (see Sumner 2004 and 2006). My own view is that we need a democratization and rationalization of social censures. For example, we might incarcerate the investment bankers who so recklessly destroyed our economy, with the MPs who fiddled their expenses so outrageously, as well as the rioters who engaged in violence, arson and serious malicious damage. If our sentencing tariff prioritized damage to society over public disorder, the sentences for reckless bankers would be much longer than those of most rioters. We need to debate the censures we wish to enforce and those that we can relax.

The society of censure

From deviance to censure is not just a shift in sociological theory, but also a change in the way societies operate. From 1945 to 1980, the difficulty was finding justifiable and effective methods of punishment. In today's world, the task for authorities, including those in micro-systems, is to find censures that will connect, win respect, bind, justify, authorize and, ultimately, evoke self-discipline and motivation. It is no longer a case of who censures wins but whose censures win. The battle for control of societies has become a slanging match; the question is whether stigma can, like mud, be made to stick. Censure has become a key weapon in politics; almost a mode of politics. Politics has moved from prudent governance in the offices of power, via a struggle for hegemony on the streets, to a virtual battle or e-conflict between the politically active, intellectuals, 'spin doctors', lawyers, bloggers, tweeters, 'smartphone' users, online voters and the chattering classes.

Deviance was developed originally as a generic concept for a number of behaviours found socially problematic by authorities. It does not, and never did, refer to objective statistical variations but to highly acculturated, negative, authoritative, moral assessments of behaviour, demeanour, status, attribute, style, ideas, intention or state of mind. But today moral judgments are no longer authoritative and very few pronunciations from authorities are granted any moral weight. Like the staircase outside the building in 'postmodern' architecture, morality is now on the outside of society trying to get back in. It is no longer a key foundation of the whole structure.

By the late 1960s, any notion of normative consensus had become history. Sustained decolonization in the Third World fired nails deep into the coffin. Mandela went from terrorist to global statesman, and Pol Pot went from political science doctorate to mass murderer. Heroes became villains and vice versa. The idea of social deviance disappeared into the vortex of the globalized, culturally diverse, world that produced it. General norms may exist but there is so little consensus on their application: all international censures and criminal laws need constant vigilance, armies of lawyers and expensive courts – and even then only selected, counter-hegemonic villains are paraded through them, never Western leaders or generals. We may all deplore murder and torture but will disagree on exactly who the murderers and torturers are; never mind the differences between homicide, suicide, accident, natural disaster, negligence, medical termination, provocation and self-defence.

Deviance, along with morality and respect, had been buried by the time that many realized that the world was dominated by dysfunctional and irrational markets, regulated by few agreed and enforced trading rules. By the end of the 1970s, after the decolonizations and the first oil crisis, we knew that large-scale theft, in so many ways, could be hailed as wealth-creation and nation-building. Kleptocracy became a sociological concept (Andreski 1972). By the end of the 1980s, our depoliticized cynicism meant that some had the confidence to celebrate their own censure, turning fate humorously and sardonically into the positive prize of identity. For after all, in the meaningless entropy of post-modernity, you were lucky to have an identity.

We also discovered excess in the 1980s and 1990s, whether in finances, politics or sexuality, and some even rediscovered life-balance. Excessive deviance really was painful, leading to disease and damage, dysfunctional relationships, or just plain ruin. This of course is the world that Goode and Hendershott understandably rail against. This was not just a stern parental warning; it was for real. We entered a new age of 'no pain no gain'. We went from protest and self-indulgence to realizations that we had to restrain our selves, that we should sometimes censure and draw a line, and that we had to censure in a responsible manner. Our children of course ensured that we were truly uncertain of the basis upon which we censured in many areas. We had moved from moral conflict to deep uncertainty about the idea of morality itself, yet at the same time many new social conditions, such as lack of trust, heightened insecurity and perceived proximity and degree of risk, have maximized an inclination to censure, wherever and whenever, always others first of course, and in that quagmire of censoriousness without normative security we try to find our judgmental feet to this day. We live in a world of censure.[2]

The censure of the recent English riots

The UK riots of summer 2011 were volcanic magma waiting to burst the surface. Indeed, once the cooling-down processes stop, there is every reason to expect further eruptions both here and abroad.[3] After all, there are no signs that our ruling

Etonians know anything about sociological volcanoes.[4] They are mistaken in seeing the 'riots' as purely criminal; romantics would be equally wrong to see them as political protest. They were neither, although the politically active of all colours might just yet inflate them into part of a general anti-capitalist movement. Insofar as you can sensibly lump the different behaviours together under one censorious umbrella, the 'riots' are to some extent a direct expression of a free market economy working as you would expect it to, i.e. chaotically. They are not a clear sign of sickness in society, nor that it is broken; they are a sign it is working fairly normally, with opportunistic materialism as the norm and unequal access to goods as the fact. The shops most targeted seem to show that the adverts have worked.

At a superficial level, the moral of the story for the authorities was: don't all go on holiday at the same time and especially at the same time as the kids are off school! Clearly, the authorities had no idea how much anger people feel currently. If they had, they would realize that not everyone is going to sit on it. They don't just need to reintroduce the idea of paying for goods at the till, they need to understand that conventional commodity circuits for many of us were already fractured in many places. For example, many prices are unreachable legally, much is available on the black market, much is free on the 'green' circuit, 'posh' people often get in free anyway, and politics seems to be a licence to print money. When we go over our authorized overdraft levels we get heavily fined but when the banks do it they are given billions of our money to rebuild. Governments everywhere do not seem to realize the full implications of most people being very angry with the investment bankers, and their political friends and relatives, who have blown our future so recklessly and unprofessionally.[5] We want parity with the bankers, either in the form of being given money to recapitalize our balance sheets or in the form of them being punished for their financial errors.

The comfortable cluelessness of the politicians, intermarried and interlocked with the bankers and other wealthier classes in a culture of educated idiocy, is a major problem for us: they are out of touch and probably cannot hear even when they listen, because their world is so remote from ours. The 'riots' are undoubtedly testimony to the current distance between politicians, police and authorities generally, on the one hand, and just about everyone else in the country on the other. Their capacity to steer the ship of hegemony appears to have gone. Indeed, most of them do not seem to give a flying four-x for hegemony. Existing models of political domination through the power of ideology need re-writing. No one in casino capitalism is really 'in charge': there are just angry people censuring each other across various chasms. Those who can, leave for a beach, anywhere.

In an aggressively entrepreneurial free-market economy that openly and committedly despises state regulation and worships de-regulation, how can anyone be surprised when street people behave with scant respect for law or justice? Few at the top recently have displayed any sense that there were any rules or commonsense about when and how you did acquisitive opportunism. Indeed, the message from the top for years has been 'help yourself'. Whether it be Russian businessmen buying up under-priced state assets via relations with politicians, or UK companies ripping off the state through PFI contracts, or politicians giving themselves the best pension system in the land and informally milking their office, the bad example has been set repeatedly: 'take your chance, help yourself is OK and it works'.

The 'rioters' have copied the rich well: they saw a niche in the market and drove a coach and horses through it, creating what you might call a broken window of opportunity. Those officially censured as 'rioters' included a millionaire's daughter, an ex-Olympics ambassador, a children's charity volunteer, a man who accepted a stolen bottle of beer whilst helping someone out of a fire; and there were many others who could hardly be described as criminals or underclass. They made the most of a moment involving summer holidays, absent policing, smart phones and new media. This was 'aggravated shopping' at a time of global under-consumption, with politicians and banks still encouraging consumer spending despite high levels of unemployment and indebtedness, with authorities elsewhere, or in plain disarray with police, politicians and media in particular at each others' throats.

Some of the rioters' behaviour was so disrespectful, violent and dangerous and it showed as much sign of radical consciousness as your local Tory MP. Many actually did seem conservative or at least depoliticized in outlook: opportunist consumers rather than street-fighting alternative culture, Thatcher's babies not Trotsky's cadres (see Hall *et al.* 2008). This was not a consciously political protest nor did it exhibit clues towards any subliminal political message. This was not even an incoherent attempt to stick two fingers up to the establishment; rather, it stuck two fingers into the pie of Western affluence.

The riots stood in contrast to the hard work and principles of all those people who try to resolve their problems without damaging others. In a country where strong community and family bonds are in sharp decline, attacking community members, damaging community institutions and destroying neighbours' property is hardly the answer, and actually is part of the problem; machine-breaking by Luddites did not rid us of industrial alienation.

Historically, what happens now is that the ruling classes respond with hastily formulated special measures and emergency powers, lashing out wildly and punishing disproportionately, after which it takes several generations to return the laws of the land to their normal state. The unlucky, the naïve and the weak get caught and receive heavy sentences; most of the organized criminals will not. This is exactly what is happening right now. Authority tries to restore itself with force, overlooking the fact that force alone does not restore authority. If we want to prevent further riots, we should address issues around polarization of wealth, advertising standards and the proliferation of advertising, the need for protection of our core values and services from the remorseless logic of business, the concentration of jobs in already privileged regions, the declining health and integrity of families, and the public provision for young unemployed in a post-manufacturing world of vastly different life chances.

The riots and their censure do, however, have something else to tell us: it's easy to dismiss Stalinistic socialism but a raw business culture is toxic and could produce the same type of civil wars that Mexico and Central America are now experiencing over their illegal drugs industry. Societal stability requires a re-constitution of society via a re-insertion of social values at all points. We need protection from business: the censure and punishment of the bankers could be the starting point of a new moral order or at least the recognition of the idea and reality of the moral economy.

Notes

1 I had a few years earlier been dismissed as a 'crackpot', so clearly Goode is prone to the unprofessional habit of dismissing his opponents as mentally ill. This matters because it demonstrates how much the concept of deviance, and the concomitant sense of moral superiority, meant to – what to the rest of us looks like – a redneck, imperialist, America threatened by its decline and the rise of a new world order.
2 There is much yet to be said about the social-psychoanalytical dimension of increased censure in a world where self-discipline and the inner father struggle to find their normative basis or drive.
3 A fuller sociological explanation and interpretation of the riots, with video comments on their meaning inside the UK, can be found in Sumner (2011a) upon which this last section is closely based. For details and other comments on the riots, by participants and leading sociologists, such as Bauman and Žižek, see Sumner (2011b).
4 See   www.independent.co.uk/opinion/commentators/adrian-hamilton/adrian-hamilton-never-mind-leadership-ndash-this-is-all-about-branding-2336853.html   (Accessed September 2011).
5 I believe many disagree with the view of the then chancellor of the exchequer, Alistair Darling, that his Labour government could not let the banks fail because of the potential domino effect of all the banks collapsing. Darling wrote recently: 'Banks . . . had made catastrophic errors of judgment and in some cases they did not even know what they were doing'. He said: 'In normal times, a bank failure is manageable. . . . these were not normal times . . . The risk of one bank collapsing and taking all the others with it was acute' (excerpted from Darling 2011). Many of us believe that was a risk we could afford to take, because it was imperative and much cheaper to create a state bank and compensate everyone who would lose savings directly. Levels of savings statutorily insured in the UK against bank failure are much lower than, say, in the USA; they should have been doubled long ago to around £100,000 – that apparent generosity would have saved the UK a fortune.

References

Ackroyd, P. and McSmith, A. (2011) 'Rioting has been a London tradition for centuries'. *Independent*, 22 August.
Andreski, S. (1972) *Social Sciences as Sorcery*. London: Andre Deutsch.
Bauman, Z. (1973) *Culture as Praxis*. London: Routledge and Kegan Paul.
Bendle, M. F. (1999) 'The death of the sociology of deviance?' *Journal of Sociology*, 35: 42–59.
Bergalli, R. and Sumner, C. S. (eds) (1997) *Social Control and Political Order: European Perspectives at the End of the Century*. London: Sage.
Best, J. (2004) 'Deviance may be alive, but is it intellectually lively? A reaction to Goode', *Deviant Behavior*, 25: 483–92.
Darling, A. (2011) *Back from the Brink*. London: Atlantic.

Finestone, H. (1964) 'Cats, kicks and color', in Becker, H. S. (ed.) *The Other Side*. New York: Free Press.

Foucault, M. (1967) *Madness and Civilization: A History of Insanity in the Age of Reason*. London: Tavistock.

—— (1977) *Discipline and Punish: The Birth of the Prison*. London: Allen Lane.

Goffman, E. (1968a) *Asylums*. Harmondsworth: Penguin.

—— (1968b) *Stigma*. Harmondsworth: Penguin.

Goode, E. (1995) 'Review of Sumner's Sociology of Deviance', *Social Forces*, 73: 1629–30.

—— (2002) 'Does the death of the sociology of deviance make sense?' *The American Sociologist*, 33: 116–28.

—— (2003) 'The MacGuffin that refuses to die: an investigation into the condition of the sociology of deviance', *Deviant Behavior*, 24: 507–33.

—— (2004a) 'Is the sociology of deviance still relevant?' *The American Sociologist*, 35: 46–57.

—— (2004b) 'The "death" macguffin redux: comments on Best', *Deviant Behaviour*, 25: 493–509.

Habermas, J. (1974) *Theory and Practice*. London: Heinemann.

Hall, S., Winlow, S. and Ancrum, C. (2008) *Criminal Identities and Consumer Culture: Crime, Exclusion and the New Culture of Narcissism*. London: Willan/Routledge.

Hendershott, A. (2002) *The Politics of Deviance*. San Francisco: Encounter.

Lemert, E. M. (1951) *Social Pathology*. New York: McGraw-Hill.

—— (1972) *Human Deviance, Social Problems, and Social Control*. Englewood Cliffs, NJ: Prentice Hall.

—— (1995) Personal communication to Colin Sumner.

Loader, I. (1995) 'Review of Sumner's Sociology of Deviance', *The Sociological Review*, 43: 400–404.

Marshall, H., Douglas, K. and McDonnell, D. (2007) *Deviance and Social Control*. Melbourne: Oxford University Press.

Mitchell Miller, J., Wright, R. A. and Dannels, D. (2001) 'Is deviance dead? The decline of a research specialization', *The American Sociologist*, 32: 43–59.

Moxon, D. (2010) 'Marxism and the definition of crime', *In-Spire Journal of Law, Politics and Societies* (online), 5.

O'Connell, M. (1995) 'Review of Sumner's Sociology of Deviance', *Discourse and Society*, 6: 549–50.

Roberts, P. (1996) 'From deviance to censure: a "new" criminology for the nineties', *Modern Law Review*, 59: 125–44.

Sumner, C. S. (1979) *Reading Ideologies*. London: Academic Press.

—— (1983a) 'Rethinking deviance', in Spitzer, S. (ed.) *Research in Law, Deviance and Social Control, Vol. 5*. Greenwich, CT: JAI Press.

—— (1983b) 'Law, legitimation, and the advanced capitalist state: the jurisprudence and social theory of Jurgen Habermas', in Sugarman, D. (ed.) *Legality, Ideology and the State*. London: Academic Press.

—— (1990a) *Censure, Politics and Criminal Justice*. Milton Keynes: Open University Press.

—— (1990b) 'Foucault, gender and the censure of deviance', in Gelsthorpe, L. and Morris, A. (eds) *Feminist Perspectives in Criminology*. Milton Keynes: Open University Press.

—— (1994) *The Sociology of Deviance: An Obituary*. Buckingham: Open University Press.

—— (1997) *Violence, Censure and Culture*. London: Taylor and Francis.

—— (2006) 'Censure, criminology and politics', in Rivera I., S., H.C., Bodelón, E. and Recasens, A. (eds) *Contornos y Pliegues del Derecho: Homenaje a Roberto Bergalli*. Barcelona: Anthropos.

—— (2011a) 'Riots, aggravated shopping and 30 years of opportunism', www.crimetalk. org.uk/library/section-list/38-frontpage-articles/427-riots-aggravated-shopping-and-30-years-of-opportunism.html (Accessed September 2011).

—— (2011b) 'Gus John letter to the PM, more riot info, analysis and data maps', www.crimetalk.org.uk/research/using-typography/905-social-data/431-more-riots-analyses-and-data-maps.html (Accessed September 2011).

—— (ed.) (2004) *The Blackwell Companion to Criminology*. Oxford: Blackwell.

Taylor, I. R., Walton, P. and Young, J. (1973) *The New Criminology*. London: Routledge and Kegan Paul.

Thompson, E. P. (1975) *Whigs and Hunters: The Origin of the Black Act*. London: Allen Lane.

Venkatesh, S. A. (1995) 'Review of Sumner's Sociology of Deviance', *American Journal of Sociology*, 100: 1632–34.

Part III

Criminological theory and violence

11 Psychosocial perspectives

Men, madness and violence

David W. Jones

The premise of this book is that there is something amiss in the way criminology has developed as a discipline. This chapter addresses the particular problem of the failure to integrate psychological theorisation within criminological thinking. Despite the fact that attention has been drawn to this gap for some time (Gelsthorpe 2009), it is still highly evident even amongst strains of criminological thought that are avowedly cross-disciplinary. For example, Ferrell *et al.* (2008: 5) in outlining their case for a revitalised 'cultural criminology' suggest that it is necessary to go well beyond 'orientations in sociology and criminology', in order to 'incorporate[s] perspectives from urban studies, media studies, existential philosophy, cultural and human geography, postmodern critical theory, anthropology, social movements theory – even from the historical praxis of earlier political agitators like the Wobblies and the Situationists'. The absence of any notion of psychological theorisation from this, otherwise inclusive, list is suggestive of the deep antipathy between the disciplines of criminology and psychology. And yet there is recognition within this strain of contemporary criminology that we need to understand the complex motivations that underpin criminality. It is not possible to engage with the full range of ideas of cultural criminology here but there are a couple of important issues that emerge. It is acknowledged that crime now has to be understood as 'expressive' phenomena rather than as ones that emerge from apparently rational processes concerned with material acquisition. What is being expressed is connected to some complex dynamics of exclusion and inclusion (Young 2007). One of the most arresting advocates of a stronger emphasis on the expressive and sensual aspects of criminality has been Jack Katz (1988: 3), who called for a revitalisation of criminology through greater attention being paid to what it 'feels, sounds, tastes, or looks like to commit a particular crime'. His focus on the expressivity of crime is notable, in particular the link between violence and humiliation which has been picked up by a number of theorists since (Fonagy *et al.* 2003; Gilligan 2003). These issues will be returned to through a psychosocial exploration of what might appear to be a very particular examination of the issue of 'personality disorder' and its relation to crime and the criminal justice system.

The call for a psychosocial criminology (Gadd and Jefferson 2007; Jones 2008) points towards dissatisfaction with the continuing exclusion of psychological theorisation from mainstream criminology. The purpose of a psychosocial approach is not just that psychological theory ought to be considered alongside the commonly considered social and cultural issues but that an understanding of the individual that incorporates their internal world needs to be integral to analysis of the cultural and social circumstances of crime. The schism between the psyche and the social that is evident within criminology is only one aspect of a much deeper polarisation of our understanding of what it is to be human that has emerged from the development of the human sciences over the past 200 years. The separate developmental trajectories of the disciplines of sociology versus psychology represent a persistent tendency to see human beings as either psychological and therefore individualised, or as social phenomena where there is little room for consideration of individual subjectivity (Jones 2011; Rustin 2009). It seems more difficult to conceptualise us as an amalgam of the social and psychological. Yet it is just this kind of conceptualisation that is important to our understanding of a great deal of criminality. Whilst there are a number of different problems created by the exclusion of psychological thought that might be explored (Jones 2008), this chapter will reflect on the problematic relationship between criminal justice policies, criminology and issues of mental illness; particularly in connection to the problem of 'personality disorder'. Criminal justice processes have taken into account the insanity of perpetrators for many centuries (Walker 1968). Indeed it is arguable that the roots of criminology can be most clearly traced in debates about the relationship between mental disorder and crime – particularly through discussion about the problem of personality disorder in its earlier manifestation of 'moral insanity' (Rafter 2004). Given the influence of those with clinical backgrounds in medicine and most notably psychoanalysis at the end of the nineteenth and beginning of the twentieth centuries, the irony of the exclusion of psychological theory by the middle of the twentieth century thus becomes clearer (Garland 2002). By examining the phenomenon of 'personality disorder' (particularly 'anti-social personality disorder' associated with violent conduct) using a psychosocial lens that can capture the internal world of the individual, we can begin to grasp the substantial links that exist between the expressivity of crime and gendered manifestations of violent crime. The so called 'personality disorders' need to be understood as failures of relationship that exist in the connections between people and not within individuals.

This chapter will briefly review the relationship between psychology and criminology; it will then consider the particular and problematic history of the diagnosis of 'personality disorder' before arguing that a psychosocial under-standing that incorporates psychoanalytic forms of understanding (that are rooted in clinical observation) can not only help us understand that particular phenomenon but throws light on commonplace dynamics of exclusion/inclusion, humiliation and violence.

Criminology and the turn away from mind

By the middle of the twentieth century, within the newly instituted discipline of criminology (Garland 2002), the notion that criminality could be understood in terms of individual pathology, particularly psychological pathology, had become virtually taboo. As criminology established itself in terms of theoretical orientation as a largely sociological discipline the figure of Caesare Lombroso emerged as an almost totemic figure (Rock [2007] has referred to him as a 'signal criminologist' in relation to debates about gender and criminology). The nineteenth-century Italian medic argued that criminality could be explained in terms of the inherited characteristics of the offenders (Lombroso 1876). The enthusiastic claims that Lombroso and colleagues made about the genetic faults of the miscreants were adorned with drawings of offenders that illustrated the physiological characteristics. The following is an often quoted paragraph (e.g. Wolfgang 1961: 369) from Lombroso's description of how he came to his insights from a post-mortem examination of a particularly notorious criminal. The febrile language used here is helpful in explaining both the initial appeal of Lombroso's work, but also its notoriety:

> This was not merely an idea, but a revelation. At the sight of that skull, I seemed to see all of a sudden, lighted up as a vast plain under a flaming sky, the problem of the nature of the criminal – an atavistic being who reproduces in his person the ferocious instincts of primitive humanity and the inferior animals. Thus were explained anatomically the enormous jaws, high cheek-bones, prominent superciliary arches, solitary lines in the palms, extreme size of the orbits, handle-shaped or sessile ears found in criminals, savages, and apes, insensibility to pain, extremely acute sight, tattooing, excessive idleness, love of orgies, and the irresistible craving for evil for its own sake, the desire not only to extinguish life in the victim, but to mutilate the corpse, tear its flesh, and drink its blood.

The writing style has much in common with the popular gothic horror genre of the nineteenth century (Rafter and Ystehede 2010). Indeed, despite the appeals to scientific rhetoric it quickly became evident that most of Lombroso's claims were simply not sustainable when subjected to empirical review (Goring 1913). Despite this, Lombroso continues to appear regularly in criminology text books, suggesting that he is a useful 'straw man' in the debates on the nature of criminology (e.g. Fattah 1997: 228). Conversely, Lombroso's name does not even appear in the index of Ronald Blackburn's otherwise comprehensive *The Psychology of Criminal Conduct*. To such advocates of psychological approaches Lombroso's name has become something of an embarrassment. To mainstream, sociologically inclined criminology, Lombroso himself has come to represent a characterisation of a psychological approach that crudely and absurdly places the cause of criminality within the individual. It certainly has to be recognised that these Lombrosian theories that located criminality in the inherited characteristics of individuals sailed into treacherous waters. The links that do exist between Lombrosian theory, eugenics movements, Nazi ideologies and gas chambers should not be forgotten. It can be argued, however, that the wholesale rejection of any approach that takes into account what an individual brings to any encounter in the social and cultural realm is problematic. As criminology began to establish itself as an independent field of enquiry in the middle of the twentieth century, shaped no doubt by that ideological watershed of the Second World War, it came to be largely dominated by on the one hand various sociological schools, and on the other by administrative concerns (Garland 2002; Gelsthorpe 2009). There is further irony here, for the post-war decades on both sides of the Atlantic witnessed the growth of the 'psy-complex' through which, as Rose (1989) puts it, 'the human psyche itself has become a possible domain for systematic government in the pursuit of socio-political ends'. The spread of the psy-complex occurred notably through the growth of child guidance clinics and the spread of counselling and therapy facilities that have led some to argue (in both negative and positive terms) that we live in a 'therapy culture' (Nolan 1998; Richards 2007). By refusing to engage with any psychological theorisation, the emergent discipline of criminology thus began to lose the tools to engage with significant aspects of debate of import to social policy and crime. One obvious failure of engagement in the UK has been in connection with the development of the Mental Health Act (MHA) that began to have ever increasing implications for the criminal justice system through the 1950s (Ramon 1989). The 1959 MHA proposed that the judgement of significant aspects of criminal culpability, through diagnosis of mental disorder, be entrusted to the medical profession. There are now compelling reasons to think that the problematic relationship between crime and notions of mental illness has become more central to concerns of the criminal justice system. The problem is manifest within the prison system itself (Fazel and Danesh 2002) and in public and political anxiety over 'dangerousness' (DoH 1999). The discipline of criminology that maintained either a 'sociological' or administrative analysis has been unable to fully engage with debates that have shaped these developments.

Moral insanity and crime

There is not the space here for any detailed analysis of the history of the diagnosis of personality disorder (Jones 2009; Ramon 1989) but it is worth drawing attention to the longevity of the diagnosis. It first appeared albeit in slightly different form, around 200 years ago, thus it is arguably an older diagnosis than that of schizophrenia (Kraepelin, for example, defined *dementia praecox* around 1896 [Porter 2002]). The longevity suggests that the diagnosis cannot be dismissed as an example of a mere 'transient' mental illness which appeared at a very specific historical point (Hacking 1998).This is despite the fact that it has remained a highly controversial diagnosis, often greeted with great scepticism from medical colleagues (Arieff and Rotman 1948), the legal professions (Hakeem 1958; Hall *et al*. 1960) and academia (Pilgrim 2001).

There is little doubt that ideas of 'moral insanity' grew out of practical problems that were emerging in the criminal justice system and it is these instrumental issues that have propagated the diagnosis to this day. The defence of insanity, as a mitigation against the death penalty, was being used increasingly through the eighteenth century before there was anything like an organised psychiatric profession, which only really emerged in the nineteenth century. There were individual medics who took insanity to be their specialism (Eigen 2004), and one of these was the Frenchman Philippe Pinel, whose name has become associated with the development of 'moral treatment' and more 'enlightened' approaches to the treatment of insanity. Based on his observations of patients at the Salpêtrière hospital in Paris, as part of a systematic nosology of insanity he defined *manie sans délire* as being characterised by there being 'no sensible change in the functions of the understanding; but perversion of the active faculties, marked by abstract and sanguinary fury, with a blind propensity to acts of violence' (Pinel 1806: 156). Pinel's work was rooted in legal concerns and he commented in detail on a number of notorious murder cases. Pinel's *manie sans délire* prefigures the notion of the violent psychopath of the twentieth century. The English medic Prichard wrote what is now taken to be the first published definitions of more general personality disorders in 1835 (Elliott and Gillett 1992: 53). Prichard described people who seemed to have normal intellectual functioning but their behaviour was clearly abnormally antisocial. In a famous and often quoted passage Prichard (1835) described 'moral insanity' in the following terms:

> A form of mental derangement in which the intellectual faculties appear to have sustained little or no injury, while the disorder is manifested principally or alone, in the state of the feelings, temper, or habits. . . . [T]he moral and active principles of the mind are strangely perverted and depraved; the power of self-government is lost or greatly impaired; and the individual is found to be incapable, not of talking or reasoning upon any subject proposed to him, for this he will often do with great shrewdness and volubility, but of conducting himself with decency and propriety in the business of life . . .
>
> (Prichard, *A Treatise on Insanity*, 1835: 4)

The essence of the 'condition' described by Prichard is that despite a rational understanding of the world around them, such individuals appear to be capable of acting without regard for the feelings of others, or of social norms of decency. There is considerable continuity here with the later diagnostic categories of 'psychopathy' and the various 'personality disorders', but most particularly 'anti-social personality' disorder. Although the term 'psychopathy' was used in the nineteenth century to describe general psychological dysfunction and was particularly associated with ideas of congenital mental defect, under the growing influence of psychoanalytic thought 'psychopathy' came to be used to describe a psychological disposition towards disordered relations with others. David Henderson's (1939) overtly psychoanalytic work influenced professional practice, but it was Harvey Cleckley's (1941) more accessible book that had the more enduring impact in establishing the idea of the rational but ruthlessly amoral personality type that received legislative recognition both in the US (Sutherland 1950) and the UK. The term 'psychopathy' itself had become unfashionable in psychiatry by the 1970s, such that the UK government-sponsored Butler Committee (DSS 1975) recommended that the term be replaced with that of 'personality disorder'. As it happened the term 'psychopathy' still survived in the MHA of England and Wales until 2007 (DoH 2007). However, there is now a plethora of personality disorder diagnoses recognised by DSM (the *Diagnostic and Statistical Manual* published by the American Psychiatric Association, and the *ICD* [*International Classificiation of Disease*] published by the World Health Organization). At the heart of the diagnosis is the perception of disturbance of affect and personal relationships. The medical definition of 'anti-social personality disorder' provided by the American Psychiatric Association (DSM IV, APA) is of a:

> pervasive pattern of disregard for and violation of the rights of others occurring for as long as either childhood, or in the case of many who are influenced by environmental factors, around age 15, as indicated by three or more of the following:
> * failure to conform to social norms with respect to lawful behaviours as indicated by repeatedly performing acts that are grounds for arrest;
> * deceitfulness, as indicated by repeatedly lying, use of aliases, or conning others for personal profit or pleasure;
> * impulsivity or failure to plan ahead;
> * irritability and aggressiveness, as indicated by repeated physical fights or assaults;
> * reckless disregard for safety of self or others;
> * consistent irresponsibility, as indicated by repeated failure to sustain consistent work behaviour or honour financial obligations;
> * lack of remorse, as indicated by being indifferent to or rationalizing having hurt, mistreated, or stolen from another.

Critics of the diagnosis (Kendell 2002; Pilgrim 2001) can find plenty of evidence just within this definition to bolster their argument that this is a diagnosis that has more to do with the social constructions of normality and regulation than anything else. The whole definition is steeped in subjective notions of morality. What do such notions as 'deceit', 'impulsivity', 'aggressiveness', and 'honour' have to do with a medical diagnosis? On the face of it, it would appear hard to argue with the notion that this is really just a descriptive label that we are putting on people that 'we' of the mainstream do not like very much and that 'we' need an excuse to medicalise, intervene, treat and incarcerate. Nevertheless, further engagement with this issue reveals that it does have historical and social resonance that can help us understand something more about contemporary criminality and our responses to it.

Despite the longer history, there does seem good reason to agree with Ramon's contention that a 'major change in the social position of psychopathy occurred during and soon after the Second World War' (1989: 219) which led to the remarkable inclusion of the category of 'psychopathy' in the 1959 Mental Health Act, as:

a persistent disorder or disability of mind (whether or not including subnormality of intelligence) which results in abnormally aggressive or seriously irresponsible conduct.

If an individual could be so diagnosed and judged to be, through that condition, at risk of harming themselves or others then they could be detained in hospital under the various sections of the MHA. The category of 'psychopathy' remained as the MHA was revised in 1983, and debate over its status was a highly significant factor in the difficulties encountered in properly revising the MHA between 1997 and 2007 (Eastman 2006). This remarkable movement in government thinking about criminality came about through the confluence of two forces. On the one hand the experiences of military psychiatrists trying to rehabilitate the veterans of combat reinforced the theories of those who emphasised the significance of past events (particularly of trauma) on psychological health. On the other hand the shift of resources and the growth of welfare state meant that 'it was confidently believed that poverty would soon be eradicated, . . . The poor were no longer viewed as irresponsible rascals . . . they were victims of circumstances' (Ramon 1989: 222). The recalcitrant few who were to evade the best efforts of benign welfarism were to be understood in psychiatric terms.

At the same time as these remarkable shifts in welfare and legal policy were occurring, the newly emerging discipline of criminology had little to say about the issue of psychopathy. This lack of engagement has endured, despite huge government interest in the issue of personality disorder since the late 1900s. A survey of the contents of the *British Journal of Criminology* between January 1996 and March 2011 turned up just one article substantially concerned with 'personality disorder'. This was an article describing a survey of the presence of psychopathy amongst the population of HMP Grendon (Hobson and Shine 1998). Another two articles refer briefly to the problem. One article on recidivism rates amongst former special hospital residents (Jamieson and Taylor 2004) noted that the rate of reconviction was seven times higher amongst those with a diagnosis of personality disorder, compared to the rest. The other by Hebenton and Seddon (2009) merely referred to 'Dangerous and Severe Personality Disorder' in an article that is a critique of risk culture in relation to sex offending. I suggest that this, albeit unscientific, survey signals a remarkable neglect of a topic over a period of time when government in the UK has been extremely interested in the category. An important trigger for the announcement of a review of the 1983 MHA was UK government concern over the issue of the relationship between personality disorder, criminality and the mental health system. One significant reason for the collapse of the process that was intended to produce a new MHA and the subsequent acceptance of a series of amendments instead in 2007, was the failure to agree to how the issue of personality disorder should be dealt with. In the meantime a whole serious of initiatives established the intention to encourage the health service to take responsibility for 'personality disorder' (DoH 2003; Scanlon and Adlam 2008).

The contemporary problem of personality disorder

Government interest in personality disorder was prompted by the murder investigations that eventually led to the conviction of Michael Stone (Jones 2008: 61–62). In July 1996 a mother and her two young daughters were viciously attacked in what seemed to be a motiveless crime. Lin Russell and her elder daughter were killed, whilst 9-year-old Josie was left for dead. The contrast between the evident innocence of the victims and the viciousness of the motiveless assault on them in such a bucolic setting as a country lane in Kent meant that the case was met with 'justifiable national horror' (in the words of the subsequent *Inquiry* [2006: 4][1]).

The lack of witnesses or any apparently orthodox 'motivation' for the attack ensured the case was difficult to prosecute. Stone only emerged as a suspect following a televised appeal for information, a year after the attack. The lack of forensic or witness evidence, or indeed ostensible motive, meant that Stone's eventual conviction has been contested (the conviction has been quashed once, only to be reinstated at the subsequent retrial). Despite the controversy, his case is in many ways an exemplar of the difficulties posed by people who lead disturbed and disturbing lives on the margins (Scanlon and Adlam 2008). It emerged during the trial that Stone not only had a history of violence, but he was well known to psychiatric services, receiving various diagnoses including that of 'personality disorder'. The report into Stone's care, treatment and detention quotes from a psychiatric assessment made in January 1995, some 18 months before the killings:

> A tough minded man . . . [who] . . . at no point displayed any features of a psychotic illness. He had credible explanations for apparently psychotic episodes . . . [and] . . . denied ever hearing voices. The most striking abnormality was his extremely callous attitude towards victims and anger and contempt towards several professionals involved with him. . . . My impression is that he has committed major violent crimes in the past and is likely to do so in the future . . . He fulfills the criteria for anti-social personality disorder and there may also be a paranoid mental illness.
>
> (p. 196)

The psychiatrist argued that Stone's detention under the MHA was 'highly inappropriate' and that further it would not appear to be 'appropriate to offer [Mr Stone] a bed as firstly he is no longer mentally ill and secondly he is unlikely to respond to a graded rehabilitation package'. The fact that psychiatrists were allowed by the MHA to distinguish between 'mental illness' and the kinds of difficulties that Stone exhibited came to be a target of government attention. The then home secretary Jack Straw argued that it was 'extraordinary' that psychiatrists should only take patients who they regarded as 'treatable' and that if this 'philosophy applied anywhere else in medicine there would be no progress whatsoever'. He went on to argue that it was 'time, quite frankly, that the psychiatric profession seriously examined their own practices and tried to modernise them in a way that they have so far failed to do' (Warden 1998: 1270).

If the government might have been concerned about pursuing policy initiatives on the grounds of a single case, they did not have to look far for further evidence of the significance of the diagnostic category. It is fairly commonplace in discussion of the relationship between mental illness and crime to point to the high levels of mental illness evident in the prison system. Closer inspection of these figures suggests that the overwhelmingly most common problem of mental health difficulty is in the form of 'personality disorder' (Fazel and Danesh 2002). It is at this point that critics of the concept can simply point to the apparent circularity of the definition and its application to people who are so evidently antisocial. I want to question this easy dismissal, however. Instead, attention to the individuals who come to be so diagnosed reveals other ways of understanding the phenomena and the predicament that we are all in. By focusing on the individual, their history and psychology, we are led not into some Lombrossian eugenic circular argument, but instead we are led inexorably to the social and cultural context of crime.

One of the most striking features of the inquiry report is that despite its length, only a rather murky picture of Michael Stone's chaotic life emerges. He is considered in the words of the report to be 'one of the group of patients who are among the most difficult and challenging for the health, social and probation services to deal with'. His life is documented by his contact with the various services of the modern welfare state from cradle to the prison. And yet paradoxically the report notes that, 'even after a searching investigation by this inquiry, it is not possible to describe a full picture of the man, his history and his life, for much of it remains unknown' (*Report of the Independent Inquiry*: 4). Yet, what we can gather is that Stone's life was marked by chaos, disruption and violence from the beginning. He grew up with his mother and initially with a man who Stone had reason to think was not his father. There were then various disruptions, including a period in care at the age of 7. His early home life seems to have been disordered and filled with violence. The case files are described as containing repeated descriptions of the young Michael's exposure to violence in the home, including witnessing an attack involving an axe (*Inquiry*: 47). By the age of 11 he was more or less in permanent local authority 'care' or detention. At 12, following a number of offences, a social work report describes him as an unhappy child who:

> speaks of the week in which the offences were committed in a flat, motionless way, and maintains that at the time he gave no thought to the consequences of his actions. He talks bitterly of his father and the home situation, and appears to be ambivalent in his feelings towards his mother. He is adamant that he does not wish to return home.
>
> (*Inquiry*: 47)

The adult life that emerges from the report is one that appears to be stumble from crisis to crisis, from violence to institution to institution. His life appears as a collage made up of the brief notes and observations of the various professionals of the modern welfare system: social workers, GPs, probation officers, community psychiatric nurses, prison officers, police officers, registered mental health nurses, addiction workers, consultant psychiatrists, senior registrars, junior doctors, clinical psychologists and psychotherapists. Between them they provide an account of trying to restrain, contain and support someone who is alternatively depressed, pathetic, violent, threatening and dangerous. The report catalogues his medicinal history, the consumption of an ever changing cocktail of pharmaceutical brands and categories that included depixol, cannabis, methadone, temazepam, diazepam, benzodiazepine, alcohol, melleril, nitrazepam, heroin, amphetamine and mogadon.

His offences escalate from theft and burglary to arson, robbery, grievous bodily harm and armed robbery. He spends most of life from mid-teens until the age of 32 in borstal or prison. He is threatening and violent when out of prison. The years between his release from prison and his arrest for murder appear to be characterised by taking an apparently vast range of prescribed and street medication. On at least three separate occasions he describes fantasies of killing children. He threatens to kill his probation officer and to rape his wife; despite at other times having a good relationship with him. Whilst the *Inquiry* catalogues the various attempts of professionals to help, and engage with Stone, the difficulty is that Stone is precisely the kind of person that Scanlon and Adlam (2008) describe as one of the many who are 'socially excluded' and might appear dangerous, violent, self harming, homeless, or drug addicted – but whose stance is essentially one of refusing to 'join in'. Scanlon and Adlam argue that this apparent refusal to be part of society has to be understood as a psychosocial dynamic. Such 'refusal' is a state of mind based on their experience of being 'psychosocially dis-membered and un-housed as a result of the complex reciprocal relationship played out between "us" and "them" within the psychosocial organizations that are "our" families, communities and societies' (2008: 539). Jock Young (2007) has argued that complex dynamics of exclusion/inclusion, particularly as they are played out in the lives of young men, need to be grappled with if we are to understand the experience of deviance and criminality in 'late modernity'. Indeed they do, but to properly do this we have to take into account the internal worlds of individuals where the dynamics are, in part, played out.

A psychosocial understanding of personality disorder, masculinity and shame

Much of the construction of our concepts of personality disorder have come through particular strains of psychoanalytic thought that broadly fit into the category of object relations (Kernberg 1975; Klein 1957) which can make a couple of relevant contributions here. First, such schools of psychoanalysis offer an understanding of the internal worlds of individuals, and how those 'internal' worlds both interact and determine our perceptions of and understanding of the 'external' world. Second, a great deal of the psychoanalytic project has been concerned with understanding the significance of individual history on psychic development. There is now a considerable weight of empirical evidence that points to the significance of early negative experiences. Those experiences, of course, have to be understood as occurring in specific social and cultural contexts.

We know from a mass of evidence that the association between Stone's childhood experiences of neglect and violence and his own later violent, impulsive and chaotic behaviour are commonplace amongst those who come to be violent and excluded (Jones 2008; Moffitt *et al.* (2002); Widom 1989). We are understanding more about how those mechanisms work, and they may help us understand more about the particular dynamics of gender, violence and exclusion in the contemporary period. Fonagy *et al.* (2003), for example propose a developmental theory of 'personality disorder'. They argue that the ability to process and reflect on emotions is a developmental achievement that is dependent upon close and empathic interaction between carer and young child. Through interaction with responsive adults children can learn to think about how they feel and plan how to act accordingly. Without this kind of ability people can be left only with the recourse to act, rather than think, when they feel. Such individuals can be left to act in ways characteristic of 'personality disorder', marked by seemingly impulsive, inconsistent and sometimes hostile behaviour that might lead to violence that masks a very insecure sense of themselves. Lansky (2003) suggests that Fonagy and colleagues are correct to point towards the significance of the early years of life being crucial to the development of the capacity to process emotions but argues that it is more particularly an inability to tolerate feelings of shame that underlies many of the problems characteristic of personality disorder. In a parallel argument Schore (1994, 1998) suggests that the ability to process shame is a particularly key aspect of the capacity to inhibit violence and has its roots in the very early years of interaction with adults. According to Schore's formulation shame is an alarm that signals the threat of abandonment. It first manifests around the end of the first year of life as young children first commonly experience disapproval as they begin to be able to behave in ways that might need control (by being able to put themselves in danger for example). Disapproval from a carer is experienced as a deadly threat to one that is so utterly dependent on the love and care of others. Thus shame is arguably a very primitive feeling, that as Gilligan (2003: 1168) argues, even in adulthood evokes:

> the fear that one will be abandoned, rejected, or ignored and will therefore die because one is so weak, helpless, dependent, unskilled, and incompetent that one cannot take care of oneself, because of which one is also inferior, unlovable, and unworthy of love that one probably will be abandoned.

A young child experiencing shame will directly communicate this distress through typical shame responses – 'the child's facial display, postural collapse and gaze aversion act as non-verbal signals of his or her internal distress state' (Schore 1998: 65). The very visibility of shame thus makes it a psychosocial phenomenon as it is powerfully communicated to others who can then respond. It is the response that Schore argues is crucial if an individual is going to develop the ability to experience and cope with the feeling of shame later in life:

> If the caregiver is sensitive, responsive, and emotionally approachable especially if she re-initiates and re-enters into mutual gaze visual affect regulating transaction . . . , shame is metabolized and regulated, and the attachment bond is re-established.

Thus the capacity to tolerate feelings of shame grows through relationship with others. If the individual is not helped to develop this capacity to metabolise shame they can be left simply to respond to it when they experience it. The experience of shame has been identified as a common trigger for violence (Gilligan 1997, 2003; Katz 1988; Scheff and Retzinger 1997). This psychosocial formulation of shame helps us understand why it is that shame can be such a trigger for violence as it poses such an existential threat to worth and existence to those who have little experience of connection and worth. One obvious way that an individual can ward off feelings of helplessness and worthlessness that are evoked in a potentially shaming situation is to attack those that threaten them with shame.

A number of commentators have noted the significance of the defence of reputation that underlies a lot of street violence (Gilligan 1997; Katz 1988; Polk 1994). This psychosocial understanding of shame points us towards the significance of shame in contemporary culture. Bearing in mind that shame is fundamentally the experience of alarm at the threat of social isolation, then, arguably, in conditions of late modernity when we are freer of the bonds of class, religion, community and extended families, the threat of isolation is ever present. The threat of shame is very present to those who already feel isolated and have never had the experience of feelings of shame leading to re-connection with others. To those who have little experience of attachment, survival depends not on connection to others but to a more literal and aggressive defence of the self – that can easily manifest in violence. Whether it is useful or not to provide a medical diagnosis of 'personality disorder' for such dynamics is not clear. What is more certain is that to understand the dynamics of exclusion and inclusion that are surely so important to our understanding of contemporary expressive criminality, we do need to be able to take account of an understanding of the individual, their internal world, and their history.

Note

1 *The Report of the Independent Inquiry into the Care and Treatment of Michael Stone* (2006), South East Coast Strategic Health Authority, Kent County Council, Kent Probation Area.

References

Arieff, A. and Rotman, D. B. (1948) 'Psychopathic Personality: Some Social and Psychiatric Aspects.' *Journal of Criminal Law 39 (2) 158–166.*

Augstein, H. F. (1996) 'J. C. Prichard's Concept of Moral Insanity: A Medical Theory of the Corruption of Human Nature.' *Medical History 40: 311–343.*

Bandelow, B., Krause, J., Wedekind, D., Broocks, A., Hajak, G. and Ruther, E. (2005) 'Early Traumatic Life Events, Parental Attitudes, Family History, and Birth Risk Factors in Patients with Borderline Personality Disorder and Healthy Controls.' *Psychiatry Research 134 169–179.*

Blackburn, R. (1993) *The Psychology of Criminal Conduct: Theory, Research and Practice.* Wiley: Chichester.

Brown, P. (2006) 'Risk Versus Need in Revising the 1983 Mental Health Act: Conflicting Claims, Muddled Policy.' *Health, Risk and Society 8 (4) 343–58.*

Buchanan, A. and Leese, M. (2001) 'Detention of People with Dangerous Severe Personality Disorders: A Systematic Review.' *The Lancet 358 December 8 1955–1959.*

Cabinet Office (2006) *Reaching Out: An Action Plan On Social Exclusion.* HM Government Cabinet Office: London.

Cleckley, H. (1941) *The Mask of Sanity: An Attempt to Re-interpret the Social Psychopathic Personality.* Henry Kimpton: London.

DoH (1999) 'Managing Dangerous People With Severe Personality Disorder: Proposals for Policy Development'. Joint Home Office/Department of Health Working Group. Department of Health : London.

—— (2003) *Personality Disorder: No Longer a Diagnosis of Exclusion.* Department of Health: London.

—— (2006) *The Mental Health Bill: Plans to amend the Mental Health Act 1983.* Department of Health: London.

—— (2007) *Mental Health (Amendment) Act.* HMSO: London.

DSS (1975) *Report of the Committee on the Mentally Abnormal Offenders.* (Butler). HMSO: London.

Eastman, N. (2006) 'Reforming Mental Health Law in England and Wales: The Government's Recent Climb Down Is Not a Victory: The Real Battle Is About to Begin.' *British Medical Journal 332 (7544) 737–738.*

Eichner, E. (1982) 'The Rise of Modern Science and the Genesis of Romanticism.' *PMLA 97 (1) 8–30.*

Eigen, P. J. (2004) 'Delusion's Odyssey: Charting the Course of Victorian Forensic Psychiatry.' *International Journal of Law and Psychiatry 27 395–412.*

Elliott, C. and Gillett, G. (1992) 'Moral Insanity and Practical Reason.' *Philosophical Psychology 5 (1) 53–64.*

Fattah, E. A. (1997) *Criminology: Past Present and Future: A Critical Overview.* Macmillan: Basingstoke.

Fazel, S. and Danesh, J. (2002) 'Serious Mental Disorder in 23,000 Prisoners: A Systematic Review of 62 Surveys.' *The Lancet 359 Feb 16 545–550.*

Ferrell, J., Hayward, K. and Young, J. (2008) *Cultural Criminology.* Sage: London.

Fonagy, P. (1999) 'Male Perpetrators of Violence Against Women: An Attachment Theory Perspective.' *Journal of Applied Psychoanalytic Studies 1 7–27.*

Fonagy, P., Gergely, G., Jurist, E. L. and Target, M. (2004) *Affect Regulation, Mentalization, and the Development of the Self.* Karnac: London.

Fonagy, P., Target, M., Gergely, G., Allenn, J. and Batemen, A. (2003) 'The Developmental

Roots of Borderline Personality Disorder in Early Attachment Relationships: A Theory and Some Evidence.' *Psychoanalytic Enquiry 23 (3) 412–459.*

Gadd, D. and Jefferson, T. (2007) *Psychosocial Criminology: An Introduction.* Sage: London.

Garland, D. (2002) 'Of Crimes and Criminals: The Development of Criminology In Britain.' In *The Oxford Handbook of Criminology.* 3rd ed. Eds Maguire, M., Morgan, M. and Reiner, R. Oxford University Press: Oxford.

Gelsthorpe, L. (2009) 'Emotions and Contemporary Developments in Criminology.' In *Emotion: New Psychosocial Perspectives.* Eds Day Sclater, S., Jones, D., Price, H. and Yates, C. Palgrave: Basingstoke.

Gilligan, J. (1997) *Violence: Reflections on a National Epidemic.* Vintage Books: New York.

—— (2003) 'Shame, Guilt, and Violence.' *Social Research 70 (4) 1149–1180.*

Goring, C. (1913) *The English Convict: A Statistical Study.* London: HMSO.

Hacking, I. (1998) *Mad Travelers :Reflections on the Reality of Transient Mental Illnesses.* University Press of Virginia: Charlottesville and London.

Hakeem, M. (1958) 'A Critique of the Psychiatric Approach to Crime and Correction.' *Law and Contemporary Problems 23 (4) Crime and Correction. 650–82.*

Hall William, J. M. E., Gibbens, T. C. N. and Jennings, R. (1960) 'The Mental Health Act, 1959.' *The Modern Law Review 23 (4) 410–424.*

Hebenton, B. and Seddon, T. (2009) 'From Dangerousness to Precaution: Managing Sexual and Violent Offenders in an Insecure and Uncertain Age.' *British Journal of Criminology 49(3): 343–362.*

Henderson, D. K. (1939) *Psychopathic States.* Chapman and Hall: London.

Hobson, J. and Shine, J. (1998) 'Measurement of Psychopathy in a UK Prison Population Referred for Long-term Psychotherapy.' *British Journal of Criminology 38 (3) 504–15.*

House of Lords/House of Commons (2005) *Joint Committee on the Draft Mental Health Bill – First Report.* www.Parliament.uk: London.

Jamieson, L. and Taylor, P. (2004) 'A Re-Conviction Study of Special (High Security) Hospital Patients.' *British Journal of Criminology 44 (5) 783–802.*

Jones, D. W. (2008) *Understanding Criminal Behaviour: Psychosocial Approaches to Criminality.* Willan: Cullompton.

—— (2009) 'A Psychosocial Understanding of Personality Disorder: The Historical Problem of Moral Insanity.' In *Emotions: Psychosocial Approaches.* Eds Day Sclater, S., Jones, D. W., Price, H. and Yates, C. Palgrave: Basingstoke.

—— (2011) 'Bubbles and Bees: Historical Exploration of Psychosocial Thinking.' *Journal of Psychosocial Studies 5 (1).* http://hls.uwe.ac.uk/research/current-volume.aspx

Katz, J. (1988) *Seductions of Crime: Moral and Sensual Attractions in Doing Evil.* Basic Books: New York.

Kendell, R. E. (2002) 'The Distinction Between Personality Disorder and Mental Illness.' *British Journal of Psychiatry 180 110–115.*

Kernberg, O. (1975) 'Borderline Conditions and Pathological Narcissisms.' Jason Aronson: New York.

Klein, M. (1957) 'Envy and Gratitude.' In *Envy and Gratitude and Other Works 1946–1963.* Virago: London.

Lansky, M. R. (2003) 'Discussion of Peter Fonagy *et al.*'s "The Developmental Roots of BDP".' *Psychoanalytic Enquiry 23 (3) 460.*

Lombroso, C. (1876) *The Criminal Man.* Translated and edited by Mary Gibson and Nicole Hahn Rafter [2006]. Duke University Press: Chesham.

Moffitt, T. E., Caspi, A., Harrington, H. and Milne, B. (2002) 'Males on the Life-course Persistent Pathways: Follow-up at Age 26 Years.' *Development and Psychopathology 4 179–207.*

Nolan, J. L. (1998) *The Therapeutic State: Justifying Government at Century's End.* New York University Press: London.

Pilgrim, D. (2001) 'Disordered Personalities and Disordered Concepts.' *Journal of Mental Health 10 (3) 253–265.*

Pinel, P. H. (1806) *A Treatise on Insanity.* Translated by D. D. Davis. W. Todd for Calwell and Davis: London.

Polk, K. (1994) *When Men Kill: Scenarios of Masculine Violence.* Cambridge University Press: Cambridge.

Porter, R. (2002) *A Brief History of Madness.* Oxford University Press: Oxford.

Prichard, J. C. (1835) *A Treatise on Insanity and Other Disorders Affecting the Mind.* Sherwood, Gilbert and Piper: London.

Rafter, N. (2004) 'The Unrepentant Horse-slasher: Moral Insanity and the Origins of Criminological Thought.' *Criminology 42 (4) 979–1008.*

Rafter, N. and Ystehede, P. (2010) 'Here Be Dragons: Lombroso, the Gothic, and Social Control.' In *Popular Culture, Crime and Social Control.* Ed. Mathieu Deflem. Emerald Group: Bingley.

Ramon, S. (1989) 'Psychopathy: Its Professional and Social Context in Britain.' In Miller, P. and Rose, N. *The Power of Psychiatry.* Polity: Cambridge.

Report of the Independent Inquiry into the Care and Treatment of Michael Stone (2006), South East Coast Strategic Health Authority, Kent County Council, Kent Probation Area.

Richards, B. (2007) *Emotional Governance: Politics, Media and Terror.* Palgrave Macmillan: Basingstoke.

Rock, P. (2007) 'Caesare Lombroso as a Signal Criminologist.' *Criminology and Criminal Justice 7 (2) 117–133.*

Rose, N. (1989) *Governing the Soul: The Shaping of the Private Self.* Routledge: London.

Rustin, M. (2009) 'The Missing Dimension: Emotions in the Social Sciences.' In *Emotions: Psychosocial Approaches.* Eds Day Sclater, S., Jones, D., Price, H. and Yates, C. Palgrave: Basingstoke.

Scanlon, C. and Adlam, J. (2008) 'Refusal, Social Exclusion and the Cycle of Rejection: A Cynical Analysis?' *Critical Social Policy 28 (4) 529–49.*

Scheff, T. and Retzinger, S. (1997) 'Shame, Anger and the Social Bond: A Theory of Sexual Offenders and Treatment.' *Electronic Journal of Sociology 3 (1).* www.sociology.org/content/vol003.001/sheff.html

Schore, A. (1994) *Affect Regulation and the Origin of Self: The Neurobiology of Emotional Development.* Lawrence Erlbaum and Associates: New Jersey.

—— (1998) 'Early Shame Experiences and Infant Brain Development.' In Gilbert, P. and Andrews, B. *Shame: Interpersonal Behaviour, Psychopathology, and Culture.* Oxford University Press: Oxford.

Sutherland, E. H. (1950) 'The Sexual Psychopath Laws.' *Journal of Criminal Law and Criminology 40 (5) 543–554.*

Walker, N. (1968) *Crime and Insanity in England: Volume One: The Historical Perspectives.* Edinburgh University Press: Edinburgh.

Warden, J. (1998) 'Psychiatrists Hit Back at Home Secretary.' *British Medical Journal 317 (1270) 10.*

White, S. M. (2002) 'Preventive Detention Must Be Resisted by the Medical Profession.' *Journal of Medical Ethics 28 95–98*.

Widom, C. S. (1989) 'The Cycle of Violence.' *Science 244 160–166*.

Wolfgang, M. E. (1961) 'Pioneers in Criminology: Cesare Lombroso (1835–1909).' *Journal of Criminal Law, Criminology, and Police Science 52 (4) 361–91*.

Young, J. (1999) *The Exclusive Society: Social Exclusion, Crime and Difference in Late Modernity*. Sage: London.

—— (2007) *The Vertigo of Late Modernity*. Sage: London.

12 'All that is sacred is profaned'

Towards a theory of subjective violence

Simon Winlow

Introduction: the limits of 'objective' criminological analysis

Let me begin with a rather simple heuristic claim: Much of the work in mainstream criminology that addresses subjective violence falls into one of three camps. First, there are those who highlight the exhilarating nature of physical confrontation. Here it is often suggested that the subject is seduced by the illicit thrill that accompanies the transgression of conduct norms: pushed by the oppressive sameness of everyday social reality, and pulled by the possibility of rupturing this dull regimentation with a sudden explosion of visceral energy, the violent subject becomes enamoured with a self-image that inspires fear. Second, there are scholars who have sought to chart and explicate changing levels of violence historically, often relating these changes to civility and control and the development of modern subjectivity. We should also include in this group those who have attempted to identify and explain the differing rates of violence between cultures, societies and nations. Third, there are criminologists who have sought to situate violence within a broader process of social learning. Here a pathological attachment to violence is passed from one generation to the next, or violence itself is integrated into a complex assortment of class-based 'solutions' to the pressures of the social field. While each one of these camps has produced important ideas and empirical data that have illuminated our understanding of subjective violence, criminology as a discipline has yet to adequately integrate this material into its corpus. Instead, criminology tends to treat subjective violence as a tangent to some other dis-cussion: drug markets, drinking cultures, urban marginality and so on. In this short paper I offer a rather basic but integrated theory of subjective violence, a theory that is firmly planted in the discipline of criminology, and one that attempts to draw these three basic areas of study together.

These notes on subjective violence are situated within a context of political and cultural inertia – the time after the great transformation; a time in which the traditional symbolic universe has imploded. We have lived through a period in which traditional forms of personal and community restraint and regulation have undergone profound change, and this has had a huge impact upon both the occurrence of subjective violence and social experience more generally. But that change is now complete. We now occupy an anti-utopian era that has hollowed out political ontology and turned academics, politicians and 'the people' into pragmatists and cynics. Until political universality can return, we seem to be marooned here. It is not so much that history has ended; *rather, we act as if it has ended.* For example, many liberal academics treat Fukuyama's (1993) thesis with disdain while at the same time acting as if history has reached its end, in the sense that they appear to accept that all historical change must occur within a system of capitalism and liberal democracy. This is where ideology resides these days. If modernism approached ideology as a problem of knowledge, contemporary ideology exists as a problem of social action (and inaction). We seem to believe that our pragmatic knowledge and cynical bearing will protect us from the harms that are an unavoidable by-product of global capitalism. We believe we know 'reality', that we see through all the cynical attempts to invest in particular versions of truth. The excesses and harms of social power are no longer 'hidden' as such. They are already 'out there' in the symbolic order and circulate in every-day culture – we know about the grotesque inequalities of global capitalism, we know that parliamentary democracy is a hollow and corrupt spectacle, but we act as if this knowledge magically distances us from these processes. Of course capitalism doesn't care about this awareness, as long as we continue to work and consume, and parliamentary democracy can survive the degradation of its image, as long as we continue to vote. For the moment at least, and until universality returns, individuals imagine themselves all-knowing but powerless to intervene.

The West these days is all about the language of formal freedom in the absence of any real concept of social justice and genuine inclusivity. We must view our lives as instrumental projects geared towards maximising personal pleasure and reward; we must view morality, ethics and 'values' as external systems of control that impede freedom, rather than an embodied truth that structures our behaviour. Gradually the symbolic substance that makes life relatively civilised and sustain-able is being reduced to mere representation. All of these general trends are exhib-ited in contemporary liberal democracies, but it seems reasonable to suggest they take on a darker hue when they become demonstrable characteristics of those places of excision that are so indicative of the contemporary capitalism. While I will offer no empirical evidence in this paper, my analysis of subjective violence is built upon my previous work with groups who occupy such places.

Before I begin, let me offer a pre-emptive defence. It is, in my view, totally inadequate for liberal social scientists to suggest that any theory that attempts to universalise the meaning of violence immediately fails to take into account the innumerable particularities that together constitute contemporary social reality. Many criminologists continue to thoughtlessly adopt this position, as if recourse to the infinite diversity of our cultural life immediately invalidates the claims made by those who might risk a generalised theory. First, I totally refute the sug-gestion that our world is one of total fluidity, and that our cultural life is unendingly 'diverse'. This postmodern submission to the supposed infinite complexity of the world suggests a powerful desire for *atonality* (Badiou 2009), a desire to live in a world that is devoid of a master-signifier and lacks a determining logic. But beneath the shallow surface of multicultural diversity lies a durable universality.

This universality is not a generalised homogeneous mass, but a *universal singularity* that can allow us to bypass the ceaseless and entirely unproductive charting of shifting cultural particularities. Changes to the surface of contemporary consumer culture appear to draw our attention away from those underlying factors that structure contemporary culture itself. We must be willing to explore the possibility that we are exposed to an image of change *so that nothing has to change*, and that surface cultural diversity masks a sameness at the political and economic level. The change between one musical trend and another, or between one elected government and another, is simply the appearance of change that occurs within a system that never changes. Second, the rush to declare all meta-theory 'deterministic' seems to be a hastily constructed and deeply ideological excuse that is offered to cover up the absence of thought itself. Liberal pluralists and affirmative postmodernists tell us we can discount all grand theory because it generalises, and fails to take into account the boundless diversity of human experience and the increased ability of individuals to define their lives in their own terms. A corollary of this position is that the liberal critic of meta-theory demands *more evidence*. How can we dare to risk a truth claim without first completing an exhaustive, expansive and multi-faceted piece of social research that acknowledges the specificities of particular communities and integrates these specificities into a careful and thoroughly dispassionate final analysis? Shouldn't we withhold a firm conclusion until we have carried out yet more 'evidence based research'? This push for ever more data has had an intellectually immobilising effect upon criminology. Our discipline is now awash with what Roger Matthews (2009) has called 'so what?' criminology: pointless, banal, story-telling social research that contributes nothing and serves only to advance the academic career of the individual. The development of this 'so what?' criminology has contributed to a strangely anti-intellectual academic climate that discourages genuinely inquisitive theorists from asking searching questions about contemporary social problems. This restrictive focus upon empirical data contributes to a prevailing atmosphere of defensiveness and tentative theorisation, in which we dare not say anything that does not fit immediately into one of the already established 'schools' of the criminological mainstream. Third and most problematic of all, the refutation of 'deterministic' theorisation, the immediate denial of all truth claims and the championing of boundless pluralism represent a refusal to engage in a genuinely progressive ideological and dialectical discussion. Instead, it seeks to discard this process and in its place install its own meta-discourse, the ideological content of which has become almost entirely 'naturalised': this is the perverse meta-discourse of 'abstracted empiricism' (see Mills 1999), a pseudo-scientific discourse that is firmly rooted in the dominant ideology of liberalism.

What this means for criminology is that we get the constant reiteration of what already exists. There is little sense of forward motion in the discipline as a whole, despite the heroic work of some on the margins. Instead, dedicated careerist criminologists engage in an endless cycle of micro-studies. The majority of those theorists who adopt a 'critical' approach tend to focus on systems of control that pathologise or restrict the freedoms of marginalised populations. What is missing, of course, is any critical and properly philosophical consideration of subjectivity, about the complexity of our internal life and criminal motivations (which the dominant liberal discourse encourages us to believe are infinitely complex and entirely subjective, and therefore always beyond a general theoretical analysis), or how we might approach universality in economic, political and ontological terms. So, I am intensely comfortable with the suggestion that I am 'generalising', and that the brief analysis of subjective violence that follows is 'deterministic'. Despite a clear focus upon the violence of men who come from working-class, marginalised or excluded backgrounds, I am attempting to produce a general account of social processes that extend well beyond this narrow social field. I am also happy to acknowledge my truth claims are approached through the field of ideology. Ideology may involve a manipulation and distortion of the objective world, but it also colours that world, and it does not close off access to 'truth' as such. Those criminologists who scoff at political commitment and grand theorisation, only to turn their attention to the world of pseudo-scientific 'objective' empirical analysis, as if this field is magically free from a corrupting ideology, are labouring under a profound misapprehension about the nature of social reality. We can also speculate that these criminologists are engaged in an act of fetishistic disavowal (Žižek 2008a; 2010), an act of lying to oneself, of 'choosing to forget', or refusing to acknowledge what the subject knows to be true. What they are refusing to acknowledge, of course, is their own ideological commitment. Despite the swirling rhetoric that proclaims the rise of a new pragmatic post-ideological age, ideology continues to exist in criminology, and not just for those who acknowledge a clear political affiliation. The commitment these 'so what?' criminologists hold is to a dominant ideology that seeks its own perpetuation by establishing an always-already-present ironic, smirking scepticism towards genuinely new intellectual directions in criminology. Rather than seeking to address the real questions of our time, too many criminologists prefer instead the comfortable repose of yet another empirical study, yet another tentative conclusion, yet another Home Office report, yet another tacit endorsement of established ideas. In criminology, the ideologies of liberal pluralism and abstract empiricism provide the critic with a well-stocked armoury of put-downs that allow them the comfort of refusing to engage with new ideas in any real sense, and the growing anti-intellectual climate of Western criminology grants them leave to continue onwards in the firm belief that they are the stoic defenders of academic propriety.

All of this is a reflection of the fact that for too many criminologists these days liberal democracy and free market capitalism represents an intellectual horizon. It is as if, for them, we have found the formula – democratic freedom mixed with individual enterprise – and all we now need to do is encourage people to be a little more respectful and tolerant of each other. Much criminology these days involves a critique of culturally oppressive social practices followed by a repetitive request that we all try to be a little nicer to each other. Of course, it is vital that our discipline sees beyond this horizon. Criminology must once again be filled with vigorous debate and serious theorisation. We must be ambitious enough to construct new ways of explaining the world and courageous enough to battle against the criminological mainstream and imagine a world that lies beyond 'parliamentary capitalism' (Badiou 2008).

The intellectual stasis we now face is at least partly reflective of the fact that criminology has allowed itself to become responsive to social and governmental agendas relating to 'social problems'. Rather than empirically seeking an answer to that which is defined as 'problematic', it is incumbent upon the critical criminologist to ask whether the identified 'problem' is indeed a true problem. We must also continually encourage society and government to see the 'problem' itself in different and new ways, while at the same time excavating the social for ever more issues for society and government to worry about (see Badiou and Žižek [2009] on this point). In this way, by retaining what is proper to academic enterprise, we can attempt to avoid creeping deprofessionalisation and the gradual mutation of 'the intellectual' into the 'occupational specialist'.

So, while first of all encouraging critics to begin with a thoughtful investigation of their own intellectual position, I invite criticism that seeks to identify flaws with, and advance upon, the claims I make here. Critical criminologists should have no time for those who would sabotage this dialectical process.

A world without world

Innumerable authors have noted that there exists a subsection of the overall male population who value physical violence and place its enactment and broader symbolism close to the centre of self-identity. It is this specific population that I am most concerned with in this paper. It is not at all contentious to claim that the majority of these men come from working-class, marginalised or excluded social locations. However, one must also immediately supplement this claim with an acknowledgement that those social groups who sit atop the precipitous hierarchies of the contemporary politico-economic order are themselves not free from aggressive and violent impulses. The differences that exist between these two groups are important and they are partially addressed in this chapter, but before we continue it is perhaps best to offer an initial justification for focusing so directly upon working- and lower-class men.

We can do this quite quickly. First, there are practical issues: those who are the beneficiaries of contemporary liberal capitalism attempt to create for themselves rather sanitised and segregated lives, free from the pressing actuality of the revanchist city with its almost palpable sense of desperation, aggressivity and conflict. They rarely, if ever, encounter situations in which physical violence is an obvious requirement. This is simply not the case for those who exist upon the lower reaches of the allegedly fluid social hierarchy of contemporary liberal democracy. Second, there are cultural issues: they have not been socialised to accept the inevitability of violent confrontation, and have instead become attuned to the deployment of *symbolic violence* – a violence of language, a violence that hides behind smiles, handshakes, business deals and expressions of sincerity. This is the violence that is forever missing from contemporary analyses of the successes of liberal democracy and the significant statistical declines in twenty-first century serious crime rates in both Britain and America. We may be beating and shooting each other a little less than 10 years ago, but our societies are awash with corrosive forms of symbolic violence. The desperate struggle to reduce the other and elevate the self, to inspire envy in others, is essential to the social order of contemporary liberal capitalism. The trans-historic sublimation of aggressive impulses has dispersed rather than extinguished the raw energy of these impulses. This energy 'returns' and continues to inform our current way of life (see for example Sloterdijk 2010, on the sublimation and return of rage). In the economic sphere, these sublimated impulses have driven the globalisation of an aggressive and competitive marketplace; in the cultural sphere, they have contributed to the prevailing leaden atmosphere of institutionalised instrumentalism; and, in terms of our psychical life, they inform the development of our rather desperate scramble for recognition and social distinction (Hall *et al.* 2008). Elias's (2000) civilising hypothesis omits this crucial insight, that the barbarism of the dark ages does not melt into air, but instead is sublimated and pacified and is forever connected to the development of capitalist political economy (Hall 2007; 2012). The huge growth of symbolic violence throughout the twentieth century is reflective of the return of these suppressed thymotic passions, and the consequences of this broad historical process have yet to be fully understood by criminologists. So, my point here is not that the ex-working classes are free from forms of symbolic violence, but rather that some of their number occupy a *visceral habitus* (Hall 1997) that rests on the embodiment of codes relating to physical conflict, and the meanings and contexts through which the subject comes to appreciate involvement in it.

My initial proposal is that gendered elements of what is commonly referred to as the 'working-class habitus' structure the development of *far more specific* processes that establish and reproduce the self-identity of persistently violent men. As many others have noted, in these cultures the desire to retain dignity and self-respect are elevated in significance. If twentieth-century Western modernism – with its internalised truths, its sense of community, its utopian politics, and so on – attempted to contain the thymotic drive towards recognition and reputation by encouraging the individual to see himself and his interests in relation to collective projects, it now seems reasonable to speculate that thymotic passion has been at least partially released by an ideological order that encourages possessive individualism and the aggressive pursuit of personal interests in order to drive its economy. These concerns with reputation and social distinction seem to be expressed most clearly in contemporary forms of symbolic violence, but there also seems to be enough evidence to suggest that thymos contributes to cultures of violence in a variety of contexts. Here, even in places of social excision, this imperative not to be dominated by another, to aggressively defend the basic essence of the self in a socio-economic context in which virtually all battles are lost in advance, can play a crucial role in the structuring of masculine identity for those who occupy areas of permanent recession beset by high rates of interpersonal violence.

If the traditional symbolic order of twentieth-century modernism enabled the establishment of institutionalised forms of violence, a violence that allowed individual troubles to be folded into collective, politicised projects (Wieviorka 2009; Wieviorka, this volume), the new world of advanced twenty-first-century capitalism offers the individual no such opportunity. A complex assortment of social, economic and political transformations, ranging from the development of cultures of cynicism, atomisation and competition to the expurgation of utopianism from politics, now means that ever greater numbers of individuals experience social reality free from the restrictions and obligations of traditional community life. The codes and rituals that structured the traditional working-class habitus are entirely absent, in any real sense, from the social experience of those men who concern us here. These codes and rituals continue to linger on in shadow form and tend to be addressed in an almost sociopathic manner – a rational choice of expression, an internal narrative of self-creation, or a tool of impression management, rather than a reflection of an enclosed identity and fidelity to a deep, internalised truth. Without a fixed root in a structuring symbolic order these expressions of traditional working-class culture are essentially hauntological (Derrida 2006), a spectre of what once was, deprived of its traditional symbolic substance. Problems experienced by the individual are rarely understood in relation to matters external to immediate social experience, and feelings of exploitation, humiliation and subordination weigh heavily upon the psyche of marginalised men who are unable to find a controlled or institutionalised means of divesting the self of this raw energy. The result is a general climate of aggressivity and occasional explosions of impotent rage.

This broader picture frames the way the subject engages with the masculinist injunctions of a transformed working-class habitus. Winlow and Hall (2009: 288) claim that:

> generations of working class men have been instructed to 'look after yourself' and 'not to take any shit'. These injunctions were and still are a practical and entirely necessary response to everyday life in a cultural environment in which threats to the individual's physical integrity issued by a minority of persistently violent individuals are an unavoidable part of everyday life.

It is not necessarily physical violence and aggression that is 'valued' by the culture, but rather the ability to retain dignity in the face of it. Within the broader working-class habitus these injunctions are structured in such a way as to emphasise their cautionary and defensive element, but it is also entirely reasonable to suggest that *particular individuals* can misinterpret this logic and react aggressively to any suggestion that another is attempting to impose his or her will upon them.

Why do these 'particular individuals' misinterpret these defensive cultural injunctions, and use them to justify their own violence and aggression? Why is it they so often draw upon physical violence when given only the flimsiest provocation? In what follows I offer a very basic assessment of how the experience of *specific but quite common* biographical events can shape the self-identities of persistently violent men.

Death drive

I will begin with a straightforward claim: many persistently violent men have been raised in a climate of pronounced insecurity. As Lacan recognised, anxiety is the only affect that does not lie. It signifies the close proximity of the Real, and communicates to the subject that the symbolic world can be immediately ruptured by the intrusion of this Real, this raw force that defies comprehension. Often this anxiety and insecurity is generated by the fear the child has for their immediate physical safety, but this insecurity can also be the result of exposure to broader social and environmental pressures that create in the child a general sense of uncertainty and anxiety. For some of these men this experience relates directly to a relationship with a father who, reflecting a pathological and distorted attachment to the cultural requirements of the gendered habitus, sought to 'toughen the boy up' by exposing them to threats, dangers or direct physical abuse (see Winlow and Hall 2006; 2009). Of course, a domineering and violent father need not always be present and assume the role of encouraging the toughening up of the boy's psycho-somatic disposition. This role can be played by anybody that provides important input during the child's socialisation. It is also worth noting that the narrative of 'toughening the boy up' is not a universal requirement, and that merely being raised in a climate of advanced insecurity may be enough to push the child in the direction of violent action if other cultural pressures are present. Similarly, the process of becoming committed to aggressive physical violence need not be rooted in childhood experience. Anyone transported into an environment of constant threat and occasional brutality can find themselves on a similar path towards barbarism.

These micro-climates of hostility and insecurity also involve far more subtle processes that deprive the child of the emotional support that might allow them to grow into civilised and sociable adults. Outside of the home, the young boy also operates within a culture that advocates a particular enclassed version of tough masculinity that appears to sanction and reinforce the dominant narrative of sustained aggressivity that exists within the home. I am not suggesting that working class-masculinities are necessarily violent. Rather, working-class men tend to be raised with a deep appreciation of the gravity of violence, and some aspects of working-class masculinity are closely connected to the visceral energy and cultural power of physical conflict. This external cultural climate of robust, no-nonsense masculinity is not a requirement of the passage of the innocent boy to a violent adult male, but in those sections of society that are the focus of this paper, this culture always exists as a contextual background. The crucial point to note here is that the individual who is socialised in this climate of insecurity and aggression becomes attuned to the ephemeral cultural and tangible material benefits that accrue for those who are successfully violent. They learn something that is withheld from those children raised in more secure environments – that violence is real and does actually happen, and that some people will use physical violence in order to secure a benefit for the self. For them, violence is not an unearthly and unfathomable spectacle, some distant, mythical Thing that happens elsewhere and to others. Despite the heightened emotions that accompany violence, its ugliness and crudity can become routine, profoundly ordinary, a mere aspect of everyday social engagement. The child that is exposed to insecurity and violence at an early age, in a very practical way, is consciously and subconsciously encouraged to see violence as a social resource stripped of its usual civilised associations.

The child that grows into the violent man is exposed to a general climate of insecurity and a constant stream of threats. These threats can be quite clear and direct, perhaps articulating the bodily harm that will result if an instruction is not carried out. They can also feed the general climate of insecurity in more subtle ways, like the kind of uncertainty the child feels when is in the presence of someone he knows can be incredibly violent. Even when this violent individual is calm and reasonable, an uncertainty borne of the intensity of emotion during violent interludes continues to hang over social encounters.

One powerful aspect of this atmosphere of insecurity is the experience of humiliation. The raw emotional fury of capitulating to a more physically powerful foe returns to haunt social experience, and the dread and fear that one might feel these emotions again can be a powerful impetus to violent action, even when the process of transforming the innocent child into the persistently violent adult is complete. There is also a background cultural context that requires the individual to understand the external world as inherently dangerous and competitive, a space in which the battle for dignity and respect is waged constantly. Many of the persistently violent men I have interviewed and observed recount tales of being told, while still very young, that the world is populated by nakedly instrumental others who will attempt to wrestle dignity from the self. As they grow they become attuned to this image of the external world and retain it as an explanatory structure when attempting to elucidate what they perceive to be the defensive nature of their adult violence (Winlow and Hall 2006). There also seem to be specific violent events and images that reinforce the understanding that violence itself has a powerful utility in relation to social action: the violent father who dominates, the schoolyard fighter who wins respect, the local gangster surrounded by sycophants and subordinates. These narratives are quite common in interview accounts of the experience of becoming violent. The super-ego forms of restraint that encourage the individual to avoid engagement in violence and to be considerate of the interests of others are often already in a weakened state, and are made weaker by this evidence that seems to suggest violence is indeed possible and can in fact be beneficial. The moral and ethical problems that accompany physical violence are now muddied and unclear. The persistently violent man is not subject to a powerful moral injunction that demands he treats others with respect and is considerate of their welfare.

This theme is crucial to the development of my overall theory. My claim is that the cultural forms of control that are internalised in the super-ego are no longer 'embodied' as such, and are increasingly experienced as a yoke that impedes egoistic expression. Those sociologists who have identified the problematic nature of new freedoms, in which the subject is compelled to engage in processes of self-creation, offer a useful insight into the nature of contemporary subjectivity and sociability. They are right to suggest that the subject feels a weight of expectation and can become anxious and deeply insecure about the responsibility they have to create a good and satisfying life for themselves and their families. But those who suggest that these new freedoms prompt individuals to remove themselves from this this situation and create new worlds of certainty, a process often associated with the rise of nationalism across Europe, miss something important about the subjective experience of these new freedoms. First, most people do not experience contemporary social reality as a world of boundless freedoms. I would suggest that most people who inhabit the places of excision that are the focus on this chapter feel a general sense of *unfreedom*, that they are in their everyday lives controlled and over-policed, surrounded by a matrix that stultifies their own self-expression. This, I think, is reflective of the fact that freedom and enslavement are far more closely connected than we seem willing to admit. What is crucial is that 'the people' lack the very language necessary to articulate this unfreedom. What is freedom today if not the freedom to consume, the freedom to vote, the freedom to pursue individual life projects?

There is much to be said about the place of freedom in contemporary Western societies, but the point I am particularly keen to get across is that something far more fundamental is also at work here. Many left-liberal criminologists have argued passionately that prevailing structures of power seek to restrict freedom, creativity and spontaneity, but now, it seems, these are the very tools that are used in ensure that the social and economic system of contemporary capitalism can continue onwards. Our creativity, our fight for freedom, our desire for self-expression is the fuel the system needs to postpone its ultimate end-point. In this situation, the subject experiences all ethical injunctions as oppressive interventions that seek to impose a universality upon the messy business of everyday life. To use the language of the time, those who demand that we submit to these rules are 'terrorising' us, harassing us with what are merely their own subjective viewpoints. If god is dead, if we have no faith in science or politics or anything else, who are you to say what is moral and what is not? These days, the subject committed to expressive individualism believes that what is right and wrong in relation to their own behaviour, or what is ethical and unethical, is essentially a decision for the individual and therefore nobody else's business.

The advent of postmodernism has changed human subjectivity, and it has done so in important ways. We are, it seems, edging closer to a world equivalent to that faced by Nietzsche's 'last men': a world in which the paradigmatic citizen of Western liberal democracies fears an excessive intensity of life, restricts herself to a life of shallow pleasures, adopts a darkly cynical attitude to all truth claims, and rejects the intrusive nature of conventional morality as a fetter placed upon individual expression. Here I endorse Žižek's (2008a; 2008b, etc.) model of postmodern subjectivity, in which the Cartesian subject returns only to be deprived to the symbolic substance that might allow her to construct an identity she can believe in and fully commit to. Without these things, all that remains is the formal respect for freedom, reflected in our obsession with individual 'rights', and a tolerance of otherness, which is a mode of address that ensures the neighbour is always kept at a safe distance. For the postmodern subject then, morality is not something that emanates from within, or reflects a deep, bodily conviction that cannot be ignored. Rather, the postmodern subject is painfully 'rational', unable to believe, compelled to cynically calculate, but without a commitment to truth that might allow those calculations to drive the subject forward and out of the darkness of that enveloped Nietzsche's 'last men'. The same is true of the violent subject: what remains of internal psychological forces that act against violence must be negotiated or avoided or rendered inapplicable if the subject is to become violent and feel justified in doing so. The violent subject does not believe that violence is 'fundamentally wrong'. Their attitude towards it is complex and dependent upon context. They are conversant with normative attitudes that define violence in these terms, but believe those attitudes to be hopelessly unworldly and divorced from the pressing actuality of life in the 'real' world. They will also construct a narrative of a challenge, or an attempt to humiliate, degrade or demean, and this provides the self with an opportunity to bypass conventional attitudes towards violence and respond with aggression and rage.

Homo homini lupus

The child who is socialised in an atmosphere of constant insecurity, and who is also subject to the gendered narratives of this specific masculine habitus, will eventually reach a point at which he tries out violence, perhaps in a social situation that is understood as immediately threatening, or in a context that is assumed to be a potential site for testing out this new behavioural hypothesis. For many of the violent men I have spoken to, this first experience of their own aggressive violence is powerfully memorable. In many cases they articulate this experience as an act of self-becoming, in which they 'learn' that which everyone should know: that violence is necessary and one has to accept and deal with this actuality. The persistently violent individual often feels that humiliation and subordination waits for all who fail to acknowledge and deal with the fact that violence is a requirement forced upon the individual by the heartless brutality of the external world. If they fail to defend an image of themselves as someone who will respond adequately to threats, insults and attempts to humiliate, they believe that their identity, rooted in class-based masculine concerns with reputation and respect, will be gradually washed away and their lives will count for nothing.

The child comes through this first experience of aggressive physical violence intact. They learn that many people will go to great lengths to avoid violence, and that even in run-down inner city neighbourhoods a sudden burst of violence can transform the ways others see and interact with the self. They also learn that it is possible to fight against forms of internal behavioural regulation and overcome them. The violence of others, the violence that during childhood seemed so alien and threatening, can be adopted and made one's own. This incredible ethereal power can be harnessed and controlled and sent out to make others cower and squirm, forcing them to acknowledge the supremacy of the self. This realisation can be powerfully intoxicating and can encourage them to believe that they have accessed some hidden truth or that they have moved beyond the boundaries that hold other men in expressive servitude. This realisation often has significant consequences for the self-image of men who pass through this process, and can have a profound effect upon their unfolding social engagement.

Together with Steve Hall (Winlow and Hall 2009) I have recently claimed that persistently violent men often search social interaction looking for the merest indication that another is attempting to humiliate the self. This can often result in immediate aggressive action, but the feeling that one has been slighted might also take some time to fully form in the mind. Violence can therefore be removed from the immediacy of its specific interactive context and *transported into the future*. The violent subject has 'stewed' on some aspect of interaction and eventually arrived at the conclusion that the other has attempted to demean or subordinate the self. This may not have been a fully conscious behavioural tactic deployed by the other but this is how that behaviour has been interpreted by the violent subject. Months may pass, and the violent subject's antagonist may have no idea that they have caused deep offence. The next time they meet the violent subject may explode into violence in what is understood by the audience as an act of random aggression. In fact, it is anything but. It is an act of self-rescuing violence that is deeply reflective of the psychical processes that are particular to individuals who are willing to invest everything in a self-image built upon violence, fearlessness and domination. For the violent subject this violence is understood as a continuation of, or response to, the initial incident and, for them, *had to take place* if they are to avoid the emotional pain that accompanies this humiliation. The nagging, clawing sense that they have been taken for a fool, that they are being laughed at or that their cultural capital is under threat, circulates in the mind, shifting and mutating until the violent subject is left with a clear choice between acting against those who would humiliate the self or relinquishing an image of the self that is built around fearlessness and domination. For the violent subject this is no choice at all. When the punches are thrown it is as if the humiliation the violent subject has painstakingly constructed from the fragments of the initial interaction is right there in the immediacy of the moment, being expressed directly in the most aggressively demeaning manner possible, even though their victim stands mute in front of them. No words have passed between the two, but the violent subject is red-faced, furious, filled with righteous indignation and attacking an adversary whose often mythical attempt to humiliate cannot be borne by the violent subject any longer.

An unusual example of this process can be seen in the film *Casino*, directed by Martin Scorsese. In this film Joe Pesci plays a gangster who displays many similarities with the image of the violent subject I outline here. In a key scene, Pesci's character and a number of subordinates have been torturing a rival gangster in order to extract information. Pesci's character expresses admiration for his rival gangster's steadfastness, but realises he must bring the torture to a conclusion. Pesci places his rival's head in a vice and begins to tighten it. Crucially, Pesci's tone is quite conciliatory at this stage: he doesn't want to do what he is doing, and he asks his adversary to provide them both with a way of avoiding what must come. He asks 'don't make me have to do this. Don't make me be a bad guy'. The adversary issues a final 'fuck you'. In the rest of the scene it is possible for the viewer to gain some insight into the ways the violent subject can utilise a sense of humiliation, and the rage that results, in order to enact the raw brutality that is so central of his self-identity. The encounter is no longer interactional as such, and this is why a sociologically informed psychoanalytic approach is crucial in understanding the internal dynamics and hypercomplexities of subjective violence. Pesci's character deliberately summons up a sense of humiliation, and its rage accompaniment, so that he might engage in an incredibly brutal act that, were he not filled with a sense of justifiable rage, would be extremely difficult for him to accomplish. He sighs at the bravery of his adversary one final time, and then abandons this respectful, pacific mode and wilfully summons up from within himself the emotions that might allow him to take the next step. Pesci responds 'Fuck me? Fuck me, you motherfucker?! Fuck my mother?! That's what you going to tell me?!' This speech begins quietly and rises quickly to a shout. His adversary has said nothing about Pesci's mother, but Pesci creates a brutal insult that can support that rapid rise of his own rage. Eventually the torture victim divulges the required information, and Pesci exhumes from this tiny sliver of speech yet another insult. Pesci is now furious that the victim, his head squashed in a vice, has wasted his time and compelled him to engage in this act of savagery in order to protect another gangster whom Pesci judges to be totally unworthy of the victim's loyalty.

What is unusual about this scene is what appears to be the Pesci character's agency in relation to his own sense of humiliation. He is capable of summoning up a sense of humiliation and indignation that might allow him to engage in violent acts, even when humiliation is not a demonstrable part of unfolding social interaction. Here, to all intents and purposes, the victim of Pesci's violence has not sought to humiliate. He has doggedly sought to cling on to an image of himself as loyal and tough, even when staring death in the face. The Pesci character admires his victim, but he knows he must overcome this reaction if he is to be able to traverse super-ego restraints and move into a new mode that sanctions the use of brutal violence. He therefore *chooses to feel humiliation* and anger in a manner that is neither fully conscious nor fully subconscious. In most cases, evidence seems to suggest the feeling of humiliation rises immediately as a reaction to actual social interaction. In other cases it can build slowly as the violent subject reflects upon events they have already experienced. I am also willing to risk the hypothesis that this *decision to feel humiliated*, and the almost calculated summoning up of the emotions that accompany this experience, may also be a part of the armoury of some persistently violent men.

Barbarous freedom

The appreciation of the benefits of violence often inspires the violent individual to believe that their capacity for and skill in violent combat generates respect and inspires envy in others. This belief is complex and multifaceted. For violent men who inhabit those marginalised socio-economic environments in which concerns with generating respect and retaining dignity are paramount, it is entirely reasonable for the violent subject to assume that his skill in combat has a powerful impact upon the image others hold of the self. Men who are successfully violent are often granted forms of respect that are specific to this cultural milieu (Winlow 2001). There may also be a measure of envy that results from the ability of the violent subject to secure this culturally informed respect. But it is also reasonable to claim that the violent subject can misconstrue the messages that are carried in the refracted images that bounce back at him from the social mirror. In this situation the fear, dread and barely concealed antagonism that the persistently violent subject produces in his immediate social circle can be mistakenly interpreted as respect and envy borne of the stoic, robust, ready-to-fight identity adopted in his wilful creation of self. Here, the violent subject sees himself as the man who is willing to do what is necessary, the man who will not compromise or debase himself by yielding to the will of others. This grandiose, egoistic self-image is both a profound consolation and self-justification, and the driving force which assures self-destruction.

Once the violent subject has made the momentous step into aggressive violence and discovered its deep utility, it becomes progressively easier for him to overcome internal inhibitions and draw upon violence in everyday social interaction. By this stage, the violent subject has learnt that internal inhibitions can be overcome, and that using violence allows him to dominate interaction and impose his will upon others. The decision to react aggressively to any sense of threat or challenge is not always fully conscious, and appears to depend upon the extent to which the subject has detected the motive to humiliate within the context of the interaction. Once the subject has triumphed in the battle against forms of super-ego restraint, these restraints have significantly less power over the subject and recourse to violence can seem almost 'natural' and therefore unencumbered by moral or ethical questions.

The internal psychological restraints that keep civilised people from bursting into aggressive violence as soon as they encounter a problem are, in the violent subject, in a poor state of repair. As I have suggested above, the violent men who are the focus of this chapter also inhabit a culture in which readiness to fight and skill in combat are highly prized. These aspects of the culture are fully internalised and become 'real' to the violent subject as they are essentially a tool of freedom that allows and encourages the subject to do what they want to do. Systems of control and regulation which can also be internalised and become 'real' are understood differently as they tend to restrict the social engagement of the individual. These control mechanisms are therefore not fully drawn into the identity of persistently violent men. Instead, these systems of control exist in a space in which there are no hard and fast 'answers'. Here the subject recognises that it is always possible to resort to mitigating factors and complex contextual indicators that transform the hard restriction against violence into a soft suggestion that violence should be avoided, unless particular contextual imperatives are in place that suggest violence is actually permissible. In this way, the broader cultural imperative that forbids violence against women becomes a general observation that violence against women is not advisable and should be restricted to those occasions when the women in question has made the avoidance of violence impossible. This image is one of a possessive subjectivity in which the fundamentally narcissistic individual effectively arrives at a point at which it seems reasonable to choose which controls and prohibitions are followed, which are not, and under what circumstances that decision is to be made. The problem is of course that once the subject reaches a stage of such narcissistic self-identification, it is then impossible for them to absorb the stabilising imperatives of the traditional symbolic order in an unproblematic manner.

Persistent involvement in violence has encouraged the violent subject to develop some of the practical skills that are likely to increase the chances of a successful outcome when one becomes involved in physical conflict. Anger and aggression now rise quickly and are slow to dissipate. The violent subject has also by this stage fully integrated violence into their on-going processes of self-identification, and empirical evidence seems to confirm that many persistently violent men are driven by a powerful mimetic admiration for the dominant other, and, consciously or subconsciously, attempt to recreate the self in his image (Winlow and Hall 2009). From this point onwards, if the violent subject encounters one of the infinite number of mild frustrations that are so indicative of contemporary urban life they will find it relatively easy to deploy the 'master fix' of immediate aggressive violence to address the problem. Violence, they are now sure, *works*. It has a function, and it can be a disturbingly practical answer to many of the difficulties faced by the violent subject who inhabits a marginalised social space. Rather than the gradual build up to violence, in which the civilised individual becomes progressively more frustrated and exhausts all rational alternatives to violence before turning to it as the last available option, the violent subject can leap straight in with an immediate burst of raw brutality, secure in the knowledge that violence was in fact *always inevitable*, that any attempt to resolve the problem in a non-violent way simply *could not work*, and any attempt to do so would reflect a weakness that the violent subject is unable to countenance.

'My father is beating me'

Lacan's work on the subjective experience of shame is instructive here. For Lacan (1988), desire is mostly experienced as that which we *do not* want. All desire symbolises a lack, an absence, signalled by the fact that achieving the object of our desire immediately extinguishes our desire for it. For Lacan, we tend to orbit around the object of our desire, intoxicated by it but mindful of the fact that as soon as we reach out and attempt to grasp it, it will disappear instantly. Desire is therefore rooted in the experience of *jouissance* – those acts of 'pleasure' that extend into pain; those pleasure-seeking behaviours that sabotage the interests of the self, or reveal something that the subject would prefer remained hidden. For Lacan, shame is inevitably connected to this jouissance, and always involves a fantasy element. If we take this to its limit, the central harm of the shame emotion is delivered not by our acquiescence to another, but by our experience of jouissance as a result of this acquiescence. We are so appalled that our experience of passivity subconsciously thrills us in some way, that our brutalisation has somehow tapped into the hidden desires of our fantasy space, that the shame we feel is fundamentally a reflection of this self-revulsion rather than simply a 'natural' result of our abuse at the hands of another. Žižek (2005: 147) offers a troubling example: 'shame is not simply passivity, but an actively assumed passivity: if I am raped, I have nothing to be ashamed of; but if I enjoy being raped, then I deserve to feel ashamed.' Žižek's point is that there always exists a gap between our everyday, outward identity and the 'fantasmatic kernel of the subject's being' (ibid.). The act of drawing close to this hidden truth is always traumatic and often causes the subject's outward identity to disintegrate. Being forced to live out a hidden fantasy in this passive mode, in which one is reduced to a mere body to be used by the other is, for Žižek (ibid.: 148), 'perhaps, the worst, most humiliating kind of violence, a violence which undermines the very basis of my identity ... by exposing me to an unbearable shame'.

Space restricts me from offering a framework that might allow us to better understand this possible dimension of the child's understanding, in which shame and humiliation reflect the indirect experience of the child's desire. All I will say is that the standard philosophical positioning of subjective shame, in which our social identity is disturbed by the Real of our bodily experience, must be supplemented by new ways of thinking about this problem.

Conclusion

The rambling, speculative nature of this chapter is driven by a desire to rethink the problem of subjective violence. What I have attempted to do here is identify for criminologists one or two new ways of addressing this problem. Too often in criminology the motivations of the violent criminal are removed from our critical analysis. The violent criminal is often positioned as a cypher, being pushed and pulled, driven and induced by the nature of specific social contexts. This, I think, reflects our discipline's unwillingness to engage with subjectivity in a properly philosophical manner. It also reflects an unwillingness to see subjective violence in relation to those other forms of violence that are a part of the way we live now. Specifically, the systemic violence of the current order, which acts as a zero-point against which we measure subjective violence, and symbolic violence, which includes those forms of violence that wound and shame but never move beyond the realm of language (see Žižek 2008a). The systemic violence of global capitalism, for example, creates for us in the West the appearance of relative calm and continuity. Subjective violence upsets this calm, and we usually experience it as a visceral interruption by social, political or subjective pathology. But this experience of calm is itself built upon violence, the violence that needs to take place in order to give Western citizens the experience of regulated, rule-governed civility. This systemic violence is not simply the violence we in the West do not see, but create – for example the staggering harms that are visited upon the natural environment, or the violence of mindless consumption upon workers in developing countries. It is also the violence of a capitalist system which endlessly seeks its own renewal, blindly rumbling forwards, totally inconsiderate of its impact upon human populations, or the historical and ecological limits of its own enterprise. This systemic violence of global capitalism and the everyday symbolic violence of culture and language must be implicated in the structuring of subjective violence if we are to move towards a more complete understanding of human violence itself.

References

Badiou, A. (2008) *The Meaning of Sarkozy*, London: Verso.

—— (2009) *Logics of Worlds*, London: Continuum.

Badiou, A. and Žižek, S. (2009) *Philosophy in the Present*, Oxford: Polity.

Derrida, J. (2006) *Spectres of Marx*, London: Routledge.

Elias, N. (2000) *The Civilising Process*, Oxford: Blackwell.

Fukuyama, F. (1993) *The End of History and the Last Man*, London: HarperPerrenial.

Hall, S. (1997) 'Visceral Cultures and Criminal Practices', *Theoretical Criminology*, 4, 1: 453–78.

—— (2007) 'The Emergence and Breakdown of the Pseudo-Pacification Process', in Katherine Watson (ed.) *Assaulting the Past: Violence and Civilisation in Historical Context*, Newcastle Upon Tyne: Cambridge Scholars Publishing.

Hall, S., Winlow, S. and Ancrum, C. (2008) *Criminal Identities and Consumer Culture: Crime, Exclusion and the New Culture of Narcissism*, Cullompton: Willan.

—— (2012) *Theorizing Crime and Deviance: A New Perspective*, London: Sage.

Lacan, J. (1988) *The Seminar of Jacques Lacan, Book 2: The Ego in Freud's Theory and in the Technique of Psychoanalysis 1954–1955*, ed. J-A. Miller. Cambridge: Cambridge University Press.

Matthews, R. (2009) 'Beyond "So What?" Criminology: Rediscovering Realism', *Theoretical Criminology*, 13, 3: 341–62.

Mills, C. W. (1999) *The Sociological Imagination*, Oxford: Oxford University Press.

Sloterdijk, P. (2010) *Rage and Time*, New York: Columbia University Press.

Wieviorka, M. (2009) *Violence*, London: Sage.

Winlow, S. (2001) *Badfellas: Crime, Tradition and New Masculinities*, Oxford: Berg.

Winlow, S. and Hall, S. (2006) *Violent Night: Urban Leisure and Contemporary Culture*, Oxford: Berg.

—— (2009) 'Retaliate First: Memory, Humiliation and Male Violence', *Crime, Media, Culture*, 5, 3: 285–304.

Žižek, S. (2005) 'Neighbors and Other Monsters: A Plea for Ethical Violence', in S. Žižek, E. Santner and K. Reinhard, *The Neighbor: Three Inquiries in Political Theology*, Chicago: University of Chicago Press.

—— (2008a) *Violence*, London: Verso.

—— (2008b) *In Defense of Lost Causes*, London: Verso.

—— (2010) *Living in the End Times*, London: Verso.

13 Late capitalism, vulnerable populations and violent predatory crime

David Wilson

Few people have heard of John Barr.[1] Even fewer will associate his name with late capitalism, vulnerable populations and crime – even if his crimes were neither violent nor predatory in any orthodox criminological sense. Yet Barr was responsible for the deaths of twenty-one people – many of them elderly – in Wishaw, Scotland, in circumstances that started ordinarily enough. In November 1996 a group of pensioners gathered for lunch in their local church hall and ate stewed steak in puff pastry, all of which had been supplied by their local, prize-winning butcher, John M. Barr and Son. Within weeks, six of the lunch party were dead. More deaths followed, and even today many others in Wishaw who had been supplied with meat from this same source still suffer from kidney problems and fatigue as a result of what has been described as 'the world's worst recorded outbreak of fatal E coli food poisoning' (Seenan, 1999).

In a report conducted into the events surrounding this outbreak, Sheriff Principal Graham Cox criticised Barr, suggesting that he had only paid 'lip service to environmental health officers so that he could conceal the full extent of his business operations. In this way he was able to avoid very tight food regulations set out in 1994', (BBC News, 19 August 1998). Sheriff Cox also criticised local environmental health officers (EHOs) who had failed to issue Barr with an emergency prohibition notice, which would have immediately stopped the sale of cooked meat from his shop. As a result Barr was able to continue to supply more cooked meat a few days later to an 18th birthday party, where there were over 100 guests. When some of these guests started to fall ill, EHOs once again interviewed Barr but they did not record their meeting, make notes for a transcript, or caution Barr that anything that he said could be used in court. As a result, a trial in November 1997 against Barr for culpable, wilful and reckless supply of contaminated meat to the birthday party collapsed and, to date, Barr has simply been fined £2,250.

Barr's story is of interest because it is illustrative of a number of issues which are important to highlight before considering the phenomenon of serial killing – a type of multiple murder and the most notorious form of violent, predatory crime which is the focus of this chapter. First, it reminds us that what we call 'crime' – including violent, predatory crime – is essentially socially constructed. Rarely do we think of a small, local butcher's shop, or a much larger multi-national corporation, deliberately ignoring health and safety legislation, and rarely does it occur to us that the state itself may be a source of unlawful homicide, through, for example, the leaking or dumping of toxic waste (Slapper and Tombs, 1999). The law – and criminology – rarely considers deaths caused in this way to be worthy of scrutiny, or in any way troublesome, problematic or unlawful (Tombs and Whyte, 2007; 2008). As a result there was and has been no moral panic about John Barr, and nor, frankly, was there very much press interest, even though the twenty-one deaths that resulted from his sale of contaminated cooked meats would have ranked him third highest on a list of British serial killers since 1888, with more deaths attributable to him than Jack the Ripper, John Haigh, Reg Christie, Peter Manuel, Peter Sutcliffe, Dennis Nilsen, the Wests and Ian Brady and Myra Hindley (see Wilson, 2009 and Table 13.1 overleaf).

On the other hand, it has recently been argued that 'a symbiotic relationship exists between the media and serial killers. In the quest for audience share the media have become addicted to portrayals of serial killers' (Haggerty, 2009: 174). Part of this addiction stems from the fact that serial killers offer:

> rich opportunities to capture public attention by capitalizing on deeply resonate themes of innocent victims, dangerous strangers, unsolved murders, all coalescing around a narrative of evasion and given moral force through implied personal threats to audience members. Serial killers were apparently ready-made for prime time.
>
> (Haggerty, 2009: 174)

Barr occasionally made it onto the regional news bulletins, but he was certainly never considered to be prime time, and nor has he been the subject of a documentary, or the inspiration for any number of TV series, films or true crime books (for accounts of how serial killers are presented in the media see Schmidt, 2005; Gibson, 2006; Jarvis, 2007).

Finally, when we try to apportion responsibility for these twenty-one deaths in Wishaw there is an understandable – 'common sense' – tendency to hold Barr personally responsible. Indeed, this individualisation of criminal behaviour has become a dominant trend in positivist criminology and questions of how responsibility might be broadened to include public policy more generally – especially underlying and structural economic and social factors – is rarely considered. As Coleman *et al.* (2009: 5) have recently put it, 'the violence that concerns criminology is individual violence'. Yet, as Barr's case demonstrates, responsibility for the deaths that resulted from this outbreak of E. coli poisoning could equally be placed at the door of the behaviour of the state's EHOs who took inappropriate action initially, and then failed to deal with the situation adequately after the birthday party. In short, responsibility for these deaths is more complicated than simply seeing Barr as personally culpable. After all, what made those who were poisoned at the birthday party vulnerable to illness was a failure to act appropriately by preventing Barr from continuing to sell cooked meats.

This issue of how certain groups are made 'vulnerable' by the state, or by wider social, economic and cultural processes – and how, as a consequence, that

Table 13.1 British serial killers, 1888–2009

Name	Year Tried	Occupation	Victims	Number
'Jack the Ripper'	N/A	N/K	Prostitutes	5
Thomas Neill Cream	1891	Doctor	Prostitutes	3
George Chapman	1903	Publican	Women	3
George Smith	1916	Petty Criminal	Women	3
John Haigh	1949	Businessman	Random	6
John Christie	1953	Clerk	Women	7
Peter Manuel	1958	Petty Criminal	Random	8
Michael Copeland	1965	Soldier	Young person/gay men	3
Ian Brady/ Myra Hindley	1966	Clerk/ typist	Children/young people	5
Patrick Mackay	1975	Gardener	Elderly women/priest	3
Donald Neilson	1976	Builder	Men/young person	3
Trevor Hardy	1977	Petty Criminal	Young women	3
Archibald Hall/ Micheal Kitto	1978	Butler/ unemployed	Acquaintances/ employer	5
Peter Dinsdale	1981	Unemployed	Random	26
Peter Sutcliffe	1981	Lorry Driver	Women/prostitutes	13
Dennis Nilsen	1983	Civil servant	Gay men	15
John Duffy	1988	Unemployed	Women/young person	3
Kenneth Erskine	1988	Unemployed	Elderly	7
Beverly Allitt	1993	Nurse	Children	4
Colin Ireland	1993	Unemployed	Gay men	5
Robert Black	1994	Van driver	Children	3
Fred West/ Rose West	1995	Builder/ housewife[1]	Young people/family member	10
Peter Moore	1996	Cinema owner	Gay men/random[2]	4
Steve Grieveson	1996	Unemployed	Young men	3
Harold Shipman	2000	Doctor	Elderly	215
Mark Martin[3]	2006	Unemployed	Women	3
Steve Wright	2007	Van Driver	Prostitutes	5
Colin Norris	2008	Nurse	Elderly	4
Peter Tobin	2009	Odd Job Man	Women	3

Notes
1 Rose West might also be described as a 'part-time prostitute'.
2 One of Moore's victims was a security guard on a building site that Moore simply chanced upon.
3 Martin killed two of his victims in the company of two other men – Dean Carr and John Ashley.

vulnerability makes them more likely to become a victim of a serial killer – is a recurring theme throughout this chapter. The chapter is based on what we know about the phenomenon of serial killing in Britain from 1888, although there is a particular focus on the victims of serial killers after 1960 and then much closer to the late modernity of our own time. This focus has been deliberately chosen for, as Haggerty (2009) has recently suggested, 'serial killing is patterned in modernity's self-image' and that as a result, modernity provides 'the key institutional frameworks, motivations, and opportunity structures characteristic of contemporary forms of serial killing' (Haggerty, 2009: 170).

I start by covering some familiar criminological territory about this subject, prior to developing the argument that I have introduced through using the story of James Barr.

Individual serial killers and the definition question

Until relatively recently serial killing has been almost exclusively dominated by theorising that considers the biography of the individual serial killer and his aetiology, or by questions of definition (Egger, 1984; Holmes and De Burger, 1988; Dietz, 1996; Hale, 1998; Holmes and Holmes, 1998; Ferguson *et al.*, 2003; Canter and Wentink, 2004). As a result of this type of theorising it has become accepted that we label a serial killer as someone who has killed three or more victims in a period of greater than 30 days, usually with a 'cooling off' period between each murder. Identifying serial killers in this way allows us to differentiate, for example, between those people who murder a large number of people – such as Michael Ryan at Hungerford in August 1987 who shot and killed sixteen people, or Thomas Hamilton at Dunblane who shot and killed sixteen children and their school teacher in March 1996 – and who thus qualify in terms of the numeric threshold, but not in relation to the element of time. Indeed, Hamilton or Ryan would be described in the academic literature as 'spree', 'mass' or 'multiple' murderers.

However, defining 'serial killing' remains an inexact science. Even this simplistic time/numeric threshold hides a variety of criminological debates. Some criminologists, for example, suggest that there should be a six-point identification of the serial killer; that there need only be two victims; that the murders should occur at different locations; and, crucially, that there should be no relation between the victim and the perpetrator. These stipulations seem too prescriptive, and would in the British context exclude some perpetrators such as Dennis Nilsen and Fred and Rosemary West (for general introductions to these cases see Masters, 1986; Sounes, 1995). Both Nilsen and the Wests, for example, had prior relationships with many of their victims, and they also murdered their victims in the same locations, in London and Gloucester respectively.

Perhaps because definitions of serial killing are so problematic there have been few attempts to devise a typology of serial murders. The most comprehensive remains that devised by two American criminologists – Ronald Holmes and James DeBurger. Their typology also has the added advantage of being based on interviews and analysis of more than 400 cases of serial murder. They concluded that there were four main types of serial murderer – visionary, mission, hedonistic and power/control (see Table 13.2). However, there are other typologies and, for example, other criminologists have suggested that there are 'place/specific' serial killers who murder in particular physical locations, such as hospitals or nursing homes. We should also note that the typology devised by Holmes and DeBurger is not necessarily fixed, or mutually exclusive, and so a serial killer might display characteristics of more than one type.

Other criminologists have attempted to understand the behaviour of serial

Table 13.2 Types of serial killer (male)

Visionary	Killer is impelled to murder because he has heard voices or seen visions demanding that he kill a particular person, or category of people. The voice or vision may be for some a demon, but for others may be perceived as coming from God.
Mission	Killer has a conscious goal in his life to eliminate a certain identifiable group of people. He does not hear voices, or have visions. The mission is self-imposed.
Hedonistic	Killer kills simply for the thrill of it – because he enjoys it. The thrill becomes an end in itself.
Power/control	Killer receives gratification from the complete control of the victim. This type of murderer experiences pleasure and excitement not from sexual acts carried out on the victim, but from his belief that he has the power to do whatever he wishes to another human being who is completely helpless to stop him.

Source: Adapted from Holmes and DeBurger (1988).

killers from the perspective of their 'intrinsic' and 'extrinsic' motivations. In other words, whether their motivation to kill lies outside of their personality (such as with 'hit men', those fighting for a political cause, or the nineteenth-century body snatchers Burke and Hare who murdered for financial gain), or deep within their psychological make-up. Ronald Holmes – on this occasion writing with Stephen Holmes – concluded that most serial killers are motivated by intrinsic considerations, but that it is useful to try and understand what a given killer 'has to gain from the commission of a particular crime' either materially or psychologically. They suggest that, through the interviews that they have conducted with serial killers, most murder for psychological reasons. They go on:

> In interviews, many [serial killers] have told us that the principal motivating factor in their killing was that they simply enjoyed killing. Others have stated that they were motivated by the intense feeling they got out of holding the fate of other persons in their hands. The more a person kills, the greater becomes his need to experience those feelings of gratification or power. The feeling becomes more than a compulsion, it becomes an addiction.
>
> (Holmes and Holmes, 1994: 115)

Of course this addiction is easy to feed if there is a ready supply of victims. Sadly those who have been murdered by serial killers rarely manage to get a mention in the mass of true-crime books devoted to the subject and which are almost universally dominated by the so-called 'medical-psychological' tradition. This tradition attempts to understand the phenomenon of serial killing from the perspective of the individual serial killer. In other words, how he – and it is usually a 'he' – was born and raised, whether he had good relationships with his father, mother, siblings, and how he might have responded to moments of crisis or trauma in his life, such as when a parent, grandparent, partner and so forth died.

Theorising that places serial killers and the phenomenon of serial killing into a broader framework that accommodates social, economic and cultural factors has been almost totally neglected. However, a small group of scholars – largely inspired by, but not slavishly following, the work of Elliott Leyton (1986) – have begun to investigate the phenomenon of serial killing from a 'structural', rather than from the medical-psychological perspective. So, for example, in the case of Britain, it has been suggested that

> the responsibility for serial killing does not lie so much with the individual serial killer, but can be better found within the social and economic structure of Britain since the 1960s, which . . . does not reward the efforts of all and in particular marginalised large sections of society.
>
> (Wilson, 2007: 17; and also see Grover and Soothill, 1999; Soothill, 2001; Soothill and Wilson, 2005; Wilson, 2009)

Let's investigate this structural approach further in relation to serial killing in Britain.

Applying these definitions to Britain

Using this time/numeric threshold as a basis for investigating the phenomenon of serial murder in Britain, what issues, patterns and themes emerge about the 32 serial killers and their 370 victims? Some general points about Table 13.1 can be made immediately. First, the victims of British serial killers are clearly drawn from certain groups: the elderly, gay men, babies and infants, young people moving away from home and prostitutes. Of course there are overlaps between these general categorisations, and so, for example, the description 'the elderly' masks the fact that many of the elderly in question were elderly women, rather than elderly men. So too 'young person/people' is a very broad description, although it is being employed here so as to capture those young people – as opposed to babies and infants – who have by and large left home, and are attempting for various reasons to make their own way in the world. Here too there is a gender imbalance, but while some serial killers, such as the Wests, concentrated their efforts on young women, others, like Dennis Nilsen, were more interested in young men.

Second, gay men have been regular targets of serial killers, especially in the latter part of our time-frame – despite the fact that civil partnerships have become common, and gay relationships are far more open. Perhaps this suggests something about the persistence of homophobia at a time when homosexuality is no longer illegal. (Indeed if I had included the case of the Italian born and raised Lupo – who killed four gay men in London in 1986 – the numbers of gay victims would have been higher still.) However, it is also worth noting here that whilst two of the serial killers are open about their sexuality – Peter Moore and Dennis Nilsen – we do not know if Michael Copeland was gay, and press reports suggested that Steven Grieveson murdered his victims to hide his sexuality. However, Colin Ireland seems to have chosen to kill gay men only because they were vulnerable to attack, and therefore suitable targets which would allow him to achieve his objective of becoming famous through their serial murder (*The Times*, 21 December 1993).

Third, it is important to acknowledge that the elderly are the group that has been attacked most regularly by British serial killers. Some 225 elderly people have been murdered by serial killers – a figure that constitutes just over 60 per cent of the total number of victims since 1888. Finally, we should consider absences. For example, there are no Asian, or black British serial killers, and with the exceptions of Myra Hindley, Beverly Allitt and Rosemary West (two of whom killed in conjunction with male partners in a *folie à deux*), all of the British serial killers mentioned here are male.

It is also interesting to note when the serial killers that I have identified in Table 13.1 were active. In other words, when the victims of these serial killers were murdered.[2] This also helps us to chart peaks and troughs in their activities, and it is clear that the numbers of victims increases over our time-frame – despite the relatively few numbers of victims between 1960 and 1972, and between 1999 and 2010. So too, there were no serial killers active in Britain in the 1920s and 1930s (for a discussion of why this might be the case, see Wilson, 2009: 84–110). It is also obvious that the numbers of serial killers and their victims rises as the time-frame moves closer to the present. Indeed, we could divide the time-frame into four distinct phases – *Victorian/Pre-War*; *Inter-War*; *Post-War*; and *Thatcher/Consensus* – which roughly corresponds to the periods *1888–1914*; *1915–1945*; *1946–1978*; and finally *1979–present day*. The first phase produced three serial killers and eleven victims, while the last has produced seventeen serial killers and 272 victims, despite the fact that these phases are roughly comparable in terms of time.

Statistically, 1986 emerges as one of the most interesting years, as it was during this year that the greatest numbers of serial killers were known to be active over the period under discussion. In 1986, Duffy and Mulcahy murdered their three victims, Kenneth Erskine murdered seven, and Robert Black murdered 10-year-old Sarah Harper. Harold Shipman murdered eight people in 1986. Indeed if we had included Lupo's victims in this graph the number of serial killers active in Britain in this year would have been six, compared to an average over our time-frame of two per year.

Above all, the pattern that emerges from looking at the history of the phenomenon of serial killing in Britain is that the explanation for this phenomenon does not lie so much with the individual serial killer, but can be better found within the changing social and economic structure of Britain between 1888 and 2010, which – generalising on a theme that will be discussed more fully – does not reward the efforts of all, and in particular has marginalised large sections of society. In short, as late capitalism has begun to widen the gap between the 'haves' and the 'have nots', the numbers of serial killers and their victims has grown accordingly.

Given all of this, should it come as any surprise that the victims of British serial killers have been exclusively confined to certain marginalised groups in our culture – the elderly, gay men, prostitutes, babies and infants, and young people moving home and finding their feet elsewhere in the country – and that women make up a significant number in all but one of these categories? It is people from within these marginalised groups that are the focus of this chapter. In my attempt to explore the reasons why individuals from within these groups come to be victimised, I draw upon more familiar criminological territory – such as policing initiatives, 'cop culture', and the work of the criminal justice system more generally – to develop my argument more fully. In doing so, I want to reveal how these groups are made vulnerable by the state, or by state officials – a vulnerability that serial killers are only too happy to exploit. For reasons of space I will concentrate on the group that is most regularly attacked by serial killers in Britain – the elderly – although I will also make allusions to how vulnerability is created in the other four groups that have been identified.

The elderly

Some 229 elderly people (mostly women) have been killed in Britain by serial killers since 1960. Indeed, the most prolific British serial killer – Harold Shipman, who worked as a General Practitioner – specifically targeted the elderly, and unsurprisingly his story and the issues that it raises dominate what follows. However, three other British serial killers – Patrick Mackay, Kenneth Erskine and Colin Norris – also targeted older people, and I use aspects of their stories to gain further insight into the Shipman case. Indeed, in one of those twists of fate that history seems to so often throw up, four days after Shipman murdered for the first time, Mackay killed his final victim – Father Anthony Crean, a 64-year-old Catholic priest who had befriended him.[3] We can only speculate if Shipman followed this case in the news, but while Mackay's crimes were coming to an end, Shipman had only just started on a journey that would see him become this country's worst serial killer.

This group of elderly people can hardly be described as a representative sample of the elderly in Britain. However, it is important to remember that there is no fixed 'old age' – from which a representative sample might be drawn – but rather a variety of cultures of old age, some of which might compete with each other. There is also a growing disparity of wealth within the retired population, who are now living for longer, and some of whom are richer than ever before. As a consequence the fact that the group that I have chosen to consider might not be representative of the whole does not seem to be too problematic. Indeed the diversity within the older population, and the transformation of 'old age' more generally, are important points to bear in mind, but even so, as recently as 2005 the *Guardian* reported that, according to the National Pensioners Convention campaign group, there were 2.2 million older people living below the poverty line in the UK, and that around 1.5 million of Britain's older citizens were either malnourished, or at serious risk of it (*Guardian*, 8 June 2005).

As with the relative absence of comment about John Barr, there has also been a remarkable failure to analyse and understand our worst ever serial killer, or the circumstances that allowed him to kill so many people. 'How was Shipman able to repeatedly kill?' would seem to be a perfectly legitimate question to ask. However, beyond some very vague notions related to his desire to have 'the power of life and death', a desire to 'get what he wants', 'difficulties in his childhood', and his 'arrogance' – all aspects of the medical–psychological tradition – there has been little attempt to question the circumstances that allowed Shipman to kill and in doing so broaden out responsibility for his crimes (but see Soothill and Wilson, 2005). In short there have been relatively few attempts to see Shipman's crimes from a structural perspective.

Perhaps this failure to investigate the circumstances that allowed Shipman to repeatedly kill was a by-product of the announcement after Shipman's conviction on 31 January 2000 by the secretary of state for health of an independent (albeit private) inquiry into Shipman's crimes, and which was to be chaired by Lord Laming. By September 2000 the inquiry – after a great deal of pressure – was made public, and was thereafter chaired by Dame Janet Smith. Her inquiry began work in February 2001, and her final report was published in January 2005, before the inquiry was formally decommissioned in Easter of that year. The terms of reference for the inquiry were four-fold: to enquire into the actions of the statutory bodies, authorities, other organisations and responsible individuals concerned in the procedures and investigations which followed the deaths of those of Harold Shipman's patients who died in unlawful or suspicious circumstances; after receiving the existing evidence and hearing such further evidence as necessary, to consider the extent of Harold Shipman's unlawful activities; by reference to the case of Harold Shipman, to enquire into the performance of the functions of those statutory bodies, authorities, other organisations and individuals with responsibility for monitoring primary care provision and the use of controlled drugs; and following those enquiries, to recommend what steps, if any, should be taken to protect patients in the future, and to report its findings to the secretary of state for the Home Department and to the secretary of state for health. Without doubt it is this final component of the inquiry's terms of reference that is the most important.

So too the comparative silence on the question as to why Shipman killed might also have been the convenient consequence of a general acceptance that Shipman was 'evil', and therefore that the whole Shipman 'phenomenon' was such a freak of nature that it was thought unlikely to re-occur. Within this type of theorising Shipman is viewed as a lone, rogue predator. Why, therefore, waste too much energy in considering the grossly bizarre? In fact, these three apparently easy explanations are both contradictory, and not worth supporting.

First, the authoritative explanation about why Shipman committed his crimes from Dame Janet Smith's inquiry was not forthcoming. Despite the massive amount of time and money spent on the inquiry, there was no real answer to this key question. Indeed, even though the inquiry produced six reports between 2002 and 2005, Dame Janet, in her first report – *Death Disguised* – published in July

2002, which contains a chapter on Shipman's character and motivation, reminds her readers that:

> The Inquiry's Terms of Reference require me to consider the extent of Shipman's unlawful activities. They do not expressly require me to consider the motives behind Shipman's crimes, or the psychological factors that underlay them. However, I decided that I ought to consider and report on those matters, as well as I am able.
>
> (unless otherwise indicated all quotes are taken from www.the-shipman-inquiry.org)

Thus, with a team of forensic psychiatrists to support her – which included Professors John Gunn and Pamela Taylor and Drs Clive Meux and Alec Buchanan – Dame Janet had originally raised hopes and expectations that an authoritative explanation about Shipman's motivation might emerge. However, those reading Dame Janet's various reports will have these expectations dashed almost immediately, as Shipman refused to have anything to do with the inquiry, or indeed with Dame Janet's team of forensic psychiatrists. This meant that they could not interview him and had to rely on, at best, second-hand information about Shipman. Dame Janet points out that the psychiatrists could not 'gain any real insight into Shipman's character', and so had been 'unable to reach any conclusions' and thus 'in the end I have been unable to attempt any detailed explanation of the psychological factors underlying Shipman's conduct'.

Nor have the media tried particularly hard to investigate the Shipman phenomenon, perhaps because they had to deal with the same issue as Dame Janet – Shipman's refusal to speak. ITV's *To Kill and Kill Again*, which was broadcast on 1 March 2005, did not markedly help reveal any deeper understanding as to why Shipman killed, despite a whole plethora of 'experts' (mostly forensic psychologists) offering opinions. However, Carole Peters (2005) – the producer/ director of *To Kill and Kill Again*, and in her subsequent book called *Harold Shipman: Mind Set on Murder* – has attempted to go beyond the confines of the broadcast documentary. Ultimately all she could conclude was that Shipman became a serial killer because 'he enjoyed what he did'.

The third possibility for this silence – that the Shipman 'phenomenon' is a freak of nature and that Shipman himself was a lone, rogue predator who is unlikely to appear again – will be a hope that is shared by everyone, for it helps to secure the defences of our comfort zone. Thinking in this way makes us feel better about those elderly relatives or friends that we might have – but have not necessarily seen in some time – and for whom we have devolved responsibility to care and residential home owners, trusted local GPs and community nurses. However, we also know that this hope might not be realised. Indeed, the setting up of an inquiry (and it should be remembered that initially the inquiry was going to be held in private), in part suggests an official view that it could happen again. And, of course, an inquiry can also be used to dampen down speculation and contribute to a conspiracy of silence – 'we can't say anything until the inquiry has reported'

– but by the time that it does report, serious interest in the topic will have all but disappeared, and the media agenda moved elsewhere.

Nonetheless it is very important to understand why Shipman was able to murder so many elderly people, for this should allow us to then do something to stop others following in his footsteps. For if we do not understand the circumstances in which Shipman was able to repeatedly murder, then we will always remain in the position of trying to mend a leak without knowing the cause; of never really putting right the awful circumstances that allow the elderly to be targeted by serial killers.

First and last victims

Eva Lyons was Shipman's first victim. She had lived in Todmorden all her life – it was where she was born, raised, married and had a child – and it would also be where she died. Like most of her contemporaries, when Eva left school she had started to work as a weaver in one of the cotton mills that dominated the town, and which were once a source of its prosperity. The mills have long since disappeared, and Todmorden now mostly serves as a commuter town for people working in Manchester, Leeds, Bradford and Huddersfield. When Eva was 28 years old she met her husband Dick, a shuttle-maker at another factory, and they soon produced a child – a girl they named Norma. By early 1975 Eva was ill with cancer, although a new drug regime that she had started at Halifax Royal Infirmary was helping her with her condition. Eva's hair had started to grow back, and she was eating again. Even so, on the night of 17 March she was in some discomfort, and so Dick called out the doctor. Their local GP soon arrived at the house, and he told Dick that he was going to give Eva something to 'ease the pain'. He took a syringe from his bag, and injected it into Eva's hand, all the time maintaining a regular conversation with Dick. Five minutes later Eva was dead.

Eva's doctor would eventually be convicted at Preston Crown Court on 31 January 2000 of the murder of fifteen of his patients, whilst he was working as a GP from a singleton practice in Market Street, Hyde, near Manchester, and with one count of forging a will. Shipman was sentenced to life imprisonment, but ultimately took his own life while serving his sentence at HMP Wakefield, in January 2004.[4] Following his training at the University of Leeds Medical School, Shipman acted as a pre-registration house officer at Pontefract General Infirmary and then moved to the Abraham Ormerod Medical Practice in Todmorden in 1974. Perhaps during his student days, but certainly during this time, he developed an addiction to pethidine for which he was ultimately charged, and appeared before Halifax Magistrates' Court in 1976, where he pleaded guilty to three offences of obtaining ten ampoules of 100mg pethidine by deception, three charges of unlawfully possessing pethidine and two of forging prescriptions. He asked for seventy-four further offences to be taken into consideration and was fined £600. Shipman thereafter moved to Newton Aycliffe Health Centre, where he worked as a clinical medical officer, before moving to Hyde in 1978.

In Hyde Shipman originally worked at the Donneybrook Practice, before setting up his solo practice in Market Street in 1992. During his time in the town he rapidly gained a reputation as being a particularly good, 'old fashioned' doctor – especially with elderly people – whom he was prepared to visit in their own homes. A measure of his esteem in the Hyde community can be gleaned from the fact that there was a 'Shipman's Patient Fund', which raised money to buy medical equipment for his practice. When allegations about the murders started to circulate, a group of incredulous patients formed a support group for their erstwhile GP. At the time of his arrest over 3,000 patients were registered with his practice, a not inconsiderable number for a sole practitioner.

It would seem that Shipman was caught largely through a bungled attempt to forge the will of his last victim – Kathleen Grundy – whom he murdered on 24 June 1998, and which raised the suspicions of Mrs Grundy's lawyer daughter, Angela Woodruff. So poorly was the will forged that it could be suggested that Shipman may have wanted to have been caught, although equally this raises the issue that there may have been a financial motive for Shipman's killings. When he was arrested for the murder of Mrs Grundy it would seem that Shipman was killing at the rate of once every 10 days, and Dame Janet concludes that by that time Shipman was 'no longer in touch with reality'. Starting with the murder of Eva Lyons, and then for the next 23 years until the death of Mrs Grundy it has been calculated that Shipman killed 215 people – mostly elderly women (171 women and 44 men) – and Dame Janet harboured suspicions about the deaths of another forty-five of his former patients, making a total of some 260 people whom he may have killed.

It is worth reflecting here on Shipman's last offence – the murder of Mrs Grundy – and how this was exposed. So too we should also consider other less celebrated locals in Hyde who also harboured suspicions about Shipman and who had tried to make those in authority listen to their concerns. These reflections also allow us to consider more generally who it is that has a 'voice' and is listened to in late modernity, and who in comparison is 'silenced'; which deaths are deemed to be worthy of the state's investigation, and which do not prompt comment or further inquiries.

For example, John Shaw, a former policeman, started K Cabs in Hyde in 1988, having spotted the niche business of driving elderly clients around the town in his blue Volvo. His business prospered – largely because these elderly ladies grew to trust him – and over time most of his clients came to be on first name terms with their taxi driver, who would also sometimes do odd jobs for the ladies that he ferried to and fro. However, Shaw started to notice that not only were significant numbers of his 'ladies' suddenly dying in very similar circumstances – always at home, and 'posed' in an easy chair – but that they were all also Shipman's patients. So he started to compile a list dating back to the death of Monica Sparkes in October 1992 and would periodically voice his concerns to those who would listen. Few did. Accusing a doctor of murder was not something that could be done lightly, and so his list of sudden deaths, and the dates that these had happened were ignored during a first police investigation into Shipman, which had been conducted by Detective Inspector Smith of Greater Manchester Police. Ann

Alexander – the solicitor who would eventually represent the families of Shipman's victims – suggested that as far as this investigation was concerned: 'I had always believed that it was a policeman's job to go out and ask questions. And in this particular case Smith didn't ask any questions.' She continued:

> He sat and waited for information to be given to him. He just completely failed to get to the bottom of it, failed to make any notes, and because of the way in which he approached the whole thing it was inevitable that he wasn't going to get anything that would have given rise to an earlier arrest.
>
> (BBC Radio 4, 12 February 2009)

Shaw and his concerns were only taken seriously after the awful truth about Shipman began to emerge. In other words, John Shaw was silenced until those with more powerful voices were able to make a complaint that was given credence by those in authority.

But there is another silence that is only occasionally mentioned in the Shipman case – a silence related to the class of most of his victims. Those that Shipman killed were overwhelmingly working-class people – 'ordinary' women and men – who perhaps more than most had been socialised into trusting and respecting a doctor. Their very 'ordinariness' can be compared with Shipman's final victim – Kathleen Grundy – a former mayor of Hyde (who had also been married to a mayor of Hyde), a local councillor, who owned property in the town and also in the Lake District, and had some well chosen investments. Indeed Mrs Grundy's daughter – Angela Woodruff – was a solicitor and it was her legal knowledge (and her familiarity with police, coroners, and magistrates), which allowed her suspicions about the forgery of her mother's will to begin the process of unravelling Shipman's crimes. Even so Mrs Woodruff and her husband had to begin the investigation of Mrs Grundy's will themselves, before handing over their findings to the police.

So it was a forged will that brought Shipman to justice, and concerns over inheritance being voiced by professionals who understood how to make their anxieties known, rather than the suspicions of a taxi driver who recognised that there was a surprisingly high number of the local GP's patients who were suddenly dying for no apparent reason. This conclusion is not intended to be disrespectful to either Mr or Mrs Woodruff, but rather is meant to encourage us to reflect on who it is that has the power to complain and demand action, and who it is that has to shut up and make do.

Was the Shipman case a 'freak event'? The stance of the inquiry seems to have been that they wanted to deal with those issues that could be definitively 'proven' one way or another – where evidence could be weighed up and a decision about that evidence delivered. Thus, for example, the first of Dame Janet's reports concentrated on the numbers of patients who had been murdered; the second on the conduct of the police investigation; the third about the conduct of coroners and death certificates; the fourth about the regulation of controlled drugs in the community; the fifth which made suggestions about how patients might be protected in the future; and the sixth and last concerned Shipman's career as a junior doctor in Pontefract.

Shipman overwhelmingly chose victims who were poor, elderly, vulnerable and female. Peters (2005: 216) also suggests that Shipman may have chosen his victims because 'the elderly or infirm would go first because they simply ceased to be as valuable as human beings and so there was no reason to keep them'. In this way they could be perceived as living outside the moral order of a competitive capitalist society, and were therefore increasingly seen as a socio-economic 'burden'. A great many elderly people are increasingly marginalised and isolated, and while acknowledging Shipman's advantages of being seen as a 'respected' GP – which certainly provided cover for his murders – it is noteworthy that he was able to continue killing his patients for over two decades precisely because they were often out of touch with family members. Indeed, the very fact that he gained respect – which allowed him to build up his practice – was largely because he was seen as 'old fashioned', which in effect meant that he was willing to visit his patients in their homes. This simple reality not only provided Shipman with access to his victims, but also the opportunity to kill them as he pleased and where he in turn expected a silence about these deaths to be guaranteed by his good name.

Over Shipman's lifetime, there were both continuities but also many more changes in British culture and society which provided the context for his crimes. In many respects the dominant economic change was the move from production to consumption, which left in its wake large numbers of poor people who were no longer 'useful' as their labour wasn't needed. Nor could they consume to the same extent as those who had money, or as they might have done previously. In short, they were a burden. So too in Shipman's lifetime Britain was becoming a more secular society, and thus the sanctity of life is now less preserved by religious conviction. In contrast doctors – both in appearance and in reality – are increasingly becoming the moral arbiters of life. Shipman was simply demonstrating this power in an outrageous way. Exactly *why* he wanted to demonstrate this power will now probably never be known. However, the messages emanating from the Shipman case are the total failure to control his performance as a medical professional and our inadequate protection of the poor and the vulnerable – especially of the poor and vulnerable elderly – to whom he had access, and the opportunity to use that access, to kill again and again.

Other victims

The concentration on the victims of Britain's most prolific serial killer is justified not just by the numbers of elderly people whom Shipman murdered, but also by reflecting on how their vulnerability to attack was specifically socially constructed. This construction has a number of dimensions which are mirrored when considering the other four groups of victims of British serial killers – gay men, prostitutes, runaways and throwaways and babies and infants. In particular the failure of a number of state agencies to provide adequate protection to these four groups – in particular the failures of the police – is a recurring theme. For example,

Peter Sutcliffe – the so-called 'Yorkshire Ripper' – was interviewed nine times as part of the ongoing police investigation into the murders of thirteen women between 1975 and 1981 but was never arrested as a result of these interviews (Bilton, 2003). In the Steven Grieveson case, Northumbria Police wrongly claimed that Grieveson's three victims had died as a result of 'glue sniffing' and only launched a murder investigation some seven months after the death of his first victim. Douglas Stewart – who survived an attack by Dennis Nilsen – also encountered problems with the police, and found them to be be extremely unhelpful when he reported the attack. As he survived, his story is especially interesting and helps to throw further light on how vulnerability is created in late modernity.

Douglas Stewart is from Wick in the Highlands of Scotland, and moved to London in the 1970s having trained as a chef at the Gleneagles Hotel in Auctherarder in Perthshire (all quotes taken from Wilson, 2007). In London he worked at the Holland Park Hotel in Ladbroke Terrace, and found himself a girlfriend called Dawn, who worked at the same hotel as a chambermaid. Douglas drank in the Golden Lion where he met other Scottish people – including Dennis Nilsen – who had also trained as a chef in the army. On one particular evening they had both drunk a great deal, and when the pub closed Nilsen invited Douglas back to his flat – at that time in Melrose Avenue, prior to his move to Cranley Gardens. Whilst in the flat Nilsen gave Douglas a large glass of vodka, and very soon he had fallen asleep in an armchair. He woke up, and realising that it was now very late, accepted Nilsen's offer to stay until the morning. Nilsen also suggested that they should sleep together, but Douglas declined the offer.

Some time later Douglas woke again. He was aching from sleeping in the armchair, and so wanted to stretch, but immediately realised that he couldn't because his ankles were tied to the leg of the chair. He then sensed that his tie was being loosened and knotted around his throat; Nilsen was throttling him. Somehow Douglas managed to aim a blow at Nilsen's face, and was then able to struggle out of the chair. There was an exchange of words, with Nilsen suggesting that Douglas should just take his money and get out, and Douglas accusing Nilsen of trying to murder him. Interestingly, Nilsen pointed out to Douglas that if he went to the police 'they'll never believe you. They're bound to take my word for it. Like I told you in the pub, I'm a respectable civil servant.'[5] Nilsen then managed to get a knife, but Douglas was able to calm the situation down, so that Nilsen put the knife away. He then offered Douglas another drink, which was declined, and even though it was only 03:30, Douglas left Nilsen's flat and walked down Melrose Avenue.

Douglas walked the length of two or three houses, and then broke into a run. He soon found a telephone box, and dialled 999. When the police car arrived Douglas reported that Nilsen had tried to kill him, and showed the two police officers the red marks on his throat. One of the police officers stayed with Douglas whilst the other went and knocked on Nilsen's door. As Douglas was later to recall, 'Nilsen denied everything I had told the police. He gave them the impression that we were going out together and it was just a lovers' quarrel in a homosexual romance'.

Douglas maintains that as soon as the word 'homosexual' was mentioned the police lost all interest, and that despite leaving his brother's address so that they could contact him, he never heard from them again. It was only after Nilsen's arrest that the police eventually got in touch with Douglas, via his mother who was now living in Milton Keynes, and traced him to a house in Thurso in the North of Scotland. As Douglas later stated:

> The police made a bad mistake. They let him off when he attacked me. Now we don't know how many more he killed at Melrose Avenue after he took me back there. Or Cranley Gardens after that.

In fact we know that Nilsen would murder another ten young men and assault another three after this attack on Douglas Stewart.

What should we make of the failure of the police to pursue the attack on Douglas after it was reported to them? Nilsen – the former policeman, soldier and civil servant – is able to deflect the police by presenting what had happened as a 'lovers' quarrel in a homosexual romance', and that as soon as the word 'homosexual' was used the police lost all interest. Indeed, perhaps Douglas was prompted to report the attack precisely because he was not gay. Incensed at what had happened to him, his first thought was to dial 999 and – as an heterosexual who therefore presumed that he would be taken seriously – he expected the police to arrest the person responsible. The fact that they did not – for whatever reason – was a 'bad mistake', especially as it led to the deaths of several others. Indeed the failure of the police to act can also be seen as part of the invisibility of gay men, and specifically the violence that takes place in their lives. For if the police had arrested Nilsen they would have had to have made public what had taken place 'behind closed doors', and in doing so it would have exposed a world that they would seem to have wanted to remain hidden. So too, in making this private world public, the police would have been in effect delivering the protection of the state by offering an equality of service and protection to gay men, in exactly the same way that heterosexuals can expect to be treated by the police if they are attacked and assaulted.

Is it fair to conclude that the police do not take seriously violence against gay men and women? Are gay men and women given the protection of the state by being offered the same quality of service from the police as heterosexuals? To try to make sense of Douglas's complaint, and consider more generally how the police aim to support and assist the gay community, let's consider the whole issue of 'cop culture'.

Reiner (1992) suggests that 'an understanding of how police officers see the social world and their role in it – "cop culture" – is crucial to an analysis of what they do, and their broader political function'. In other words, 'cop culture' – now more commonly referred to as 'cop cultures' – shapes police practice. Whilst some academics are reluctant to accept that what one says and what one actually does are directly related, and others are more 'appreciative' of 'cop culture' (see, for example, Waddington, 1999), which is usually seen as a 'bad thing', we have to remember that given the great discretionary powers that the police have over individuals, or in shaping investigations, it is not unreasonable to presume that what police officers write, say, and how they socialise would mould their responses to what they find in the streets, or how they attempt to solve problems. Here too we should acknowledge that there exist a variety of 'cop cultures'; for example, between operational and non-operational police, civilian staff, detectives, and staff divided by hierarchy, gender, race and even sexuality (see Chan, 1996; Fielding, 1994; Foster, 2003; O'Neill, Marks and Singh 2007; Skolnick, 2008; Westmarland, 2008; Young, 1999).

In its original formulation Reiner suggested that the main characteristics of 'cop culture' are: Mission–action–cynicism–pessimism; Suspicion; Isolation/solidarity; Conservatism; Machismo; Prejudice; Pragmatism. He argues that the central characteristic of 'cop culture' is a sense of 'mission'. In other words that being a police officer is not simply just another job, but one that has a worthwhile purpose of protecting the weak from the predatory. The police are an indispensable 'thin blue line' protecting society, and this inevitably means that they have on occasions to take action. Indeed, some police officers might want to take rather more action than is often necessary, and will pursue exciting and thrill-seeking activities, rather than repetitive, mundane or boring police tasks such as filling in paperwork.

Over time, Reiner suggests, police officers will become more cynical and pessimistic; they have 'seen it all before', with each new development in society seen in almost apocalyptic terms, with the potential to destroy the moral world that has shaped the sense of mission that the police have developed. So too they are trained to be suspicious, but the worry here is that this suspicion can lead to stereotyping potential offenders, which in turn means that this stereotyping becomes a self-fulfilling prophecy. For example, a disproportionate number of young black men get stopped and searched in the streets, which leads to more young black men being arrested, which in turn 'confirms' the stereotype that more young black men are offenders than young white men. Indeed, given that police officers are often socially isolated, there is little likelihood that they will encounter young black men who play the piano, read books, or who might wish to become police officers themselves. Similarly the need to rely on one's colleagues in a 'tight spot' means that a great deal of internal solidarity exists, which does little to erode their sense of isolation from other members of society that police officers might encounter.

Of note, Reiner also argues that police officers tend to be conservative both politically and morally, and thus culturally would distrust those groups, such as gay men and prostitutes, which might be seen as challenging conventional morality. However, this does not mean that 'cop culture' is puritanical. Rather, it is dominated by what Reiner describes as 'old fashioned machismo', and there are high levels of stress, drinking and divorce. Based on his own research from Bristol in the early 1970s, Reiner also suggests that the police were hostile to and suspicious of black people, and this issue was again to come to the fore with the Macpherson Inquiry into the murder of the black teenager Stephen Lawrence in

April 1993 (Macpherson, 1999). The last aspect of 'cop culture' that Reiner draws attention to is pragmatism. By this he means the simple desire that a police officer has to get through the day as easily as possible. A police officer does not want fuss – especially paperwork – and would rather stress the practical, 'no-nonsense' aspects of the job. Reiner describes this as 'conceptual conservatism', given that this pragmatism often masks a common sense culture that dislikes research, innovation and change.

I have spent some time discussing cop culture because it provides a way of understanding what happened after Douglas Stewart reported Nilsen's attack on him to the police. In short, the pragmatic desire of the officers to whom he spoke to simply get through the day with the minimum of fuss and paperwork, and their moral conservatism about homosexuality seems to have allowed them to dismiss this attack as simply a 'lovers' quarrel' that they would rather leave 'behind closed doors'. More broadly analysing cop culture allows us to look behind the culture of policing, and see more clearly the quality of service that is provided not only to the gay community but also to other people whose lifestyles might not sit comfortably with a moral conservatism.

Of course the background to all of this is homophobia, and whether from the earlier decades of our time-frame – when homosexuality was still illegal – or from nearer our own time when gay men and women have become more visible, and can, for example, engage in civil partnerships, antipathy towards the gay community seems as virulent as ever.

Conclusion

The numbers of serial killers and the numbers of people that they kill have increased over time. Why should that be so? Why also did 1986 produce so many victims of British serial killers? Here I am not implying some crude economic determinism but it is surely more than coincidence that the most recent high-point of British serial killing coincided with the high point of 'Thatcherism'. By 'Thatcherism' I do not just mean the coming to power of Mrs Thatcher in 1979, but also a 'new right' ideology – based on ideas popularised by Friedrich von Hayek (1944), Milton Friedman (1953) and Robert Nozick (1974) – which gained ascendancy under her leadership. This 'new right' ideology emphasised that the British state had become involved in too many areas of civil society, and specifically that too many national resources were being spent on welfare. In turn the demands on government were increasing, and as a consequence taxes on business had become too high, limiting the private sector's profit-making and wealth-creating potential. As a result, it was argued, there should be less government regulation and intervention in the economy, and far less provision for those who were poor and unemployed, from fear that this would create 'welfare dependency'.

While this broad outline seems fair enough, I do not seek to push this analysis too far, and it also has to be remembered that, for example, much of the welfare state did survive Thatcherism. Nonetheless, it is scarcely controversial to suggest that Britain did change after 1979, and that those changes are related to policy directions influenced by 'new right' thinking. The economist Will Hutton (1995) suggests that, as a consequence of this type of thinking dominating the policy agenda of government, we became a '40/30/30' society, or a society of 'us and them', where the rich have got richer, and the poor got left behind. By '40/30/30' Hutton is suggesting that only 40 per cent of the workforce is in full-time, secure employment; 30 per cent are insecurely self-employed, or working casually; and the remaining 30 per cent – the 'marginalised' – are unemployed, or working for 'poverty' wages. Hutton has gone further and argues that since 1979 'capitalism has been left to its own devices'. By this he means that Britain has become a low-cost, deregulated producer, with correspondingly low social overheads, and a minimalist welfare state. Thus, for example, supplementary benefit for the unemployed as a proportion of full time earnings dropped from 26 per cent in 1979 to 19 per cent in 1993; union membership was discouraged and fell dramatically from 13.3 million to 9 million over the same period; and Hutton argues that the state was also trying to 'wash its hands of future generations of old people'. So too Nick Davies (1997) draws attention to the 3 million people who were unemployed by 1993, and the fact that between 1966 and 1977 wages of all men in all social classes grew at the same rate. However, from 1979 they started to diverge, and between 1979 and 1992 those already on the highest wages saw their income grow by 50 per cent, whilst those on the lowest wages were actually worse off than they had been in 1975.

Of course Hutton and Davies were writing before New Labour's victory in 1997, but their coming to power does not seem to have particularly altered the course that was being pursued by their Tory predecessors (for a general introduction see McAnulla, 2006). So too there would seem to have been a continuation of the social and economic policies of their predecessors, albeit that these have been characterised as a 'Third Way' bringing together social justice and a dynamic economy. Nonetheless, New Labour has drawn directly from neo-liberal discourses in its analysis of the global economy. Indeed 'globalisation' has become a favourite justification of the New Labour 'project', and thus the British economy, it is argued, has to continue to make itself as attractive to investors as possible by maintaining a deregulated economic approach, and limiting any social interventionist strategies.

By far the most vulnerable of the groups that I have identified that will remain targets for serial killers are likely to be women working in the sex industry, and the elderly. Quite simply, nothing has happened in our public policy that would seem to extend greater state protection to these groups, either in relation to the former by, for example, introducing safe zones for prostitutes to work within, or with regard to the latter by tackling the poverty, isolation and powerlessness that many elderly people experience. And so they will remain targets for those individuals who want to exploit that isolation and powerlessness for their own ends, and in extreme circumstances this will mean that they are murdered by serial killers.

Above all what emerges from the history of serial killing in Britain is that we need to learn that serial killers exploit the fractured communities of late modernity, in which some lives are seen as more valuable than others and where increasingly people have to struggle simply to survive. So too we must learn that serial killers exploit police incompetence and public indifference to the young, vulnerable women who sell sexual services, or gay men who have a lifestyle that is seen to be challenging to the status quo; that they exploit the isolation, loneliness and powerlessness of the elderly; and that they exploit the public policies of successive governments which no longer sees value in the young or the old, and which prioritise the rich over the poor.

In this dreadful way serial killing tells us something about our culture, our values and our civic society. It emerges as the elephant in the sitting room of public policies that create a culture of 'them' and 'us' and a society where there is a widening gap between the 'haves' and the 'have nots'. In such societies it is presumed that some people simply don't have value for the development of that society, and can therefore be cast adrift as challenging the status quo and unrepresentative, or as a burden on the state's resources. It is these circumstances and those groups that are characterised in this way that serial killers target. After all, surely it can come as no surprise that there were no heart surgeons, TV producers, journalists, bankers and accountants, lawyers, or academics in our list of the victims of British serial killers, and that instead the list was dominated by gay men, the elderly, prostitutes, babies and infants and young people leaving home for one reason or another, or that the vulnerability of some of these groups has been remarkably constant whether we were describing 2010 or 1888?

Notes

1 I am grateful to Professor Steve Tombs of Liverpool John Moores University for bringing this case to my attention.
2 It was not always possible to identify the specific date of a death, and this accounts for the different totals used in this graph from Table 13.1.
3 Interestingly Martin Fido (2001: 141) suggests that Mackay killed Crean because they were rumours that the priest may have been gay and the thought that this might be so had 'enraged' Mackay. I discuss the victimisation of gay men later in this chapter.
4 *Inside Time* – the prison newspaper produced by the charity New Bridge – claims that Shipman was in fact murdered and draws attention to the unexplained bruises on his body and the inordinate time that staff took to find his body (*Inside Time*, November 2004: 1, 18).
5 Nilsen was also a former police constable; he served in the Metropolitan Police between December 1972 and December 1973.

References

Bilton, M. (2003) *Wicked Beyond Belief: The Hunt for the Yorkshire Ripper*. London: HarperCollins.
Canter, D. and Wentink, N. (2004) 'An Empirical Test of Holmes and Holmes's Serial Murder Typology', *Criminal Justice and Behavior* 31(4): 489–515.
Chan, J. (1996) 'Changing Police Culture', *British Journal of Criminology* 36(1): 109–34.

Coleman, R., Sim, J., Tombs, S. and Whyte, D. (eds) (2009) *State, Crime, Power*. London: Sage.

Davies, N. (1997) *Dark Heart: The Shocking Truth about Hidden Britain*. London: Chatto & Windus.

Dietz, M. L. (1996) 'Killing Sequentially: Expanding the Parameters of the Conceptualization of Serial and Mass Murder', in O'Reilly Fleming, T. (ed.) *Serial and Mass Murder*. Toronto: Canadian Scholar's Press.

Donaldson, L. (2001) *Harold Shipman's Clinical Practice, 1974–1998*. London: Department of Health.

Egger, S. (1984) 'A Working Definition of Serial Murder and the Reduction of Linkage Blindness', *Journal of Police Science and Administration* 12(3): 348–57.

Ferguson, C., White, D. E., Cherry, S., Lorenz, M. and Bhimain, Z. (2003) 'Defining and Classifying Serial Murder in the Context of Perpetrator Motivation', *Journal of Criminal Justice* 31: 287–92.

Fido, M. (2001) *A History of British Serial Killing*. London: Carlton Books.

Fielding, N. G. (1994) 'Cop Canteen Culture', in Newburn, T. and Stanko, B. (eds) *Just Boys Doing Business? Men, Masculinities and Crime*. London: Routledge.

Foster, J. (2003) 'Police Cultures', in Newburn, T. (ed.) *Handbook of Policing*. London: Willan/Routledge.

Fox, J. and Levin, J. (2005) *Extreme Killing: Understanding Serial and Mass Murder*. Thousand Oaks, CA: Sage.

Freidson, M. (1970) *Profession of Medicine: A Study of the Sociology of Applied Knowledge*. New York: Harper and Row.

Friedman, M. (1953) *The Methodology of Positive Economics*. Chicago: University of Chicago Press.

Gibson, D. C. (2006) *Serial Murder and Media Circuses*. Westport, CT: Praeger.

Grover, C. and Soothill, K. (1999) 'British Serial Killing: Towards a Structural Explanation', *The British Criminology Conferences: Selected Proceedings, Volume 2*, http://www.lboro.ac.uk/departments/ss/bccsp/vol02/08grove.htm

Haggerty, K. (2009) 'Modern Serial Killers', *Crime, Media, Culture* 5(2): 168–87.

Hale, Robert (1998) 'The Application of Learning Theory to Serial Murder, or "You Too Can Learn to be a Serial Killer"', in R. M. Holmes and S. T. Holmes (eds) *Contemporary Perspectives on Serial Murder*, pp. 75–84. Thousand Oaks, CA: Sage.

von Hayek, F. (1944) *The Road to Serfdom*. London: Routledge.

Hickey, E. (1991) *Serial Murderers and Their Victims*. Pacific Grove, CA: Brookes/Cole Publishing.

Holmes, R. and Holmes, S. (1994) *Profiling Violent Crimes*. Thousand Oaks, CA: Sage.

Holmes, R. and Holmes, S. (eds) (1998) *Contemporary Perspectives on Serial Murder*. Thousand Oaks, CA: Sage.

Holmes, S. and de Burger, W. (1988) *Serial Murder*. Newbury Park, CA: Sage.

Hutton, W. (1995) *The State We're In*. London: Jonathan Cape.

Jarvis, B. (2007) 'Monsters Inc.: Serial Killers and Consumer Culture', *Crime, Media, Culture* 3(3): 326–44.

Jenkins, P. (1988) 'Serial Murder in England, 1940–85', *Journal of Criminal Justice* 16: 1–15.

Leyton, E. (1986) *Hunting Humans: The Rise of the Modern Multiple Murderer*. Toronto: McClelland & Stewart.

Macpherson, W. (1999) *The Stephen Lawrence Inquiry: Report of an Inquiry by Sir William Macpherson of Cluny*. CM 4262, London: HMSO.

McAnulla, S. (2006) *British Politics: A Critical Introduction*. London: Continuum.

Masters, B. (1986) *Killing for Company: The Case of Dennis Nilsen*. London: Coronet Books.

Nozick, R. (1974) *Anarchy, State and Utopia*. Oxford: Blackwell.

O'Neill, M., Marks, M. and Singh, A-M. (eds) (2007) *Police Occupational Culture: New Debates and Directions*. Amsterdam: Elsevier JAI Press.

Peters, C. (2005) *Harold Shipman: Mind Set on Murder*. London: Carlton Books.

Reiner, R. (1992) *The Politics of the Police*. Hemel Hempstead: Harvester Wheatsheaf.

Rose, N. (1989) *Governing the Soul*. London: Routledge.

Schmidt, D. (2005) *Natural Born Celebrities: Serial Killers in American Culture*. Chicago: University of Chicago Press.

Seenan, G. (1999) 'Killer Food Bug's Legacy of Suffering', *Guardian*, 10 February.

Seltzer, M. (1998) *Serial Killers: Death and Life in America's Wound Culture*. London: Routledge.

Skolnick, J. (2008) 'Enduring Issues of Police Culture and Demographics', *Policing and Society* 18(1): 34–45.

Slapper, G. and Tombs, S. (1999) *Corporate Crime*. London: Longman.

Smith, J. (2002–5) All reports taken from www.the-shipman-inquiry.org

Soothill, K. (2001) 'The Harold Shipman Case: A Sociological Perspective', *The Journal of Forensic Psychiatry* 12(2): 260–62.

Soothill, K. and Wilson, D. (2005) 'Theorising the Puzzle That Is Harold Shipman', *Journal of Forensic Psychiatry and Psychology*, 16(4): 658–98.

Sounes, H. (1995) *Fred and Rose: The Full Story of Fred and Rosemary West and the Gloucester House of Horrors*. London: Time Warner Books.

Tombs, S. and Whyte, D. (2007) *Safety Crimes*. London: Willan/Routledge.

—— (2008) *A Crisis of Enforcement: The Decriminalisation of Death and Injury at Work*. London: Centre for Crime and Justice Studies.

Waddington, P. (1999) 'Police (Canteen) Sub-Culture: An Appreciation', *British Journal of Criminology* 39(2): 286–309.

Westmarland, L. (2008) 'Police Cultures', in Newburn, T. (ed.) *Handbook of Policing*. London: Willan/Routledge.

Wilson, D. (2007) *Serial Killers: Hunting Britons and Their Victims*. Winchester: Waterside Press.

—— (2009) *A History of British Serial Killing, 1888–2008*. London: Sphere.

Winlow, S. and Hall, S. (2006) *Violent Night: Urban Leisure and Contemporary Culture*. Oxford: Berg.

Young, J. (1999) *The Exclusive Society*. London: Sage.

Part IV

Crime and criminological theory in the global age

14 Outline of a criminology of drift

Jeff Ferrell

On the good days, anyway, we might hope that new directions in criminological theory would evolve from our critical engagement with the new directions taken by the social world that surrounds us. With this in mind, I've to some degree set aside my usual analytic work on crime and culture recently, as I've tried to make sense of the current crisis – a crisis that interweaves economic collapse, dislocation, and ecological decay with conflicts over immigration, development, and consumption, and all of it shot through with an overdose of profound uncertainty. Of course this crisis is moving along more than one trajectory, and it's certainly not my intent to suggest that any single analysis can account for it. Yet it does seem to me that one significant direction emerging within the contemporary global crisis is a certain lack of direction – that is, drift. Drift seems to pervade current experience, to exist as both normative and spatial dislocation, to result from both economic development and economic collapse, to flourish in precisely those situations meant to contain it. Consequently, I've lately been thinking through a criminological theory of contemporary drift, not from any pre-existing expertise or interest (as I fear this chapter may make evident), but from a desire to understand where we're heading, if we're heading anywhere at all.

Certainly a plethora of contemporary social dynamics serves to cast people and populations adrift. Ongoing civil and transnational warfare spawns swelling refugee populations. Repressive governmental regimes engage in the forced expulsion of dissidents and minority groups – and when these regimes are confronted, even successfully, further dislocation often results. Within China, across Europe, and around the globe, economic migrants wander in search of work, or are simply moved en masse from one work locale to another as economic demand changes. In the U.K., Europe, and the United States, the corporate criminality of the mortgage/banking crisis, the ongoing destruction of low-cost housing as part of urban redevelopment schemes, and the proliferation of part-time and low-wage service work all conspire to preclude certainty as to home, shelter, or destination. Moving from house to house or country to country, sleeping in cars or temporary shelters, haunting streets and train stations, those cut loose from certainty find little in the way of spatial or normative stability.

In this world, impoverished Central Americans risk assault and extortion to hitch rides through Mexico atop U.S.-bound freight trains. Trafficked children and migratory sex workers subsist as perpetual 'new arrivals', dislocated both from home communities and new areas of residence (Oude Breuil, 2008; Sanders *et al.*, 2009). Migrants from rural areas pour into sprawling encampments outside Rio de Janeiro, Mumbai, and Ulan Bator, or find themselves shuttled between one country and the next by political and economic upheaval. Young Arabs argue that 'it's impossible for us to get ahead here – there are no opportunities', and dream of moving abroad; North African refugees in search of work or safety crowd rickety boats to cross the Mediterranean, only to find themselves bounced back and forth across the Italian/French border, lacking always the right permit or sufficiency of funds, 'a kind of Ping-Pong ball in a French-Italian soap opera' (Erlanger, 2011: A8; Saunders, 2010; Shenker *et al.*, 2011: 28; Gillet, 2011). In southern Europe itself, a native-born generation finds that today, even advanced degrees leave them lost between dead-end jobs and unemployment – and so they sleep in their car, when not considering 'driving it into a wall', or make plans to travel abroad in search of work (Donadio, 2011; Thomas, 2011: A1; Younge, 2011). In Japan – even before the recent tsunami and nuclear crisis – almost half of the country's young workers are consigned to temporary, 'irregular' jobs amidst a collapsing career structure; in Germany, a 'shadow labor market' of poorly paid temporary workers is now seen as essential to the country's 'global competiveness'; in China, migrant workers from rural areas now make up a third of Beijing's population, and with no place to live, occupy abandoned air-defense tunnels underneath the city (Fackler, 2011; Ewing, 2011: B6; Wong, 2011). In post-Soviet, free-market Russia, 'the *bomzh* – a homeless person in dirty clothes, begging in the metro underpasses, at churches, lying on park benches or scavenging near train stations – has become omnipresent in Russian cities and towns' (Stephenson, 2006: 113). Meanwhile, in the United States, migrant farmworkers continue to face family disruption, limited educational opportunities, and deportation; graduate students, part-time instructors, and non-tenure-track instructors now make up three quarters of college faculty; the newly homeless and unemployed drift from city to city, sleep in flood drains beneath the streets of Las Vegas, or become semi-permanent residents of cheap motels; and an economist reports that, in general, 'we're in a period where uncertainty seems to be going on forever. So this period of temporary employment seems to be going on forever' (Rich, 2010: A1; Lewin, 2011: A15; Brown, 2011: 17, 21; Raymer, 2011).

Unsurprisingly, then, Bauman (2002: 343) describes refugees as 'perhaps the most rapidly swelling of all the categories of world population' today, and Saunders (2010: 1, 21) estimates current worldwide rural-to-urban migration as involving 'two or three billion humans, perhaps a third of the world's population', with China alone producing some '150 to 200 million . . . peasants "floating" between village and city'. In some ways this pervasive dislocation does indeed constitute a new and immediate problem of astounding magnitude, one brought on by the ongoing globalization of capital, the collapse of housing and financial markets, population shifts to urban areas, land and water crises associated with global warming, and upheavals in the Middle East, North Africa, and elsewhere. Yet a number of scholars concerned with the uncertain dynamics of contemporary social life argue that this instability is in fact not some recent aberration. Instead, it was the period of twentieth-century Fordism – with its regulatory controls, relative stability, and social welfare state – that constitutes the exception within the long and chaotic history of modern capitalist development (Fantone, 2007; Neilson and Rossiter, 2008). From this perspective, itinerant labor, unstable career opportunity, and spatial dislocation are not simply dimensions of 'late capitalism' or 'liquid modernity' (Bauman, 2000); likewise, a vertiginous sense of disorientation is not only symptomatic of the late modern condition (Young, 2007). Rather, they are a return to the sort of predatory uncertainty that has long defined capitalism, and that was interrupted, briefly and partially, by the decades of Fordism in the United States and Europe. Widening this view, it might be argued that modernity itself, with its corporate nation states and war machines, has produced and continues to produce profound and ongoing dislocation – and with it an endless stream of migrants, refugees, and lost souls – as much as it has produced bureaucratic stability, rationalized labor, and regimes of political power. Certainly, if we look past the masking ideologies of social stability and social progress, there is evidence for all of this – from the aggressive dislocations of early industrial capitalism to the lost generation of World War I, from Soviet collectivized farms to Nazi death trains, from Depression-era drifters in the United States and displaced persons' camps in post-World War II Europe to homeless vets from Viet Nam and Iraq. And to the extent that this is so, it seems to me that theorizing drift takes on even greater urgency, as a way of understanding both where we may be heading and where we've been.

Criminology and drift

Sifting through existing criminological theory suggests an analytic angle from which drift might be approached. Durkheim's (1984 [1893]) model of anomie, and Merton's (1938) subsequent interpretation of it, offer an obvious starting point. Together, they show that the unraveling of social order can produce a dangerous sort of normlessness, a cultural disorientation that can leave individuals and groups afflicted with what Garfinkel (1967: 45) would later call an 'amnesia for . . . common sense knowledge of social structures'. As Merton emphasizes especially, this tendency toward normative disorientation may, ironically, be embedded in the very structure of society itself; if the gap between culturally approved aspirations and legitimate means to achieve them is sufficiently great – if the strain of unmet and unmeetable goals is sharply enough felt – then the social order carries within itself the seeds of its own failure, its own potential for crime, desperation, innovation, and dislocation. The brief travelogue of despair already seen suggests something of this; time and again, from Syria to southern Europe, Japan and the United States, young people today report that their deeply inculcated goals of education and career have been blocked – betrayed, actually – through no fault of their own, and so they are left to innovate, to wander away, or simply to give up.

Within criminology these themes of normative uncertainty, criminality, and drift have been most fully explored by David Matza and Gresham Sykes, most famously in their article 'Techniques of Neutralization: A Theory of Delinquency' (Sykes and Matza, 2003 [1957]). Taken at face value, their theory sets out to explain how would-be delinquents go about temporarily neutralizing their bonds to a shared moral order, with successful neutralization then leaving them free to drift into delinquent behavior. Examined more closely, theirs is in reality more a theory and critique of the normative order itself. For them, the apparent moral solidity of the shared social order is an illusion; the social order is in fact a tangle of contradictions permeated by moral ambiguity. 'The normative system of a society is marked by . . . *flexibility*', they contend. 'It does not consist of a set of rules held to be binding under all conditions' (Sykes and Matza, 2003: 233–34, emphasis in original). Significantly, then, potential delinquents neutralize their bonds to an ambiguous social order by employing the same moral ambiguities already extant in social life – and, as Sykes and Matza (2003: 234) note, these ambiguities themselves constitute 'cultural constructions' closer to Mills' (1940) vocabularies of motive than to isolated individual beliefs. As they explicate more fully in subsequent works (Matza and Sykes, 1961; Matza 1964: 60–61), the social order incorporates its own self-made contradictions – and so, again, the seeds of its own disorder.

Writing in mid-1950s America, at the pinnacle of America's presumed post-war normative consensus and Fordist success, Sykes and Matza were arguing not only against Cohen's (1955) theory of subculturally grounded delinquency; they were arguing against the reality of this successful and consensual order. Even *within* the Fordist period, the mechanisms of drift were present; even here, Sykes and Matza were saying, the boundaries between normal and abnormal, law and crime were slippery and shifting. By Sykes and Matza's reckoning, drift is *inherent* in an already compromised moral order, awaiting only the neutralizing touch of the potential delinquent. The prerequisites for drifting away from the illusion of moral certainty are structurally in place: the ambiguity of dominant moral claims, the situational flexibility of allegedly absolute legal and religious codes. The potential delinquent senses these contradictions and hypocrisies, draws on them – but does not invent them. Seeing the holes in the moral order, the potential delinquent only wedges them open a bit wider so as to set a course of autonomous social action, making manifest existing moral contradictions in an attempt to exit, if momentarily, existing social constraints. The moral compromises and subterranean values (Matza and Sykes, 1961) that circulate through daily life constitute the shifting cultural milieu from which crime and delinquency emerge.

In this sense a compromised moral order spawns drift as surely as a constipated social order spawns strain. Mixing Merton with Sykes and Matza, we can say that the moral order of contemporary society is itself *anomic* – not only at the level of the structural contradictions that Merton charted, but within the experience of everyday moral uncertainty. Echoing Merton's analysis, Sykes and Matza (2003: 237) speculate that, 'on a priori grounds it might be assumed that these justifications for deviance [techniques of neutralization] will be more readily seized by segments of society for whom a discrepancy between common social ideals and social practice is most apparent'. Or, it may be that 'this habit of "bending" the dominant normative system – if not "breaking" it – cuts across our cruder social categories. . . .' In either case the gap between 'social ideals and social practice' – that is to say, the *strain* of pronounced moral absolutes grinding against the reality of everyday moral contradictions – opens a path to delinquency and drift. The path may not be taken – in the same way that for Merton the structural contradictions that spawn strain may or may not be addressed through theft or drugs, so the moral contradictions that underlie drift may or may not result in delinquency – but there can be no doubt as to its origins. The path has been paved with cultural contradictions.

Like Merton, then, Sykes and Matza locate the potential for drift within the order of society – or more particularly, in the tensions and contradictions that suffuse it. Consequently, to understand the drifter – the temp worker, the unemployed college graduate, the global migrant – we must first understand the prerequisites of their drift: the host of gaps and contradictions that permeate social and cultural arrangements, and so spawn disorientation and dislocation. This is of course a classic sociological analysis of individual and group pathology, and so a sturdy foundation for a criminology of drift and its consequences. But it is hardly enough. To outline a criminology of contemporary drift, it seems to me, we must at least begin to build three analytic edifices on this foundation. The first concerns the particular dynamics by which contemporary law and economy engender drift. The second attempts to account for the spatial dimensions of drift, and to imagine the ways in which normative and spatial drift intertwine. The third explores the experiential politics of drift – on the assumption, following Merton and Sykes and Matza, that while structural contradictions may set the conditions for social action, they do not determine its meaning for those engaged in it.

A political economy of drift

There are certainly multiple political economies of contemporary drift, each shaped by the particular intersections of global and local dynamics. Here I highlight one: the degree to which, amidst the dynamics that define late capitalist economies, both failure and success engender dislocation. The links between economic failure and drift are perhaps easier to imagine, and have to some extent already been glimpsed in previous discussions. A multi-country banking crisis evicts millions from their over-mortgaged homes, leaves millions more unemployed or piecing together part-time work. Ecological crises brought on by global warming, global oil, and global agri-business push small farmers off their land, turn fishing communities into welfare recipients, and force itinerant farm workers into ever-wider arcs in search for work. Amidst collapsing national economies or civil wars, refugees – some of them already migrants from elsewhere – leave belongings behind to flee in crowded boats or on commercial airlines. With economic failure come, often enough, the anomic disorientation and structural strain of Durkheim and Merton, and with them profound moral uncertainty and spatial dislocation.

And yet with contemporary economic 'success' many of the same problems arrive. Increasingly, cities throughout Europe, the United States and elsewhere in the developed and developing world 'succeed' by way of economies organized around service work, entertainment, tourism, and consumption. Researchers like Markusen and Schrock (2009: 345, 353) argue that this sort of new 'consumption-driven urban development ... help[s] to attract skilled workers, managers, entrepreneurs, and retirees', and they emphasize the 'significance of lifestyle preferences of skilled workers as an important determinant of economic development'. As David Harvey (2008: 31) notes, 'quality of urban life' has in this sense 'become a commodity, as has the city itself, in a world where consumerism, tourism, [and] cultural and knowledge-based industries have become major aspects of the urban political economy'. But if these retail urban economies and commodified 'lifestyle preferences' benefit the managers and skilled workers privileged enough to consume them, they are distinctly less helpful to the far larger population of low-end retail workers who provide them. For them, the Fordist model is indeed finished; their work lives are now defined by the uncertainty of part-time and temporary employment, flex scheduling, missing medical and retirement benefits, and aborted careers. For them the old social contract has been annulled, as has the link between long work hours and long career. Accompanying every 'successful' urban redevelopment scheme, every old factory converted into high-end lofts and retail spaces, is an increase in the number of workers left with few options but to drift between unstable employment and economic failure.

Once Western cities took shape around the economic interests of industrial capitalists and the relative stability of long-term employment; now they are reshaped by developers and city planners who carve from them integrated lifestyle zones of high-end consumption. Within existing urban arrangements, though, these 'consumption spaces' (Zukin, 1997) are rarely carved from open land; instead, they are built on the revanchist reclaiming of urban space for privileged populations (Smith, 1996). Recalling those displaced by Haussmann's grand reconfiguration of nineteenth-century Paris, and by the 'brutal modernism' that Robert Moses imposed on twentieth-century New York City, Harvey (2008: 28, 34) emphasizes that this sort of urban development is predicated on 'the capture of valuable land from low-income populations that may have lived there for years'. And with this land captured, with its low-cost housing obliterated and local shops bought out, there are all but sure to be ongoing spatial consequences for those dispossessed – put simply, the great likelihood that they and their neighborhoods will now be cut loose and cast adrift in ways that they were not before. It's not just that the new boutique hotel, built in place of the old warehouse or neighborhood center, signals a shift in the city's class character and the terms of its employment; it's that its built stability mocks the drifting instability of those it has displaced. For many in the economically 'successful' late modern city, instability of occupation is echoed in the displacement of neighborhood and home.

A third development promotes yet again the inequitable instability inherent in 'consumption-driven urban development'. As I and others have documented (Ferrell, 1996, 2001, 2006; MacLeod, 2002; Mitchell, 2003; Amster, 2008), the policing of these new consumption spaces – more broadly, the policing of these late modern urban economies – emerges as aesthetic policing. That is, the goal is to police the meaning and appearance of the city and its new consumption spaces, to protect the city's 'quality of life' from those whose public presence would intrude on its ensemble of attractions and profitability. Here policing comes to focus on perceptions as much as populations, on minimizing risk and intrusion as much as solving crimes (O'Malley, 2010). So, for example, an economic official in the U.S. argues during an urban revitalization campaign that panhandling is a problem precisely because 'it's part of an image issue for the city' – and an American legal scholar agrees, positing that 'the most serious of the attendant problems of homelessness is its devastating effect on a city's image' (in Ferrell, 2001: 45; in Mitchell, 2003: 201). As Aspden (2008: 13) concludes in regard to the recent transformation of a decaying British industrial city into a 'corporate city of conspicuous consumption': 'There seems to be no place in the new Leeds for those who disturb the rhythms of the consumer-oriented society'.

At times this ideology is implemented with startling simplicity: existing streets, sidewalks, or parks are deeded to private developers, and so made unavailable to the unprofitable (Amster, 2008). More generally it is enforced though a host of popular crime control approaches. In Britain, authorities use Anti-Social Behavior Orders, dispersal orders, and curfews to push undesirables away from consumerist havens. In the United States and elsewhere, built-environment policing programs like CPTED (Crime Prevention Through Environmental Design) seek to reduce certain forms of crime by building social control into the spatial environment; such programs are regularly employed to discourage 'loitering' by the homeless and other vulnerable populations in public areas or transit stations. By removing waiting facilities, installing uncomfortable benches, and closing public toilets, authorities are indeed often able to force such populations from public parks or town squares, thereby 'cleansing' these spaces for preferred populations of tourists and short-stay retail consumers. But in doing so, of course, such programs undermine even the fragile spatial communities that emerge among the vulnerable populations that occupy such spaces, and so put these populations back on the move once again. Recalling the old U.S. 'move on' laws used to roust laborers and labor organizers a century ago, CPTED programs force vulnerable populations to move on, again and again, in search of even minimal comfort or convenience (Ferrell, 2001).

Likewise, the contemporary criminal justice emphasis on 'broken windows' policing and 'place-based' crime prevention produces programs like the Los Angeles Safer Cities Initiative (SCI). This 'place-based policing intervention' deploys police officers to move through Skid Row areas with entrenched homeless populations, 'breaking up homeless encampments, issuing citations, and making arrests for violations of the law' (Berk and McDonald, 2010: 813, 817) for the purpose of dispersal. Such initiatives are designed specifically to address the alleged problem of 'spatial concentration' among the homeless – with such initiatives to be complemented by the 'dispersal of homeless facilities' and support services throughout urban areas as well (Culhane, 2010: 853). Vitale (2010: 868, 870) argues that, due to aggressive fines and arrests, such initiatives only further entrap those targeted in homelessness. To this I would add that such initiatives also force the homeless into ever more dislocated ways of living; as before, they are 'moved on' whenever and wherever they settle. Revealingly, Vitale also wonders if

> the primary goal of the SCI [is] really to reduce crime and homelessness or instead to remove a large concentration of poor people forcibly from Skid Row in hope of encouraging the subsequent gentrification of the area. . . . A major effort to gentrify Skid Row has been underway for years.

In these ways a political economy of drift becomes also a criminology of drift. Global corporate criminality in the form of mortgage fraud and insider trading costs millions their homes and their livelihoods, cutting them loose from neighborhood and career; others lose home, neighborhood, or career to the economic bulldozer of 'consumption-driven urban development'. Cast adrift, they find themselves pushed off privatized sidewalks, driven from public spaces, cited for loitering or trespass, rounded up and arrested for the crime of spatial concentration. As criminologists, we might note in such situations the iatrogenic effects of law and economy, and as with the cultural contradictions already seen, the 'ironies of social control' (Marx, 1981). The spatial controls meant to contain urban space, to protect it from transient populations, only serve to make such populations more transient; the closure of urban space to drifters exacerbates urban drift. The reconstitution of urban economies around managed meaning and consumption dislocates the very sorts of citizens whose peripatetic presence is thought to threaten consumption and its meanings.

Drift, space, and law

While classic works in criminology can usefully attune us to the social and cultural contradictions that are the progenitors of drift, they nonetheless tend to conceptualize drift as an oddly de-spatialized phenomenon. For Durkheim, Merton, Matza and Sykes, the dislocations brought about by structural contradictions are normative in nature, and the fixed locations from which the normative drifter departs are imagined primarily in terms of moral certainty or social cohesion. In this sense such conceptualizations are essentially metaphorical; they draw evocatively from the physicality of the rudderless boat lost to the ocean, even the wayfaring stranger wandering from town to town, but fail to situate this metaphorical drift in the physical spatiality of human action. Other threads in existing criminological theory – theories of social ecology and social disorganization, for example, with their ecological metaphors, 'zones of transition', and grounding of crime in place rather than person – certainly introduce spatiality into criminological analysis. Yet despite their invocation of 'disorganization' and 'transition', these are primarily analyses of locations – humanly constructed locations, certainly, but locations nonetheless – rather than analyses of drifting human movement through and beyond them. It remains, it seems, to suggest some of the dynamics linking drift as normative anomie and drift as dislocated spatial experience.

One dynamic has already been glimpsed more than once in the preceding discussions: the likelihood that normative dislocation and spatial dislocation will intertwine in the lived experience of drift. Bankrupt economic aspirations lead young people to imagine a better life elsewhere, and often to set out in search of it; the dissolution of agricultural economies, and with them long-standing ways of village life, drive rural families toward urban slums or maquiladoras. Retail temp workers and part-time university instructors forfeit both their career aspirations and their ability to settle in any one job setting or neighborhood. As a civil war unravels ideologies of national unity and multi-generational familial ties, it also pushes those so afflicted to seek refuge beyond its borders. But more than this, the economic migrant or war refugee now arrives in a spatial environment whose symbolic coordinates, unreadable and unknowable to the culturally uninitiated, confirm the anomie of being a stranger in a strange land. Social space is cultural space (Ferrell, 1997), encoded with meaning and memory, and to flee from Tunisia to southern Italy, to cross from rural Mexico to a North American metropolis, to wander the country chasing employment, is to lose oneself in ways that are at the same time spatial and normative.

Other dynamics directly interweave the pains of cultural and spatial dislocation with the dangers of legal marginality, and so create a redoubling of initial drift. From the homeless of Los Angeles to Tunisian refugees lost along the Italian–French border, there is often by law simply no legitimate place to settle. Beyond this, the strict household-registration system in China means that the hundreds of millions of citizens now moving illicitly from village to city occupy 'an uncomfortable world that is neither urban nor rural, isolating them from their own children, [and] preventing them from becoming full members of the country's economy' (Saunders, 2010: 16); in Russia, a similar system of 'administratively organized territorial affiliations' guarantees that for homeless populations 'a lack of place also means a lack of any social recognition, employment rights or recourse to public welfare' (Stephenson, 2006: 145). The millions of global refugees whose drifting journeys pause in refugee aid camps nonetheless remain adrift in similar ways. As Bauman (2002: 344; 2000: 102) argues, such 'non-places' or 'nowherevilles' originate as 'a totally artificial creation located in a social void', and so incorporate an 'extra-territoriality' absent meaning or belonging for those forced to occupy them. Describing these massive collectivities as 'city-camps' (*camps-villes*), Agier (2002: 322) likewise notes that they are designed to induce 'the social and political non-existence of the recipients' of their aid, and quoting Michael Pollack, sketches a striking intersection of spatial and normative drift that occurs within them:

> Identity becomes a preoccupation . . . only where it is no longer taken-for-granted, when common sense is no longer given in advance and when the

actors involved can no longer agree on the meaning of the situation and the roles they are supposed to be playing in it.

A particularly complex intersection of cultural, spatial, and legal drift emerges with the global mass migration of rural populations to urban areas. As such populations begin to accumulate in an urban area, they often first settle in the relatively unplanned, unregulated zones that surround it – thereby forming emergent 'arrival cities', as Saunders (2010) calls them. These areas function as tenuous, informal footholds for those seeking a life in the city, and with their links to both rural areas and the city itself, operate as ongoing conduits for subsequent generations of migrants. Unlike the anonymous dependency of refugee camps, they often operate as do-it-yourself cultural and economic accomplishments, with their warrens of homemade architecture, their cultural affirmations of urban life and rural tradition, and their networks of informal aid and economic innovation. At the same time, they suffer from the benign neglect of urban authorities; allowed to exist, they nonetheless remain outside the orbit of water and sanitation services, legal protection, and urban citizenship. In this sense such arrival cities are not so much illegal as *extra-legal*; and over time, this legal and spatial marginality may move either in the direction of incorporation into the formal urban grid, or outright criminalization and demolition. Adding further complexity is Saunders' argument that the occupants of such areas are generally not aimless wanderers, but highly motivated seekers of a better life in the city; adapting Merton, we might say that they respond to the strain of blocked aspirations by a form of *spatial innovation*. In doing so, though, they often spend generations only tenuously connected to the city of their aspirations, consigned to a space of marginality and fluctuation. The arrival city is 'both populated with people in transition . . . and is itself a place in transition' – yet it is also 'a place of upward mobility – or at least a calculated grasp for the best hope of mobility' (Saunders, 2010: 11, 50).

Two concepts would seem of some utility for thinking through these interplays of normative and spatial drift in the context of law and crime. The notion of alienation, in both its Marxist formulations and its more general usage, has long denoted the distance that separates people from their work, their family, or their identity; alienation suggests the experience of estrangement, the sense of being a stranger in one's own life. For the drifter this experience is often one of *spatial alienation*. The drifter occupies space temporarily and provisionally, in it but not of it, distanced from it by unreadable cultural codes and enforced anonymity. The drifter's physical presence hides a cultural and legal absence; for those who control such space the drifter is invisible, non-existent, or at best a category of law or administration. Because of this, drift also invokes multiple moments of *transgression*. Transgression involves a crossing over, a breaching of boundaries established by law, custom, or morality. Drifting takes those involved in it across such boundaries as they are encoded in individual identity, as they are enforced within sedentary associations – and as they are mapped into spatial arrangements. In drift the morality and spatiality of transgression intersect, and the threats posed by transgression double.

Drift as experiential politics

To this point I've conceptualized contemporary drift largely as a product of cultural contradictions, economic arrangements, and strategies of legal enforcement; the drifter has in turn been imagined to be a cultural stranger, and in the eyes of the law, either outlaw or non-entity. The notion of transgression suggests something further: that the drifter might wander across boundaries with an emerging intentionality, might begin to see the world differently because of boundaries breached, might even learn to turn marginality and estrangement back on those whose arrangements engender it. About this let me be clear: The experience of drift for many, perhaps for most – the political refugee, the impoverished migrant, the homeless family – is undoubtedly suffused with sorrow, anger, and a sense of irretrievable loss. In such cases alienation from home, career, or cultural history produces a degree of existential disempowerment and emotional pain that defines drift as anything but a romantic adventure. Yet as I've found in my own ethnographies of peripatetic outsiders (Ferrell, 1996, 2001, 2006), sharply subversive lessons are sometimes interwoven with this loss and pain, along with a sense of self and society unavailable to the sedentary. These closing remarks, then, are neither a comprehensive catalogue of drift's experiential dimensions nor a celebration of drift as such, but rather a brief inquiry into some of these lessons, and their potential for a politics of drift.

Whatever the forces that cast and keep one adrift, whatever the mix of structural victimization and human agency, the experience of drifting tends to produce also the sequenced experience of exclusion and alienation. In this sense the drifter exists as a perpetual outsider – outside the boundaries of home country, conventional labour market, or legal citizenship. As this drifting continues across time and space the exclusions accumulate, and in so doing reinforce the drifter's identity as always outside the frame – an outsider many times over. Here is the sorrow, loss and alienation of the drifter, the emptiness of anomie as well – but here also is the potential for living and learning beyond the usual bounds of the social order. A serial transgressor by law or by choice, the drifter is able to see – forced to see – the order of things from the other side over and over again, to understand that the truth claims of one gate keeper are as suspect as those of the next. Like Sykes and Matza's neutralized delinquent, the drifter sees social and cultural contradictions, and in seeing them is freed from them – at least for a while. Little wonder, then, that the economic dislocation forced on young people in Europe, Asia and the Middle East leads them to imagine radical alternatives, to think beyond their parents, to make plans for escape. Little wonder that kids involved in the American punk/traveler culture mix unemployment, squatting, and train hopping with 'dumpster diving, hitchhiking, shoplifting, and scams' – or that they argue that 'to revolt against work and thus boredom, routine, wage slavery, the exchange economy with your *body* as well as your mind, to recognize and legitimize your heart's longing to escape by *trying to*, is to declare openly that we are *not* crazy for wanting more than the scraps of self [that] capitalism leaves us' (Powell, 2003: 51; Commando, 2003, emphasis in original). Little wonder, perhaps, that an old train hobo three times their age voices a similar outsider's critique:

> They say this country is based on hard work and integrity and worshiping God. That's a lie. It's built on murder, man. Mayhem, slavery, oppression, lies, stealin' and killin'. That's what it's based on. And you can't change it after it started. Just stay away from it. Try to get away from it. Be independent of it. Cause if you try to deal in it, you become part of it. Stay away from it, you diminish it by one. By one.
>
> (in Daniel, 2008: 99)

A representative sample of drifters and their orientations toward the social order? Maybe not, or more to the point, how would we know, given the amorphous dynamics of drift and drifting? But there are other bits of evidence. Richard Grant's (2003: 263) summation of his years wandering America with itinerant rodeo cowboys, freight train hobos, and neo-hippies is one, notable for its inter-weaving of attitude, law, and spatial arrangement. 'They have a quintessentially nomadic attitude toward sedentary society', he concludes.

> They don't pay taxes, they don't vote, and they don't consider themselves bound by the social contract. And thanks to vagrancy laws, begging laws, laws against sleeping in parks, laws against hitchhiking and riding freight trains – laws, in short, that make it illegal to be poor and nomadic – they are locked into conflict with the sedentary state and its coercive power.

As with traveling punks and young migrants, an interesting sort of politics can be seen among Grant's nomads – one whose critical distance, like the drifter's own experiences, emerges from the interplay of abandoning and engaging with the dominant social order. Cultural geographers and literary scholars have noted a similar interplay, both in studies of spatial mobility and attitude (Prince, 1973) and in their broader invocation of the flâneur (Keith, 1997). As a subversive model of urban citizenship, the flâneur embodies both the notion of drifting movement though a city – the abandonment of fixed coordinates and stable hierarchies of knowledge, that is (see de Certeau, 1984) – but also a critical re-engagement with the city by way of the holistic, comparative understandings that emerge from such drift. Raising the political stakes, Situationists and psychogeographers similarly propose that the *dérive* – an intentionally disorienting drift though urban space that mixes 'letting go' of the 'usual motives for movement and action' with a 'knowledge and calculation' of possibility – can usefully undermine taken-for-granted exercises of power while simultaneously reinventing one's world as a landscape of possibility and surprise (Debord, 1958; see Makeworlds, 2003).[1]

This is of course quite a drifter hodgepodge – from Middle Eastern youth and American punks to old hobos and French Situationists – and among them various issues remain unresolved, including the degree to which attitude and intentionality shape, and are shaped by, the experience of drift. Yet despite this, it does seem that drift in its various forms often fosters a type of comparative, outsider politics especially attuned to the tension between critical engagement and radical disengagement. Moreover, it seems that this drifting politics at times coalesces into collective action – or, from the view of the authorities, collective criminality. Critical Mass, for example, is a global urban bicycling movement intent on challenging automotive dominance and promoting collective bicycling, and determined to do so by way of anarchic, do-it-yourself 'dis-organization'. Consequently, those involved in large Critical Mass rides offer up no leaders with whom public officials can negotiate, disavow the need for police protection or assistance, and decline to designate pre-established routes, all in hopes that each ride will emerge as a drifting exercise in spontaneous self-determination. Collectively cutting loose amidst the tightly controlled consumption spaces of the contemporary city – another time ignoring the spatial controls undergirding a national political convention – Critical Mass riders engage a politics of 'assertive desertion', and as a result face ongoing police harassment and arrest (Ferrell, 2011; Carlsson, 2002: 75; Shepard and Smithsimon, 2011). In Southern Europe, the precarity movement likewise confronts the inherent uncertainty of post-Fordist economies, particularly for a young generation lost between the twin instabilities of long-term unemployment and 'flexible', part-time work. Interestingly, theorists of this movement speculate that the sheer extent of precarious circumstances among young people, migrants, refugees and others may be such that the 'precariat' is now emerging globally as 'the post-Fordist successor to the proletariat' (Ross, 2008: 34–35); put another way, they suggest that 'perhaps all this precarity is not new. What is new though is the use of this concept to create a common understanding for people to organize around' (Kruglanski, 2005; see Neilson and Rossiter, 2008). Such organizing acknowledges the systematic disengagement of young people and others from any stable social contract, while advocating new terms of fluid, disobedient engagement: computer hacking, collective squatting, urban train hopping, and corporate shoplifting, with all this a means of raiding the few amenities that remain, and of creating 'a commons for people who do strange, illegal things' (Kruglanski, 2005).

Maybe the young generation involved in these emerging movements is onto something. Maybe drift, as old as it is new, is once again becoming a collective commons of the dispossessed, a non-place where young workers, homeless populations, migrants, and refugees can shape a shifting commonality of experience. Or maybe drift is now emerging as the ill-defined field of post-Fordist engagement – engendered by inequality, forced on vulnerable populations by law and economy, but in turn utilized by them as a weapon of assertive desertion and radical reengagement. In any case, this much seems clear: a host of contemporary social and cultural contradictions permeate drift, propel it forward, and entangle it with critical issues of crime, control, and global politics. As criminologists, we would do well to wander along with the drifters – just to see where they might take us.

Note

1 Deleuze and Guattari (1987: 380) propose in a different context that 'the life of the nomad is in the intermezzo' – that the nomad's knowledge of the world becomes 'smooth', uncontained, and comparative as it forms between and beyond particular places.

References

Agier, M. (2002) 'Between War and City: Towards an Urban Anthropology of Refugee Camps', *Ethnography* 3(3): 317–41.

Amster, R. (2008) *Lost in Space*. New York: LFB.

Aspden, K. (2008) *The Hounding of David Oluwale*. London: Vintage.

Bauman, Z. (2002) 'In the Lowly Nowherevilles of Liquid Modernity', *Ethnography* 3(3): 343–49.

—— (2000) *Liquid Modernity*. Cambridge: Polity.

Berk, R. and McDonald, J. (2010) 'Policing the Homeless', *Criminology and Public Policy* 9(4): 813–40.

Brown, P. L. (2011) 'Itinerant Life Weighs on Farmworkers' Children', *New York Times* (13 March): 17, 21.

Carlsson, C. (2002) 'Cycling Under the Radar – Assertive Desertion', in Chris Carlsson (ed.) *Critical Mass*. Oakland, CA: AK Press, pp. 75–82.

Cohen, A. (1955) *Delinquent Boys*. New York: Free Press.

Commando, Holden Caulfield (2003) 'How Much Can You Get Away With?' in Anonymous, *Evasion*. Atlanta, GA: CrimethInc, no page number.

Culhane, D. (2010) 'Tackling Homelessness in Los Angeles' Skid Row', *Criminology and Public Policy* 9(4): 851–57.

Daniel, B. (2008) *Mostly True*. Bloomington, IN: Microcosm Publishing.

Debord, G. (1958) 'Theory of the Dérive', at www.bopsecrets/org, accessed 12 April 2011.

de Certeau, M. (1984) *The Practice of Everyday Life*. Berkeley: University of California Press.

Deleuze, G. and Guattari, F. (1987) *A Thousand Plateaus: Capitalism and Schizophrenia*. Minneapolis: University of Minnesota Press.

Donadio, R. (2011) 'Young, Smart and Fearing for the Future', *New York Times* (2 January): 6.

Durkheim, E. (1984 [1893]) *The Division of Labour in Society*. Basingstoke: Macmillan.

Erlanger, S. (2011) 'On Journey to New Lives, Young Tunisians Need Only a Final Destination', *New York Times* (20 April): A8.

Ewing, J. (2011) 'Temp Workers in Germany Dismay Unions', *New York Times* (20 April): B1, B6.

Fackler, M. (2011) 'Japan Blocks Young, Stifling the Economy', *New York Times* (28 January): A1, A9.

Fantone, L. (2007) 'Precarious Changes: Gender and Generational Politics in Contemporary Italy', *Feminist Review* 87: 5–20.

Ferrell, J. (2011) 'Corking as Community Policing', *Contemporary Justice Review* 14(1): 95–98.

—— (2006) *Empire of Scrounge*. New York: NYU Press.

—— (2001) *Tearing Down the Streets*. New York: Palgrave/St. Martin's.

—— (1997) 'Youth, Crime, and Cultural Space', *Social Justice* 24(4): 21–38.

—— (1996) *Crimes of Style*. Boston: Northeastern University Press.

Garfinkel, H. (1967) *Studies in Ethnomethodology*. Englewood Cliffs, NJ: Prentice-Hall.

Gillet, K. (2011) 'Fast-growing Mongolian Shantytown Holds Quarter of National Population', *Guardian Weekly* (20 May): 9.

Grant, R. (2003) *American Nomads*. New York: Grove.

Harvey, D. (2008) 'The Right to the City', *New Left Review* 53: 23–40.

Keith, M. (1997) 'Street Sensibility? Negotiating the Political by Articulating the Spatial', in A. Merrifield and E. Swyngedouw (eds) *The Urbanization of Injustice*. New York: NYU Press.

Kruglanski, A. (2005) 'Precarity Explained for Kids (a Medley)', *Journal of Aesthetics and Protest* 4, at www.journalofaestheticsandprotest.org, accessed 8 June 2011.

Lewin, T. (2011) 'Survey Finds Small Increase in Professors' Pay', *New York Times* (11 April): A15.

MacLeod, G. (2002) 'From Urban Entrepreneurialism to a "Revanchist City"?', *Antipode* 34(3): 602–24.

Makeworlds (2003) 'Precarias: First Stutterings of Precarias a la Deriva', at www.makeworlds.org/node/61, accessed 25 March 2011.

Markusen, A. and Schrock, G. (2009) 'Consumption-Driven Urban Development', *Urban Geography* 30(4): 344–67.

Marx, G. (1981) 'Ironies of Social Control', *Social Problems* 28(3): 221–46.

Matza, D. (1964) *Delinquency and Drift*. New York: Wiley.

Matza, D. and Sykes, G. (1961) 'Juvenile Delinquency and Subterranean Values', *American Sociological Review* 26: 712–19.

Merton, R. K. (1938) 'Social Structure and Anomie', *American Sociological Review* 3: 672–82.

Mills, C. W. (1940) 'Situated Actions and Vocabularies of Motive', *American Sociological Review* 5(6): 904–13.

Mitchell, D. (2003) *The Right to the City*. New York: Guilford.

Neilson, B. and Rossiter, N. (2008) 'Precarity as a Political Concept, or, Fordism as Exception', *Theory, Culture and Society* 25(7–8): 51–72.

O'Malley, P. (2010) *Crime and Risk*. London: Sage.

Oude Breuil, B. (2008) ' "Precious Children in a Heartless World"? The Complexities of Child Trafficking in Marseille', *Children and Society* 22: 223–34.

Powell, R. (2003) 'Having a Few Words with the Author of *Evasion*', *Clamor* (September/October): 51–52.

Prince, H. (1973) 'Scepticism, Mobility and Attitudes to Environment', *Antipode* 5(3): 40–44.

Raymer, B. (2011) 'The Upside of Foreclosure', *New York Times Magazine* (10 April): 23.

Rich, M. (2010) 'Weighing Costs, Companies Favor Temporary Help', *New York Times* (20 December): A1, A4.

Ross, A. (2008) 'The New Geography of Work: Power to the Precarious?', *Theory, Culture and Society* 25(7–8): 31–49.

Sanders, T., O'Neill, M. and Pitcher, J. (2009) *Prostitution*. London: Sage.

Saunders, D. (2010) *Arrival City*. Toronto: Knopf.

Shenker, J., Angelique Chrisafis, L. W., Finn, T., Tremlett, G. and Chulov, M. (2011) 'Arab Youth Anger in the Ascendancy', *Guardian Weekly* (25 February): 28–29.

Shepard, B. and Smithsimon, G. (2011) *The Beach Beneath the Streets: Contesting New York City's Public Spaces*. Albany: SUNY Press.

Smith, N. (1996) *The New Urban Frontier: Gentrification and the Revanchist City*. London: Routledge.

Stephenson, S. (2006) *Crossing the Line: Vagrancy, Homelessness and Social Displacement in Russia*. Aldershot: Ashgate.

Sykes, G. and Matza, D. (2003 [1957]) 'Techniques of Neutralization: A Theory of Delinquency', reprinted in E. McLaughlin, J. Muncie and G. Hughes (eds) *Criminological Perspectives*. London: Sage.

Thomas, L. (2011) 'Continuing Money Troubles Take Personal Toll in Greece', *New York Times* (16 May): A1, A3.

Vitale, A. (2010) 'The Safe Cities Initiative and the Removal of the Homeless', *Criminology and Public Policy* 9(4): 867–73.

Wong, E. (2011) 'The Labyrinth', *New York Times Magazine* (24 April): 16.

Young, J. (2007) *The Vertigo of Late Modernity*. London: Sage.

Younge, G. (2011) 'With Slender Job Prospects, Nation's Young Look To Leave', *Guardian Weekly* (8 April): 13.

Zukin, S. (1997) 'Cultural Strategies of Economic Development and the Hegemony of Vision', in A. Merrifield and E. Swyngedouw (eds) *The Urbanization of Injustice*. New York: New York University Press.

15 'It was never about the money'

Market society, organised crime and UK criminology

Dick Hobbs

> It was never about the money, never, not for me. It was about what I could buy with it.
>
> (Terry Jackson, counterfeiter of £20 notes)[1]

> Capital is not a thing but a process in which money is perpetually sent in search of more money.
>
> (Harvey, 2010: 40)

Alien conspiracy

Although occasionally perceived by the British police as a problem experienced in a few cities (Levi 2005: 825), and resulting in a range of essentially local solutions, based on specialised local knowledge (Sillitoe 1955), historically organised crime is hard to locate in either political or academic discourse in the UK. However, specific illegal pleasures and various forms of vice did trigger a racial pathology locating certain ethnic groups as being culpable for the corruption and degradation of white British society (Hobbs 2012; Knepper 2007). Indeed images of collaborations of foreign criminals imposing themselves upon the UK were especially alarming (Slater 2007), as 'alien conspiracy theory' settled at the foundations of what was to become the UK's policy on organised crime.

The formalisation of these underlying fears into the social construction of organised crime can be traced to the rapidly expanding industrial cities of nineteenth-century USA, where concerns for the moral condition of a workforce made up of European immigrants and southern Black migrants contributed to the identification of 'organised evil' (Woodiwiss and Hobbs 2009). Following the 1919 Volstead Act, the illegal market in alcohol that lasted until the repeal of the Amendment in 1933 was a chaotic, criminogenic free-for-all that featured a wide range of nationalities. However, it was Italians who were targeted by the state as the main players (Block 1983: 130–41, Critchley 2009), ignoring the culpability of established political forces (Landesco 1929: 169–90; Fox 1989: 51),[2] and establishing an enduring template for the essentially alien nature of organised criminality.

War

Conspiracies abounded in the intense Cold War period that pervaded after the Second World War. For instance, it was claimed that the People's Republic of China was importing drugs to the US in order to fund a future war, while simultaneously weakening the 'health and moral fibre of its enemies' (Woodiwiss 1993: 3). This Cold War paranoia was played out in a series of set piece government investigations and commissions that revealed a national conspiracy run by: 'a sinister criminal organisation known as the Mafia operating throughout the country . . . a direct descendant of a criminal organisation of the same name originating in the island of Sicily' (United States Senate 1951: 2). The conspiracy, which was later given its academic benediction by Cressey (1969),[3] was based upon testimony from law enforcement witnesses (Moore 1974), and although subsequently criticised by American scholars,[4] the Mafia was presented as 'the expression of a moral conspiracy aimed at the vitals of American life' (Block 1983: 123). Together these conspiracies created a powerful vision of threat that legitimised exclusionary policies at home, and violent oppression abroad (Picketing 2001: 48–49), typified by President Nixon's declaration in 1971 of a 'war on drugs' (Woodiwiss 1988: 221–22; see Elwood 1994). A decade later the Reagan presidency increased pressure on the international community to recognise and respond to organised crime (Woodiwiss and Hobbs 2009), also using metaphors of war as he vowed to 'cripple organized crime' (Woodiwiss 1988: 200).

The morality of drug markets had long figured in American foreign policy rhetoric (McAllister 2000: 27–30; Mena and Hobbs 2010: 74), and pressure on European states to mimic the conspiracy theories of the USA intensified. The war on crime, in particular the drug trade, was enthusiastically embraced by Prime Minister Margaret Thatcher (Woodiwiss 1988: 222),[5] and American-inspired policies abounded (Hencke, 1985). One result was that by the 1990s the notion of organised crime had become common currency in British political and media circles, especially in relation to any form of non-white acquisitive crime (Gardner 1987; Murji 1999).

The cessation of the Cold War opened up new political and security spaces in Europe (Edwards and Gill 2003: 264), and after the United Nations Convention Against Transnational Organised Crime in 2000, organised crime was redefined as a major internal threat within European states (Gachevska 2009). Although evidence was as weak as it had been in the USA during the 1960s (Fijnaut 1989: 76; see also Buzan *et al.* 1998; Raine and Cilluffo 1994), in 1997 the EU action plan against organised crime was published, and a range of legislative tools and institutional arrangements followed (see Edwards and Levi 2008; Sheptycki 1995). While the EU demanded police cooperation across a borderless continental Europe, the version of organised crime that emerged had a clearly identifiable USA copyright, and helped set a precedent for the next two decades of anti-organised crime policies.

The National Criminal Intelligence Service (NCIS), dubbed as a 'British FBI', (Burrell 1996), was created in 1992, and was fiercely opposed by established law enforcement agencies (Dunnighan and Hobbs 1996). NCIS collated and processed intelligence and acted as a nexus for anti-organised crime co-operation and the exchange of information and intelligence between British and overseas agencies, as the UK emerged as a major voice in global organised crime policing, albeit a voice heavily influenced by the USA (Hobbs 2012). When the National Crime Squad took over from the existing regional crime squads in England and Wales in 1998, a degree of police centralisation that would have been unthinkable a mere decade earlier was created (Dorn *et al.* 1992: 203; von Lampe 1995: 2), and a batch of measures designed to combat financial crime, in particular money laundering, rapidly followed (Gold and Levi 1994; Levi 1991) as joint operations between competing agencies produced complaints of a lack of co-ordination and resources (Dunnighan and Hobbs 1996).

Confusion marked the concept of organised crime (Home Affairs Committee 1994), although early products of NCIS clearly indicated the influence of both American-based alien conspiracies, and post-Cold War demonology, as NCIS threat assessments opted for the exotic big brands of global organised crime: Triads, Yardies, Russians, Colombians, Italians and Turks (NCIS 1993a; 1993b). As in the USA, these threats were not home-grown, nor did they stem from the everyday logic of the political economy (Bell 1953: 152; see Block and Chambliss 1981). For the USA and its European satellite states, the organised crime threat was imminent, and transnational.

British criminology, for all its liberal conceits, chose to ignore organised crime and the related creation of large, secretive, democratically unaccountable institutions until the concept was fully embedded in British political discourse.[6] A full decade after the creation of NCIS, political scientist Frank Gregory (2003) produced a withering critique of the evidence base upon which British organised crime policy relied, and in particular exposed the notion of foreign criminal invasion to be a fallacy. Yet generally there was little interest amongst UK scholars in interrogating the viability of the transnational threat (Edwards and Gill 2003; Hobbs 1998; Sheptycki 1995, 1998) as organised crime was vigorously promoted by secretive state institutions hungry for funding.

Why do we have SOCA?

Less than 20 years after NCIS was created against a backdrop of fierce hostility from across the political divide and the mass media, as well as from within the law enforcement community, a young criminology lecturer in a British university explained to me that, 'of course we have organised crime in this country, that is why we have SOCA' (Serious Organised Crime Agency). The unaccountable policing of alien conspiracies as the model for British anti-organised crime policy was expanded when Sir Stephen Lander, ex-director general of M15, took over as chairman of the fabulously expensive, ludicrously secretive Serious Organised Crime Agency in 2006. SOCA is a non-police agency that combined the National Crime Squad, the National Criminal Intelligence Service, the National Hi-Tech Crime Unit (NHTCU), the investigative arm of HM Revenue & Customs on serious drug trafficking, and the Immigration Service's unit dealing with people trafficking. During Lander's bemused cavalry cut time in charge of SOCA, operatives were dispatched gunboat style to open up offices in problematic parts of the world;[7] as staff resigned, details of internal disputes were leaked to the media, drug seizures plummeted and generally the 'British FBI' failed to convince either their political masters or the general public that they were value for money (Barrett 2008; Lashmar 2008; O'Neill 2008).

Threats and claims

The UK organised crime threat stemmed from a particularly alarming rendition of globalisation (Findlay 2008: 151–52), which 'suggest that righteous citizens are being perverted, intimidated, and forced into vice by alien forces' (Potter 1994). In 2009, a government report called *Extending Our Reach* (Cabinet Office 2009) featured a map of organised crime in the UK, described international criminal organisations as 'cartels', and extended potential threats to include the Taliban, Somali pirates and delinquent youth gangs. In response to pressure from within the UK law enforcement community, *Extending Our Reach* also acknowledged the importance of local police involvement, and recommended a multi-agency strategy designed to fit the priorities of regional police forces (Hobbs 2012: ch. 3). However, the transnational trope was by now well embedded, leaving little room for national political interventions (Bowling 2009; Sheptycki 2007), establishing a continuum of crisis (Bigo 1994) which enabled the establishment of global norms for the policing of organised crime (Woodiwiss and Hobbs 2009) that shrouded local demand, the intricacies of local markets, and the centrality of predatory economic activity in post-industrial cultures.

In 2008 *The National Security Strategy of the United Kingdom* identified 'transnational organised crime' as a 'security challenge' (Cabinet Office 2008: 4), establishing an 'existential threat, requiring emerging measures and justifying actions outside of the normal bounds of political procedure' (Buzan *et al.* 1998: 23–24). For scholars this is especially problematic, for when presented as a vaguely drawn national security issue (Findlay 2008) shrouded in a cloak of secrecy, both the social construction of the threat and the state's response become difficult to debate critically. Equally, the deafening silence from British criminology remains hard to credit.

Policy convergence with American political interests is now very much the norm (Sparks 2001: 165), and within organised crime narratives globalisation should be understood as, 'the universalization of the particular characteristics of an economy embedded in a particular history and social structure, that of the United States' (Bourdieu 2003: 87; see also Slater and Tonkiss 2001: 188). While uniquely European collaborations on organised crime policing have been important (Elvins 2003), American pressures have proved to be dominant in the UK, albeit often in conjunction with the United Nations (Mena and Hobbs 2010). This combination of American and European anxieties (Bigo 2000) produced a powerful set of claims (Best 1990: 41) regarding threats to western security that have resulted in global interventions that are designed to protect physical, moral and economic borders.

Tainted fruit

It is clear that, 'Reliance on unsubstantiated accounts and the lawman's ideological preconceptions has mired the study of organised crime in the bog of conspiracy, allowing the term itself to be carelessly transformed to stand for the monolithic organisation of criminals' (Block 1994: 15). Indeed, academic research into illegal market activities portrays a situation that is at odds with the alien conspiracies of NCIS and early SOCA threat assessments, suggesting chaotic sets of personal and business affiliations featuring both settled and transient relationships (Hobbs 2012; van Duyne 2006, 2011). However, this chaos is not easily translated into the network analysis charts of the type so beloved of both police and police science (Natarajan 2006; Sparrow 1991), for these increasingly popular socio-metric methodologies fail to acknowledge the organisational decisions, assumptions and prior knowledge that impact upon the sampling of the cases that are selected for analysis.[8] Evidence of phone tapping, or physical surveillance, are lodged in case files constructed with a view to gain convictions, and fabricating visual representations of criminal activity based solely upon such flawed 'data' can give the impression of a stable and mappable community of the guilty, rather than a volatile market-based series of fluid collaborations.

Police-generated data are not designed to construct theoretically nuanced presentations of market-based cultures, and all aspects of the accused existence, apart from material relevant to the evidential base of a specific police case, are excluded, rendering the subsequent network analysis useless to all but those engaged in the law enforcement project.[9] Consequently, products of law enforcement agencies should carry the warning: 'The contents of this file are the fruits of police activity' (Kitsuse and Cicourel 1963), the kind of sceptical disclaimer that was built into the study of crime and control when it was taught and researched from within an intellectually rigorous, self-consciously oppositional sociology of deviance.

Ordering human activity (Bauman 1989: 44; 1991: 15) via the creation of a meta-order renders crime predictable (Bauman 1999: 79), and implies order and consistency in an increasingly chaotic world (Bauman 1973: 70). Matza (1969: 1) once warned us against imposing order where none existed, but that was during an era when the scepticism of the sociology of deviance briefly held sway over the unimaginative rigidity of criminology, and before the study of crime and control was reduced to a liberal karaoke. As late as the 1980s, criminology in the UK was associated almost exclusively with the Cambridge Institute and the Home Office, while the study of deviance was hosted by departments of sociology, and encountered by students alongside the sociologies of education, housing, race, gender and so on, and theory lay at the core of both undergraduate and postgraduate study. This made it impossible for a student to complete a sociology degree without encountering a wide gamut of theoretical frameworks that usually manifested themselves as distinctly political stances. Sometimes simplistic, and often turgid, nonetheless, alongside an equally purist and theoretically informed education in sociological methodology, a sense of craft and disciplinary induction was inculcated.

The commodification of higher education in the UK, and the subsequent expansion of the university sector that followed the years of shrinkage under Thatcher, created criminology degrees, lectureships, departments, journals, conferences, publishers, and the invention of a criminological tradition.[10] For British sociologists, who through the 1980s and much of the 1990s were bemused by the corporately themed monotony of the American Criminology Conference, with its book exhibitions flogging simplistic handbooks, and featuring breakfast meetings where well-scrubbed clones of Wall Street negotiated grants and jobs before presenting numerically indecipherable reports of research designed to eliminate crime, it was all a mystery to be mocked on the long flight home. However, back in Blighty the political and social profile of crime increased inexorably throughout the 1980s, and while the sociology of deviance had been sceptical, imaginative and distinctly of the left, albeit with a pronounced liberal underbelly, the expansion of state engagement in various wars on crime enabled the involvement of a wide range of essentially pragmatic professionals in policy formation, and criminology became a cash cow for an expanded university sector. The new administrative tendency marginalised critical writing and reduced theory from a live contested quality that ran like a thread through all aspects of scholarship, to a niche or specialism (Maruna 2008), as criminology evolved into 'a practical pursuit, devoted to helping society deal with those it found troublesome' (Becker 1964: 1), as a criminological mainstream evolved as a result of the popularity of undergraduate criminology courses, a development that was largely an acknowledgment of the popularity of options offered in the sociology of deviance.

One of the consequences of this loss of its sociological soul, is the tendency identified more generally within sociology towards disciplinary fragmentation, as criminologists come together under the umbrella of various sobriquets in an attempt to establish some measure of hegemony over the chaotic criminological terrain, or more modestly to maintain a platform for their work. Time and space do not allow me to list those criminological scholars whose work retains sociological relevance,[11] but the tendency of criminologists to Balkanise themselves, often preaching to the converted via specialist outlets and citation clubs, has drastically reduced the potential impact of their scholarship, exacerbating the retreat from sociology, and severely restricting criminology's range. Consequently, amongst criminologists, debates concerning the construction of expensive, secretive and unaccountable state institutions inspired barely a whisper, and reviews of the development of British organised crime policy only became more substantial when the relevant institutions were well embedded in law enforcement orthodoxy (Bowling and Ross 2006; Harfield 2006; Hobbs and Hobbs 2011; Levi 2005).

A slack-jawed economy

The ragbag of disparate criminality that constitutes organised crime, usually refers to some kind of acquisitive illegal activity, an area in which for the most part British criminologists have shown little interest, the major exception being a small group of British scholars who have focused upon fraud (Levi 1981),[12] white collar crime (Croall 2001), and variations on corporate crime (Slapper and Tombs 2007; Tombs and Whyte 2007).[13] The work of these academics is rooted in an identifiable sociological and political tradition that stands in stark opposition to that of the criminological mainstream, whose commitment to providing repair kits for the criminal justice system enables the criminogenic practices of capitalism to be ignored.

Along with an equally small group of British scholars who have looked at street drug markets (Coomber 2006),[14] these scholars of corporate and white collar deviance have addressed aspects of acquisitive criminality which are particularly notable for their absence within criminological writings that are designated as 'theoretical'. One reason for this omission is the false dichotomy that has been created in British criminology between the economic and the cultural, and the subsequent blind eye that is turned to the manner in which the mongrel concept of organised crime resides at the intersection of the two (Hobbs 2012; see also Kubrin and Weitzer 2003). The multifarious activities that constitute organised crime are committed neither by monetary programmed 'economic man' (Tobias 1968), nor by slack-jawed hedonists focused on the next drink/fuck/drug (Shover and Honaker 1991), and the ground in between positivism and rational choice (Young 1999) can be occupied by ethnographic work exploring everyman performances that are inspired by economic and hedonistic motivations that overlap with a complex set of emotional engagements embedded in everyday post-industrial life (Hobbs 2012).

Not Guy Ritchie

The underworld narratives of the industrial age, when professional criminals resided in a highly distinctive physical and moral space (Hobbs 1997),[15] have been adapted to present organised crime as a global underworld alliance of dark skinned and ex-Cold War enemies (Shelley 1995; Sterling 1994). This exoticises activity that has been woven into the everyday routines of post-industrial consumer society (Hobbs 2012), and where illegal leisure in particular has become normalised (Winlow and Hall 2006). Indeed, when viewed from a perspective that regards crime not as separate, exclusive and essentially removed from normative civil society, but as one of its central props (Chambliss 1978), what emerges is a loose system of power relationships (Albini 1971) interacting seamlessly with both upper and underworlds, and normalised in the evolving complexities of urban life emptied out of all but the residue of the restraints, disciplines and culture of industrialism (Hall *et al.* 2008). The wider impacts of neo-conservatism and de-industrialisation, and the subsequent decline of the cultures and dependent institutions of proletarian society have produced an entrepreneurial free-for-all, and much of the culture and modus operandi of what was once an exclusive underworld has leaked into the mainstream of the political economy (Hall 2012; Hornsby and Hobbs 2007).

However, important work on aspects of acquisitive crime by British scholars exists in isolated, partly forgotten alcoves that seldom feature in the numerous summaries of criminological work, nor are they central to the concerns of scholars intent on contriving a unitary, overarching theory of all things criminological. The work of a small number of scholars who were interested in the culture and practices of professional criminals (Mack 1964; McIntosh 1971, 1975; Taylor 1984), have been either forgotten or lodged into the academic equivalent of a care home (Rock 2005). Yet a generation ago scholars were producing valuable work on a range of subjects that are central to the illegal trading that is now fundamental to the concept of organised crime.

For instance, Henry's (1978) study of stolen goods trading networks established the moral ambiguity that is at the core of 'normal crime', and his identification of reciprocity as being as important as the desire to reap a profit, is a hearty slap in the face to those who insist that economic rationality resides at the heart of illegal trading. Ditton's study of fiddling in a bread factory (1977) is echoed within contemporary British drug markets in that his subjects are following a moral career, in which they learn and apply sometimes quite intricate techniques while avoiding the adoption of a deviant identity. Further, the bread salesmen's fiddling was carried out within an informal series of interlocking networks of knowledge and competence, which describes perfectly the loose-knit nature of a whole range of relations within illegal trading (Hobbs 2012). However, these important studies, along with others that explain aspects of informal entrepreneurship, are ignored despite their crucial relevance to a realm of social practice that is now central within UK society.

Current British organised crime narratives are based upon a set of global assumptions that seldom adequately take on board local renditions of global trade, or the relationship between space, place, and local political and economic history (see Hobbs 1988, 1998; Samuel 1981). For instance Winlow's (2001) ethnography of crime and masculinity only makes sense when placed in the context of the political economy of northeast England, and Ruggiero and Khan's (2006) study of British South Asian drug supply networks would have little impact were it not grounded in an understanding of the BSA diaspora. Similarly Hallsworth and Silverstone's (2009) work situates the notion of 'gun culture' firmly within a distinctively British context that is sceptical of the gang orthodoxy that is increasingly being associated with a range of social ills, including organised crime (Pitts 2008). Researchers must be prepared to respect the chaos of post-industrial lives that do not conform to the simplistic aetiological ambitions of criminologists who are reluctant or unable to acknowledge the way in which the world has changed, yet such work is at best peripheral to the concerns of most mainstream criminology.

Market trading

Taylor stressed the rise of market society and its relevance to the study of crime, and acknowledged the importance of a wide range of related fields: for instance, work and employment, housing and planning, and even the sharper edges of cultural studies (Taylor 1999; see also Currie 1997). This suggests that market relations may be a sufficiently sturdy aetiological hook to hang both the construction of organised crime, and the lived experience that constitutes its disparate cultures. It also provides a reminder that the rise of the market is not some novelty, arbitrarily driven by 'global forces', but part of an ongoing process identified nearly half a century ago as an anomic threat (Downes 1966) that is now being played out throughout British society (Ruggiero 1995), and not merely amongst working-class youth (Hobbs 2012; see Pitts 2008: 110–25). Predatory market engagement is the name of the game.

The cultural illiteracy of rational choice theory should not blind us to the attractions of market behaviour that makes nonsense of the often arbitrary distinctions between legal and illegal business. Hedonistic business is not of course the exclusive preserve of illegal enterprise, as any Friday night in a Canary Wharf bar will attest (Anderson 2009), while the sensuality of 'earning and burning money' (Katz 1988: 215) is not restricted to working-class villains. The entire range of experiences associated with crime (Young 2004: 13) is shared by benefit claimants, wage slaves, Pooters, shooters and corporate looters alike. Similarly, committed professional criminals also have families, get divorced, get drunk, get sick, and need their double-glazing replaced (Hobbs 1995: 60–73). Respectable nine-to-five family men engage in little earners that turn into something more substantial (Hobbs 2012: ch. 10), and men and women excluded from viable legitimate employment keep their families clothed, fed and sheltered, and retain self-respect by dealing in drugs (ibid.: ch. 8). However, promoting the notion of organised crime has done little more than intensify the hysterical reinforcement of national borders, and provide yet more news footage of handcuffed young men in their underwear being led into the back of a police van as the result of another dawn raid on a council house (ibid.: ch. 3).

Industrial society restricted serious criminal market engagement to the super-predators, who periodically emerged from both the criminal underworld and the City of London to plunder opportunities across the economic spectrum. However, the end of industrial society signalled the gloves coming off, and predatory entre-preneurship is now the norm in a society emptied out of the flawed certainties of industrial society. Many of the 'little earners' that enhanced the spirits and pockets of the working classes (Hobbs 1988) now translate into opportunities connected to Holland, Colombia, Turkey and beyond, as the demand for cheap goods and labour inspires engagement beyond the realm of the usual suspects (Matrix 2008).

Particularly via ethnography, there is plenty of scope for appreciative socio-logical exploration of the joys and miseries of entrepreneurial engagement. From the buzz of carving out a small niche within economic structures that otherwise suffocate and ultimately destroy, to earning and burning in a blaze of nihilism, the previously exclusive semi-mythical realm of the underworld is now available to all, and the full range of blurred hedonistic entrepreneurialism is ripe for ethnographic investigation. However, there is a sense of déjà vu crossed with amnesia here, for ethnography was also enthusiastically promoted during the pomp of the sociology of deviance (Cohen 1971: 9–24) as an alternative to the instrumental positivism typified by 'mainstream criminology' (Cohen 1974: 1–40). Yet despite the National Deviancy Conferences' championing of ethnography, of the seventy papers presented at the first fourteen symposia, fewer than ten featured ethnographic work (Hobbs 2001). Forty years on, and engagement with ethnographic work remains a rarity in a discipline that shies away from the intensity of life in market society.

Sociologically trained qualitative researchers, and in particular ethnographers, have long laboured to present deviance/transgression/crime as a complex, messy, dull, exciting, pleasurable and painful set of experiences. However, the appreciative stance that is integral to competent ethnographic practice, and the sensitive, careful and sometimes dangerous work carried out by urban ethnographers from across a range of disciplines is often ignored by criminology's umpteen citation clubs. Criminology is a 'rendezvous discipline' but it has traditionally met under the sociological clock, and rather than consign valuable work to the edges of the academic domain, contributing further to the intellectual fragmentation of the study of crime and control, we should acknowledge its embeddedness in sociology, the discipline that provides criminology's methodological and empirical base, as well as many of its theoretical cues. Yet this is not to suggest a retrenchment in a unitary, isolated discipline; but if aetiology is to be a primary concern, we must 'abandon criminology to sociology' (Smart 1990: 77), and utilise a proven platform from which scholars can stage forays from their besieged disciplinary silos. With British criminology increasingly self-obsessed, its efforts focused by a vague sense of déjà vu couched in amnesia,[16] the pace of social change will require thinking outside of criminology's fractious little box to cope for instance with the impact of the market on social relations (Harman 2009: 325–28), the increased securitisation of policing (Fussey *et al.* 2011), the recalibration of hedonism in the wake of post-industrialism (Winlow and Hall 2006) and the privatisation of formal control (Hobbs *et al.* 2003), as well as many other related developments fostered by neo-liberalism (Hall 2012)

The term organised crime is as much use as a chocolate teapot in understanding market-driven chaos in environments where, for instance, population churn stands at 30 per cent (Armstrong *et al.*, in progress), and where the complexity of culture, language and faith make the bland 'samosas, saris, and steel bands' (Younge 2005) orthodoxy of post-colonial liberalism redundant. Engagement from across the entire range of the social sciences is vital if we are to understand the interactions between global cultures and toxic bazaars (Ruggiero and South 1997), of stocks, drugs or people. Scholars of crime and control will need to understand how global diasporas and cross-border migrations feed the legal and illegal markets (Turner and Kelly 2009) that are integral to 'countergeographies of globalization' (Sassen 1998), rather than adopting vacuous law enforcement sanctified terminology such as 'transnational organised crime'. Additionally scholars should consider the impact of housing policies and consequent markets on the emergent cultures of the post-industrial working class (Hobbs 2012: ch. 10), and extend the emerging interest in consumerism (Hall *et al.* 2008; Hayward 2004) and its impact on property relations, communality, and our understanding of nihilistic violent predation in the suites as well as the streets, all the time acknowledging the role of the law in negotiating market behaviours (Bancroft 2009).

The concept of organised crime is intrinsically linked to the condition of the so-called legitimate economic sphere, which in its de-industrialised form requires a flexibility that includes considerable scope for disintegrated economic collaborations unfettered by 'nostalgic paradigms' (Robertson 1995), and is prone to chaotic and incoherent interludes (Reuter 1984). These collaborations operate within multiple, interwoven webs of both legitimate and illegitimate opportunity which, contrary to much crude criminological theory, are neither simply social, nor strictly economic (Tonkiss 2000), and crucially constitute 'small, fragmented, and ephemeral enterprises . . . not large corporate syndicates' (Potter 1994: 13). These networks thrive on flexible labour, and the informal sector feeds enterprises engaged in activities of all sorts – from construction work and fruit picking, to the sex trade (Sanders 2008) and drug dealing (Seddon 2008), to the multiple employment opportunities offered by the night-time economy (Colosi 2010).

Organised crime is an unhelpful construct that perpetrates the myth of the pantomime villain threatening the morally pristine assets of 'normal' society. Such diversions shift attention away from the insistent predatory culture that permeates every niche and alcove of class society, and scholarship intent on examining this culture cannot restrict itself to the tools available to a discipline whose very existence suggests a comfort blanket for the 'congregation of the gullible' (van Duyne 2011), distinguishing between the 'values and lifestyles of the untamed savages' (Polsky 1971: 145) and the law-abiding majority. Perhaps we should abandon the delusional grandiosity of criminology altogether and replace it with a politically engaged sociology of harm (Hillyard *et al.* 2004), leaving the entire range of post-industrial adaptations – institutional, economic and cultural – to scholars unencumbered by criminological orthodoxy to explore activities where, more than ever, 'deviance is normal' (Taylor *et al.* 1973: 282).

From financial centres (Levi and Burrows 2008), to urban estates (Pitts 2008), and the terrain in between (Ruggiero 2000), the genie is out of the bottle and it resides neither in an underworld (Taylor 1984), nor a secret society (Varese 2011). An ounce of this, a gram of that, 200 'Albanian Marlboro' and a DVD of a yet-to-be premiered Hollywood blockbuster courtesy of an extremely polite Chinese youth who delivers the goods at nine o'clock every Friday. It is this demand for cheap goods and contraband, whether it be drugs, cigarettes, sex, or somebody cheap to pick up the kids from school and do a little light dusting, that drives 'organised crime', a concept which functions as little more than 'a passive screen on to which the righteous project their own inhibited lusts and rapacities . . . [giving] respectable people the illusion of living in an overworld' (Benney 1936: 194–95).

Meanwhile we should celebrate the work of those scholars, both past and present, who have retained their sociological sensitivity, and from this sociological base reach out and plunder a wide range of other academic areas, assuring the construction of a less restrictive, yet more disciplined orthodoxy. For the real threat comes not from expanding the vocabulary of criminology, but from turning it into a zombie discipline oblivious to the changes that have enveloped the social world.

Notes

1 Terry has recently been released from prison after serving a sentence for his part in a £14 million counterfeiting operation which according to the prosecution, 'constituted a threat of the highest order to the integrity of the banking system'. While he served his time the British government expanded the amount of money in the system by £200 billion through a process known as 'quantitative easing'.

2 For a further discussion of prohibition see Hamm 1995; Kyvig 2000; Kobler 1971; Woodiwiss 1993.

3 For a critique of alien conspiracy theory see Hobbs 2012: ch. 2.

4 See Albini 1971; Block 1983; Smith 1975, 1980.

5 For an update on the ubiquitous war metaphor, see the discussion in, 'Rising Jamaican Death Toll Rooted in So-called "War on Drugs"', *Democracy Now!* 28 May 2010.

6 During the early days of NCIS the Home Office commissioned a small pilot study for a 'British Organised Crime Survey'. The subsequent report indicated a huge amount of chaos with regard to the very concept of organised crime, and an intense hostility to NCIS amongst the law enforcement community (Dunnighan and Hobbs 1996; Hobbs and Dunnighan 1998). The report was highly critical of every aspect of the NCIS project, and was 'flung into the long grass' by the Home Secretary. Given the infighting within British law enforcement, it was inevitable that the report was subsequently leaked, and on the last day of the ruling Conservative Party's annual conference a headline on the front page of the *Independent* newspaper (11 October 1996), stated 'Leak reveals contempt for British "FBI"'.

7 When I interviewed Lander in 2006 he spoke about the predictability of the IRA, whom he had encountered in his previous employment as head of MI5, claiming that compared to organised criminals they had 'played by the rules'.

8 See Klerks (2001), Coles (2001), Chattoe and Hamill (2005) for discussions of the merits of network analysis in relation to organised crime.

9 However, network-based methodologies can be useful as a descriptive tool (Potter 1994: 116), and in this respect stand in direct opposition to the monolithic hierarchical studies that dominate traditional studies and media accounts. See also McIlwain's (1999) use of network analysis in relation to media reports, and Morselli's (2005) use of the methodology as an intriguing way of looking at criminal careers using data gleaned from 'true crime' sources.

10 This tradition has mysteriously ignored interesting areas of transgression such as football hooliganism, a field which, with few exceptions (Taylor 1971) was left to sociologists and anthropologists. For a flavour of British football hooliganism at the height of its notoriety see the special edition of the *Sociological Review* (1991). No criminologist made a contribution.

11 Such an exercise would inevitably be yet another list of mentors, mates, collaborators and fellow citation club members.

12 Levi has produced a huge body of work on detailed aspects of the fraud/white collar/ organised crime nexus.

13 Frank Pearce (1976) seldom receives credit for pioneering this field. For an outstanding overview of this area see Whyte (2009).
14 For an overview see McSweeney *et al.* (2008). See also Ward (2010) for a distinctly normalising take on the drug trade, and Aldridge *et al.* (2011), for their take on normalisation and the war on drugs.
15 A crucial text that neatly documents the cultural response to control factors that marked the end of the old underworld is Matthews (2002).
16 See *British Journal of Criminology* (2011) 'A Symposium of Reviews of Public Criminology', 51(4): 707–38.

References

Albini, J. (1971) *The American Mafia: Genesis of a Legend.* New York: Appleton-Century-Crofts.
Aldridge, J., Measham, F. and Williams, L. (2011) *Illegal Leisure Revisited.* London: Routledge.
Anderson, G. (2009) *Cityboy.* London: Headline.
Armstrong, G., Guilianotti, R., Hales, G. and Hobbs, D. (in progress) 'Policing and Community Relations in the 2012 Olympics (ESRC)'.
Bancroft, A. (2009) *Drugs, Intoxication and Society.* Cambridge: Polity.
Barrett, D. (15 May 2008) 'Organised Crime Chief Attacks "Disgraceful" Staff', *Independent.*
Bauman, Z. (1999) *In Search of Politics.* Cambridge: Polity.
—— (1991) *Modernity and Ambivalence.* Ithaca, NY: Cornell University Press.
—— (1989) *Legislators and Interpreters*, Cambridge: Polity.
—— (1973) *Culture as Praxis.* 2nd edn. London: Sage.
Becker, H. (ed.) (1964) *The Other Side.* New York: Macmillan.
Bell, D. (1953) 'Crime as an American Way of Life', *The Antioch Review*, 13: 131–54.
Benney, M. (1936) *Low Company.* Facsimile edn., Sussex: Caliban Books, 1981.
Best, J. (1990) *Threatened Children: Rhetoric and Concern About Child-Victims.* Chicago: University of Chicago Press.
Bigo, D. (2000) 'When Two Becomes One: Internal and External Securitizations in Europe', in M. Kelstrup and M. C. Williams (eds) *International Relations Theory and the Politics of European Integration*, London: Routledge, 171–205.
—— (1994) 'The European Internal Security Field: Stakes and Rivalries in a Newly Developing Area of Police Intervention', in M. Anderson and M. den Boer (eds) *Policing Across National Boundaries*, pp. 161–73, London: Pinter.
Block, A. (1983) *East Side–West Side: Organizing Crime in New York, 1930–1950.* Newark, NJ: Transaction.
—— (1994) *Space Time and Organised Crime.* New Brunswick, NJ: Transaction.
Block, A. and Chambliss, W. (1981) *Organizing Crime.* New York: Elsevier.
Bourdieu, P. (2003) *Firing Back: Against the Tyranny of the Market 2.* London: Verso.
Bowling, B. (2009) 'Transnational Policing: The Globalisation Thesis, a Typology and a Research Agenda', *Policing: A Journal of Policy and Practice*, 3(2): 1–12.
Bowling, B. and Ross, J. (2006) 'The Serious Organised Crime Agency: Should We Be Afraid?' *Criminal Law Review*, December, 1019–34.
Burrell, I. (1996) 'Leak Reveals Contempt for British "FBI"', *Independent*, 11 October.
Buzan, B., Wæver, O. and de Wilde, J. (1998) *Security: A New Framework for Analysis.* Boulder, CO: Lynne Rienner.

Cabinet Office (2008) *The National Security Strategy of the United Kingdom: Security in an Interdependent World*. London: The Stationery Office.

—— (2009) *Extending Our Reach: A Comprehensive Approach to Tackling Serious Organised Crime*. Norwich: The Stationery Office.

Chambliss, W. (1978) *On the Take*. Bloomington: Indiana University Press.

Chattoe, E. and Hamill, H. (2005) 'It's Not Who You Know – It's What You Know About People You Don't Know That Counts: Extending the Analysis of Crime Groups as Social Networks', *British Journal of Criminology*, 45(6): 860–76.

Cohen, S. (1974) 'Criminology and the Sociology of Deviance in Britain', in P. Rock and M. McIntosh (eds) *Deviance and Social Control*. London: Tavistock.

Cohen, S. (ed.) (1971) *Images of Deviance*. Harmondsworth: Penguin.

Coles, N. (2001) 'It's Not *What* You Know – It's *Who* You Know That Counts: Analysing Serious Crime Groups as Social Networks', *British Journal of Criminology*, 41: 580–94.

Colosi, R. (2010) *Dirty Dancing? An Ethnography of Lap-Dancing*. Cullompton: Willan.

Coomber, R. (2006) *Pusher Myths: Re-Situating the Drug Dealer*. London: Free Association Books.

Cressey, D. (1969) *Theft of the Nation: The Structure and Operations of Organized Crime in America*. New York: Harper and Row.

Critchley, D. (2009) *The Origin of Organised Crime in America: The New York City Mafia,1981–1931*. London: Routledge.

Croall, H. (2001) *Understanding White Collar Crime*. Open University Press.

Currie, E. (1997) 'Market, Crime and Community: Toward a Mid-range Theory of Post-Industrial Violence,' *Theoretical Criminology*, 1(2): 147–72.

Ditton, J. (1977) *Part Time Crime*. London: Macmillan.

Dorn, N., South, N. and Murji, K. (1992) *Traffickers*. London: Routledge.

Downes, D. (1966) *The Delinquent Solution: A Study in Subcultural Theory*. London: Routledge and Kegan Paul.

Dunnighan, C. and Hobbs, D. (1996) *A Report on the NCIS Pilot Organised Crime Notification Survey*. London: Home Office.

Edwards, A. and Gill, P. (eds) (2003) *Transnational Organised Crime: Perspectives on Global Security*. London: Routledge.

Edwards, A. and Levi, M. (2008) 'Researching the Organisation of Serious Crimes', *Criminology and Criminal Justice*, 8(4): 363–88.

Elvins, M. (2003) 'Europe's Response to Transnational Organised Crime', in A. Edwards and P. Gill (eds) *Policy Responses to Transnational Organised Crime*. London: Routledge.

Elwood, W. (1994) *Rhetoric in the War on Drugs: The Triumphs and Tragedies of Public Relations*. Westport, CT: Praeger.

Fijnaut, C. (1989) 'Researching Organised Crime', in R. Morgan (ed.) *Policing Organised Crime and Crime Prevention*. British Criminology Conference, 1989, vol. 4., pp. 75–85. Bristol and Bath Centre for Criminal Justice.

Findlay, M. (2008) *Governing Through Globalised Crime*. Cullompton: Willan.

Fox, S. (1989) *Blood and Power: Organized Crime in 20th century America*. New York: William Morrow.

Fussey, P., Coafee, J., Armstrong, G. and Hobbs, D. (2011) *Securing the Olympic Site*. Aldershot: Ashgate.

Gachevska, K. (2009) 'Building the New Europe: Soft Security and Organised Crime in EU Enlargement', Unpublished Ph.D. thesis, University of Wolverhampton.

Gardner, D. (1987) 'Black Mafia in Gang War', *Daily Mail*, 28 December.

Gold, M. and Levi, M. (1994) *Money Laundering in the UK: An Appraisal of Suspicion-Based Reporting*. London: Police Foundation.

Gregory, F. (2003) 'Classify, Report and Measure: The UK Organised Crime Notification Scheme,' in A. Edwards and P. Gill (eds) *Transnational Organised Crime*, pp. 78–96. London: Routledge.

Hacking, I. (1999) *The Social Construction of What?* Cambridge, MA: Harvard University Press.

Hall, S. (2012) *Theorizing Crime and Deviance: A New Perspective*. London: Sage.

Hall, S., Winlow, S. and Ancrum, C. (2008) *Criminal Identities and Contemporary Culture*. Cullompton: Willan.

Hallsworth, S. and Silverstone, D. (2009) ' "That's Life Innit?"': A British Perspective on Guns, Crime and Social Order', *Criminology and Criminal Justice*, 9(3): 359–77.

Hamm, R. (1995) *Shaping the Eighteenth Amendment: Temperance Reform Legal Culture, and the Polity, 1880–1920*. Chapel Hill: University of North Carolina Press.

Harfield, C. (2006) 'SOCA: A Paradigm Shift in British Policing', *British Journal of Criminology*, 46: 743–61.

Harman, C. (2009) *Zombie Capitalism*. London: Bookmark.

Harvey, D. (2010) *The Enigma of Capital*. London: Profile Books.

Hayward, K. (2004) *City Limits: Crime, Consumer Culture and the Urban Experience*. London: Glasshouse Press.

Hencke, D. (1985) 'MPs Urge Harsher Heroin Penalties', *Guardian*, 24 May.

Henry, S. (1978) *The Hidden Economy*. Oxford: Martin Robertson.

Hillyard, P., Pantazis, C., Tombs, T. and Gordon, D. (eds) (2004) *Beyond Criminology: Taking Crime Seriously*. London: Pluto.

Hobbs, D. (2012) *Lush Life: Organised Crime as a Community of Practice*. Oxford: Oxford University Press.

—— (2001) 'Deviance and Ethnography', in P. Atkinson, S. Delamont, A. Coffey, J. Lofland and L. Lofland (eds) *The Sage Handbook of Ethnography*, pp. 204–19. London: Sage.

—— (1998) 'Going Down the Glocal: The Local Context of Organised Crime', *Howard Journal of Criminal Justice*, 37(4): 407–22.

—— (1997) 'Professional Crime and the Myth of the Underworld', *Sociology*, 31(1): 57–72.

—— (1995) *Bad Business: Professional Crime in Modern Britain*. Oxford: Oxford University Press.

—— (1988) *Doing the Business: Entrepreneurship, Detectives and the Working Class in the East End of London*. Oxford: Clarendon Press.

Hobbs, D. and Dunnighan, C. (1999) 'Organised Crime and the Organisation of Police Intelligence', in P. Carlen and R. Morgan (eds) *Crime Unlimited: Post Modernity and Social Control*. Basingstoke: Macmillan.

—— (1998) 'Glocal Organised Crime: Context and Pretext', in V. Ruggiero, N. South and I. Taylor (eds) *The New European Criminology*, pp. 289–303. London: Routledge.

Hobbs, D. Hadfield, P. Lister, S. and Winlow, S. (2003) *Bouncers: Violence, Governance and the Night-time Economy*. Oxford: Oxford University Press.

Hobbs, D. and Hobbs, S. (2011) 'A Bog of Conspiracy: The Institutional Evolution of Organised Crime in the UK', in F. Allum and S. Gilmour (eds) *The Handbook of Transnational Organized Crime*. London: Routledge.

Home Affairs Committee (1994) *Organised Crime: Minutes and Memoranda*. London: Home Office.

Howard, M. (1996) *Speech as Home Secretary to ACPO Summer Conference*. London: Conservative Central Office.

Hornsby, R. and Hobbs, D. (2007) 'A Zone of Ambiguity: The Political Economy of Cigarette Bootlegging', *British Journal of Criminology*, 47(4): 551–71.

Katz, J. (1988) *Seductions of Crime*. New York: Basic Books.

Kitsuse, J. and Cicourel, A. (1963) 'A Note on the Uses of Official Statistics', *Social Problems*, 11(2): 131–39.

Klerks, P. (2001) 'The Network Paradigm Applied to Criminal Organizations: Theoretical Nitpicking or a Relevant Doctrine for Investigators? Recent Developments in the Netherlands', *Connections*, 24(3): 53–65.

Knepper, J. (2007) 'British Jews and the Racialisation of Crime in the Age of Empire', *British Journal of Criminology*, 47(1): 61–79.

Kobler, J. (1971) *Capone: The Life and World of Al Capone*. Greenwich, CT: Fawcett.

Kubrin, C. and Weitzer, R. (2003) 'New Directions in Social Disorganization Theory', *Journal of Research in Crime and Delinquency*, 40:374–402.

Kyvig, D. (2000) *Repealing National Prohibition*. 2nd edn. Kent, OH: Kent State University Press.

Landesco, J. (1929) [1968] *Organised Crime in Chicago*. 2nd edn. Chicago: University of Chicago Press.

Lashmar, P. (2008) 'Britain's FBI "Is a Dismal Failure"' *Independent on Sunday*, 18 May.

Levi, M. (2005) 'The Making of the United Kingdom's Organised Crime Policies', in Cyrille Fijnaut and Letizia Paoli (eds) *Organised Crime in Europe*, pp. 823–52. Dordrecht: Kluwer.

—— (1991) 'Developments in Business Crime Control in Europe', in F. Heidensohn and M. Farrell (eds) *Crime in Europe*. London: Routledge.

—— (1981) *The Phantom Capitalists*. Aldershot: Gower.

Levi, M. and Burrows, J. (2008) 'Measuring the Impact of Fraud: A Conceptual and Empirical Journey', *British Journal of Criminology*, 48(3): 293–318.

Mack, J. (1964) 'Full-time Miscreants, Delinquent Neighbourhoods and Criminal Networks', *British Journal of Sociology*, 15: 38–53.

Maruna, S. (2008) 'Review Symposium: Merton with Energy, Katz with Structure, Jock Young with Data', *Theoretical Criminology*, 12(4): 534–37.

Matrix (2008) *The Illicit Drug Trade in the United Kingdom*. London: Home Office.

Matthews, R. (2002) *Armed Robbery*. Cullompton: Willan.

Matza, D. (1969) *Becoming Deviant*. Englewood Cliffs, NJ: Prentice Hall.

McAllister, W. (2000) *Drug Diplomacy in the Twentieth Century: An International History*. London: Routledge.

McIlwain, J. (1999) 'Organized Crime: A Social Network Approach', *Crime, Law and Social Change*, 32(4): 301–23.

McIntosh, M. (1975) *The Organisation of Crime*. London: Macmillan.

—— (1971) 'Changes in the Organisation of Thieving', in S. Cohen (ed.) *Images of Deviance*. Harmondsworth: Penguin.

McSweeney, T., Turnbull, P. J. and Hough, M. (2008) *Tackling Drug Markets and Distribution Networks in the UK: A Review of the Recent Literature*. London: UK Drug Policy Commission.

Mena, F. and Hobbs, D. (2010) 'Narcophobia: Drugs Prohibition and the Generation of Human Rights Abuses', *Trends in Organised Crime*, 13: 60–74.

Moore, W. (1974) *Kefauver and the Politics of Crime*. Columbia: University of Missouri Press.

Morselli, C. (2005) *Contacts, Opportunities, and Criminal Enterprise*. Toronto: University of Toronto Press.

Murji, K. (1999) 'Wild Life: Constructions and Representations of Yardies', in J. Ferrell and N. Websdale (eds) *Making Trouble: Cultural Constructions of Crime, Deviance, and Control*. New York: Aldine de Gruyter.

Natarajan, M. (2006) 'Understanding the Structure of a Large Heroin Distribution Network: A Quantitative Analysis of Qualitative Data', *Quantitative Journal of Criminology*, 22(2): 171–92.

NCIS (1993a) *An Outline Assessment of the Threat and Impact by Organised/Enterprise Crime Upon United Kingdom Interests*. London: NCIS.

—— (1993b) *Organised Crime Conference: A Threat Assessment*. London: NCIS.

O'Neill, S. (2008) 'Soca Abandons Hunt for Crime Lords', *The Times Online*, 13 May.

Pearce, F. (1976) *Crimes of the Powerful: Marxism, Crime and Deviance*. London: Pluto Press.

Picketing, M. (2001) *Stereotyping and the Politics of Representation*. Houndmills: Macmillan.

Pitts, J. (2008) *Reluctant Gangsters: The Changing Face of Youth Crime*. Cullompton: Willan.

Polsky, N. (1971) *Hustlers, Beats and Others*. Harmondsworth: Pelican (1st edn 1967).

Potter, G. W. (1994) *Criminal Organisations*. Prospect Heights, IL: Waveland Press.

Raine, L. and Cilluffo, F. (eds) (1994) *Global Organized Crime: The New Empire of Evil*. Washington, DC: Center for Strategic and International Studies.

Reuter, P. (1984) *Disorganised Crime*. Cambridge, MA: MIT Press.

Robertson, R. (1995) 'Glocalisation: Time-Space and Homogeneity-Heterogeneity', in M. Featherstone, S. Lash and R. Robertson (eds) *Global Modernities*. London: Sage.

Rock, P. (2005) 'Chronocentrism and British Criminology', *British Journal of Sociology*, 56(3): 473–91.

Ruggiero, V. (2000) *Crime and Markets*. Oxford: Oxford University Press.

—— (1995) 'Drug Economics: A Fordist Model of Criminal Capital', *Capital and Class*, 55: 131–50.

Ruggiero, V. and Khan, K. (2006) 'British South Asian Communities and Drug Supply Networks in the UK: A Qualitative Study', *The International Journal of Drug Policy*, 17: 473–83.

Ruggiero, V. and South, N. (1997) 'The Late Modern City as a Bazaar', *British Journal of Sociology*, 48/1: 55–71.

Samuel, R. (1981) *East End Underworld: The Life and Times of Arthur Harding*. London: Routledge & Kegan Paul.

Sanders, T. (2008) *Paying for Pleasure: Men Who Buy Sex*. Cullompton: Willan.

Sassen, S. (1998) *Globalisation and Its Discontents: Essays on the New Mobility of People and Money*. New York: The New Press.

Seddon, T. (2008) 'Drugs, the Informal Economy and Globalization', *International Journal of Social Economics*, 35(10): 717–28.

Shelley, L. (1995) 'Transnational Organized Crime: An Imminent Threat to the Nation-State', *Journal of International Affairs*, 48(2): 463–89.

Sheptycki, J. (2007) 'Police Ethnography in the House of Serious Organized Crime', in A. Henry and D. J. Smith (eds) *Transformations of Policing*, pp. 51–79. Aldershot: Ashgate.

—— (1998) 'The Global Cops Cometh', *British Journal of Sociology*, 49(1): 57–74.

—— (1995) 'Transnational Policing and the Making of a Postmodern State', *British Journal of Criminology*, 35(4): 613–35.

Shover, N. and Honaker, D. (1991) 'The Socially Bounded Decision Making of Persistent Property Offenders', *The Howard Journal*, 31(November): 276–93.

Sillitoe, P. (1955) *Cloak Without Dagger*. London: Cassell.

Slapper, G. and Tombs, S. (1999) *Corporate Crime*. London: Longman.

Slater, D. and Tonkiss, F. (2001) *Market Society*. Cambridge: Polity.

Slater, S. (2007) 'Pimps, Police and Filles de Joie: Foreign Prostitution in Interwar London', *The London Journal*, 32(1): 53–74.

Smart, C. (1990) 'Feminist Approaches to Criminology: Or Postmodern Woman Meets Atavistic Man', in L. Gelsthorpe and A. Morris (eds) *Feminist Perspectives in Criminology*. Milton Keynes: Open University Press.

Smith, D. (1980) 'Paragons, Pariahs, and Pirates: A Spectrum based Theory of Enterprise', *Crime and Delinquency*, 26: 358–86.

—— (1975) *The Mafia Mystique*. New York: Basic Books.

Sociological Review (1991) Special issue on football culture, 39(3): 427–695.

Sparks, R. (2001) 'Degrees of Estrangement: The Cultural Theory of Risk and Comparative Penology', *Theoretical Criminology*, 5(2): 159–76.

Sparrow, M. K. (1991) 'Network Vulnerabilities and Strategic Intelligence in Law Enforcement', *International Journal of Intelligence and Counter Intelligence*, 65: 255–74.

Sterling, C. (1994) *Crime Without Frontiers*. London: Little, Brown.

Sutherland, E. (1937) *The Professional Thief*. Chicago: University of Chicago Press.

Taylor, I. (1999) *Crime in Context*. Cambridge: Polity.

—— (1971) 'Soccer Consciousness and Soccer Hooliganism', in S. Cohen (ed.) *Images of Deviance*. Harmondsworth: Penguin.

Taylor, I., Walton, P. and Young, J. (1973) *The New Criminology*. London: Routledge and Kegan Paul.

Taylor, L. (1984) *In the Underworld*. Oxford: Blackwell.

Tobias, J. (1968) 'The Crime Industry', *British Journal of Criminology*, 2: 247–58.

Tombs, S. and Whyte, D. (2007) *Safety Crimes*. Cullompton: Willan.

Tonkiss, F. (2000) 'Trust, Social Capital and Economy', in F. Tonkiss and A. Passey (eds) *Trust and Civil Society*. Basingstoke: Macmillan.

Turner, J. and Kelly, L. (2009) 'Trade Secrets Intersections between Diasporas and Crime Groups in the Constitution of the Human Trafficking Chain', *British Journal of Criminology*, 49(2): 184–201.

United States Senate (1951) *Special Committee to Investigate Organized Crime in Interstate Commerce*. New York: Didier.

van Duyne, P. C. (2011) *(Transnational) Organised Crime, Laundering and the Congregation of the Gullible*. Valedictory, 14 March, Tilburg University.

—— (2003) 'Medieval Thinking and Organized Crime Economy', in E. Viano, J. Magallanes and L. Bridel (eds) *Transnational Organized Crime*, pp. 23–44. Durham, NC: Duke University Press.

—— (1996) 'The Phantom and Threat of Organized Crime', *Crime, Law and Social Change*, 24(4): 341–77.

Varese, F. (2011) *Mafias on the Move: How Organized Crime Conquers New Territories*. Princeton, NJ: Princeton University Press.

von Lampe, K. (1995) 'Understanding Organised Crime: A German View', Paper presented at the Academy of Criminal Justice Sciences, Boston.

Ward, J. (2010) *Flashback: Drugs and Dealing in the Golden Age of the London Rave Scene.* Cullompton: Willan.

Whyte, D. (ed.) (2009) *Crimes of the Powerful: A Reader.* Maidenhead: Open University Press.

Winlow, S. (2001) *Badfellas: Crime Tradition and New Masculinities.* Oxford: Berg.

Winlow, S. and Hall, S. (2006) *Violent Night: Urban Leisure and Contemporary Culture.* Oxford: Berg.

Woodiwiss, M. (1988) *Crime, Crusades and Corruption: Prohibitions in the United States 1900–1987.* London: Pinter.

Woodiwiss, M. and Hobbs, D. (2009) 'Organized Evil and the Atlantic Alliance: Moral Panics and the Rhetoric of Organized Crime Policing in America and Britain', *British Journal of Criminology*, 49(1): 106–28.

Woodiwiss, M. (1993) 'Crime's Global Reach', in F. Pearce and M. Woodiwiss, *Global Crime Connections*, pp. 1–31. London: Macmillan.

Young, J. (2004) 'Voodoo Criminology and the Numbers Game', in J. Ferrell, J. Hayward, W. Morrison and M. Presdee (eds) *Cultural Criminology Unleashed*, pp. 13–28. London: Glasshouse Press.

—— (1999) *The Exclusive Society.* London: Sage.

Younge, G. (2005) 'Cricket Test to Citizenship: How the War on Terror is Wrecking Britain's Racial Landscape', Hobhouse Lecture Series, Wednesday 30 November, LSE.

16 After the crisis

New directions in theorising corporate and white-collar crime

Kate Burdis and Steve Tombs

Introduction

Something is rotten in the body of criminology. At a time when evidence of corporate harm, white-collar criminality and corruption abound, our discipline finds itself in a state of paralysis; a state in which we seem unable to offer credible explanations for developing forms of crime and criminality, precisely when such explanations are urgently required. We do not appear to possess the theoretical tools to respond to crucial contemporary events such as the ongoing global economic crisis, the endemic criminality in the News International empire, the explosion and subsequent haemorrhaging of oil from the *Deepwater Horizon*, or the seemingly unending series of international financial frauds which have emerged over the past quarter of a century (see Levi, 2008). Moreover, not only have we failed to generate adequate critical insights into the genesis of these harmful activities and events, we have also failed to theorise the contexts in which they are reproduced and virtually given up suggesting alternative forms of social and economic organisation which may reduce their incidence (Dean, 2009). If this latter aspiration is thought to lie outside the remit of the criminological discipline (see Loader and Sparks, 2011), it is our contention that we must re-incorporate broader political aims and ideals into the criminological enterprise.

The absence of truly transformative political ideals in criminology is indicative of the current poverty of the discipline. In particular, criminological thinking has, in recent years, increasingly channelled its efforts into discussing and responding to particular 'criminals', rather than the persistent forms of criminality which systematically cause widespread social harm (Hillyard *et al.*, 2004). There also appears to be an impasse reached in terms of innovative thinking around corporate and white-collar crime: scholars in this area (and we include ourselves) still struggle to demonstrate to an increasingly formulaic and empiricist criminological mainstream the crucial importance of this area of study. Our efforts have relapsed, to some extent, into auto poiesis (isolated self-reproduction) rather than being outward-looking and interdisciplinary.

In this chapter, we suggest three directions in which the theorisation of white-collar and corporate crimes could be developed. We begin, in the following section, by providing a context for this discussion; we argue that the current crisis is one in which the material opportunities and psychological motivations for white-collar and corporate offending have been both reproduced and strengthened. This in itself creates a change of direction for those who tend to theorise such forms of offending mainly in the context of regulation. We then set out three new directions along which such work must proceed. First, in 'Theorising the White-Collar Criminal', we argue that there is a need to transcend the 'black box' or 'rational actor' model of the individual offender, and seek to understand more fully the relationship between the individual and dominant economic and cultural conditions. Then, in the section that follows, we advocate the study of criminal subjectivities as crucial to the formation of more complete and coherent accounts of white-collar criminality. Second, we consider how neoliberalism has reshaped opportunity structures for corporate and white-collar crime, and we argue here that the challenge for criminology is to move beyond existing state–market dichotomies and simple accounts of deregulation, while conceptualising the relationship between states and markets as an ongoing and complex process of interdependence, which provides new opportunities for criminality and contexts for criminal subjectivities. We develop this in the following section by considering, third, the unfolding moralities of neoliberal capitalism, arguing that we need to grasp the dynamic cultural and symbolic aspects of any society that makes white-collar and corporate crime more (or less) likely, their effects on the level of regulation of corporate activity, and their effects on the popular, political and academic consciousness. We conclude with a short section that advocates the repoliticisation of the study of white-collar and corporate criminality.

The current crisis

Dominant responses to the current economic crisis have demonstrated the unwavering ideological power of private capital; paradoxically, increasing free-dom for capital has been prescribed as the solution to the problems created in the first place by the excessive freedoms of capital. Thus, across all the mainstream political and economic agendas concerned with economic recovery, the minimally regulated circulation of private capital is virtually the only game in town. Nowhere has this been more clearly in evidence than in the 'golden parachutes' (Žižek, 2009a: 12) handed out to the UK banking system, the first tranche of which had amounted to the tune of £850 billion before the end of 2009 (National Audit Office, 2009). At the same time, it is worth emphasising, in the United Kingdom, certainly, that there has been no thoroughgoing attempt to re-regulate the financial services sector, save the Vickers Report's belated proposal for a flimsy fence between retail and investment banking – not to be erected until 2019 (well beyond the life of the present government); nor any inclination to alter radically those parts of it that are now effectively under state ownership; no thoroughgoing inquiry into the potential illegalities involved in the near collapse of this sector; no significant prosecutions developed by the Serious Fraud Office or the Financial Services Authority; and certainly no ideological or material undermining of political faith in 'light touch' regulation across all other areas that 'affect' business life in the light of our current collective experience of its manifest failures. More specifically, we do not know, nor are we likely to know, to what extent criminal activity was implicated in the events leading up to the crisis. A significant and growing body of literature on the causes of the crisis is accruing across the social sciences, accompanied by some particularly insightful accounts offered by investigative journalists, yet, with only a few important exceptions (see for instance Hall, 2012), penetrative criminological analyses of the crisis are notable only by their absence.

To return to the paradox noted above, it is absolutely clear that the prevailing idea of what constitutes 'feasible' regulation of relatively powerful individuals and organisations, firmly set in place from the 1970s onwards, appears to be remarkably robust even in the wake of its manifest failure. This new 'common sense' seems to have been barely dented by the financial collapse and global recessions that unfolded at the end of the last decade (Crouch, 2011). Thus, despite having overseen an unprecedented bailout of the banking system – a massive state subsidy funded by the taxpayer that effectively socialised the consequences of long-term, systematic private greed and possible illegality – the UK's Labour government underscored their commitment to the 'free-market system' and 'light-touch regulation', while again declaring their continued faith in business morality and corporate social responsibility:

> Our government is pro business; I believe in markets [and] entrepreneurship, and there are many areas of the economy that need the spur of more competition. But the events of the past months bear witness, more than anything in my lifetime, to one simple truth: markets need morals.
>
> (Brown, 2008)

On one level the claim that 'the markets' – a purely reified entity – need morals is just *non*-sense; on the other hand, the fact that such a statement can be made attests to the power of the hitherto constructed *common*-sense. For Brown is claiming, of course, that if there were lessons to be learned, they were to be learnt on the terrain constructed for capital in the previous years: thus the emphasis was upon eliminating bad apples, not the necessity of restructuring the market or the key private actors within it.

Yet, to emphasise, the period following the crisis that unfolded from late 2008 was one of unprecedented levels of state intervention in (parts of) the corporate sector. The financial commitments made by governments since September 2008 have included purchasing shares in banks to enable re-capitalisation, indemnifying the Bank of England against losses incurred in providing liquidity support, under-writing borrowing by banks to strengthen liquidity, and providing insurance cover for assets. Moreover, during this period, governments effectively allowed the banks to ignore competition law – the supposed bedrock of neoliberal markets – in order to broker a merger between HBOS and Lloyds, two of the country's largest banks.

That it was *only* the state which could respond to the crisis – under the guise of creating 'the conditions for a new expansion' – is not in itself at all remarkable (Gamble, 2009: 97). What *is* remarkable, however, is that in so doing, the idea of the necessity and desirability of regulatory retreat has persisted across the mainstream political spectrum.[1] Going into the British general election of 2010, all three major political parties were committed to reducing regulation in general, while each referred to the need to 'do something' about regulating banks and financial services; a remarkable (if unremarked upon) balancing act. Yet the key terrain upon which approaches to regulation were set out comprised the following two elements: first, that regulation in general was inherently burdensome and only to be an option of last resort, a minimalist necessary evil; and second, that in any case regulation entailed costs for both the state and for business, costs that had to be restricted in the new 'Age of Austerity'. Thus regulatory costs *had* to be minimised on the one hand as part of the overall attempt to tackle the new fiscal crisis of the state, and on the other hand to reduce the costs for the private sector, which was seen as the only vehicle for economic recovery. This in turn underscores perhaps a central achievement of the neoliberal period; that the key institutional form of capital, the corporation, has been reified as *the* quintessential agent of economic success. Absent from this discursive terrain was any consideration of the forms of state regulation which had fuelled unsustainable levels of profit maximisation on the part of financial services operating in the shadow-economy of derivatives and securities, a toxic process which created the very crisis to which more of the same poison was to prove the necessary cure, in the form of economic recovery. Finance-centred neoliberal capitalism seems to have taken on the form of the ancient *pharmakon*, the strange body that is both toxic and curative to the community (see Stiegler, 2010).

Thus, the ideological foundations upon which our economy is based have somewhat paradoxically been strengthened by the recent economic crisis; the moral and practical strength of private capital has been increased by its triumph as the only feasible response to economic crisis. Consequently, we find ourselves in a position in which the material opportunities and psychological motivations for white-collar and corporate offending have been both reproduced and strengthened. If general observations about the ways in which these conditions are conducive to such forms of criminality have been well documented, the precise ways in which such structural and cultural conditions combine with individual characteristics of white-collar criminals remain an under-theorised area of criminology. There remains a real need to understand more fully the relationships between the individual subject and dominant economic cultural conditions. In the following section, we advocate the study of criminal subjectivities as crucial to the formation of more complete and coherent accounts of the criminality of the powerful.

Theorising the white-collar offender

One of the common features of the plethora of behaviours defined as 'white-collar crimes' is that, by their very nature, they often remain inaccessible to public, political and academic scrutiny. The social positions of perpetrators often provide opportunities for the successful concealment of offences, or for the avoidance of prosecution either by having access to expensive lawyers or by being, quite literally, above the law (witness Berlusconi's legal immunity legislation, *Telegraph*, 2003). Consequently, an important task of criminology has been to expose some of these forms of criminality and to gain some sense of the extent and nature of this elusive phenomenon. This tradition – stretching back to the work of E. A. Ross and the 'muckrakers' of the early 1900s – has provided the discipline with countless illuminating examples of corporate and white-collar criminality which combine to demonstrate the pervasiveness of the phenomenon. However, despite the development of case studies, the 'dark figure' of white-collar crime remains even more unquantifiable than that pertaining to 'street' crime. Nevertheless, the application of almost journalistic curiosity to the exploration and exposure of white-collar crimes is a tradition which has made an important contribution to the discipline, initially by raising awareness of the criminality of those with power, and then by progressively providing insight into the pervasiveness of corruption, or serious incompetence from the level of the individual (see Arvelund, 2009; Zuckoff, 2006), the corporation (see Bakan, 2005; Pearce, 1976; Sutherland, 1985), the regulatory authority (see Fooks, 2003) and the government and political class (see McCoy, 2003; Pearce, 1976; Wilson and Lindsey, 2009). This forensic tradition within criminology is an important one, and one which ought to continue not only within the field of academia – where its role in tracking the changing shape of criminality is essential – but also within the public domain, to underpin popular recognition of the actual nature of the organisations and institutions which pervade our lives, not to mention the powerful individuals who operate within them.

Within the burgeoning sphere of blogging and social media, such a critical stance is already well-established. However, despite the important contributions of several dedicated journalists (see for example Monbiot, 2011), the accounts of white-collar criminality offered by mainstream, corporate-controlled media often reflect the 'official line' of the business world. These interpretations largely remain at the level of rare individual pathology, allowing for the public flagellation of occasional 'bad apples' but not the systematic investigation of wider economic and business culture. The invocation of individual pathology as occasional aberration within this realm is of clear political utility; the deracination of action from its socio-economic context means that ameliorative intervention need not focus at any level other than the individual and that the systemic violence of capitalism remains distinctly off the agenda. Through the vilification of 'pathological' individuals such as Bernard Madoff, capitalism's role in the cultivation of criminality and social pathologies remains hidden (Žižek, 2009a: 35–37), and it is possibly for this reason that many academics have remained wary of the underlying logic that frames such explanations.

As a result of the tendency within rightist criminology to bind inextricably notions of pathology and criminality with biological, moral or economic deficit, the dominance of leftist theorists within white-collar crime debates becomes almost axiomatic. As noted above, theoretical claims implicating the economic and cultural features of late capitalism in the generation of corporate and white-collar crime are now well established. However, the *specific ways* in which these cultures manifest themselves at the level of the individual white-collar criminal has been subject to far less academic scrutiny. Whilst this may be the result of the notorious difficulties in gaining access to high-status offenders as research subjects, it is possibly more closely related to the fear that the study of criminal subjectivities may lead towards accounts of criminality rooted within 'rightist' notions of individual pathology. Whatever the reason, we believe that there is a real need to understand more fully the ways in which the human psyche and human action are shaped by the cultural contexts within which they exist. This will inevitably require moving beyond the restatement of simplistic statements about the relationships between dominant structural and cultural forms and white-collar criminality; rather, using qualitative methods, criminology must extend its enquiry to the mechanisms by which dominant cultural and socio-economic forms interact with personal and biographical details in order to form criminal motivations at the level of the individual.

Such a focus does not shirk from recognising structural pathology. Rather, the successful theorisation of criminal subjectivities will allow us to understand more fully the pathological features of the capitalist system, even those which manifest themselves at the level of the individual. This entails a more detailed analysis of how prevailing cultures of greed, competition and profit interact with, and manifest themselves within, the individual subject. Through a focus upon criminal subjectivities, we may be able to shake off accusations of economic determinism and over-prediction by being able to account for how particular individuals become involved in crime. Indeed, development of theory in this direction seems especially important in light of emerging theories which posit correlations and causal relations between ideology, everyday experience, external structures and the individual's neurological make-up (see Hall, 2012; Johnston, 2008; Žižek, 2009a: 55). Central to the leftist thesis on white-collar criminality is the way in which capitalism's profit imperative has systematically evaded or eroded meaningful regulation within the business and financial sectors, opening up chasms in which criminal subjectivities are allowed to flourish. However, without interrogation of criminal subjectivities themselves, and some insight into their desires, it is only by appeal to the rational actor that this area of theory is able to 'shed light' on the motivational aspect of white-collar offending. Undoubtedly, within these conditions the rewards for criminality can be potentially very lucrative, whilst the likelihood of detection is low and the consequences of detection relatively minor. Add to this the consideration that following prosecution, high-status offenders are able to avoid being stigmatised as 'criminal' amongst peers (Benson, 1985), then one could be forgiven for assuming that this is motivation enough for the engagement in white-collar criminality. However, we cannot *assume* rational calculating subjectivity; we must theorise the conditions under which humans might act rationally, while at the same time it seems reasonable to accept that at best 'rational action' cannot fully account for involvement in criminal activity on the part of actors who are in fact far less calculating and predictable than this position assumes. Indeed one might argue that the rational actor model of motivation be abandoned given its central role in dominant ideologies around all kinds of offending. That is, by beginning from the core ontological assumption that the pursuit of advancement over others and of profit and gain ('benefits') at any cost is 'rational', many of the criminogenic features of late-capitalist ideology become naturalised and therefore unavailable to critical scrutiny. At the same time, we fail to account for the (irrational) drives and desires that underlie human choice and action, and give meaning and forge libidinal attachment to what the actor regards as 'benefits', *and* the cultural and economic forces which, in turn, shape and are shaped by these drives and desires.

There is a further point to be made here. We need to put the rational actor model as applied to the corporation in its place. This does not mean abandoning this characterisation altogether, as there remain good *political* reasons for challenging the actions of corporations on the basis of their claims of rationality. However, anthropomorphising the corporation has also generated political and theoretical costs: it allows the continuation of disavowal of responsibility among individuals involved in corporate offending; it has obscured the need to theorise the individual offender; and it lends support to views of corporations which endow them with the actuality or possibility of a personality, good citizenship and social responsibility, the latter in fact being legal, social and political constructions which empower the corporate form to prevail as a structure of irresponsibility (Glasbeek, 2007).

In order to move towards this more holistic understanding of corporate and white-collar criminality, it is also necessary to avoid focusing simply upon contemporary cultural dynamics. Theorising, therefore, needs to take account of the shape and nature of white-collar criminality beyond the relatively short period of late capitalism and to understand the complex interaction of human proclivities with various cultural and socio-economic forms. It is only in doing so that we can come to fully comprehend the effects of late-capitalist culture on human subjectivities and vice-versa. The lack of theoretical development in this direction is inextricably linked to another shortcoming of much of our discipline, namely the unwillingness to engage in an interdisciplinary approach to the explanation of criminality. By stepping outside of the boundaries of late capitalism, the theorist is simultaneously forced to move beyond the normal boundaries of their discipline, which stress the role of socialisation into contemporary cultural and economic forms. Rather, by reconnecting sociology with its philosophical and historical roots, theorising can move more towards the 'theory of society' model employed by the Frankfurt School theorists, in which sociology is merely one contributory discipline (Tar, 1977: 137). There are, of course, already examples of interdisciplinary theorising within this area, but it tends to remain as the preserve of the few (see for examples Gadd and Jefferson, 2007; Hall *et al.*, 2008; Ruggiero, 2009). Thus, it is our contention that criminology, as a discipline, must extend both its temporal and disciplinary frames of reference in order to move forward and that changes in this direction would facilitate more successful theorisation of the white-collar criminal.

The neoliberal reshaping of opportunity structures for corporate and white-collar crime

Following Jameson's suggestion that late capitalism represents 'a *purer* stage of capitalism than any of the moments that preceded it' (Jameson, 1991: 3), we must understand our current epoch and the recent restoration of neoliberal economics and elite privilege (see Badiou, 2008; Harvey, 2007) within its historical context. The cultural and economic features of our own period are best viewed in terms of their role in the 'purification' of the capitalist system, paving the way for the absolute 'freedom' of capital: the cultivation and reproduction of criminogenic values and the 'deregulation' of business and finance must no longer be conceived of as dysfunctions of the system but rather as playing a pivotal role in the expansion of capital. For this reason, Monbiot (2011) has recently suggested that our failure effectively to regulate capital can no longer be seen as a 'perversion of the system'; rather, he suggests, 'it is the system'.

Despite dominant political and academic consensus surrounding this failure in regulation, the development of neoliberalism is not to be understood simply as a story of deregulation. On such a reading, the contraction of the state is central to the restoration of neoliberal economics; private capital is granted free rein to operate with little or no interference from the state and its regulatory bodies. Thus, as distance between markets and regulatory oversight appears to increase, and as private capital becomes more heavily involved in the provision of 'public' service, opportunities for white-collar criminality proliferate. However, neoliberalism is not synonymous with *laissez-faire* (Amable, 2011), notwithstanding many of the claims of its advocates. Simplistic accounts based on a 'state–market' dichotomy obscure the fact that 'neoliberal' states have engaged and must continue to engage in an awful lot of work to construct free corporations in free markets.[2] During the years of Conservative rule, rather than acting simply to deregulate markets as is often suggested, governments introduced a series of regulatory forms that feverishly *promoted* market activity. Thus, the privatisation of energy, telecommunications and rail was accompanied by a mass of regulatory institutions designed to establish and maintain what were effectively new, state-constructed markets (Prosser, 1997). Consequently, government's role increasingly shifted from service provider to the chief architect in the construction and regulation of markets. The rhetoric which accompanied this period of neoliberalism gave little acknowledgement to the state's role in the creation and maintenance of these markets, focusing instead, upon the need to *reduce* government 'interference' in the economy, maintaining the fiction of an ontological separation between state and market (Crouch, 2011). In other words, the empirical evidence suggests that the period spanned by the Conservative governments was a complex, and at times incoherent, era of re-regulation. Nevertheless, the idea of deregulation, itself claimed as economically determined by the seemingly naturally unfolding of neoliberalism-as-globalisation, strengthened during this period.

Under the guise of greater 'choice' and 'efficiency', the interweaving of state and private capital continued at pace under the New Labour government. The arrangements involved in transfers of ownership from the state – which had created *new* and significant popular and political dependencies upon private capital, given the centrality of the goods and services now in private hands – continued to become more opaque. Crudely, such arrangements represented mechanisms for effectively privatising profits while socialising financial risks in areas previously untouched by private sector involvement, a paradigmatic and infamous instance being in the health care sector. The case of the Private Finance Initiative is paradigmatic here: literally hundreds of billions of pounds at stake within an oligopolistic and opaque bidding and contractual process[3] represents significant, new material opportunity structures for corporate and white-collar crime, overseen by states at both national and local level. Indeed, the very form of these relationships can be viewed, from a criminological point of view, as crime-facilitative – despite the fact that criminology has been silent about these criminogenic contractual relationships.

Furthermore, as part of Prime Minister Tony Blair's commitment to cultivate a 'deeper and intensified relationship' with business (Blair, cited in Osler, 2002: 212), the Labour Party embarked on a material and ideological assault on regulation. In the material sense, this agenda can be discerned in the powers of the Regulatory Reform Act 2001, which aimed to remove or reduce regulatory 'burdens'. In 2004, whilst launching the Hampton Review, Gordon Brown advocated the introduction of a new system of regulation which would be characterised by 'not just a light touch, but a limited touch' (Brown, 2005). This 'limited touch' being proposed by Brown had the potential to be catastrophic in terms of the state's ability to combat white-collar and corporate criminality, as the review's remit encompassed sixty-three major regulatory bodies including the Financial Services Authority, the Health and Safety Executive and the Environment Agency (Hampton, 2005, 13); in other words, every agency which played a role in the detection of white-collar and corporate criminality.

This shift in the state's regulatory capabilities was simultaneously accompanied by an ideological assault which took the form of a long term, drip-drip type of discursive framing – which was rapidly accepted as common sense – of regulation as 'red tape' that created a 'burden on business'. Thus, if political myth would have it that it was the Thatcher governments which were generally deregulatory, the reality was much more complex: it is in fact the last decade where we see the most sustained series of *actually* deregulatory initiatives, even if the latter tended to be unfolded somewhat below the political and popular radar.

The implications of these brief observations for new directions in theorising corporate and white-collar criminality are two-fold, yet intimately related. First, we need to think beyond state–market dichotomies and simple accounts of deregulation which suggest an ongoing withdrawal of the state from markets. Second, in the ongoing state creation of re-regulated markets, we need to assign greater centrality to a refashioned concept of state–corporate crime, albeit one which understands the relationship between the two as an ongoing and complex process of interdependence, which facilitates new opportunities for criminality (Tombs, 2011). In other words, markets were created and recreated in which material factors created greater physical opportunities for criminal activity and the predominance of private capital within these markets, which, moreover, meant that in this overall context psychological drivers for criminality also flourished, a point to which we now turn.

The 'moral capital' of capital: the unfolding moralities of neoliberal capitalism

Forty years after the first governmental experiment in neoliberalism, the political – and some might argue academic – consensus is that the era of state management of national economies has clearly passed; so too has the moral collectivism upon which it was founded, replaced by a trenchant ethos of individualism. For neoliberal ideologues, the claim is that these shifts have been economically *determined*; they represent the triumph of capitalist expansion and efficiency over the inefficiency of state interference within mixed economies, and 'totalitarian' regimes committed to centrally planned economies. Globalisation, then, is the necessary consequence of the national successes and inherent dynamism of neoliberalism. In this Randian form of logic, healthy societies are a product of the competitive self-reliance of men, women and their families. Here, too, we recognise that the neoliberal project cannot be simply defined in terms of economics; it has, too, a moral core (Amable, 2011).

Thus, with the emergence to dominance of neoliberalism, one can discern a *moral* aspect to the new status of private capital: private economic activity was elevated to the status of an intrinsically worthy end in itself (Frank, 2001), as opposed to a *means* to some other end. Consequently, the 'moral capital' attached to business activity has increased dramatically over the past 30 years. Private enterprise, entrepreneurship, the pursuit of wealth, and the 'market' have all become valorised *as ends in themselves*. Just as paid work came to be invested with moral meaning throughout the industrial epoch, private individuals and institutions that control work and business activity have increasingly come to be seen as moral agents within our own society. One index of this development is that as citizens we are constantly encouraged to believe that the 'success' or 'failure' of business activity matters to us. Witness, for example, the massive growth in business reporting across a range of media over the past quarter-century. Far from being restricted to the economic and business spheres, however, the hegemonic status of private capital has also come to permeate the world of popular culture. Taking on the identity of celebrity, 'successful' entrepreneurs – Brady, Branson, Sugar, Trump, to name but a few – have entered popular consciousness through fronting or participating in entertainment shows such as *The Apprentice* or *Dragon's Den*. Through a plethora of synoptic vehicles, they are represented as *ego ideal*, valorising atomism, acquisitiveness, avarice and ruthless 'undertaking' (see Hall, 2012). Somewhat differently, on his death in 2011, Steve Jobs was hailed as an innovator of style who had changed people's lives and the ways 'we' live our world, rather than as the driving force behind a ruthless, profit-maximising, global entity. Indeed, not content with being models of 'entrepreneurialism', many such figures have sought also to represent themselves as figures involved in both political and charitable spheres. Thus while heading a corporation mired in a long running refusal to pay European Commission-levied fines for anti-competitive practices, to the tune of hundreds of millions of US dollars, popular representations of Bill Gates tend more to focus on his Foundation which, amongst various 'philanthropic' activities, is currently freeing the under-developed world from malaria. Such is the power of Žižek's 'liberal communists' (Žižek, 2009b); their cultural as well as economic domination ensures that they are often perceived as a panacea to economic and social problems, and this domination is more than just hegemonic, as we have said, but inscribed in the neurological systems and desires of many of the children of neoliberalism.

Indeed, Peter Mandelson, as secretary of state for trade and industry, attempted to forge an inextricable link between the idea of the business-person-as-celebrity with the wider economic health of the 'country':

> We want a society that celebrates and values its business heroes as much it does its pop stars and footballers. So we must remove the barriers to enterprise in this country, reward risk-taking, and encourage innovation and creativity.
> (Mandelson, 2 November 1998, cited in Elliott and Atkinson, 2007: 47)

Now, it is crucial to emphasise that the increasing salience of private capital is not 'mere' ideology or appearance (Fisher, 2009; Geras, 1972). In a real sense, the business world affects a much greater number of us than was the case 30 years ago. As we have seen, private capital has come to dominate in the provision of both essential and peripheral services within late capitalism, creating a new class of dependent consumers, often in oligopolistic markets where there is in fact little 'choice' to be exercised. In addition, as social insurance has diminished, people have increasingly come to have stakes in either private pensions or in savings schemes linked directly to company and stock exchange performance. This has created both a real and an exaggerated belief amongst many of us that we have a major stake in the effective functioning of the central institutions of the corporate world in general, and the financial sector in particular. This furthers the ideology that business interests – which are by definition sectional interests arising out of activity conducted for clear motives – are synonymous with 'general' or 'national' interests.

In short, private capital has become so heavily involved in the provision of goods and services in late capitalism that both practical and psychological dependencies upon it have come to be an intractable part of late-modern life. This is of crucial import in the production of new opportunity structures for corporate and white-collar crime. Raising the status – the moral and cultural capital – of private business and of the men and women who control, manage and work successfully within it according to its core logic creates new opportunities for the ruthless psychological motivations of the entrepreneurial 'undertakers' to cross the border into criminality: to put this in familiar criminological terms, new, intensified and ubiquitous forms of motivations and techniques of neutralisation simultaneously become socially produced and available. At the same time, these shifts also serve to undermine the legitimacy of those charged with preventing and responding to such crimes. Inevitably, state regulators now operate upon a terrain in which their cultural capital and leverage has been significantly reduced. As these new realities interact, what is deemed acceptable in and on behalf of the corporate world shifts, which in turn shifts cultural definitions of illegality towards support for greater freedoms for corporate activities from the anti-entrepreneurial instincts of states and their regulators.

The ideological transformation to which we have alluded has involved ascribing a moral status not so much to *particular* businesses – this would be a difficult task given the evidence of amorality, immorality or criminality on the part of individual business organisations – but to business, or rather 'capital', in general. The superiority of the private over the allegedly wasteful, inefficient, intrusive and freedom-negating public sector is now *obvious*. At the same time, this distinction between capital in general and specific companies or businessmen and women at specific times allows a further paradox to be ideologically resolved. If, as we have claimed, popular investment (literally and metaphorically) in the private sector is real as well as ideological, then this creates a challenge where corporate wrong-doing is in fact exposed. In other words, how can wrongdoing on the part of particular companies be managed politically in an era where minimal regulation is deemed preferable? The answer is an ideological one, provided by the increasingly ubiquitous claims of 'corporate social responsibility' (CSR). That is, the rise of CSR discourse squares the circle of greater risk and less regulation; or, more accurately, both deregulation *and* forms of re-regulation which in themselves create greater risk in the form of opportunity structures for criminal motivations and activity. At the same time, it allows for normal business behaviour to be decried as aberrant or marginal.

Let us be clear about the challenges that the claims presented in this section pose for theorising white-collar and corporate crime. The increasing 'moral capital' of capitalism itself in recent decades is indeed a cultural transformation, but it is only comprehensible in relation to a series of material *and* subjective changes. Thus we need to grasp the dynamic cultural and symbolic aspects of any society which make white-collar and corporate crime more (or less) likely, as well as the ways in which these impact upon the level of regulation of corporate activity. Further, we need more generally to reflect upon the extent to which such changes become so entrenched and generalised that they prevent us from thinking about alternative forms of organisation (Fisher, 2009), even in fairly limited respects, for example the acceptance of state definitions of feasible levels and forms of regulation as creating the parameters within which regulatory 'reform' can be proposed and achieved (Tombs and Whyte, 2010: 47–50). As we indicate in our concluding section, a criminology of corporate and white-collar crime must break free from such cultural shackles.

Some concluding comments: a post-crisis criminology of the crimes of the powerful?

The study of white-collar and corporate crime found its natural home within the critical and radical branches of the discipline of criminology. From this position, academics were able to transcend criminology's traditional focus on street criminality and, instead, set their sights upon the criminal acts of powerful members of society, which had historically remained absent from criminological agendas. Some, in the tradition of Bonger (1916), went further, identifying the criminogenic nature of capitalism itself. Thus, certain branches of criminology came to be rooted in a politicised, transformative agenda. This properly radical/critical approach is, for us, the logical extension of the study of crime and criminality. As criminologists, charged with the business of identifying and explaining some of the key maladies and dysfunctions of our society, we have an obligation to explore critically the relative weight attached to such maladies. Acting on these obligations is not necessarily to engage in moral entrepreneurship, but it must entail reflecting upon and engaging with the political implications of our role as social 'scientists'.

In the latter context, there are many forms of political action that can come from our role as theorists. Here we note two, which will be familiar to many readers. One form of political action which can originate from criminological enquiry is an area in which radical criminologists have achieved some successes, albeit never secure – an obvious and important area to point to here are the achievements of feminist social scientists and criminologists, working as part of wider social movements against forms of domestic and sexual violence. In relation to white-collar and corporate criminality, progressive work will continue to seek to identify and expose areas in which harm occurs, and to apply pressure towards more meaningful regulation and the reduction of harm within these particular settings. This can produce improvements in the protection of individuals as employees, consumers and so on, reducing opportunities for criminality, corruption and exploitation. We might term this form of political intervention, with no claim of originality, as reformist – at one extreme as *merely* reformist, and at its most radical variant, as proposing *non-reformist reforms* (Gorz, 1980). A second, distinct type of political action involves the development of social and political ideals with which to change society in accordance with the unmasking of the systemic causes of corporate and white-collar criminality. This *transformative* approach is one generally absent from corporate and white-collar crime agendas. This is perhaps curious. For those working in these areas have striven tirelessly to produce detailed accounts of the ways in which the capitalist form cultivates criminality: states' dependence upon capital necessarily undermines effective regulatory efforts; the ways in which the legally constructed and politically maintained corporate form *per se* is criminogenic, albeit to greater or lesser extents; and the various aspects of late-capitalist culture which play a role in the cultivation of criminal motivations in the subject (so that we are now well aware of the ways in which short-termism, narcissism, competitive individualism, the valorisation of material success, or the pursuit of profit above all other goals may combine to form conditions in which criminality becomes all the more likely). Thus, criminology has been unambiguous in its suggestion that the socio-economic, psychological and cultural features of capitalism play an instrumental role in the cultivation of white-collar and corporate criminality. Yet involvement in the search for alternatives remains limited, and the lack of participation in debates regarding wider political ideals is particularly curious.

The two forms of political action we identified above – versions of reformist and transformative criminology – are not, of course, mutually exclusive. Reformist work can contribute to effecting real, progressive changes to people's lives. However, without a simultaneous commitment to a transformative project, reformism remains limited to working towards a capitalism that is a little less socially and ecologically harmful. It is only if and when we can address the overhaul of the current form of economic organisation that the reduction of the deep cultural malaise and systemic violence inherent within contemporary capitalism becomes possible. Therefore, we must also contribute as criminologists to debates about alternative forms of political and economic organisation. Moreover, this is a pressing task. There is a tendency to refer to current crises in the past, and to bemoan the fact that the political opportunities presented by them have also passed. In contrast, for us, the lived experiences of people across the world indicate that the human suffering caused by the crimes of neoliberal capitalism has barely begun. Thus it would seem that there has never been a more appropriate time to focus new forms of critical scrutiny upon corporate and white-collar crimes and harms.

Notes

1 Not to mention that it continues to dominate academic thinking in the guise of 'responsive regulation'; see Tombs and Whyte (2010: 47–50).
2 Albeit there are quite distinct views of how such activity proceeds; see, for example, Polanyi (1971/1944); Sayer (1995); Vogel (1996).
3 See Pollock (2011), for an excellent overview critique of the costs, lack of accountability and opaqueness associated with such contracts.

References

Amable, B. (2011) 'Morals and Politics in the Ideology of Neo-liberalism', *Socio-Economic Review* 9(1): 3–30.

Arvelund, E. (2009) *Madoff: The Man Who Stole $65 Billion*. London: Penguin.

Badiou, A. (2008) *The Century*. Cambridge: Polity.

Bakan, J. (2005) *The Corporation: The Pathological Pursuit of Profit and Power*. London: Constable.

Benson, M. (1985) 'Denying the Guilty Mind: Accounting for Involvement in a White-Collar Crime', *Criminology* 23(4): 583–607.

Bonger, W. (1916) *Criminality and Economic Conditions*. London: William Heinemann.

Brown, G. (2008) 'America Has Embraced the Values of Progress', *Observer*, 9 November. www.guardian.co.uk/commentisfree/2008/nov/09/barack-obama-gordon-brown

—— (2005) 'A Plan to Lighten the Regulatory Burden on Business', *Financial Times*, 23 May.

Crouch, C. (2011) *The Strange Non-Death of Neoliberalism*. Cambridge: Polity.

Dean, J. (2009) *Democracy and Other Neoliberal Fantasies: Communicative Capitalism and Left Politics*. Durham, NC: Duke University Press.

Elliott, L. and Atkinson, D. (2007) *Fantasy Island: Waking Up to the Incredible Economic, Political and Social Illusions of the Blair Legacy*. London: Constable.

Fisher, M. (2009) *Capitalist Realism: Is There Really No Alternative?* Winchester: Zero Books.

Fooks, G. (2003) 'In the Valley of the Blind the One Eyed Man is King: Corporate Crime and the Myopia of Financial Regulation', in Tombs, S. and Whyte, D. (eds) *Unmasking the Crimes of the Powerful: Scrutinizing States and Corporations*. New York: Peter Lang.

Frank, T. (2001) *One Nation Under God: Extreme Capitalism, Market Populism and the End of Market Democracy*. London: Secker and Warburg.

Gadd, D. and Jefferson, T. (2007) *Psychosocial Criminology: An Introduction*. London: Sage.

Gamble, A. (2009) *The Spectre at the Feast: Capitalist Crisis and the Politics of Recession*. London: Palgrave Macmillan.

Geras, N. (1972) 'Marx and the Critique of Political Economy', in Blackburn, R. (ed.) *Ideology in Social Science: Readings in Critical Social Theory*. London: Fontana.

Glasbeek, H. (2007) 'The Corporation as a Legally Created Site of Irresponsibility', in Pontell, H. and Geis, G. (eds.) *International Handbook of White-Collar and Corporate Crime*. New York: Springer.

Gorz, A. (1980) *Ecology as Politics*. London: Pluto.

Hall, S. (2012) *Theorizing Crime and Deviance: A New Perspective*. London: Sage

Hall, S., Winlow, S. and Ancrum, C. (2008) *Criminal Identities and Consumer Culture: Crime, Exclusion and the New Culture of Narcissism*. London: Willan/Routledge.

Hampton, P. (2005) *Reducing Administrative Burdens: Effective Inspection and Enforcement*. London: HM Treasury/HMSO.

Harvey, D. (2007) *A Brief History of Neoliberalism*. Oxford: Oxford University Press.

Hay, C. and Watson, M. (1998) 'The Discourse of Globalisation and the Logic of No Alternative: Rendering the Contingent Necessary in the Downsizing of New Labour's Aspirations for Government', in Dobson, A. and Stanyer, J. (eds) *Contemporary Political Studies 1998, Volume II*. Nottingham: Political Studies Association: 812–822.

Hillyard, P., Sim, J., Tombs, S. and Whyte, D. (2004) 'Leaving a Stain Upon the Silence: Contemporary Criminology and the Politics of Dissent', *British Journal of Criminology* 44(3): 369–90.

Jameson, F. (1991) *Postmodernism: Or, the Cultural Logic of Late Capitalism*. London: Verso.

Johnston, A. (2008) *Žižek's Ontology: A Transcendental Materialist Theory of Subjectivity*. Evanston, IL: Northwestern University Press.

Levi, M. (2008) *The Phantom Capitalists: The Organisation and Control of Long-firm Fraud*. 2nd edn. Andover: Ashgate.

Loader, I. and Sparks, R. (2011) *Public Criminology?* London: Routledge.

McCoy, A. (2003) *The Politics of Heroin: CIA Complicity in the Global Drug Trade*. Chicago: Lawrence Hill.

Monbiot, G. (2011) 'To Us, It's an Obscure Shift of Tax Law. To the City, It's the Heist of the Century', *Guardian*, 7 February.

National Audit Office (2009) *Maintaining Financial Stability across the United Kingdom's Banking System*, London: The Stationery Office.

Osler, D. (2002) *Labour Party Plc. New Labour as a Party of Business*. Edinburgh: Mainstream.

Parker, D. (2004) *The UK's Privatisation Experiment: The Passage of Time Permits a Sober Assessment*. CESifo Working Paper 1126 (online). Available at: www.cesifo.de/pls/guestci/download/CESifo+Working+Papers+2004/CESifo+Working+Papers+February+2004/cesifo1_wp1126.pdf

Pearce, F. (1976) *Crimes of the Powerful: Marxism, Crime and Deviance*. London: Pluto.

Polanyi, K. (1971/1944) *The Great Transformation*. Boston: Beacon Press.

Pollock, A. (2011) *Evidence Submitted to the Treasury Committee Inquiry into the Future of the Private Finance Initiative*. Online. Available at: www.allysonpollock.co.uk/administrator/components/com_article/attach/2011-06-26/AP_2011_Pollock_TreasuryCtteePFI.pdf

Prosser, T. (1997) *Law and the Regulators*. Oxford: Clarendon Press.

Ruggiero, V. (2009) 'On Liberty and Crime: Adam Smith and John Stuart Mill', *Crime, Law and Social Change* 51: 435–50.

Sayer, A. (1995) *Radical Political Economy: A Critique*. Oxford: Blackwell.

Stiegler, B. (2010) *For a New Critique of Political Economy*. Cambridge: Polity Press.

Sutherland, E. (1985) *White Collar Crime: The Uncut Version*. New Haven, CT: Yale University Press.

Tar, Z. (1977) *The Frankfurt School: The Critical Theories of Max Horkheimer and Theodor W. Adorno*. London: Wiley.

Telegraph (2003) *Berlusconi Granted Legal Immunity*. 18 June (online). Available at www.telegraph.co.uk

Tombs, S. (2011) 'State Complicity in the Production of Corporate Crime', in Gobert, J. and Pascal, A-M. (eds) *European Developments in Corporate Criminal Liability*. London: Routledge.

Tombs, S. and Whyte, D. (2010) 'A Deadly Consensus: Worker Safety and Regulatory Degradation under New Labour', *British Journal of Criminology* 50(1): 46–65.

Vogel, S. (1996) *Freer Markets, More Rules: Regulatory Reform in Advanced Industrial Countries*. Ithaca, NY: Cornell University Press.

Wilson, E. and Lindsey, T. (eds) (2009) *Government of the Shadows: Parapolitics and Criminal Sovereignty*. London: Pluto.

Žižek, S. (2009a) *First as Tragedy, Then as Farce*. London: Verso.

—— (2009b) *Violence*. London: Profile Books.

Zuckoff, M. (2006) *Ponzi's Scheme: The True Story of a Financial Legend*. New York: Random House.

17 Crimes against reality

Parapolitics, simulation, power crime

Eric Wilson

> The question of modernity and post-modernity is superseded by that of reality and post-reality.
>
> (Paul Virilio)

If you do not know what you are looking at you will not know what to see.

All of the structural features of cyber-capitalism that have proven central to the global financial crisis – deregulation, derivatives trading, high-speed electronic finance – can only be understood from within a criminological perspective. By this I mean that the contemporary world economy bears all of the necessary attributes of a criminogenic phenomenon, one in which criminal activities – or, at the very least, processes that are of marginal legality – are effectively 'folded' into accepted institutional praxis, effecting a virtual disappearance of the 'criminal' into the 'lawful'. Here, I am expanding upon the notion of 'criminogenic asymmetries' as pioneered by Nikos Passas, for whom criminogenic phenomena constitute:

> [S]tructural disparities, mismatches and inequalities in the spheres of politics, culture, the economy and the law. Asymmetries are criminogenic in that (1) they generate or strengthen the demand for illegal goods and services; (2) they generate incentives for particular actors to participate in illegal transactions; (3) they reduce the ability of authorities to control illegal activities.
>
> (Passas 2000: 23)

There are two critical features to note in this definition. The first is the determining supply-and-demand logic at work that serves to underpin a mimetic relationship between licit and illicit market forces:

> Asymmetries generate the demand for goods that are illegal, unethical or embarrassing. Illegal markets follow the rules of supply and demand, sometimes even more strictly than legitimate markets – because the latter often enjoy protective measures introduced by nation states or groups of

states. Whenever there is a gap between local demand and supply, cross-border trade is likely to develop. If the goods or services happen to be outlawed, then illegal enterprises will emerge to meet the demand. In this respect, there is no difference between conventional and criminal enterprises.

(Passas 2000: 24)

The final sentence is the crucial one. Criminogenic asymmetries subvert orthodox conceptions of legitimacy that demarcate the conventional boundaries between the 'legal' and the 'illegal'. The mimetic effect produced by the criminogenic is that legal and illegal actors begin to imitate, and even appropriate, the reasoning and behaviour of the other (Passas and Nelken 1993). This leads to the second critical feature: the criminogenic does not merely denote the criminal but the far more subversive category of the 'supra-' or 'extra-legal' as well. The collapse of orthodox modes of juridical demarcation yields an epistemic crisis within political culture in which parallel market structures become effectively de-criminalized through the tactical alterations of public discourse; the market 'doesn't bypass the state in the deregulated financial environment. On the contrary, it is all the more central to it. State institutions ... have a powerful ability to administer the referents' (Wark 1994: 185). Employing a similar imaginary, Passas argues that 'when the business is illegal all that changes are some adjustments in *modus operandi*, technology, and the social networks that will be involved. In some cases, we have a mere re-description of practices to make them appear outside legal prohibitive provisions' (Passas 2000: 24). The realm of the criminogenic itself constitutes the site of a particular form of disappearance: the eradication of the border between Law and Crime.

This radical iterability, or reversibility, between Crime and Law necessarily forces the critical criminologist to consider the phenomenon of 'political crime' – or, even more subversively, 'politics-as-crime' – as a legitimate subject of criminological investigation (Wilson 2009a).[1] Fortunately, the criminological dimension of 'political crime' has already been usefully formulated through the academic discipline of parapolitics, the study of the 'collusion between legal and illegal forces', or, more broadly, 'all those political practices and arrangements, deliberate or not, which are usually repressed rather than acknowledged' (Scott 2008: 14). It is only through establishing a theoretically sophisticated understanding of the relationships between the criminogenic and the parapolitical that the progressive criminologist will be able to come to methodological terms with political crime.

Parapolitics: the criminological turn

> You don't notice that what you don't know isn't there.
>
> (Jerome Lindon)

The seminal figure in parapolitical studies is Peter Dale Scott, who strives to formulate a new terminology, or even a poetics, through which to convey new understandings of hitherto un-describable political phenomena. Two of Scott's signature concepts, 'parapolitics' and the 'dual state' bear a striking resemblance to Passas's notion of criminogenic asymmetries and are, therefore, of considerable criminological significance:

> Parapolitics: 1. A system or practice of politics in which accountability is consciously diminished. 2. Generally, covert politics, the conduct of public affairs not by rational debate and responsible decision-making but by indirection, collusion, and deceit. Cf. *conspiracy*. 3. The political exploitation of irresponsible agencies or parastructures, such as intelligence agencies.
>
> (Scott 2008: 238)

> The Dual State. A *State* in which one can distinguish between a *public state* and a top-down *deep state*. The deep state emerges in a false-flag violence, is organized by the military and intelligence apparatus and involves their link to organized crime. Most states exhibit this duality, but to varying degrees. In America the duality of the state has become more and more acute since World War II.
>
> (Scott 2008: 238)[2]

Scott's language has been strongly influenced by that of the Swedish national security scholar Ola Tunander, who was the first to coin the term 'security state'. Again, the vital issue is that extra-judicial convergence of the public body with covert agency which can only be described as parapolitical:

> After September 11, the U.S. 'democratic state' (characterised by openness, legal procedures and free elections) is forcefully ... subsumed under a 'security state' (characterised by secrecy and military hierarchy). Much of the public life is 'securitized' and the President and his close advisors are focused on the War on Terror, not on civilian matters. 'I am a war President. I make decisions ... with war on my mind.' President Bush said.
>
> (Tunander in Scott 2007: 244)

Although Tunander does not exhibit Scott's pronounced concern with organized crime as a central parapolitical component of the dual state, the introduction of the criminogenic into the parapolitical imaginary yields a new conceptual edifice: criminal sovereignty. This has been explored most thoroughly by Robert Cribb:

> Parapolitics, then, is the study of criminal sovereignty, of criminals behaving as sovereigns and sovereigns behaving as criminals in a systematic way. It was not just a topic but an analytical conclusion. On the one hand, it goes significantly beyond the proposition that relations between security and intelligence organisations, international criminal networks and quasi-states are occasional and incidental, the work of 'rogue elements' and the like. On

the other hand, it falls significantly short of grand conspiracy theory: it does not suggest that the world of visible, 'normal' politics is an illusion or that it is entirely subordinated to 'deep' politics. Rather, it proposes that the tripartite relationship between security and intelligence organisations, international criminal networks and quasi-states is systematic, extensive and influential. The task of parapolitics as a discipline is to identify the dynamics of that relationship and to delimit precisely the influence that it has, or does not have, on public politics.

(Cribb 2009: 8)

Understood this way, we can hypothesize that all parapolitical phenomena would possess four necessary attributes: duality (the iterable relationship between 'Law' and 'Crime'); governance (the collapse of the distinction between 'public state' and 'civil society', resulting in an open-ended 'privatization' of the state); nomadicism[3] (a chaotic proliferation of supra-statist, statist, and sub-statist entities, all of an indeterminate legal nature, that regularly traverse established juro-political boundaries); and the irrational (the invisible co-option of the 'public interest' by the 'private actor'). As radical criminologists the irrationality of parapolitics is what interests us the most; for Scott, the essence of the parapolitical is an '*intervening layer of irrationality under our political culture's rational surface*' (Scott 1993: 6–7). The submerged, or repressed nature of criminal sovereignty, is not only an ontological problem but an epistemological one as well; it is precisely because of its irrational essence that the parapolitical evades cognitive recognition, with all of the attendant ideological implications. According to Tunander:

> Liberal political science has been turned into an ideology of the 'deep state' because undisputable evidence for the [national security] 'deep state is brushed away as pure fantasy or conspiracy' (Tunander in Wilson 2009a: 29) . . . Thus, the problem with liberalism in political science and legal theory is not its ambition to defend the public sphere, political freedoms and human rights, but rather its claim that these freedoms and rights define the Western political system.

(Tunander 2009: 68)

If we were to nominate a source of a new 'post-liberal' conceptualization of the dual state, I would suggest the work of the French critical theorist Paul Virilio. Virilio's seminal notions of speed-politics and the logistics of perception not only provide us with the perfect tool for explaining the opaque nature of the parapolitical, but they also enable us to appropriate parapolitical studies as a sub-branch of criminology.

Simulation: Paul Virilio and the logistics of perception

What we see there depends not on sight as such, but on seeing as.

(Sean Cubitt)

For Virilio, and unlike Jean Baudrillard with whom he is frequently and somewhat misleadingly linked, the central feature of 'the post-modern condition' is not the mimetic replacement of reality with the virtual but, in a sort of ontological practical joke, the 'mis-taking' of the model for the reality (Cubitt 2001: 50).[4] Like Baudrillard, Virilio advances a radically circulationist notion of power. However, while simulation equals 'exchange' it does not equal 'substitution'; 'We face a duplication of reality. The virtual and the "real" reality double the relationship to the real, something that, to the best of my knowledge, results in clear pathological consequences' (Oliveira and Virilio 1995: 2). As against:

> [t]he opinion of Baudrillard, I have to say that reality never vanishes. It constantly changes. Reality is the outcome of a pre-determined epoch, science or technique. Reality must be re-invented, always. To me, it is not the simulation of reality that makes the difference, it is the replacement of a pre-determined reality by another pre-determined reality. I proceed from the antagonism between real and virtual reality, and I notice that both will shortly constitute one single reality.
>
> (Oliveira and Virilio 1995: 3)

Reality is not eliminated; however, neither is it merely being mis-perceived. Rather, the phenomenological conduits of reality/perception have themselves been fundamentally altered through both new social relations and new technologies.[5] For Virilio simulation-as-representation is the inability to maintain the dichotomy between the false and the true; Reality has not been abolished but dis-placed. This leaves a phenomenal Reality which, perhaps, affords us some scope of critical excavation of the criminogenic body-substance. Employing the terminology of theoretical physics as a source of metaphor, Virilio, contra Baudrillard, holds that:

> In the past, reality was a matter of mass; then it became mass + force. Today, reality is the outcome of mass + force + information. Matter has now become three dimensional. This is a clear break.
>
> (Oliveira and Virilio 1995: 3)

Virilio's penchant (often criticized) for the scientific imaginary leads him to formulate his central critical notion, one that effectively folds simulation/ simulacra into a much wider framework of critical re-presentation: that of speed. I would argue that Virilio's notion of speed – or, more precisely, of *speed-politics* – is a crucial innovation for two reasons. The first reason is that the concept permits us to advance beyond the neo-Marxist impasse that refuses to allow for any re-conceptualization of capitalism in a non-dialectical manner. On the one hand, speed would appear to serve as an updating of Marx's classic account of space/time compression that figures so largely in innovative contemporary Marxist scholarship, such as David Harvey's seminal *The Limits to Capital*:

> Marx depicts the consequent impulse to revolutionize transport relations in very general terms. Capital, he writes, must 'strive to tear down every spatial barrier to . . . exchange, and conquer the whole earth for its market,' it must 'annihilate this space with time' in order to reduce the turnover time of capital to 'the twinkling of an eye'.
>
> (Harvey 1999: 372)

While Marx's 'annihilation of space with time' is onto-materialist, Virilio's notion of speed as effecting a 'disappearance' of reality/truth is epistemological, annihilation corresponding to a condition that is as much phenomenological as it is historical. I understand Virilian speed as a non-dialectical expression of space/time compression in which the measurable rate, or velocity, of transaction/exchange is itself the primary mode of production and not a merely derivative aspect of production. As Mckenzie Wark perceptively points out, Marx's entire account fails to consider 'the *separation* of communication from transport, or the development of two distinct *velocities* of movement' (Wark: 1994: 221). Conceived in phenomenological terms, speed directly correlates with globalization theory's notion of the critical variable of 'real time communication', defined by Held as 'the manner in which globalization appears to shrink geographical time and distance; in a world of instantaneous communication, distance and time no longer seem to be a major constraint on patterns of social organization or interaction' (Held *et al.* 1999: 15 fn.2).[6]

The second reason is that Virilio's notion of speed grounds criminological theory more directly in the onto-material contours of globalization. I accept Held's definition of this nebulous term, which equates speed with velocity and identifies both as cardinal features of globalized political economy:

> [A] process (or set of processes) which embodies a transformation in the spatial organization of social relations and transactions – assessed in terms of their extensity, intensity, velocity and impact – generating transcontinental or interregional flows and networks of activity, interaction, and the exercise of power.
>
> (Held *et al.* 1999: 16)

Most importantly for criminologists:

> [V]elocity as the 'growing extensity and intensity of global interconnectedness may also imply a *speeding up* of global interactions and processes as the development of worldwide systems of transport and communication increase

the potential velocity of the global diffusion of ideas, goods, information, capital and people'.

(Held *et al*. 1999: 15)[7]

For Virilio, both politics and economics are understood as manifestations of a single geo-strategic phenomenon that is governed by variables of speed, not only in terms of conventional tactical considerations of military force but also in the practice of the domestic politics of the technologically developed state.[8] 'Speed is essential. The temporal compression that we've talked about before results from the power of instantaneous speed, of interactivity, of feedback, etc' (Virilio and Lotringer 2002: 102). The vital centre of Virilian analysis is, in fact, an ontology of speed, the dromosphere (Virilio: 2000: 37–54):

> [T]he true 'cosmic referent' is not light-as-substance but the speed-of-light as a maximal velocity that serves as the contour, or limit of Being. The 'speed of light' equates Being with Optics, resulting in a new 'post-Einsteinian' ontology in which 'truth' is identical with a state of total illumination.
>
> Speed is not at all a 'phenomenon' but only the relation *between* phenomena (relativity itself) . . . This precisely is the *dromosphere*: not so much the expansion of the universe 'brought to light', but a purely relativist recognition that it is speed – not just light and its spectral analysis – which enlightens the universe of perceptible and measurable phenomena.

(Virilio 2000: 45)

The political implications of this optical ontology are dangerous. Speed-politics reduces the being of the state to the panoptical effect of an unlimited transparency that is ultimately self-consuming, what Virilio calls 'the aesthetics of disappearance': 'The state's only original existence is as a visual hallucination akin to dreaming' (Virilio 1989: 33). Politics '*disappears into aesthetics*' precisely through its inability to successfully uphold the 'reality principle', which is premised upon conventional representational demarcations between the 'real', the 'visual', and the 'virtual' (Virilio 1991). Virilio identifies this ontological and political 'loss of reality' with the *kinematic*, which assumes two forms. 'Kinematic optics', or 'cinematic motion', effectively 'dissolves' substance through the acceleration of perception; time supplants space which 'deletes' Being (Virilio 2000: 45). 'Kinematic acceleration' is realized through the 'dismemberment' of space/time into isolated 'frames', or editorial 'cuts'. In both instances of the kinematic the virtual re-presentation of reality is now governed by alterations in the rate, or speed, of perception: 'It is reality [that] we have to measure in a cinematic way' (Virilio 1989: 79–89). The final outcome is a total 'virtualizing' of reality arising from 'the unprecedented limits imposed on subjective perception by the instrumental splitting of modes of perception and representation' (Virilio 1994: 49).

This optical/ontological collapse of politics into speed underlines the key Virilian notion of pure war (Virilio and Lotringer 1997), a military metaphor that signifies the centrality of the panoptical to the contemporary mode of combat. 'The primacy of speed is simultaneously the primacy of the military' (Virilio and Lotringer 1997: 51); pure war is the master-sign of a (post-) modern world-system that is governed by speed-politics, signifying the total reversibility between the 'political', the 'military', and the 'economic'. Politics disappears into a tripartite 'logistics of perception': military, tele-cinematic, and techno-scientific (Virilio 2000).[9] Virilian pure war has been doctrinally expressed by the Pentagon as 'Full-Spectrum Dominance' or 'Rapid Dominance' (Ullman and Wade 1998), or, in the vernacular, 'shock and awe':

> [I]n crude terms [the invader] should seize control of the environment and paralyse or so overload an adversary's perceptions and understanding of events so that the enemy would be incapable of resistance.
>
> (Ullman and Wade cited in Klein 2007: 147 and 333)

As is readily apparent, 'shock and awe' directly correlates with the onto-political kinematics of pure war:

> It is a war of images and sounds, rather than objects and things, in which winning is simply a matter of not losing sight of the opposition. The will to see all, know all, at every moment, everywhere, the will to universalised illumination: a scientific permutation on the eye of God which would forever rule out the surprise, the accident, the irruption of the unforeseen.
>
> (Virilio 1994: 70)

This simultaneous projection of speed into both external and internal political space yields two extremely dangerous developments. One is that it establishes manifold linkages between the pure war and the practical operations of hegemony within international politics. The second is that the logistics of perception creates the preconditions for the extra-legal manipulation of representation by entrenched political and military elites. Both of these developments culminate in the criminogenic transformation of the world system.

Power crime: the virtual state

> Once we have surrendered our senses and nervous systems to the private manipulation of those who would try to benefit from taking a lease on our eyes and ears and nerves, we don't really have any rights left.
>
> (Marshall McLuhan)

It is a profound neurological truth that 'brains more or less take everything in at the lowest levels of perception' (Jourdain 1997: 248). According to Robert Jourdain:

> Because life bombards us with far more information than our paltry

> brainpower can handle, a brain must pick and choose . . . It must work in a *serial* rather than a *parallel* fashion as it apportions scarce neurological resources first to one aspect of a [large structure] and then to another. In a word, the brain must work *strategically*.
>
> (Jourdain 1997: 249)

A 'strategic' brain that, literally, selects its 'targets' of perception is one that is governed by the 'law of similarity': 'similar objects are grouped even when far apart . . . Basically, the brain assumes that the simplest solution is the most likely one' (Jourdain 1997: 247). As a result, a strategically selective process of categorization 'is at the heart of nearly all our mental activity' (Jourdain 1997: 65).

If we were to translate neurology into the referents of the logistics of perception, then we quickly come to realize that we have invented a new form of 'camouflage'. Managed alterations in the rate of visual perception can produce an 'invisibility' that is both literal and metaphorical; vision governed by speed alters *gestalt*. Speed-politics is the medium of the criminogenic: 'This stunning effect of speed is . . . felt through and in power itself' (Virilio and Lotringer 2002: 161). Velocity facilitates pure war through the reduction of the substance of politics to speed (Virilio and Lotringer 2002: 50). Every act of acceleration is an act of violence; 'power will be invested in acceleration itself' (Virilio and Lotringer 1997: 51). In criminological terms, this equates with *power crime*.

For 'power crime', I use the definition provided by Passas (2007). Fraud and corruption:

> [B]y elites that have substantial governmental power or economic power (typically as CEOs). Often, of course, they have both forms of power simultaneously. Elite criminals ['control frauds'] have far greater ability than non-elites to act dynamically to optimize the environment for fraud while 'neutralizing' their crimes psychologically and obtaining substantial impunity.
>
> (Passas and Black 2007: 2)

Passas identifies two 'levels of dynamism' integral to power crime that are of particular interest to me. The first is spatial, 'that elites are able to *choose* to operate wherever the legal, political, economic and cultural environment is most criminogenic and the payoffs to abuse the greatest'. The second is causal, 'that elites are able to *change* the environment [and] . . . make it far more criminogenic' (Passas and Black 2007: 2). If we read this definition through Virilian 'lenses' we come to realize that the criminogenic variable that connects space with causality is speed-politics: the relationship between power and speed, therefore, is of considerable criminological importance. While Passas's account does not explicitly refer to speed, his understanding of power crime is highly conducive to a Virilian analysis, precisely because the essence of power crime is the control over definitions, perceptions, and appearances. Although certainly not reducible to the visual, any critical understanding of power crime would benefit tremendously from careful consideration of the optical dimensions of the phenomenon. 'Normal' crime, because it is a 'low-velocity' phenomenon, is highly susceptible to detection and enforcement: 'Normally, thieves face a fairly symmetrical environment: to steal more they have to take greater risks of detection, prosecution and sanction' (Passas and Black 2007: 2). By contrast, power crime, precisely because it is a 'high-velocity' phenomenon operating on the level of perception – that is, simulation – is able to effectively 'disappear' into a total criminogenic environment of its own making. Accordingly:

> '[E]lite criminals' are the very ones able to create an 'environment in which engaging in massive fraud and corruption *increases* one's political power and status and greatly reduces the risks of detection and prosecution. Elite criminals optimise by creating fraud networks that help them maximize this asymmetry of risk and reward'.
>
> (Passas and Black 2007: 2)

Speed itself facilitates the transformation of the 'real' of a wholly 'virtual' form of reality that effectively supersedes the notions of legality and political accountability.

Power crime understood as simulation – the semiotic inversion of the relationship between truth and appearance – allows us to classify it as a parapolitical phenomenon. It also strongly evokes Cribb's portrayal of the 'super criminal' attributes of the successful parapolitical operator: the 'principal dynamic of parapolitics appeared to be a personal lust for extraordinary power – and a drive to maintain that power – on the part of the parapoliticians' (Cribb 2009: 3). The criminogenic manipulation of the sign-systems that ordinarily demarcate Law from Crime is what identifies both power crime and the elite criminal as parapolitical phenomena. The 'ideal type' of the power criminal, therefore, is the 'media tycoon', enshrined in popular culture as Citizen Kane and embodied within the real-time/real-world frame as Silvio Berlusconi, the recently resigned (but, as yet, unindicted) prime minister of Italy (Ginsborg 2005: 138).

Berlusconi's 'capture' of the Italian state was an inherently criminogenic act. It is not the least of Berlusconi's criminogenic ironies that he 'hides in plain sight'. As in a *mafiosi*'s selective reading of Poe's 'The Purloined Letter', Berlusconi 'escapes' into the public domain precisely in order to avoid the detection (= prosecution) of his (private) criminogenic identity.[10] Yet, this self-same act of criminogenic 'camouflage' effected the optical re-configuration of the Italian government into a simulated 'virtual state'. So uncannily perfect is the fusion of simulation with the criminogenic in Berlusconi's Italy that if this power criminal did not exist, Virilio would have found it necessary to invent him.[11] Of critical importance to the Virilian criminologist is the notion of the elite criminal as the site of a convergence between criminogenic agency and the alteration of political perception through kinematic technique:

> To grasp the real importance of the 'analyser' that speed, especially audio-visual speed, now represents, we must turn again to the philosophical definition: 'Speed is not a phenomenon but a *relationship between*

phenomena.' In other words it is the very *relativity* or transparency of the reality of appearances, but a 'spatio-temporal transparency' that here supersedes the spatial transparency of the linear geometry of the optical lenses – hence the term *trans-appearance* to designate the transmitted electronic appearances, whatever the space interval separating them from the observer. This subject or *subjugated* observer thus becomes inseparable from the observed object, because of the very immediacy of the interface, of the aptly named 'terminal', that perfects the extension and duration of a world reduced to man-machine commutation, where the 'spatial depth' of perspectival geometry suddenly gives way to the 'temporal depth' of a *real-time perspective* superseding the old real-space perspective of the Renaissance.

(Virilio 2000: 56–57)

In an unintentionally revealing interview with journalist Alexander Stille, Berlusconi re-presents himself as the embodiment of the Virilian telematic analyser: Berlusconi's official position within the public state is determined by his unofficial domination of virtually all forms of televisual communication. This yields a 'cognitive dissonance' of parapolitical dimension – as Stille himself clearly perceives:

I . . . found Berlusconi to be psychologically one of the strangest people I had ever met. I had never before interviewed anyone who told so many obvious untruths with such enthusiastic conviction [. . .] in grappling with Berlusconi's curious relationship with factual truth, it began to dawn on me that what I was encountering was a deep anthropological difference. My obsession with factual accuracy, documentation, objective truth was all part of my baggage as a print journalist, the quaint and naive and old-fashioned credo of the age of Gutenberg and the Enlightenment, while Berlusconi is a man of a different age, of the age of television and mass media, in which image and perception are all that really matter. Berlusconi is decidedly a creature (and creator) of the post-modern world where it doesn't matter what actually happened, but what people think happened. 'Don't you understand,' he told one of his closest advisors, 'that if something is not on television it doesn't exist. Not a product, a politician or an idea.' And because the things we were discussing – his conflicts of interest, the crimes of which he and his associates have been accused (and, in some cases convicted) – have not been aired in Italian television, they, too, did not exist.

(Stille 2006: 18, 20)

Although every politician utilizes television as a political instrument, Berlusconi is the first parapolitician to evidence a belief in television as a social force, in a manner unnervingly reminiscent of Futurism (Ginsborg 2005: 33, 92–93, 185–87 and 189–90). The 'true' irony of Berlusconi's tele-Futurism is the speed in which it transits from the epistemological (simulation) to the ontological (the absence of Being), an irony that is only furthered when we recall that the temporal site of the emergence of the dual state – as opposed to merely 'covert agency', which is historically concurrent with social formation – is the Italian Renaissance. It is not a coincidence that the virtual re-presentation of the state-as-optical-phenomenon was spawned by the same 're-birth' that gave us modern politics and linear perspective. As Virilio observes, Renaissance painting (linear perspective; depth) lays the foundation for the Enlightenment 'anthropic principle, which regards the existence of any observer as inseparable from the existence of rationally observed phenomena' (Virilio 2000: 51).[12] The elaborate civic rituals of *Il Stato* established the iterability of the state as both an agent of perception and as an object of sight: public procession generated the simulacra of the 'transparent' state, whose Truth/ Being was commensurate with its entry into the collective gaze of *Il Popolo* (Muir 1981; Trexler 1980).[13] Berlusconi as a post-Futurist 'virtual prince' provides the parodic gloss upon Renaissance civic ritual: his procession through public space is commensurate with his criminogenic manipulation of judicial and parliamentary immunity. Berlusconi's public re-presentation is itself the highly self-conscious – if not cynical[14] – criminogenic simulation of lawful authority. The space that separates the Renaissance ritual *stato* from Berlusconi's 'virtual state' is the difference between the illusory and the delusional; 'The state's only original existence is as a visual hallucination akin to dreaming.' The political crisis of legitimacy of the disappearance of the Italian public state into the (politicized) aesthetics of the 'virtual state', occasioned by Berlusconi's dual capture of both the government and the media, is the real-time occurrence of the epistemic crisis of Renaissance epistemology described by Virilio:

> This *indirect light* [of telecommunications] is ultimately the result of the fusion of optics and kinematics, a fusion which now embraces the whole range of ocular, graphic, photographic and cinematographic representations, making each of our images a kind of *shadow of time* – no longer the customary 'passing time' of historical linearity but the 'exposed time' which . . . surfaces. This is the time of Niepce's photographic development, the time of the Lumière Brother's cinematographic resolution of movement, but now above all *the time of videographic high definition* of a 'real-time' representation of appearances which cancels the very usefulness of passive (geometric) optics in favour of an active optics capable of causing the decline of the direct transparency of matter. What is inordinately privileged by this process is the indirect (electro-optical) transparency of light or – to be even more precise – of the light of the speed of light . . . Thus, after the nuclear disintegration of the space of matter which led to the political situation that we know today, the disintegration of *the time of light* is now upon us. Most likely, it will bring an equally major cultural shift in its wake, so that the depth of time will finally win out over the depth of spatial perspective inherited from the Renaissance.
>
> (Virilio 2000: 61)

One can scarcely hope for a better parapolitical metaphor than 'the disintegration of the time of light'. Within Berlusconi's virtual state, political meaning, or 'truth', has been suspended by the optical negativity of the telematic. Herein, the 'deep' state – a metaphorical composition of space, crime, and light (deep = dark = crime) – disappears through the sensory bombardment of the high-speed circulation of post-political simulacra (Jones 2003: 127–28). As with Stille's mournful invocation of the obsolete cognitive tools of the Enlightenment, any lingering normative outrage over the criminogenic substance of the dual state is unveiled as yet one more archaic metaphysical superstition.

> The idea that the real forces behind or underneath the screen can be revealed is . . . based on the presumption that the media themselves do not have power, but instead are tools in the hands of manipulating third parties . . . the quest for hidden power not only underestimates the feature of media power, it also sticks to the rules of old power, which has in fact disappeared within the media.
>
> (Geert Lovink cited in Cubitt 2001: 142)

Here I am reminded of Jean Baudrillard's famous account of the alibi: the substitution of the false image as validation of the perceived absence of the thing-that-is-true. For Baudrillard, the two-party system is an 'alibi' for the one-party state; in Italy, the criminogenic one-party state is the 'alibi' of the multi-party system and the media circus that it entails. Once again, we encounter Tunander's admonition of the failure of liberal political discourse to encounter parapolitical (hyper-) reality. With Berlusconi as our exemplar, we can now appreciate more readily the criminological relevance of Virilio's radical and subversive optics:

> To admit that for the human eye the essential is invisible and that, since everything is an illusion, it follows that scientific theory,[15] like art, is merely a way of manipulating our illusions, went against the political-philosophical discourses then evolving in tandem with the imperative of convincing the greatest number, with its accompanying desire for infallibility and a strong tendency towards ideological charlatanism. Publicly to point to how mental images are formed, including the way their psycho-physiological features carry their own fragility and limitations, was to violate a state secret of the same order as a military secret, since it masked a mode of mass production that was practically infallible.
>
> (Virilio 1994: 23)

If the correlation between criminogenic asymmetry and speed-politics is correct, then the entire phenomenon of power crime, quite literally, can be viewed in terms of optical considerations of 'high resolution' or 'high definition' as factors governing the invisibility of the power crime 'event'; a constant, and rapid, alteration between foreground and background, between the visible and the invisible (see Virilio 2005b: 26–38). Conversely, the state, as the final arbiter of all definitional thresholds of criminality, may be re-conceptualized in terms of its existence as an 'optical effect'; juro-political truth is mediated through surveillance and transparency. Virilio has made this point clearly through a striking example taken from the modes of political control developed during the French Enlightenment:

> It is no longer the body of the army that passes back and forth in tight ranks beneath the regard of the intendant, now it is the inspector general that files past in review of the provinces, aligned as in a parade. Yet the repetition of these reviews that triggers *the unfolding of the regional film is only an artifice, only a cinematic special effect* which benefits the itinerant observer. Perceiving the sequence of geographic locations in this isolated fashion, the general loses sight of the local realities and immediately demands the reform of the common law in order to advance the administrative standard.
>
> (Virilio 2005b: 68)

The state is 'real' precisely to the degree that it is capable not only of perception but, also, to the same degree and in the same manner, that it is capable of being perceived. The state, in order to be 'real', must necessarily exhibit some degree of virtuality (Kroker 1992: 44–50); not the 'de-realized' projection of an illusory reality, but 'a change of identity, a displacement of the centre of ontological gravity of the object considered' (Levy 1998: 26). The paradox, then, of the 'surveillance society' is that in its optical hegemony the expansion of surveillance always stands in inverse relationship to the visibility of the state. The state creates its own virtual existence through time by means of the continuous re-circulation of the externalized signs of its visibility through space; the processions of the intendant's entourage through the geo-spatial territory of the state *both sees and is seen*. This ritualistic act of mutual constitution, however, serves as the grounds of a dangerous metaphysical 'trap' for the state: in effect, the reality of the state is reduced to its virtual *appearance*. Here, of course, 'real' means 'lawful'. The prejudice of modern Liberalism is that the mutual conditionality of the reality and legality of the state is guaranteed by the state's co-determinate existence with the visible, or 'public', realm, the onto-epistemological encumbrance inherited from the linear perspective of the Renaissance.[16] In fact, every state is a parapolitical entity that auto-defines its own parameters through its control over the discourse of legality and the praxis of visibility (Wilson 2009a). It is important to recall here that international law lacks a formal theory of the state. Instead, it substitutes hermeneutics – the close reading of the sign-systems of the state – for a political ontology. The resultant metaphysical lacuna allows for the occupation of the empty discursive space of the rule-of-law state by the parapolitical, and intensely heterological dual state. Virilio is highly cognizant of this parapolitical truth:

> The State apparatus is in fact simply an apparatus of displacement [*deplacement*], its stability appears to be assured by a series of temporary gyroscopic processes of delocalization and re-localization.
>
> (Virilio 2002b: 56)

The demarcation of the political body of the state rests largely upon its successful deployment of its arsenal of optical devices. Panoptical technique and its
variables, most crucially its velocity, serve as the parameters within which the
state regulates the politics of appearance; 'What we see arises from what is not
apparent' (Virilio 2005b: 136). Such political control of a high-velocity virtual
reality would operationally double as the power crime control of the invisibility,
or 'disappearance' of the criminogenic reality.

Power crime, a criminogenic phenomenon governed by both speed and
simulation, constitutes an example of what Virilio would classify as an 'accident'
of pure war. The accident, a signature Virilian concept, is a *'diagnostic of
technology'* (Der Derian and Virilio 1998: 20).[17] Constituting the 'revelation
of the identity of the object' (Virilio and Lotringer 1997: 39), the accident serves
as an

> indirect kind of *oeuvre*, a consequence of substance . . . *An accident is in fact
> an assault on the propriety of substance*, an unveiling of its nakedness, of the
> poverty of *whatever*, *whoever* is confronted by *what happens* unexpectedly
> – to people as much as to their creations.
>
> (Virilio 2005a: 28)

Virilio deploys the 'accident' as a Derridean pun, a textual displacement caused
by a sudden realization of the utterly fortuitous nature of all linguistic construction
that blurs the operational 'distinction between [the] surface features of the
discourse and its underlying logic' (Culler 1983: 146). The subversive work of
the 'pun' in this instance is accomplished through the deliberate conjunction
of the double meaning of 'accident': as derivative, or contingent, ontological
property and as the material result of industrial and technological praxis:

> As both Creation and Fall, the accident is an unconscious work, an *invention*
> in the classical sense of uncovering that which was hidden – before it emerges
> into the light of day. Unlike the natural accident, the man-made accident is
> the product of the introduction of a new device or material substance . . . So,
> for Aristotle in his day and for us today, if *the accident reveals the substance*,
> it is indeed *accidens* – what happens – which is a kind of analysis, a
> techno-analysis of what *'substat'* – lies beneath all knowledge.
>
> (Virilio 2003: 23–24)

Subversively punning on classical Aristotelian categories (substance = Being;
accident = the property of Being), Virilio extends his techno-centric critique of
pure war through drawing our attention to both the causal centrality and the
constructive agency of speed: 'If to invent the substance is, indirectly, to invent
the accident, then the more powerful and efficient the invention, the more dramatic
the accident' (Virilio 2003: 85).

The accident of speed-politics is power crime; the contingent property that is
hidden but that, when 'seen', or made transparent, reveals the essence of the

substance. The accident, however, because it is catastrophic, signifies substance as *negativity*; here, the optical effect of power crime, an 'accidental' property of speed, removes elite criminals from both direct perception and, therefore, from the low velocity realm of juro-political accountability (Wilson 2009b). 'Fast-moving' (i.e. private) entities accelerating through speed-as-politics supersede the capacity of the public state to exercise effective political oversight and judicial review:

> The accelerated and globally expanded time-space of private ordering regimes outside the frame of national law makes legible the fact that privatization is also a shift in spatio-temporal order.
>
> (Sassen 2006: 385)

In real-time, power crime has achieved a metaphorical 'escape velocity' (*vitesse de libération*) allowing it to operate as both the effect and the cause of pure war, signifying the emergence of the invisible criminogenic environment as a systemic feature of speed-as-politics. If my view is correct, then we have crossed the juridical threshold into new forms of legal personality and identity, 'a kind of universal State, a State in its pure form which is the result of Pure War, that is, of the intensity of the means of destruction' (Virilio and Lotringer 1997: 53). Within this trans-national condition of pure war, power crime acts as both sign and signifier. It is the sign that governs the criminogenic environment as a systemic property of the dual state; it is the signifier of the 'virtual' disappearance of the liberal state into the parapolitical condition of pure war. The 'accident' of power crime, therefore, is the sign that the public state has disappeared into a fast moving criminogenic 'post-reality', or hyper-reality. Power crime is co-extant with both simulation and criminogenic hyper-reality. As simulation, power crime is no longer the parapolitical/criminogenic manipulation of reality but the governance medium of a criminogenic hyper-reality. The transition from a political economy of the real to the hyper-reality of simulation takes us out of the criminogenic and into the domain of parapolitics.

Conclusion: the 'accident' of parapolitical truma

> The day when virtual reality becomes more powerful than reality will be the day of the big accident.
>
> (Paul Virilio)

We no longer believe in revolution, only in catastrophe. Major figures in German philosophy and French critical theory are in a state of 'mourning' or, at least, of acute nostalgia – for a beloved Other that has been pronounced 'dead': Nietzsche/God; Heidegger/Being; Barthes/the Author; Derrida/Presence; Lacan/the Phallus; Foucault/Man; Deleuze/the Body; Lyotard/Meaning; Baudrillard/Modernity. Virilio mourns the loss, or 'disappearance', of humanism, the annihilation of the human self through pure war: 'The rapidity of a phenomenon liquidates you'

(Virilio and Lotringer 2002: 161). Not only have the conceptual apparatuses needed to subordinate the world to humanism's frame of reference – a culturally necessary precondition for the discourse of 'the Human' to take place – been wholly superseded by the pure war of simulation, but the exhaustive presence of speed-politics has foreclosed the possibility of rational progress, the master-sign of the Enlightenment. Virilio, like Baudrillard, likens the capture of the world-system by simulation to a catastrophic collapse into a condition of absolute ontological and epistemological density:

> We're heading towards the unknown, toward a world that has no history. All the bases for interpretation are insufficient, not only critical sociology, or psychoanalysis, or Marxism, obviously. We're entering a world devoid of cognitive interpretation, without references that would allow us to interpret what is emerging in peace, in war, in politics, in the universe, including its genetics, which is about to replace atomic science and become the major science in the coming century. We're entering the black hole.
>
> (Virilio and Lotringer 2002: 148–49)

For the critical criminologist, the Virilian black hole is a cosmological variant of Baudrillard's post-*noir* epistemological conceit of 'the perfect crime', in which the murder of 'Reality' remains undetected (or invisible) precisely because the nature of the event exceeds the measurement capacity of our collective instruments:

> The perfect crime is that of an unconditional realization of the world by the actualization of all data, the transformation of all our acts and all events into pure information: in short, the final solution, the resolution of the world ahead of time by the closing of reality and the extermination of the real by its double.
>
> (Baudrillard 1996: 25)

Virilio's relevance to critical criminology is inseparable from his own relation to phenomenology: 'I am a phenomenologist, and I have never stopped being one' (Virilio and Lotringer 2002: 150). On the one hand, phenomenology preserves the 'truth' of the criminogenic body-substance even after the catastrophic accident of criminogenic hyper-reality. On the other, speed-politics induces a kind of phenomenological disorientation, rendering a Virilian criminology inseparable from 'traumatology'.[18] If pure war is the true substance, the contingent, or accidental, properties of pure war will manifest themselves through the effects of trauma and anomic decomposition induced by speed. Pure war creates anomie in two ways. In general terms, velocity, by increasing acceleration, can traumatize a structure through impact, which can lead to a kind of 'decomposition'. Decomposition occurs in all three of Virilio's metaphorical bodies: the territorial, the social, and the 'animal' (the phenomenological):

> Decomposition is everywhere . . . What is decomposing is the geographical

space, the psychophysical and psycho-physiological space of being. It affects at once the big territorial body, the small animal body and the social body.

(Virilio and Lotringer 2002: 165)[19]

In a more specific way, anomie results from globalization, understood by Virilio as the planetary operation of pure war:

The general effect of globalization, its most general strategic definition, could be stated as follows: the disjunction of political, military and economic criteria once coordinated by the state at the geographical [territorial] level of the state.

(Joxe 2002: 85)

Paradoxically, Virilio understands globalization not as a movement towards the exterior but towards the interior; 'The world proper is no longer only outside; it is inside' (Virilio and Lotringer 2002: 84). As a result, 'We are living in a world that is traversed by an unlimited destructive force' (Virilio and Lotringer 2002: 141), what Virilio has de-noted as 'the politics of the worst' (Virilio and Lotringer 2002: 140).

Virilio's notion of 'the politics of the worst' corresponds exceedingly well with Scott's notion of parapolitics: the post-geographical decomposition of the state is the site of the covert appropriation of the public domain by private agency. This is clearly reflected in Scott's recent account of September 11 and Washington's implementation of its emergency plan for the Continuity of Government (COG), later institutionalized as the Federal Emergency Management Agency (FEMA):

[Donald] Rumsfeld and [Dick] Cheney were principal actors in one of the most highly classified programs of the Reagan Administration. Under it, U.S. officials furtively carried out detailed planning exercises for keeping the federal government running during and after a nuclear war with the Soviet Union. *The idea was to concentrate on speed,* to preserve 'continuity of government' and to avoid *cumbersome* procedures; the Speaker of the House, the president pro tempore of the Senate, and the rest of Congress would play a greatly diminished role.

(Jonathan Mann cited in Scott 2007: 185)

The geo-strategy of nuclear deterrence reduces the time for both reflection and response, which equals speed-politics, which in turn prompts a shift of all rapid decision-making to the executive (Wilson 2009b). Of even greater parapolitical significance is a key passage in *Rebuilding America's Defenses*, prepared by the Project for the New American Century: 'The process of transformation, even if it brings revolutionary change, is likely to be a long one, absent some catastrophic and catalysing event – like a new Pearl Harbor' (Scott 2007: 193). The 'shock and awe' of the spectacle of the collapsing Twin Towers, as we all know, so paralysed and overloaded our collective perceptions and understandings of events that we were 'incapable of resistance'. September 11 and the resultant 'War on Terror' *is* Virilian pure war: 'a war of images and sounds, rather than objects and things', the manifestation of 'the unprecedented limits imposed on subjective perception by the instrumental splitting of modes of perception and representation', attaining its apotheosis in 'the will to universalised illumination'. For Scott, the chaotic irruption of parapolitical reality through catastrophic events such as 9/11 results in the:

> [C]reation of a partly illusory mental space, in which unpleasant facts, such as that all western empires have been established through major atrocities, are conveniently suppressed. (I suspect in fact that most readers will be tempted to reject and forget [parapolitical events] . . . as something which simply 'doesn't compute' with their observations of America.) I say this as one who believes passionately in civilization, and fears that by excessive denial our own civilization may indeed be becoming threatened.
>
> (Scott 2009a: 2–3)

Scott's distinctive parapolitical poetics and his emphasis upon the irrationality of the dual state are strikingly psycho-analytical in nature, creating (perhaps deliberately) a series of meaningful associations: repression, denial, the unconscious, guilt, transference. Missing though, but synonymous with all of the above, is the notion of *dream*. Revealingly, 'dream', in German, is *traum*, which evokes 'trauma'; trauma, in turn, is etymologically derived from the Greek word for 'wound', a rupturing-by-force that serves as sign of combat and violence. If the essence of neurosis is conflict, then every act of repression is a self-inflicted wound; every dream that symbolically announces the presence of the repressed is a signifier of trauma.[20]

It is unsurprising that Virilian pure war, consisting of the fast-moving manipulation of sensory bombardment, bears more than a passing resemblance to psychoanalytic theory; at some level, pure war/speed-politics merges into both dream and trauma. The public state is the 'space' of deep politics; full-spectrum dominance and 'shock and awe', the signs of pure war, inaugurate a catastrophic collapse between external and internal space(s) yielding a new 'post-liberal' unitary space of speed-politics. Pure war brutalizes us through speed and simulation; because we are brutalized we are traumatized. Because we suffer from collective trauma, we experience 'reality' in an irrational dream-like state,[21] in which the reality principle, the ontological and epistemological foundation of liberal and democratic discourse, is suspended. It is through the suspension of the reality principle that the dual state is able to exist – as the parapolitician Berlusconi makes 'transparent'.

The parapolitical scholar Scott, like the post-humanist phenomenologist Virilio, is in a state of mourning – and denial. Scott mourns the death of the public, democratic, and liberal state. His resultant denial is a symptom of the trauma inflicted upon his phenomenological self through the parapolitical irruption of pure war. Scott is the trauma 'victim' of the parapolitical disappearance of the

American democratic public state into the dualistic post-9/11 deep state. And even if Scott's prose does not display evidence of trauma, his poetry – an even more reliable guide to the 'real' of the unconscious – clearly does.[22] Employing poetics rather than prose, Scott conveys with inimical style the essence of our parapolitical being, 'split-mindedness':

> Is not my inability/to change all this/but my speaking with two voices/which cannot be compassed/having to be split-minded/in the struggle to keep communication/between the present/and the best of the past/there is not much progress/if the left hankers for the beach/and the right for Sacramento/the problem has always been/how do we live with evil/we can profit from it/we can preach against it/but if we write poetry/how not to misrepresent/the great conspiracy/of organized denial/we call civilization.
>
> (Scott 2009b: 137)

Split-mindedness is the master-sign of the dual state: the aesthetics of the disappearance of the parapolitical has been inscribed directly into our phenomenological body-self through trauma. This is the ultimate parapolitical act: the criminogenic decomposition of our modes of perception.

Notes

1 It is important to keep in mind that the criminogenic is not identical with the 'criminal'. While crime may be defined as the deliberate violation of clearly established laws and norms – as reflected in the formal legalism preferred by orthodox criminology – the criminogenic can be usefully understood as encompassing practices that would ordinarily be denoted as criminal if not but for the operation of political or judicial processes that effectively de-criminalize the illicit behaviours. Criminogenic phenomena, therefore, pose a direct challenge to the validity of mainstream criminology, which tends to reduce crime to conventional sociological categories of deviance and anti-social behaviour.

> The tendency of orthodox criminology to focus on private crimes of greed, lust and rage – perhaps we should think of this as criminology's version of the 'nuts, sluts and perverts' fetish that has impoverished the sociology of deviance – has rendered institutional crimes of power, that is, corporate, political and state crimes – relatively minor areas of study within criminology.
>
> (Michalowski 2009: 312)

2 In turn, the 'dual state' equates with a 'deep political system', which Scott defines as 'one which habitually resorts to decision-making and enforcement procedures outside as well as inside those publicly sanctioned by law and society. In popular terms, collusive secrecy and law-breaking are part of how the deep political system works' (Scott 1993: xi–xii).

3 Here, I am employing 'nomadicism' in the sense of 'the nomadic' as developed by Gilles Deleuze and Félix Guattari in *A Thousand Plateaus: Capitalism and Schizophrenia* (Deleuze and Guattari 1988: 351–423). The nomadic denotes not only a free moving material agent or agency, but also the ontological indeterminacy of the nomadic force, the equivalent of the 'un-decidable' in deconstruction.

4 We lose, in simulation, the grounds of our metaphysical certainty concerning the difference between the real and the abstraction, the real and the representation, the real and knowledge about it. The difference is the crucial thing that we have lost, since without that difference that separates the two poles of any of these systems of truth, picturing or science, we cannot distinguish one from the other. This is the profound implication of the indifference of simulation, its assimilation of all separations into an indefinite cloud of self-generating models.

(Cubitt 2001: 50)

5 This point has been forcefully made by Mike Gane in his authoritative studies of Baudrillard.

What separates Baudrillard and Virilio ... [is] essentially a dispute about the theory of the real as a referent for simulation, and particularly the social as referent ... Virilio's 'simulations' are representations of the real world, representations which are substituted for one another as technology develops. Baudrillard's conception of these relations is more complex: the real is not a brute given, but a historically and socially evolved form of appropriation of the world (and replaces other forms through their constant and systematic destruction). For Baudrillard then, '[r]epresentation stems from the principle of the equivalence of the sign and the real' whereas simulation, 'stems ... from the radical negation of the sign as value, from the sign as inversion ... of every reference.' In this new situation, 'there is no longer a Last Judgement to separate the false from the true'.

(Gane 2000: 95)

6 In Wark's own account, the 'vector' of high speed finance capitalism

responded enthusiastically to immaterial [information] technology, making one suspect a close affinity between the abstract social force that is money and the principles of the new technologies ... Now, the vector and capital are complicit in this, but the vector and capital are not identical. Capital drives the vector further and harder, forcing its technologies to innovate, but at the same time it tries to commodify the fruits of this development. The vector may have other properties, values that escape the restriction of its abstract potential to the commodity form ... the vector and capital are not the same thing ... and the vector is not always a functional tool for capital.

(Wark 1994: 168, 171 and 222)

7 Ibid.: 15.
8 For much of what follows see Wilson 2009b.
9 One way of understanding Virilio's work in terms of Marxism is that he effects a wholesale substitution of the mode of production with what might be called 'the mode of combat'. 'Virilio wavers uneasily between a *marxisant* interpretation of military conflict and an alternative line of inquiry in which the technology of modern warfare is conceived as an independent factor in the compression of space by speed' (Scheuerman 2004: 237 fn.65).
10 In the words of Fedele Confalonieri, president of Berlusconi's television company Mediaset, 'If Berlusconi hadn't entered politics, we would have ended up sleeping under a bridge, on trial for Mafia crimes' (Stille 2006: 138).
11 The more one studies Berlusconi the more he assumes the guise of a living parody of the power criminal. Not the least of his criminogenic propensities is his frequent use of fake quotations.

If you want to convince someone [Berlusconi] told his sales force, make up a quotation and attribute it to some renowned authority. 'So use this method: "As Bill Paley of CBS says. As Plato said. As Abraham Lincoln said" . . . Who's ever going to go and look it up? . . . People are incredibly gullible, they love quotations'.

(Stille 2006:16)

The same technique is a central feature of Al Pacino's hyper-kinetic portrayal of the arch-gangster boss 'Big Boy' Caprice in Warren Beatty's 1990 film *Dick Tracy*. Unnervingly, Caprice makes frequent bogus references to both Plato and Lincoln.

12 See Cubitt for 'Virilio's claim that Renaissance geometry was the basis for all subject-object relations and therefore of all critical thought and ultimately all human values' (Cubitt 2001: 86–92).

13 In placid Venice, 'the ducal procession was the constitution' (Muir 1981: 190), while in volatile Florence public processions 'were used after aborted conspiracies and when illegitimate governments were toppled' (Trexler 1980: 337).

14 Here, I adopt Peter Sloterdjik's definition of cynical reasoning as especially appropriate for Berlusconi's Italy.

Cynicism is *enlightened false consciousness*. It is that modernized, unhappy consciousness, on which enlightenment has labored both successfully and in vain. It has learned its lessons in enlightenment, but it has not, and probably was not able to, put them into practice. Well-off and miserable at the same time, this consciousness no longer feels affected by any critique of ideology; its falseness is already reflectively buffered . . . It is the stance of people who realize that the times of naivete are gone.

(Sloterdijk 1987: 5)

15 Political science?

16 The Enlightenment's 'prejudice' in favour of the optical may be the ideological basis of liberalism's refusal of 'conspiratorial' views of the state. The universal criticism of 'conspiracy theory' is 'lack of evidence'; that is, the absence of visible, and, therefore, detectible historical traces.

17 For Virilio as a techno-centric theorist, see Kroker 1992: 20–50.

18 If all is movement all is at the same time accident and our existence as metabolic vehicle can be summed up as a series of collisions, of traumatisms, some taking on the quality of slow but perceptible caresses; but all this, according to the impulsions lent them, becomes mortal shocks and apotheoses of fire, but above all *a different mode of being*. Speed is a cause of death for which we're not only responsible but of which we are also the creators and inventors.

(Virilio 1991: 103)

19 'But when we are in a decomposing world, when everything decomposes because of the acceleration of exchange, the deconstruction of instances and institutions, then there is no future' (Virilio and Lotringer 2002: 164).

20 A point not lost on Martin Scorsese in *Shutter Island*. 'Shutter', of course, is a photographic reference that denotes the inducement and re-enactment of trauma through the fast moving alteration of contending 'freeze-frame', or 'shutter-click', interpretations of reality.

21 Much like watching television, or cinema. A personal anecdote might be in order here. In February 2010 I was in New York City for the first time since 9/11. Naturally, I asked as many New Yorkers as possible concerning their experiences on September 11. Literally all of them who witnessed the Twin Towers attack in person recalled that the event was like 'watching a movie'.

Eric Wilson

22 Scott is generally considered America's foremost author of political poetry. His works include *Coming to Jakarta: A Poem About Terror* (New York: New Directions, 1988); *Listening to the Candle: A Poem on Impulse* (New York: New Directions, 1992); *Minding the Darkness: A Poem for the Year 2000* (New York: New Directions, 2000); and *Mosaic Orpheus* (Montreal: McGill-Queen's University Press, 2009).

References

Baudrillard, J. (1996) *The Perfect Crime*, trans. Chris Turner, London: Verso.

Cribb, R. (2009) 'Introduction: Parapolitics, Shadow Governance and Criminal Sovereignty', in E. Wilson (ed.) *Government of the Shadows: Parapolitics and Criminal Sovereignty*, London: Pluto Press.

Cubitt, S. (2001) *Simulation and Social Theory*, London: Sage Publications.

Culler, J. (1983) *On Deconstruction: The Theory and Criticism of Structuralism*, London: Routledge & Kegan Paul.

Deleuze, G. and Guattari, F. (1988) *A Thousand Plateaus: Capitalism and Schizophrenia*, trans. Brian Massumi, London: Athlone Press.

Der Derian, J. and Virilio, P. (1998) '"Is the Author Dead?": An Interview with Paul Virilio', in J. Der Derian (ed.) *The Virilio Reader*, Oxford: Wiley-Blackwell.

Gane, M. (2000) 'Paul Virilio's Bunker Theorizing', in J. Armitage (ed.) *Paul Virilio: From Modernism to Hypermodernism and Beyond*, London: Sage Publications.

Ginsborg, P. (2005) *Silvio Berlusconi: Television, Power and Patrimony*, new edn, London: Verso Press.

Harvey, D. (1999) *The Limits to Capital*, 2nd edn, London: Verso.

Held, D., McGew, A., Goldblatt, D. and Perraton, J. (1999) *Global Transformations: Politics, Economics and Culture*, Cambridge: Polity Press.

Jones, T. (2003) *The Dark Heart of Italy*, London: Faber and Faber.

Jourdain, R. (1997) *Music, The Brain and Ecstasy: How Music Captures Our Imagination*, New York: HarperPerennial.

Joxe, A. (2002) *Empire of Disorder*, trans. Ames Hodges, ed. Sylvere Lotringer, New York: Semiotext(e).

Klein, N. (2007) *The Shock Doctrine: The Rise of Disaster Capitalism*, London: Penguin Books.

Kroker, A. (1992) *The Possessed Individual: Technology and the French Postmodern*, New York: St. Martin's Press.

Levy, P. (1998) *Becoming Virtual: Reality in the Digital Age*, trans. Robert Bononno, New York: Plenum Trade.

Michalowski, R. (2009) 'Power Crime and Criminology in the New Imperial Age', *Crime, Law and Social Change*, 51: 303–25.

Muir, E. (1981) *Civic Ritual in Renaissance Venice*, Princeton, NJ: Princeton University Press.

Oliveira, C. and Virilio, P. (1995) 'The Silence of the Lambs: Paul Virilio in Conversation', *CTHEORY*, 19(1–2): 1–3. www.ctheory.net

Passas, N. (2000) 'Globalization and International Crime: Effects of Criminogenic Asymmetries', in P. Williams and D. Vlassis (eds) *Combating Transnational Crime: Concepts, Activities and Responses*, New York: Routledge.

—— (2007) *Corruption in the Procurement Process and the Outsourcing of Government Functions: Issues, Cases, Case Studies, Implications*, Report, Boston: Northeastern University.

Passas, N. and Black, W. (2007) *Corruption in the Procurement Process/Outsourcing Government Functions*, Report, Boston: Northeastern University.

Passas, N. and Nelken, D. (1993) 'The Thin Line Between Legitimate and Criminal Enterprises: Subsidiary Fraud in the European Community', *Crime, Law and Social Change*, 19: 223–43.

Sassen, S. (2006) *Territory, Authority, Rights: From Medieval to Global Assemblages*, Princeton, NJ: Princeton University Press.

Scheuerman, W. E. (2004) *Liberal Democracy and the Social Acceleration of Time*, Baltimore, MD: Johns Hopkins University Press.

Scott, P. D. (1993) *Deep Politics and the Death of JFK*, Berkeley: University of California Press.

—— (2000) *Minding the Darkness: A Poem in the Year 2000*, New York: New Directions.

—— (2007) *The Road to 9/11: Wealth, Empire and the Future of America*, Berkeley: University of California Press.

—— (2008) *The War Conspiracy: JFK, 9/11 and the Politics of War*, New York: Mary Ferrell Foundation Press.

—— (2009a) *Deep Politics and the CIA Global Drug Connection: Heroin and the Networks of Domination* (private copy).

—— (2009b) *Mosaic Orpheus*, Montreal: McGill-Queen's University Press.

Sloterdijk, P. (1987) *Critique of Cynical Reason*, trans. Michael Eldred, Minneapolis: University of Minnesota Press.

Stille, A. (2006) *The Sack of Rome: How a Beautiful European Country with a Fabled History and a Storied Culture Was Taken Over By a Man Named Silvio Berlusconi*, New York: Penguin Press.

Trexler, R. C. (1980) *Public Life in Renaissance Florence*, Ithaca, NY: Cornell University Press.

Tunander, O. (2009) 'Democratic State vs. Deep State: Approaching the Dual State of the West', in E. Wilson (ed.) *Government of the Shadows: Parapolitics and Criminal Sovereignty*, London: Pluto Press.

Ullman, H. K. and Wade, J. P. (1998) *Rapid Dominance – A Force for All Seasons: Technologies and Systems for Achieving Shock and Awe: A Real Revolution in Military Affairs*, London: Royal United Services Institute for Defence Studies.

Virilio, P. (1989) *War and Cinema: The Logistics of Perception*, trans. Patrick Camiller, London: Verso.

—— (1991) *The Aesthetics of Disappearance*, trans. Philip Beitchman, New York: Semiotext(e).

—— (1994) *The Vision Machine*, trans. Julie Rose, Indianapolis: Indiana University Press.

—— (2000) *Polar Inertia*, trans. Patrick Camiller, London: Sage Publications.

—— (2003) *Unknown Quantity*, London: Thames & Hudson.

—— (2005a) *City of Panic*, trans. Julie Rose, Oxford: Berg.

—— (2005b) *Negative Horizons: An Essay in Dromoscopy*, trans. Michael Degener, New York: Continuum.

Virilio, P. and Lotringer, S. (1997) *Pure War*, rev. edn, trans. Mark Polizzotti, New York: Semiotext(e).

—— (2002) *Crepuscular Dawn*, trans. Mike Taormina, New York: Semiotext(e).

Wark, M. (1994) *Virtual Geography: Living with Global Media Events*, Bloomington: Indiana University Press.

Wilson, E. (2009a) 'Deconstructing the Shadows', in E. Wilson (ed.) *Government of the Shadows: Parapolitics and Criminal Sovereignty*, London: Pluto Press.

—— (2009b) 'Speed/Pure War/Power Crime: Paul Virilio on the Criminogenic Accident and the Virtual Disappearance of the Suicidal State', *Crime, Law and Social Change*, 51: 413–34.

18 Global terrorism, risk and the state

Gabe Mythen and Sandra Walklate

Introduction

Over the last decade, Western capitalist nations have been bound up in a process of unprecedented securitization, formally designed to reduce and manage the terrorist threat (see Amoore and de Goede, 2007; Ould Mohamedou, 2007). Following on from the attacks attributed to followers of Al Qaeda in the United States, the UK, Spain and Turkey, issues of national security have assumed political prescience, with terrorism being cast as a pressing social problem. In the realm of formal politics, intelligence communities, and the mass media, the terrorist risk has been described as both historically exceptional and potentially cataclysmic (Aradau and van Munster, 2007; Mythen and Walklate, 2008). The events of 11 September 2001 have been commonly described as both a watershed and a catalyst for an intense phase of violence, legal regulation, surveillance and military expansion (Kellner, 2002; Welch, 2006). The process of counter-terrorism securitization over the last decade has been wide-ranging, impacting upon policing, law, immigration and the economy. With regards to the latter, the estimated amount spent by the American government during the course of the 'war on terror' presently exceeds a trillion dollars (Belasco, 2009). In the UK – running contra to a far-reaching programme of state cost-cutting in the public sector – the amount allocated by government to fund counter-terrorism measures for 2010–11 totals over £38 million (Travis, 2010). Both the unprecedented nature and the profound effects of policies and processes of securitization have led to terrorism being cast by some thinkers as the motif of a dangerous and volatile age. Beck (2002), for instance, has alluded to the modern world as a 'terroristic world risk society', while Borradori (2003) recounts the unsettling experience of living in 'a time of terror'. Insofar as the problem of terrorism should not be belittled, we would point out that it is but one of a range of harms that bring injury and death in the world today. Although media, political and academic attention has gravitated toward terrorism, global social problems such as drought, poverty, malnutrition and disease continue to take lives by the thousand each and every day. So we might justifiably ask why terrorism *in particular* has become such a fundamental concern, and why, in a time of 'austerity' during which we are all, apparently, 'in it together' – national security continues to command such a large slice of the state budget comparative to other areas of expenditure.

In this chapter we begin by elucidating the ways in which the terrorist threat has been expansively constructed yet narrowly defined through the discourse of 'new terrorism'. This discourse – which has served as a driver for the 'war on terror' – invokes a high magnitude risk against which pre-emptive action must be taken. Drawing upon discrete examples, we document some of the problems that have arisen out of both international military invasions conducted under the auspices of the war on terror and national counter-terrorism legislation designed in theory to reduce the terrorist threat. We argue that both the calamitous war on terror and extraordinary counter-terrorism measures have been erroneously led by the spectre of imagined future attacks. Considering the blood shed and the lives lost by innocent civilians as a direct result of the war on terror, we ask whether the state itself can be viewed as terroristic and what this might mean for the way in which criminology approaches the problem of terrorism. We conclude by asking what role critical criminology may have in promoting more expansive discussion about the uses and abuses of political violence.

(De)constructing 'new terrorism'

The term 'terrorism' needs to be understood as a culturally constructed and historically variable category rather than an immutable objective descriptor. The terms 'terrorism' and 'terrorist' can be traced back to the French Revolution and the infamous 'reign of terror' during which violence and repression were meted out by the government in an attempt to quash those seeking to overthrow the state (Ayto, 1990: 524). In contemporary parlance, the common meaning of terrorism differs considerably. As the state in Western capitalist countries retains a monopoly on the legitimate use of force, its violent actions are seldom regarded as 'terroristic', regardless of the degree of suffering they may cause. In contemporary Western society it is instead attacks on the state and its citizens that are classified as terrorism. While the historiography of terrorism is complex, terrorism is commonly defined as the use of violence and intimidation to disrupt or coerce a government and/or an identifiable community (Rehn, 2003). The United Nations (2003) defines terrorism thus: 'terrorism is in most cases essentially a political act. It is meant to inflict dramatic and deadly injury on civilians and to create an atmosphere of fear, generally for a political or ideological purpose. Terrorism is a criminal act, but it is more than mere criminality'. The allusion to being 'more than mere criminality' is important here. Nevertheless, the claim that the exceptionality of terrorism renders its progenitors as party to regulation that extends beyond the boundaries of the criminal justice system is contestable. It is governments that decide – in consultation with securocrats, lawyers and judges – how terrorism is legally defined and it is state institutions that determine whether particular acts are terroristic. As we shall see, within the formal party system, political discourses can be deployed to instrumental ends, with dominant neo-liberal discourses creating and upholding 'knowledge' of what 'terrorism' is and simultaneously preventing alternative interpretations from being recognized as legitimate. Indeed, the production of knowledge regarding the uniqueness and novelty of terrorism as a form of violence has served as a spur to the deployment of various 'states of exception' (see Agamben, 2005; Green and Ward, 2004). As the Copenhagen School (Buzan *et al.*, 1997) have articulated, the solidification of language into knowledge – understood as ideas, assumptions and metaphors that render particular actions both thinkable and justifiable – is the moment at which such social shaping comes to the surface. From this viewpoint 'terrorism' is not only a social construction, but also one which is ideologically charged and has material effects (see McCulloch and Pickering, 2010: 32). What is important to grasp is that definitions of terrorism are historically and culturally labile, thus categorizing terrorism is a relative rather than an absolute act.

Over the last decade, prominent security experts, politicians, media professionals and academics have been complicit in the identification of a historically unprecedented type of terrorism, practised by radical Islamic fundamentalist groups such as Al Qaeda, Jemaah Islamiyah and Lashkar-e-Taiba. This brand of terrorism has been variously dubbed 'new', 'super' or 'postmodern' terrorism (see Laqueur, 1997; 2003; Lesser *et al.*, 1999; Morgan, 2004; Sprinzak, 2006). In such contributions it is argued that 'new terrorism' is distinct from the violence used by traditional terrorist organizations. Where traditional terrorist groups specialized in localized attacks with the objective of damaging infrastructure, disrupting capital accumulation and deterring tourism, new terrorist groups seek to launch international attacks that deliberately target civilian populations (see Hoffman, 1999: 9; ISP/NSC Report, 2005: 3). What is explicit in the discourse of terrorism is the transformed nature of the risk, which is now global and universal. As Beck (1996: 32) puts it: 'there are no bystanders anymore'. Those adhering to the new terrorism thesis aver that the range and the type of weaponry used in attacks has changed dramatically and now includes 'all facilities including water supplies, gas stations, transport systems and the like' (Peters, 2004: 4). The specific intent of new terrorist groups is to cause mass destruction and their technological capability to commit 'high-lethality' attacks has encouraged the view that new terrorism constitutes an existential threat which, ergo, necessitates the introduction of exceptional security measures. In addition, the narrative of new terrorism also infers that there are key differences in the internal structure of traditional and new terrorist organizations. Rather than sharing united goals and operating under clear hierarchies, new terrorist groups have disparate objectives and a horizontal organizational structure (9/11 Commission Report, 2004). In this sense, Al Qaeda has been described as an 'ideology' or a 'philosophy' that has inspired individuals and small groups to launch attacks on the West rather than an organized and tightly controlled group (Burke, 2005: 1; Zedner, 2009: 128). While recruitment for traditional terrorist groups has largely operated on a local scale, new terrorist organizations recruit across continents, making use of the internet to disseminate their values and to attract followers (Leitzinger, 2004; Weimann, 2006).

Insofar as the discourse of 'new terrorism' captures certain aspects of the evolution of political violence, there are several flaws in its composition and reasons to be concerned about the political uses to which it has been put. Before we consider some of the dubious practices of control and coercion invoked by this discourse, it is first worth interrogating some of the claims made by its proponents. First, although there is some substance in the observation that the tactics, technologies and strategies used by terrorist groups have changed over time, this is unremarkable in and of itself. One would expect the methods of terrorism to change over time in line with scientific and technological developments. As it has been mobilized in political discourse, the attachment of the adjective 'new' is crucial, indicating a historical break rather than a gradual continuum of change in forms of political violence (McGhee, 2008: 5). Second, several of the features attributed to new terrorist groups are equally applicable to groups that have used political violence in the twentieth century. The IRA, for example, made optimum use of weapons technology, operated an organizational cell system and targeted areas of civilian use, as evidenced by the bomb attacks in Birmingham, Manchester and Warrington. Third, if we are to understand ideologies as distorted representations of reality that seek to reinforce power and control, it seems reasonable to posit that the discourse of new terrorism is ideological. The attempt to conceal historically important events and to present a fractional view of the world is shot through the new terrorism thesis. Despite the fact that terrorist attacks have in recent times emerged from various sources and been waged by a range of groups following different faiths and expressing different political beliefs, the terrorist recounted in the discourse of new terrorism is religiously and ethnically explicit. The terrorist imagined here is not the lone White supremacist or the disenchanted Christian fundamentalist. Rather, (s)he is the non-White, indoctrinated, fanatical Islamist committed to causing chaos and carnage. As Burnett and Whyte (2005) note, the discourse of 'new terrorism' is historically blinkered. Those who have been partial to deploying it in politics and security circles tend to avoid any reference to the root causes of terrorism, save those that explain away violence in terms of erroneous interpretations of the Koran, or the use of 'brainwashing' techniques at Jihadi training camps. We would concur with Peters (2004: 7) that 'the representation of political violence as *terrorism* – its narrativisation and its embodiment as a discourse – reifies it, cutting it off from other forms of violent behaviour and often disguising or preventing examination of claims to political legitimacy'. Such a myopic approach elides the explanations for violent actions offered by those engaging in terrorist acts. The pre-recorded videos made by the young British men responsible for the 7/7 attacks in London, for example, draw attention to the inaction of the West in defending Palestine against Israeli attacks, the illegal invasion of Iraq and the occupation of Afghanistan. These expressed motivations exist as 'elephants in the room' for the UK government, which has done its utmost to separate out the military actions of the state in Muslim countries from home-based terrorist attacks, despite evidence from its own agencies and organizations suggesting otherwise (see Gregory and Wilkinson, 2005; Vertigans, 2010).

Countering terrorism? Risk, regulation and the pre-emptive turn

Thus far we have examined the new terrorism thesis and considered some of the problems that it engenders both in terms of conceptual coherence and in relation to the narrow political focus that it produces. Post 9/11 it is clear that the discourse of new terrorism has informed both domestic and international security policies and that a process of parallel securitization is evident in the development of national and international frameworks. The UK National Security Strategy (2010: 5) states: 'when it comes to national security, foreign and domestic policy are not separate issues, but two halves of one picture'. As McCulloch and Pickering (2010: 32) observe, this coalescence of interests has become pronounced in the deployment of pre-emptive measures which have become integral facets of both international military strategy and domestic counter-terrorism policy. In what follows we wish to stitch the discourse of new terrorism to the introduction of extensive counter-terrorism measures intended to prevent future attacks.

It is indisputable that there is a risk of future terrorist attacks by Islamist groups and/or their supporters in the UK.[1] Having acknowledged this social fact, the strategies deployed in the political communication of this message to the general public have been curious, characterized by a contradictory mix of frank disclosure, denial, leaks and speculation. This inconsistent approach across state agencies has facilitated a blurring of the real and the imaginary in the communication of the terrorist risk (see Mythen and Walklate, 2006). What Vedby Rasmussen (2004) describes as the 'presence of the future' can be detected in a projective political agenda that engages in the imagining of upcoming threats. So far as terrorist attacks are concerned, a plethora of possibilities has been visualized, including the detonation of radiological dispersal devices, biological and chemical attacks, contamination of public water supplies and air strikes against nuclear facilities (see Barnaby, 2002). The consensual path for pre-emptive modes of regulation has been laid by appeals to the future catastrophic, employed to the point of being threadbare by both Tony Blair and George W. Bush. While political hyperbole around terrorism has receded somewhat since their respective departures, the logic of anticipatory risk remains pivotal in counter-terrorism strategy. Running in tandem with the militaristic 'war on terror' waged on international soil, over the course of the last decade the British government has introduced a broad range of domestic counter-terrorism legislation designed to combat terrorism.[2] The governance of terrorism has been redrafted via a succession of legislative acts, including the Terrorism Act (2000), the Anti-Terrorism, Crime and Security Act (2001), the Prevention of Terrorism Act (2005) the Terrorism Act (2006) and the Counter-Terrorism Act (2000). These forms of legislation have been imposed to reduce the risk of terrorist attacks, but pervasive concerns have been raised about the way in which elements of legislation infringe civil liberties. What is important about these counter-terrorism measures is that they are designed to reduce the terrorist risk not just in the present, but also in the future. While all laws are intended to deter would-be offenders and reduce future risks, the preventive angle has been well developed in recent legislation, through the introduction of offences such as incitement to terrorism, acts preparatory to terrorism and giving and receiving terrorist training. Such precautionary powers have been welcomed by senior police officers and intelligence agents who attest that precautionary measures are required to prevent attacks (see Clark, 2007; Evans, 2007). In its National Security Strategy, the UK government concedes that early intervention measures may result in the loss of basic rights and freedoms for some: 'to protect the security and freedom of many, the state sometimes has to encroach on the liberties of a few: those who threaten us' (2010: 23). What is clear in such statements is that the state is distancing itself from fundamental principles of human rights and gravitating toward policies that accept a zero-sum approach that the rights of some can be forfeited to defend those of others (see Hudson 2003: 65). Such governmental justifications for exceptional measures often involve attempts at ideological incorporation that appeal to 'in' groups and strive to convince the majority that measures will only affect a dangerous minority to which they do not belong. As such, the state is involved in an hegemonic effort to create a clear divide between a safe 'us' and a dangerous 'them' whose rights, by definition, are not equitable with 'ours'. In this sense, security and justice are being recast as partial and contingent not absolute and guaranteed conditions.

In addition to shifting notions of justice and rights, the redrafting of security post 9/11 has involved a pre-emptive turn in modes of regulation and control. The goal of pre-emption is to decrease the extent of the terrorist threat by deploying a mix of punitive sanctions and criminal justice legislation to defuse future harms before they actualize (McCulloch and Pickering, 2009: 4). Alongside the creation of new offences, the extension of police powers of questioning, arrest and detention rendered permissible under counter-terrorism legislation has proven to be controversial (see Durodie, 2006: 2). Arguably the most contentious preemptive measures have been the introduction of Control Orders under the Prevention of Terrorism Act (2005), the use of stop and search powers permitted under section 44 of the Terrorism Act (2000) and the extension of the period of detention without charge brought in under the Terrorism Act (2006). We will briefly consider each of these developments in turn. Section 44 of the Terrorism Act (2000) first permitted police officers to search an individual without having either evidence or 'reasonable suspicion' that an offence had been committed or was being planned. Under Section 44, the police are able to stop and search any person in a specific area without grounds for suspicion. The apparent arbitrariness of these powers has been challenged by civil rights groups such as Liberty, and their application in practice has been subject to widespread criticism. Since the implementation of Section 44, police statistics categorically show that the powers have been used unevenly across the population. In 2007/08 alone police figures showed a 322 per cent rise in Black people stopped and searched and a 277 per cent rise in Asians stopped and searched under Section 44 powers (see Ford, 2009: 1). As a direct consequence of these practices, thousands of innocent people belonging to ethnic minority groups have found themselves interrupted and questioned while going about their daily business. Unsurprisingly, Section 44 powers have been negatively received and caused anger amongst Muslim minority groups, leading to deteriorating relations between Black and Asian communities and the police force in some areas (Mythen *et al.*, 2009). Aside from disproportionately targeting Black and Asian individuals, complaints have been made about the misuse of Section 44 powers as a tool for control that extends beyond the ambit of countering terrorism. Political protestors, professional photographers, journalists and tourists have all been stop-searched under the powers while moving in the public sphere. Indeed, it was ultimately a case brought to the European Court of Human Rights by a journalist and a peace activist that led to the powers being declared illegal. Both had been subject to stop-searches under Section 44 whilst travelling to a demonstration against an arms trading fair. The Court ruled that article 8 of the European Convention on Human Rights had been broken and that the powers were insufficiently circumscribed and did not provide adequate legal safeguards against abuse. In July 2010 the government announced the suspension of Section 44 measures, and they remain subject to wider counter-terrorism review.

In addition to stop and search powers, the extension of the period of pre-charge detention has proved controversial. The Terrorism Act of 2000 raised the standard 48-hour detention limit to 7 days with the permission of the courts. This period was doubled to 14 days in 2003 and then raised to 28 days under Section 25 of the Terrorism Act 2006, subject to approval from judicial authorities. Following on from the 7/7 attacks, the UK government lobbied to raise the maximum permissible time for detention without charge to a staggering 90 days.[3] It is important to note that the UK stands out as anomalous in the length of its pre-charge detention period in comparison with other countries similarly threatened by terrorism. The maximum permissible period of detention without charge in the United States is 2 days; in Spain it is 72 hours and in Italy 24 hours. One of the primary justifications for the extension of detention without charge has been the 'ticking bomb' scenario, in which a terrorist suspect may possess information that if accessed could prevent a large-scale attack from occurring. Whilst it is debatable whether lengthier periods of detention actually enable interrogators to extract useful information – even in situations in which the parties detained may possess it – this scenario has served as a powerful metaphor mobilized to permit assorted 'states of exception' ranging from secret surveillance to torture. Consequently, the threshold of evidence required before arrests are made is diminished and the ancient right of habeas corpus has been removed (see Zedner, 2008: 19). There are no rights of redress for those detained without charge, nor are suspects allowed to know the reasons why they have been detained. In this respect, detention without charge shifts the assumption of presumption of innocence until proved guilty to presumption of guilt unless proven innocent. In effect, the dystopic future depicted in the ticking bomb situation trumps basic rights and freedoms in the present.

While the extension of detention without charge has caused much consternation amongst civil rights campaigners, Control Orders introduced in the Terrorism Act 2005 have been deemed to infringe basic human rights by the European Commission for Human Rights and have been declared illegal by the House of

Lords (see Travis, 2009). Control Orders are arguably the archetypal example of pre-emptive counter-terrorism regulation, being invoked in circumstances in which a person is suspected of being involved with terrorism but where the evidence is incomplete or cannot be made public. Control Orders permit the state to electronically tag, monitor and contain terrorist suspects without formal charges being brought. In implementation Control Orders have led to suspects being placed under house arrest for up to 16 hours per day with privacy, asylum and free movement being curtailed.[4] Without legal charges been tabled, Control Orders severely disrupt the lives of individuals subjected to them, placing curfews on association and communication and forcing subjects to comply with self-monitoring systems which interrupt normal sleeping patterns. The enforcement of the Control Order is emblematic of the mobilization of anticipatory risk to implement draconian legislation exceptional in its capacity to veto fundamental human rights. As legislation introduced in response to the conflict in Northern Ireland indicates, exceptional measures designed as a temporary response to crisis conditions can become permanent and routine over time. The palpable danger is that the exception soon becomes the norm (see McCulloch and Pickering, 2009).

The examples discussed above are but legislative headlines in a much wider sweep of securitization around the terrorist threat which involves a dramatic intensification of pre-emptive modes of policing and surveillance. Nevertheless, it is important to appreciate that this process of securitization is partial and has differential consequences. Certain communities deemed to be 'risky' are over-surveyed, while 'safe' communities retain the standard rights and privileges. Despite the ambition of enhancing security and control, pre-emptive strategies may serve to increase rather than decrease the risk of future attacks (see Diprose *et al.*, 2008: 274). Violent military incursions and counter-terrorism policies that discriminate against Muslim populations may engender the 'law of inverse consequences' whereby the very problem that the state is trying to alleviate is actually exacerbated by its actions (see Mythen, 2010). For example, if we consider the rationale for the invasions of Iraq and Afghanistan – in the first case that Saddam Hussein had weapons of mass destruction and had made an alliance with Al Qaeda and in the second that the Taliban would allow Al Qaeda to take refuge in the country – we are inclined to ask if the risk the state was attempting to tackle has been supplanted by a range of threats much greater than the original one. The human cost of military intervention has been huge, international relations between countries in the Middle East and the West have deteriorated and British Muslim communities have been ostracized and alienated. There can be little dispute that over-zealous and aggressive modes of policing and regulation around counter-terrorism have further alienated Muslim minority groups and are likely to have aggravated rather than alleviated both feelings of marginalization and the range of grievances held against government (McGhee, 2008; Mythen *et al.*, 2009).

It is important to note that the application of methods of pre-emption and pre-crime may formally be designed to aid prevention, but they do not automatically lead to it. As McCulloch and Pickering (2010: 33) note, 'prevention is an outcome while pre-crime and pre-emption are strategies. Pre-empting threats through pre-crime laws translates into prevention only if the laws are effective'. Given the human costs of the disastrous military invasions of Afghanistan and Iraq and the deleterious effects of domestic counter-terrorism legislation on minority groups, it is essential that criminologists speak up, out and against the creeping pre-emptive regime. While it is incumbent on the state to maintain conditions of public safety and to reduce the risk of terrorist attacks happening in the future, the willingness of the state to depart from the foundations of formally democratic law – for instance, as embedded in trial by jury, open proceedings, due process, habeas corpus and an appeals system – is as unprecedented as it is worrisome. So far as the development of security policies is concerned, we need to ask whether fictional future possibilities are a sensible and reasonable gauge for determining legislation in the present. If the regulation of terrorism is driven by dystopic imaginings rather than evidence, pre-emptive measures that dislodge civil liberties become nothing short of logical. Once a projective 'What if?' position is normalized, presumption of innocence is replaced by presumption of guilt. Evidence is required in refutation, not prosecution. Silence equals culpability. In such conditions of 'hyper-riskality', in which the imagined risk becomes more 'real' than the material threat, the dangers of injustices occurring are writ large (see Mythen and Walklate, 2010). No more so are these in evidence than in what Vertigans (2010: 27) dubs the 'dark side' of counter-terrorism, manifested in acts such as extrajudicial killing, extraordinary rendition and torture.

Permitting terror: the violent state

We have argued that the ideological underpinnings that support the state's intense drive toward securitization, as embedded within the discourse of 'new terrorism' and the 'war on terror', are both partial in their construction and conceal relations of domination and subordination. The UK National Security Strategy (2010: 3) proclaims:

> Our national interest requires us to stand up for the values our country believes in – the rule of law, democracy, free speech, tolerance and human rights. Those are the attributes for which Britain is admired in the world and we must continue to advance them, because Britain will be safer if our values are upheld and respected in the world. To do so requires us to project power and to use our unique network of alliances and relationships – principally with the United States of America.

Given that a range of state interventions and policies in the arena of counter-terrorism have been in direct *contravention to* rather than being *informed by* values of democracy, human rights and tolerance, it is important to ask exactly what 'power' means in this context and to contemplate whether using the term 'national interest' is apt, given that the rights and justices of 'the few' are expendable. Whilst the lens of media, academic and political interest has been heavily trained toward the actions and possible plans of groups such as Al Qaeda, as our earlier discussion suggests, it is important to acknowledge that states are themselves routinely engaging in meting out violence. It should be remembered that terrors are practised, witnessed and felt in and through both the 'asymmetrical' wars of the present and the 'regular' wars of the past. Insofar as the state reserves the legal right to use violence in warfare, well over 100 million people have perished in warfare over the course of the twentieth century (see Eagleton, 2003: 15; Green and Ward, 2004: 1). Further, while the First and Second World Wars led to huge losses of soldiers in battle, the civilian death toll has risen markedly in more recent conflicts. In the first decade of the twentieth century 90 per cent of war casualties were soldiers. In the ninety-three wars between 1990 and 1995, the same percentage were civilian casualties.[5] In effect, advances in technology and new modes of warfare have shifted the risk from soldiers to civilians. During the course of the war in Iraq, 200 British troops have died, compared to well over 100,000 civilians.[6] While neo-liberals might contest that terrorist attacks cannot be compared with military violence, the steady stream of revelations about the activities of a minority of US and UK soldiers seems to undermine such protests. We can justifiably refer to these situations where the state reproduces the behaviour it formally sets out to erase as 'risk hypocrisies'. Although these hypocrisies are numerous, we shall briefly discuss just three, namely: the use of infinite imprisonment, extraordinary rendition and torture.

While the British and American governments rebuked Saddam Hussein for illegally detaining Kurdish citizens without charge or trial, since 9/11 an alarming number of citizens have been and remain detained without charge at the behest of the UK and the US. In the US, a spike occurred directly after 9/11 with the US government rounding up and arbitrarily detaining over 1,000 people whose profiles and details the government refused to publicly declare (see Chomsky, 2002; Christian, 2008). Under the extensive powers enabled by the Patriot Act the US state subsequently arrested and incarcerated hundreds of people – largely of Middle Eastern descent – in notorious 'fishing expeditions', without levelling formal charges allowing the possibility of application for bail or the prospect of a trial (see Welch, 2006).[7] Since 9/11 around 775 prisoners – rights stripped and identities reduced to the status of 'enemy combatant' – have been held under repressive conditions without charges at the infamous military prison situated at Guantanamo Bay. Some of those that remain detained at the camp have now been imprisoned for over a decade. In the UK, aside from those detained in Iraq, to whom we will return to shortly, over fifty suspected terrorists were held indefinitely at Belmarsh prison without charges being heard, prior to such detention being declared illegal in 2004. In addition to infinite detention, the shadowy practice of 'extraordinary rendition' has been publicly exposed. Extraordinary rendition involves the kidnap, detention and movement of terrorist suspects to countries where torture is permissible (Gill, 2006: 24). Once in situ in locations with lower human rights thresholds, suspects are subjected to a mix of intense questioning and 'enhanced interrogation techniques' – read torture – by intelligence agents. Despite denials by the British state, it has since been established that aircraft used explicitly by the CIA in extraordinary renditions have flown in and out of UK territory over 200 times since the 9/11 attacks (see Norton-Taylor, 2010).[8] Aside from the objectionable moral bankruptcy of extraordinary rendition, in such cases the credibility of intelligence leading to intervention is critical (see Gill 2006).

The logic behind the practice of extraordinary rendition is that torture can be rendered legally permissible and used in attempts to gain information from suspects in countries with diminished protection of human rights. Over and above this, many of the people held at Guantanamo Bay have claimed that various forms of torture were a regular part of imprisonment, including beating, whipping, water boarding, sleep deprivation, sexual humiliation and forced exposure to pornography. US military documents disclosed in the recent 'WikiLeaks' disclosure of 400,000 military field reports reveal systematic abuse of prisoners by US and UK troops. What is shocking is both the range of methods of serious abuse and torture and the sheer number of cases that were simply stamped 'no further investigation required' (see Iraq Warlogs, 2010: 2). In the case of UK forces, allegations have emerged about the use of torture against prisoners held in a military interrogation centre near Basra. Over 200 former inmates brought high court proceedings alleging that Joint Forces Interrogation Team systematically subjected them to food and sleep deprivation, sensory deprivation and threats of execution. The ex-prisoners claim they were sexually humiliated by female soldiers, beaten, forced to kneel in stress positions for up to 30 hours, and subjected to electric shocks (Cobain, 2010). In the well publicized case of Binyamin Mohamed, the appeal court released CIA intelligence that showed that MI5 were aware that he had been subjected to treatment 'at the very least cruel, inhuman, and degrading' (see Norton-Taylor, 2010). The appeal court also rejected the subsequent demand by the government and security services that any evidence of the state's knowledge about the treatment of Guantanamo Bay inmates must be suppressed in a civil case. The recent decision to award UK citizens previously incarcerated in Guantanamo Bay compensation packages to prevent the case going to court amidst claims of maltreatment, seems at odds with the British state's denial that its agents and soldiers had no knowledge of torture being used. This decision does little to assuage the concerns of those who believe that torture was practised and sanctioned by the UK military and secret services.[9]

Of course, in Western capitalist cultures the state retains a monopoly on the use violence, but this does not mean that its actions are exempt from scrutiny or challenge. The processes and practices of infinite detention, extraordinary rendition and torture are clear examples of the capability of Western capitalist states to flout human rights, enact violence, deliberately inflict pain and suffering and to induce fear in populations – *in toto* to produce terror. Situated alongside the introduction of authoritarian domestic controls, what has transpired over the last decade has been a geopolitical power play, an attempt to re-establish hegemony, administered through the sovereign power vested in Anglo-military and foreign policy.

Conclusion

The discourse of 'new terrorism' and the 'war on terror' has permitted the state to pursue a weighty military agenda internationally whilst deflecting attention from exceptional law and order measures, systematic state violence and the root causes of political violence. There is now a palpable need to factor the role of the state more firmly into discussions about the production and escalation of terrorism (see Jackson *et al.*, 2009). This requires first recognising that Western states are both capable of committing violence which is terroristic and, second, acknowledging that the state can deploy (counter) terrorism as a political tool to secure governance and reinforce control (see Jackson *et al.*, 2009). As the state becomes inured to moving 'beyond the law' (Gill, 2009: 154), claims made regarding the protection of 'liberty' and 'security' are thrown into sharp relief. At a time in which the tendency toward spin and political manipulation of information is pronounced, it is more important than ever that abuses of power are revealed and that forms of state denial are themselves refuted (see Cohen, 2001; Welch, 2003). As Hillyard (2009) suggests, there is more than enough evidence to suggest that the UK and the US governments can reasonably be described as 'exceptional states'. The expansion of law, the increased use of informal measures of control, mass surveillance and willingness to act either outside or against law all attest to this. The various 'states of exception' outlined by Agamben (2005) are clearly present. For Agamben (2005), acts of state power that derogate from the normal rules of law appear in many guises, from *legally defined* spaces and/or times at which legal regulations are suspended *qua* the use of Section 44 powers, to *extra-legal* measures in which a government either deviates from proscribed procedures or seeks to impose new procedures as evidenced through the use of Control Orders, to *de facto* states of exception where the state does not seek to suspend or replace extant laws but instead acts in direct contravention to them, such as the use of torture (see Green and Ward, 2009).

It is important that criminology seeks to engage the political economy of states of exception and the way in which such states may be driven by complex motives that extend beyond the search for 'security'. In addition, it is important that we monitor the diffusion and transference of exceptional measures, counter-terrorism legislation and state violence. The military force actioned in the war on terror and the panoply of exceptional counter-terrorism measures implemented, have palpable ramifications for the criminal justice system. With tongue only just in cheek, Steinert (2003: 271) remarks: 'we will soon see "pre-emptive strikes" against crime and hear justifications of "collateral damage" as "regrettable but unavoidable"'. Academically, there is then a need to broaden out understandings of violence within criminology and to further probe the ways in which the state uses, justifies and perpetuates violence (see Pantazis and Pemberton, 2008; Tombs, 2007). It is the duty of criminologists to contest the casting aside of normal moral constraints to the use of violence and the underlying rationales that permit exceptional measures and the use of excessive force and torture. Politically, it is vital that the British state recognizes the cultural, religious and political values which drive the actions of those willing to resort to terrorist attacks. Groups such as Al Qaeda have made clear their objections to 'western economic imperialism', yet these are rarely aired in political or media circles (Lilleker, 2006: 200). Unless there is serious engagement with the historical role of the West in creating the conditions of anger and resentment that fuel terrorism, it is unlikely that the current cycle of violence will be broken. In defining and approaching 'terrorism' as a protean enemy, the British and US government have failed to grasp the discrete histories of particular conflicts between state and non-state actors. The hopelessly general, haphazard and haplessly executed war on terror is an indication of the state's failure to acknowledge diverse power struggles and to tackle the underlying drivers of political violence. The discrete demands and aspirations of groups using violence against the state and civilian populations – for instance in Spain, Turkey, India and Russia – have clumsily been rolled into a singular terrorist enemy. In reducing terrorism to a singular object to be defeated by force, the grievances of non-state groups using violence – including colonial exploitation, economic imperialism, religious bias and geo-political exclusion – are swept under the carpet.

So far as criminology is concerned, the recent wave of excessive legislation and over-regulation around terrorism should act as a spur, rather than a reason to retreat from debate under the expedient auspices that the subject matter is beyond the disciplinary ambit. Geo-political conflicts of interest involving violence, ideological contests and struggles over power should not be seen as out of the reaches of criminology. Indeed, we would argue that the porosity of borders and the globalization of crime and violence mean that such issues need to be situated at the centre rather than at the margins of criminological inquiry. If criminology proceeds to place primary emphasis on the local, national and the empirically quantifiable, it risks becoming something of a 'zombie discipline' that continues to function according to its own partially outmoded traditions rather than recognizing structural transformations, engaging with prescient global issues and building research agendas that scrutinize injustices, harms and inequalities.

Notes

1 In 2006 the head of the UK security service warned that there had been at least five intercepted terrorist plots since the 5 July bombings and thirty more conspiracies uncovered (see Durodie, 2006: 1).
2 Although our focus is primarily on the UK, it is worth noting that other countries – notably the United States, Spain, Germany, Italy and Australia – have strengthened terrorism laws since 9/11 (see Gill, 2006: 43).
3 At present the period remains set at 28 days and is subject to annual renewal. The current coalition government extended the powers for 6 months in June 2010, but they are now also subject to impending counter-terrorism review.
4 At the time of writing, just seventeen Control Orders remain in operation, eleven of which involve foreign nationals.
5 See volume 6 of the 2004 Open University publication *Society Matters*.
6 See www.bbc.co.uk/news/uk-10629358; and www.iraqbodycount.org/ respectively.
7 The Patriot Act also permitted the tapping of electronic and wireless communication, the

arrest of individuals without charges and the staging of secret military trials (Kellner 2002: 32).

8 Despite persistent denials by Tony Blair, the government was also forced to concede that CIA aircraft being used for extraordinary rendition had landed on British territory in Diego Garcia to refuel.

9 Further, in terms of state accountability and the serving of justice, it will seem to some that it is possible for the state to simply buy itself out of trouble using public monies. Given that the settlement deal means that no more damaging documents or information will be released by the courts, it might be argued that such money has effectively been used to suppress information that may cast the state and the security services in a negative light.

References

9/11 Commission Report (2004) *Final Report of the National Commission on Terrorist Attacks Upon the United States*. Washington: National Commission on Terrorist Attacks.

Agamben, G. (2005) *State of Exception*. Chicago: University of Chicago Press.

Amoore, L. (2007) 'Vigilant Visualities: The Watchful Politics of the War on Terror', *Security Dialogue*, 38(2): 139–56.

Amoore, L. and de Goede, M. (2007) *Risk and the War on Terror*. London: Routledge.

Aradau, C. and van Munster, R. (2007) 'Governing Terrorism Through Risk: Taking Precautions, (un)Knowing the Future', *European Journal of International Relations*, 13(1): 89–115.

Ayto, J. (1990) *Dictionary of Word Origins*. London: Arcade.

Barnaby, F. (2002) *How To Build a Nuclear Bomb and Other Weapons of Mass Destruction*. London: Granta.

Beck, U. (1996) 'Risk Society and the Provident State', in B. Szerszinski, S. Lash and B. Wynne (eds) *Risk, Environment and Modernity: Towards a New Ecology*. London: Sage, 27–43.

—— (2002) 'The Terrorist Threat: World Risk Society Revisited', *Theory, Culture and Society*, 19(4): 39–55.

Belasco, A. (2009) *The Cost of Iraq, Afghanistan and Other Global War on Terror Operations Since 9/11*. Washington, DC: Congressional Research Service.

Borger, J. (2006) 'Cost of Wars Soars to $440bn for US', *Guardian*, 4 February.

Borradori, G. (2003) *Philosophy in a Time of Terror: Dialogues with Jürgen Habermas and Jacques Derrida*. Chicago: University of Chicago Press.

Burke, J. (2005) *Al Qaeda: The True Story of Radical Islam*. London: Penguin.

Burnett, J. and Whyte, D. (2005) 'Embedded Expertise and the New Terrorism', *Journal for Crime, Conflict and the Media*, 1(4): 1–18.

Buzan, B., Waever, O. and de Wilde, J. (1997) *Security: A New Framework for Analysis*. Boulder, CO: Lynne Rienner.

Chomsky, N. (2002) *Manufacturing Consent: The Political Economy of the Mass Media*. London: Random House.

Christian, L. (2008) 'The Shame of British Complicity', *Guardian*, 22 August.

Clark, P. (2007) *Learning From Experience: Counter Terrorism in the UK since 9/11*. London: Policy Exchange.

Cobain, I. (2010) 'Iraqi Prisoners Abused at UK's Abu Ghraib', *Guardian*, 6 November.

Cohen, S. (2001) *States of Denial: Knowing About Atrocities and Suffering*. Cambridge: Polity Press.

Diprose, R., Stephenson, N., Mills, C., Race, K. and Hawkins, G. (2008) 'Governing the Future: The Paradigm of Prudence in Political Technologies of Risk Management', *Security Dialogue*, 39(2): 267–88.

Durodie, B. (2006) 'Tempted by Terror', *Spiked Online*, 14 November.

Eagleton, T. (2000) *The Gatekeeper*. London: Vintage.

Evans, J. (2007) *Intelligence, Counter-terrorism and Trust*. London: Security Service.

Ford, R. (2009) 'Blacks Bear Brunt of Rise in Stop and Search', *The Times*, 1 May.

Gill, P. (2006) 'Not Just Joining the Dots But Crossing the Borders and Bridging the Voids: Constructing Security Networks After 11 September 2001', *Policing and Society*, 16(1): 27–49.

—— (2009) 'Intelligence, Terrorism and the State', in R. Coleman, J. Sim, S. Tombs and D. Whyte (eds) *State, Power, Crime*. London: Sage.

Grabosky, P. (2010) *Crime and Terrorism*. London: Sage.

Green, P. and Ward, T. (2004) *State Crime: Governments, Violence and Corruption*. London: Pluto Press.

—— (2009) 'Violence and the State', in R. Coleman, J. Sim, S. Tombs and D. Whyte (eds) *State, Power, Crime*. London: Sage.

Gregory, F. and Wilkinson, P. (2005) 'Riding Pillion for Tackling Terrorism Is a High-risk Policy', *Security, Terrorism and the UK*. ISP/NSC Briefing Paper 05/01. London: Chatham House, pp. 2–4

Hillyard, P. (2009) 'The Exceptional State', in R. Coleman, J. Sim, S. Tombs and D. Whyte (eds) *State, Power, Crime*. London: Sage.

Hoffman, B. (1999) 'Introduction', in I. Lesser, B. Hoffman, J. Arquilla, D. Ronfeldt, M. Zanini and B. Jenkins (eds) *Countering the New Terrorism*. Santa Monica, CA: RAND.

Hudson, B. (2003) *Justice in the Risk Society*. London: Sage.

Iraq Warlogs (2010) *The Guardian Special Supplement,* 23 October.

ISP/NSC Briefing Paper 05/01 (2005) *Security, Terrorism and the UK*. London: Chatham House.

Jackson, R., Murphy, E. and Poynting, S. (2009) *Contemporary State Terrorism: Theory and Practice*. Oxford: Routledge.

Kellner, D. (2002) 'Postmodern War in the Age of Bush II', *New Political Science*, 24(1): 57–72.

Laqueur, W. (1997) 'Postmodern Terrorism', *Global Issues: An Electronic Journal of the US Information Agency*, 2(1): 1–8.

—— (2003) *No End to War: Terrorism in the 21st Century*. New York: Continuum.

Leitzinger, A. (2004) 'Postmodern Terrorism', *The Eurasian Politician*, January: 1–3.

Lesser, I., Hoffman, B., Arquilla, J., Ronfeldt, D., Zanini, M. and Jenkins, B. (eds) (1999) *Countering the New Terrorism*, Santa Monica, CA: RAND.

Lilleker, D. (2006) *Key Concepts in Political Communication*. London: Sage.

McCulloch, J. and Pickering, S. (2009) 'Pre-Crime and Counter Terrorism: Imagining Future Crime in the "War on Terror"' *British Journal of Criminology,* 49(5): 628–45.

—— (2010) 'Future Threat: Pre-crime, State Terror and Dystopia in the 21st Century', *Criminal Justice Matters*, 81: 32–33.

McGhee, D. (2008) *The End of Multiculturalism: Terrorism, Integration and Human Rights*. London: McGraw Hill.

Morgan, M. (2004) 'The Origins of Terrorism', *Parameters*, Spring: 29–43.

Mythen, G. (2010) 'Counter-Terrorism, Pre-emption and Risk: The Law of Inverse Consequences?' in F. Columbus (ed.) *Terrorism: Motivation, Threats and Prevention*. New York: Nova.

Mythen, G. and Walklate, S. (2006) 'Communicating the Terrorist Risk: Harnessing a Culture of Fear?' *Crime, Media, Culture: An International Journal*, 2(2): 123–42.

—— (2008) 'Terrorism, Risk and International Security: The Perils of Asking What if?', *Security Dialogue*, 39, 2–3: 221–42.

—— (2010) 'Pre-crime, Regulation, and Counter-terrorism: Interrogating Anticipatory Risk', *Criminal Justice Matters*, 81(1): 34–36.

Mythen, G., Walklate, S., and Khan, F. (2009) "I'm a Muslim, but I'm not a Terrorist": Victimization, Risky Identities and the Performance of Safety', *British Journal of Criminology*, 49(6): 736–54.

National Security Strategy (2010) *A Strong Britain in an Age of Uncertainty: The National Security Strategy*. London: HMSO.

Norton-Taylor, A. (2010) 'Guantánamo Payout Deal Is Climax of Years of Denials of UK Role in Rendition', *Guardian*, 16 November.

Ould Mohamedou, M. M. (2007) *Understanding Al Qaeda: The Transformation of War*. London: Pluto Press.

Pantazis, C. and Pemberton, S. (2008) 'Trading Civil Liberties for Greater Security? The Impact on Minority Communities', *Criminal Justice Matters*, 73(1): 12–14.

Peters, M. (2004) 'Postmodern Terror in a Globalized World', *Globalization*. Glasgow: University of Glasgow Press.

Rehn, E. (2003) 'Excessive Reliance on the Use of Force Does Not Stop Terrorism', in T. Hoeksema and J. ter Laak (eds) *Human Rights and Terrorism*. Holland: NHC/OSCE.

Sprinzak, E. (2006) *The Great Superterrorism Scare*, viewable at: www.radiobergen.org/ terrorism/super-2.html (Accessed 23/10/10).

Steinert, H. (2003) 'The Indispensable Metaphor of War: On Populist Politics and the Contradictions of the State's Monopoly of Force', *Theoretical Criminology*, 7(3): 265–91.

Tombs, S and Whyte, D. (2007) *Safety Crimes*. Cullompton: Willan.

Travis, A. (2009) 'Terror Control Orders Breach Human Rights, Law Lords Rule', *Guardian*, 10 June.

—— (2010) 'Government Accused of Drawing Up Secret Hit List of Embassies to Close', *Guardian*, 21st January.

United Nations (2003) *Report of the Policy Working Group on the United Nations and Terrorism* Geneva: United Nations.

Vedby Rasmussen, M. (2004) 'It Sounds Like a Riddle: Security Studies, the War on Terror and Risk', *Millennium: Journal of International Studies*, 30(2): 381–95.

Vertigans, S. (2010) 'British Muslims and the UK Government's "War on Terror" Within: Evidence of a Clash of Civilizations or Emergent De-civilizing Processes?', *British Journal of Sociology*, 61(1): 26–44.

Weimann, G. (2006) *Terror on the Internet: The New Challenges, the New Arena*. Haifa, Israel: Haifa University Press.

Welch, M. (2003) 'Trampling Human Rights in the War Against Terrorism: Implications for the Sociology of Denial', *Critical Criminology*, 12(1): 1–20.

—— (2006) 'Seeking a Safer Society: America's Anxiety in the War on Terror', *Security Journal*, 19: 93–109.

Zedner, L. (2008) 'Terrorism, the Ticking Bomb and Criminal Justice Values', *Criminal Justice Matters*, 73(1): 18–19.

—— (2009) *Security*. London: Sage.

—— (2010) 'Pre-crime and Punishment: A Health Warning', *Criminal Justice Matters*, 81: 24–25.

Index

340   *Index*

Fielding, N., 232, 236
Fijnaut, C., 258, 270, 272
Filley, C.M., 84, 95
Finder, A., 68, 77
Findlay, M., 260, 270
Finestone, H., 168, 179
Finn, T., 255
Finney, N., 117, 119
firearm, 121
Fisher, M., 147, 160, 162, 286–287, 290
FitzGerald, M., 107–109, 111, 120
Flamm, M., 146–147, 161–162
Flint, J., 142
Fonagy, P., 183, 193, 195–196
Fooks, G., 280, 290
football, 268, 274, 286
Ford, R., 322, 331
Fordism, 243–244, 246, 253, 255
Fordyce, L.R., 68, 77
foreclosure, 114, 255
forensics, 138, 190, 195, 225, 237, 280
forgery, 4, 51, 57, 117, 226–228
Forkhead box P2 (gene), 89
Foster, J., 232, 236
Foucault/Foucauldians, 2, 35, 72, 84, 86,
    90, 92–96, 131, 143, 153, 162, 167, 172,
    179, 307
foundationalism, 10, 60, 85, 92, 94
Fox, J., 236, 257, 270
Franck, K., 137, 143
Frank, R.H., 108, 120
Frank, T., 148, 160, 162, 285, 290
Frankfurt School, the, 54–56, 282, 291
fraud/s, 39, 58, 140, 248, 263, 268, 272,
    276–277, 290, 300–301, 315
Frazier, F.E., 112, 120
freedom, 54–58, 106, 108, 147, 156–157,
    164, 169, 200–202, 207–208, 211–212,
    277, 283, 287, 295, 322–323
Freese, J., 83, 95
Freidson, M., 236
Freud/Freudians, 3, 100, 215
Friedman, M., 31, 76, 233, 236
Friedrichs, D.O., 68, 77
friendship, 8, 58, 117
Fromm, E., 3
Fukuyama. F., 152, 162, 200, 215
Fullbrook, E., 31, 48
functionalism, 53, 115, 137, 159, 312
functionaries, 92, 156
fundamentalist, 171, 319–320
fury, 187, 207
fusion, 301, 303

Fussey, P., 266, 270
Futurism, 302–303

Gabbidon, S.L., 72, 77, 79, 108–109,
    116–117, 120, 122
Gachevska, K., 258, 270
Gadd, D., 183, 196, 282, 290
Gagnon, J.H., 86, 95
Gane, M., 312, 314
Gane, N., 130, 143, 159, 162
gangster/s, 163, 207, 210–211, 273, 313
Garbarino, J., 71, 77
Gardner, D., 258, 271
Garfinkel, H., 243, 255
Garland, D., 32, 37, 45, 92, 95, 130, 143,
    150, 162, 184, 186, 196
Garner, S., 118, 120
Gatrell, V., 37, 49
Geary, R., 37, 49
Geis, G., 162, 290
Gelbort, M.M., 95
Gelsthorpe, L., 179, 183, 186, 196, 274
gender, 23, 53, 60, 69–72, 75–78, 93, 108,
    110, 132, 179, 184–185, 193, 204, 206,
    209, 221, 232, 254, 261
genealogy, 50
generation/s, 4, 39, 43, 77, 112, 116,
    127–128, 139, 146, 153, 160, 177,
    199, 205, 234, 242–243, 250, 253, 264,
    272, 281
generosity, 178
genes/genetics, 1, 10, 83–96, 153, 185, 308
Genesis, 53, 195, 269, 276
genocide, 79, 101
genome, 85–86
gentrification, 248, 256
geodemographics, 142–143
geoforum, 142, 144
geography/geographers, 11, 18, 106,
    109–111, 123–137, 139, 141–144,
    183, 252, 255, 297–298, 305, 308–309,
    315, 329
geometry, 302, 313
Geras, N., 286, 290
Gergely, G., 195
Gerson, G., 57, 64
Gerstel, N., 28
Gerwitz, S., 65
gestalt, 300
ghettFo, 118
ghetto, 78, 111–115, 117–118, 122
GHS (General Household Survey), 38
Gibbens, T.C.N., 196